The Mythic Dimension

The Mythic Dimension

Selected Essays 1959–1987

Joseph Campbell

Edited by Antony Van Couvering

Collected Works of Joseph Campbell
Robert Walter, Executive Editor

HarperSanFrancisco
An Imprint of HarperCollins*Publishers*

Grateful acknowledgment is made for permission to reprint:

From *Myth, Religion, and Mother Right* by J. J. Bachofen. Copyright © 1967 by Princeton University Press. Used with permission.

From *C.G. Jung and the Humanities,* edited by Karen Barnaby and Pellegrino D'Acierno. Copyright © 1990 by Princeton University Press. Used with permission.

From *In All Her Names,* edited by Joseph Campbell and Charles Musès. Copyright © 1991 by HarperSanFrancisco. Used by permission of HarperCollins*Publishers.*

From *Myth, Dreams, and Religion.* Copyright © 1970 by Society for the Arts, Religion, and Contemporary Culture, Inc. Used with permission.

The Joseph Campbell Foundation publishes the *Collected Works of Joseph Campbell* in association with HarperSanFrancisco*Publishers.* The Joseph Campbell Foundation, dedicated to the preservation, protection, and perpetuation of the works of Joseph Campbell, offers many services and programs, and may be contacted at (800) 330-6984.

FIRST EDITION
Antony Van Couvering, Managing Editor, Collected Works of Joseph Campbell

Library of Congress Cataloging-in-Publication Data
Campbell, Joseph
The mythic dimension: selected essays 1959-1987 / Joseph Campbell
:edited by Antony Van Couvering. —1st ed.
p. cm. — (Collected works of Joseph Campbell)
Includes bibliographical references.
ISBN 0-06-096612-2 (pbk.)
1. Mythology. 2. Myth. I. Van Couvering, Antony. II. Title.
III. Series: Campbell, Joseph   Works. 1993
BL315.C269   1997   96-46156
291.1'3—dc21

98 99 00 01 /HC 10 9 8 7 6 5 4 3 2

Contents

Editor's Foreword

From 1959 until his death in 1987, Joseph Campbell wrote three major works. The multi-volume works *The Masks of God* and the *Historical Atlas of World Mythology,* and the vast *The Mythic Image* are not books about just mythology, they are books about *all* mythology, large-scale attempts to comprehend the religious expression of the human species. In them Campbell introduced many facts, stories, images, and ideas to serve his larger argument, only to let them go after they had served his purposes, frequently to the secret disappointment of his newly intrigued reader. During these most productive years of his career, however, Campbell did write about much of the material that he only touched on in his major works. He lectured prodigiously and wrote numerous essays which were either early explorations of, or mature reflections upon, material that appeared in his larger ventures. These essays were published in small-circulation magazines and journals, or as introductions or chapters in others' books. The best of them are collected here.

The essays themselves need little introduction. Written independently of each other, each can be read separately, in any order. The essays fall naturally, nonetheless, into two categories. In Mythology and History, Campbell writes about mythology from a historical perspective: its development, its uses in the past, and the mythological themes, dating from early times, that inform our lives today.

Mythology and the Arts collects the essays in which Campbell addresses his lifelong interest in how mythology is used in art to address the universal concerns of human consciousness.

As the first essay in the book, I have also included *Comparative Mythology as an Introduction to Cross-Cultural Studies,* Campbell's informal look at his teaching method for the hugely popular course on mythology he gave for thirty-five years at Sarah Lawrence College. Readers who wish they had been present for those invigorating lectures can consult, as the next-best thing, the appendix that lists the books Campbell regularly assigned to his class.

Notes on the Text

The essays are presented with a minimum of editorial change. I have not attempted to correct Joseph Campbell. He himself saw the essays presented here into print on the occasion of their initial publication, so except for the correction of infrequent spelling mistakes and other obvious errors, the essays appear as they did upon their first printing. I have, however, added footnotes where I felt an explanation would help. Footnotes that are not Campbell's I have enclosed in square brackets. Since the footnotes added for this edition make frequent reference to Campbell's other works, I have included a select bibliography of Campbell's works as an appendix. References to the first appearance of the essays in this edition may be found here.

Acknowledgments

John David Ebert was an essential collaborator from the inception of the project. He collected the originals of all the essays included here and assisted in verifying that the transcriptions were accurate. He composed the initial versions of many of the footnotes, and he read the manuscript and made suggestions and corrections at every step. Stacey Feldman did most of the transcribing and helped with the early stages of the page layout. Erik Rieselbach did the bulk of the page layout and made sure that the images were properly prepared for printing.

Mythology and History

Comparative Mythology
as an Introduction to Cross-Cultural Studies

In teaching women one is confronted with different sets of academic demands from those of men. Whereas men generally are preparing for specialized careers, the demands of which determine the order and organization of their studies, women are comparatively free to follow the lead of their own interests. In a women's college (at least, of the kind in which I have been teaching), there is, so to say, an open-field situation. We do not have required courses; nor do we have examinations. On the other hand, we do have a strict and very demanding system of education by dialogue and discussion. I see every one of my students individually, in conferences, for at least one half-hour every fortnight. This makes it possible to follow the growth, direction, and dynamics of each student's individual development.

The instructor in such a situation has to be willing not only to give generously of his time but also to participate in the student's discovery of interests—even to the point, on occasion, of abandoning his own academic plans and point of view. It was in such a fluid environment as this, then, that the course which I am going to describe came into being—in relation to a context of interests not primarily academic but experimental.

During my first two or three years, I taught a survey course in comparative literature, but at the close of the second year, three students came to me, separately, to ask for a course in mythology. Apparently my interest in this subject had become more evident in my teaching than I had supposed. I was excited by the idea and decided to give three separate courses—one to each—the following year, based on three quite different reading lists from three different approaches.

At the end of that year, four students came to me for such a course. I brought them together in one classroom, basing the readings and approach that year on what I had learned the year before. Then the year following, there were seven; and from that time on, this course has been both an established part of our curriculum and one of the great joys of my life. I have given up teaching anything else, and since about 1939, have been busily trimming it here, expanding it there, and keeping it up to date.

The departmental organization of Sarah Lawrence College is somewhat atypical. We do not have strictly separated departments. There is a literature and language faculty, which is the group with which I am officially associated. Since Sarah Lawrence students have generally professed great interest in the arts, we have strong departments in the fields of dance, theater, music, painting, and sculpture. There is, of course, a large and rather aggressive department in social science, which includes, for some reason or other, philosophy. Psychology is strong and important at Sarah Lawrence—particularly in relation to a greatly appreciated nursery school. And finally, there is a faculty of mathematics and natural science.

In describing this course, I shall be dealing with something out of an age that is long past. My observations about this course—antecedent and indifferent as it is to all academic departmentalization—may be of some use after all even to those faced with the problems of an elaborately structured university.

The course is conducted in lectures. About 50 per cent of each student's reading is directly related to the topics of the lectures. Each, however, meets me in conference at least once a fortnight, and for these meetings she reads according to her own special interest in whatever direction she has chosen to go. During the first month or so, about half the class will be at a loss. The other 50 per cent, however, will know very well what they want to do and will be off with the gun. As the year proceeds, the others gradually find their bearings.

The individual projects often are developed in relation to some aspect or other of another course, for the material can be approached from many points of view—literary, anthropological, psychological, religious. The course has served, in fact, as an effective coordinating aid for many students. And on the other hand, for those already strongly directed, there is plenty of occasion for more specialized study. I can report that a good many really impressive productions have come onto my desk. One of the most recent is now at the Viking Press and will appear as a book next year.

The readings for the class begin with Ovid's *Metamorphoses*.[1] Most students think of mythology as classical mythology, and so it has seemed to me that the logical field for a beginning would be here. Besides, Ovid's style is fluent and delightful—not a boring line in the book. The index to the volume, furthermore, provides as good a guide to classical myths as a beginner could require. But the main value of the work, from my point of view, derives from the fact that Ovid grouped his tales in clusters according to theme, so that the student sees immediately how one essential plot can be told and retold with a variety of turns and ascribed to many different heroes. Certain patterns, certain principles, a morphology, can be recognized—the kind of situation that I have expounded in my *Hero with a Thousand Faces*. There is a general pattern to the hero journey—the quest of the hero into unknown realms, the powers that he meets there and overcomes, the stages of his crises of victory, and his return then, with some boon that he has gained, for the founding of a city, religion, dynasty, or whatnot; or, on the other hand, his failure and destruction. Also in

Ovid right at the beginning, parallels with the Book of Genesis are evident with the cosmogonic cycle, the formation of the world, creation of man, the flood, the restoration of the earth, and so on.

Next, after Ovid has set us right in the middle of our subject, we go back to the *Odyssey*, as a great example and test case of what we have learned about the archetypal hero journey. And we are now being introduced, as well, to the historical backgrounds of the classical tradition. After that, we go back one great step further, with Frazer's *Golden Bough*, to pre-Hellenic times.

Frazer is considered by some to be a bit old-fashioned today. At the same time, I do not know of a better way to introduce a completely unprepared student to the whole range of this immense field—its relation to the folk as well as high traditions, the Orient and the Occident, Africa and the Arctic, the great and the little rituals, fairy tales, and all. The same motifs that have already been recognized in the classical field are here revealed as spread throughout the world, the motifs and themes of quest and return, death and rebirth, creation of the world and dissolution. Frazer deals with these in terms largely of their relationship to fertility cults, but he also gives enough material to show their relationship both to cosmological imagery and to the spiritual themes of inward quest, interior sacrifice, and the fertilization of the spirit.

Following Frazer, I used to embark on a review and discussion of theories— Tylor, Müller, Durkheim, Radcliffe-Brown, and others. After a number of years of this, however, I gave up stressing theory and began to concentrate upon direct presentations of the various mythological traditions themselves, starting with a brief review of some primitive cultures.[2]

Experience shows that it serves well, as an introduction, to classify primitive mythologies in two great categories. In the first are the mythologies of peoples who live and hunt on the great animal plains, where the basic food supply is animal meat and the chief suppliers of the food are men. Most of the hunting tribes inhabit (or once inhabited) the North and South temperate zones. The second category, in direct contrast, comprises the mythologies of peoples of the tropical equatorial belt, whose environment is a steaming jungle and where the chief food supply is vegetable, the women do nearly all the work, and the men devote themselves mainly to their leisure. I think it was Pater Wilhelm Schmidt who, in his *Ursprung der Gottesidee*, first brought out this contrast of the roles of the male in societies, respectively, of the hunt and of the plant world. In the latter, as he says, the primary work is accomplished by the women, who bring forth the children, tend the little gardens, build the houses, and take care of them—a fine situation for establishing a profound sense of inferiority in the male.

But the masculine ego, pushed back on itself, responds with that wonderful invention, the men's secret society, where no women are allowed. And there very important things are done.[3] In Melanesia, for example, the major occupation is the raising of pigs—male pigs, of course. Their upper canine teeth are knocked out so that the lower tusks can flourish, and they do grow in a beautiful curve, outward and downward and around back through the jaw. The owner of the pig celebrates certain stages of this progress by sacrificing hundreds of other porkers. And if he can get his main pig's tusks to loop around through the jaw and out again, three times, he enjoys all the prestige of a thirty-second degree Mason, entitled to such names as "He who walks above the clouds." This is a matter of great psychic importance, because when the man who has raised such a pig dies, he can present it as an offering, instead of himself, to be consumed by Sev Sev, the female guardian of the fiery way to the labyrinth of the underworld and immortality.

The survey of these primitive provinces actually starts with examples of mythology from the northern hunting peoples—North Siberian, Eskimo, and American Indian. Then, in America we confront the problem of the tropical planters and the interesting, sensitive question of a possible trans-Pacific influence.[4] American anthropologists are not as touchy on this point now as they used to be. I used to regard them as afflicted with a kind of Oedipus complex—not wishing to believe that their motherland, America, might have been fertilized by a foreign intrusion. The amount of passion that this question can generate has always amazed me. I try to be noncommittal, but it is difficult not to draw conclusions from the fact that one detail after another of the Middle American cultures has counterparts on the Asian side. After a skirmish with this problem, we return to the Old World by way of the Pacific (Polynesia, Melanesia, the Andamans, and on to Africa). And this concludes the introductory, first portion of the course, the principal aims of which have been to acquaint the student with the most common themes and patterns of the world mythology, the geography of the subject, and the modes of inflection of the common themes on the primitive, nonliterate level of culture.

The next step is to examine more closely this universality of themes, first in psychological terms. Here we begin with Freud; and since Freud's anthropologist was Frazer, an easy connection can be made with points already noted. To begin with, Frazer's conception of sympathetic magic as based on an association of ideas is not very different from Freud's. Freud simply adds the dimension of associations that are unconscious, a depth of unsuspected layers of association. The student here begins to acquire a new sense, at once of the multilayered language of myth and of its psychological force. Both Frazer and

Freud offer a psychological answer to the problem of the universality of mythic themes. The human psyche everywhere is essentially the same and, responding essentially to the same stimuli, renders patterns of association in fantasy and act that are also essentially the same.

From Freud the course moves to Jung. Personally, I find Jung as an interpreter of myths far more impressive than Freud. Freud projects a Viennese family romance of Papa, Mamma, and their boy-child into every mythology on earth, regarding myths not as symbolic of adult insights, but as symptomatic of an infantile pathology; not as revelatory, but as concealing; not as progressive, leading to maturity, but as regressive, pointing back to childhood. Jung's view, on the other hand, is that the figurations of myth are to be read as the metaphors of a necessary, almost pedagogical discipline, through which the powers of the psyche are led forward to mature relationships, first to the responsibilities of adulthood and then to the wisdom of age.

We spend something like six weeks on Freud and Jung and then move on to the Orient, for which Jung's psychology has already prepared the way. In his introductions to the *Tibetan Book of the Dead* and the Chinese *Secret of the Golden Flower,* he discusses both the similarities and the differences between a Western, psychological, scientific approach to mythology and the Oriental, mystical, and devotional. When we have clarified these points, I leave psychology behind and devote the next portion of our year's work to a descriptive historical study of the mythologies of the higher cultures.

These are separated into two great groups with the dividing line at Iran. Westward of this cultural watershed are the two provinces of Europe and the Levant; eastward, India and the Far East. In both of the Oriental provinces the essential belief concerning the ultimate truth, the ultimate substance, the ultimate mystery of being, is that it transcends all description, all naming, and all categories—which is a point not easy for our students to grasp and yet essential to an understanding of Oriental psychology as well as religion.

It is not easy for students to realize that to ask, as they often do, whether God exists and is merciful, just, good, or wrathful, is simply to project anthropomorphic concepts into a sphere to which they do not pertain. As the *Upanishads* declare: "There, words do not reach." Such queries fall short of the question. And yet—as the student must also understand—although that mystery is regarded in the Orient as transcendent of all thought and naming, it is also to be recognized as the reality of one's own being and mystery. That which is transcendent is also immanent. And the ultimate function of Oriental myths, philosophies, and social forms, therefore, is to guide the individual to an actual *experience* of his identity with *that; tat tvam asi* ("Thou art that") is the ultimate word in this connection.

By contrast, in the Western sphere—in terms of the orthodox traditions, at any rate, in which our students have been raised—God is a person, the person who has created this world. God and his creation are not of the same substance. Ontologically, they are separate and apart. We, therefore, do not find in the religions of the West, as we do in those of the East, mythologies and cult disciplines devoted to the yielding of an experience of one's *identity* with divinity. That, in fact, is heresy. Our myths and religions are concerned, rather, with establishing and maintaining an experience of *relationship*—and this is quite a different affair. Hence it is, that though the same mythological images can appear in a Western context and an Eastern, it will always be with a totally different sense. This point I regard as fundamental.

In the Orient, the gods do not stand as ultimate terms, ultimate ends, substantial beings, to be sought and regarded in and for themselves. They are more like metaphors, to serve as guides, pointing beyond themselves and leading one to an experience of one's own identity with a mystery that transcends them. I have found that the approach through Freud and Jung greatly helps to make this point clear to students brought up in the mythology of Yahweh—a jealous god, who would hold men to himself and who turned mankind *away* from the Tree of Immortality, instead of leading us to it. Such a god in the Orient would be regarded as a deluding idol. In fact, heaven itself and our desire for its joys are regarded there as the last barrier, the last obstacle to release, to be transcended. And to escort my students beyond heaven and hell, I take them first to India and then China and Japan.

For India, I begin with a bit of Heinrich Zimmer and Ananda K. Coomaraswamy and go on to the *Upanishads* and the *Gita.* We also read the *Shakuntala* and *Panchatantra.* Buddhism I introduce through Coomaraswamy's *Buddha and the Gospel of Buddhism* and Alan Watts's *The Way of Zen,* with readings in Waley's *Three Ways of Thought in Ancient China* as my introduction to the Far Eastern sphere. Readings are also assigned in Lao-tzu, Confucius, Chuang-tzu, Mencius, and Mo Te. And then, finally, for Japan, I use Lafcadio Hearn's *Japan,* Okakura Kakuso's *The Book of Tea,* Herrigel's *Zen in the Art of Archery,* selections from the *Kojiki,* some bits of Noh and Haiku, and a lot of enthusiasm of my own.

The course now turns again to the West. We have already been introduced to the classical field through Ovid and the *Odyssey;* but I want now to contrast the points of view of Europe and the Levant. It seems to me that where God and Man are viewed as opposed terms, one is inevitably faced with a final decision as to one's ultimate loyalty. Is it to be to God, or is it to be to Man? As I see it, the ultimate loyalty in the Levant has always been to God—in Zoroastrianism, Judaism, Christianity, and Islam. In the West—whether Greeks or Romans, Celts or Germans—it has been to Man.

I see the *Book of Job* as the consummate expression of the Levantine orientation.[5] There God behaves outrageously—unjustly, unmercifully, brutally, and irrationally—yet when Job is confronted with the power and boasting of his tormentor, who now adds insult to injury, he bows in admiration. "Behold," he prays, "I am of small account. I had heard of thee by the hearing of the ear, but now my eyes see thee; therefore I despise myself and repent in dust and ashes."[6]

I contrast with this abdication of human judgment the posture of Prometheus, who was also tortured by a god who could have filled Leviathan's nose with harpoons; and yet, when offered respite if he would but apologize for his aid to man and give honor to that god, he retorted: "I care less than nothing for Zeus; let him do what he likes."[7] I point out to my students that as the ethical humanism of the Greeks developed, their old gods lost stature and force. Their ultimate loyalty was to man. And yet they did not forfeit their primal religious sense of awe before the mystery and wonder of creation. They did not personify that mystery in a being before whom the human spirit should abdicate but, on the contrary, recognized that the supreme manifestation on earth of that same mystery and wonder is the human mind itself, well housed in the beautiful human body.

That is the contrast that I seek to illustrate for my students through the materials of Greece and Rome, the Celts and Germans, the Bible and Islam. And I find that it serves not only to make clear to them certain grand lines of historical stress and conflict but also to bring out some of the problems of their own lives and beliefs in this strange society of ours, where for six days a week we honor the humanistic values of Greece and Rome and on the seventh for half an hour or so, confess guilt before a jealous Levantine god. Then we wonder why so many of us must repair to the psychoanalyst.

The course comes to a close with a program of medieval and modern readings, dealing in the modern field with two or three authors who have made significant use of mythological forms and themes such as James Joyce, Thomas Mann, and T. S. Eliot. Through these I can bring Freud, Jung, and the Orient back into our picture again for a culminating summation.

And meanwhile, as already noted, the students have been developing their own projects. For some, the principal interest has been anthropological through studies of African, Polynesian, Melanesian, or American Indian mythologies. A greatly favored field is Indian mythology and philosophy; another, Buddhism; another, Far Eastern art. In fact, the arts in general are of enormous interest. My wife is a well-known modern dancer, and I always have at least one student who hopes that through my course she may learn to invoke my wife's Muse, Terpsichore. Wagner and Germanic mythology go together as another favorite topic. Greek drama is still another. Celtic mythology, Arthurian romance, Yeats, and the Celtic Twilight authors are always popular; Dante, Goethe, and Blake, as well; and every year I have two or three who work through all of Joyce and Thomas Mann. Schopenhauer, Nietzsche, and Jung likewise draw their devotees.

Before the Second World War most of the students who came into the course were of the intellectual type that was generally accused in those days of "ivory tower retreatism." These were young women interested in what I still believe college campuses were made for, namely, four years of absorption in science, the liberal arts, and philosophy. Then came the war, Pearl Harbor and all that, and since my course was the only one on the campus at that time that paid any attention whatsoever to the Orient, I suddenly found that my teaching had acquired political importance. This high dignity did not long remain to me, for we now have no end of people who know all about the Orient. And so the course is now again being patronized largely by those interested in philosophy, religion, and the arts. They are so numerous, these days, I am pleased to say, however, that I have had to confine my teaching to seniors, simply to cut down on the number of applicants for admission.

The interest in Oriental art and thought is particularly strong. The interest in Jung is on the rise. For some reason that I have not been able to determine, the psychologists on our campus have never dealt with Jung. It has always been with Freud, and if Jung's name has been mentioned, it has been only to be misinterpreted and disparaged. And so, it is to my course that students come to be introduced to Jung. The Bible, also, has become, in late years, a subject of the greatest interest. Every year, I now have two or three going through, from beginning to end, with the *Dartmouth Bible* as guide.

About ten years ago, I was invited to lecture for the State Department at the Foreign Service Institute in Washington, where I was able to test out some of the lessons that I have learned from my young women. What I found was that the same approach works with State Department officers and military men (through Freud and Jung to Oriental mythology, and through mythology to an understanding of the roots and commitments of alien culture-provinces).

And then again, at the Cooper Union in New York, I had the privilege of presenting my entire course to people of still another type: for the most part, moderately educated people, simple and direct, who just wanted to learn.[8] They were not scholars—just curious. And here again, the approach succeeded. Then, finally, three years ago, I was invited to deliver a series of lectures on educational television, and for that I simply converted this same course into thirty-four half-hour television programs.[9] Once more, the response was amazing. I would not pretend that there was anything of academic worth about such teaching. It did, however, have the value of opening the minds of people who perhaps would never have thought of such things to the meanings of other cultures and to new possibilities of thought and experience for themselves. The letters that came to the television station originated with men and women of the simplest sort, as well as professionals in many fields of learning.

This experience understandably confirms my conviction that, if we could in our academic world get away from specialization and departmentalization, at least in the introductory stages of our cross-cultural studies, a great deal would be gained—not only in understanding, but also in the rapidity with which students would find their way into branches of learning of intimate, genuine interest to themselves. I sometimes think of this course of mine, worked out in such close association with students over the past thirty years, as a kind of pilot project. It is a preliminary sketch of something that in a large university, with cooperating scholars from every one of the fields touched upon, might well take shape as a really important educational project.

While the course is now confined to seniors, it could be addressed even more profitably, I believe, to freshmen. I recall that when I entered Dartmouth there was an excellent freshmen course taught in biology. A required course, it opened up every aspect of the field. There is the need today for something comparable in relation to the rapidly increasing number of approaches to culture and cross-cultural study. Comparative mythology, as I have found, supplies an amazingly serviceable vehicle of approach to every possible aspect of this vast sphere.

Some such elementary course in comparative mythology as I have here suggested—conducted, however, by a team of scholar-specialists lecturing in their special fields and separately directing individual student projects—could be put together readily in any one of the major universities. It would serve not only to open to students a view of the whole range of possibilities before them, when they enter as wide-eyed youngsters the enchanted wood of the world's learning, but also to lead them along, through paths of their own choosing, to explorations of its deep groves.

The Historical Development of Mythology

The comparative study of the mythologies of the world compels us to view the cultural history of mankind as a unit; for we find that such themes as the Fire-theft, Deluge, Land of the Dead, Virgin Birth, and Resurrected Hero have a worldwide distribution, appearing everywhere in new combinations, while remaining, like the elements of a kaleidoscope, only a few and always the same. Furthermore, whereas in tales told for entertainment such mythical themes are taken lightly—obviously in a spirit of play—they appear also in religious contexts, where they are accepted not only as factually true but even as revelations of the verities to which the whole culture is a living witness and from which it derives both its spiritual authority and its temporal power. No human society has yet been found in which such mythological motifs have not been rehearsed in liturgies; interpreted by seers, poets, theologians, or philosophers; presented in art; magnified in song; and ecstatically experienced in life-empowering visions.[1]

Indeed the chronicle of our species, from its earliest page, has been not simply an account of the progress of man the toolmaker but—more tragically—a history of the pouring of blazing visions into the minds of seers and the efforts of earthly communities to incarnate unearthly covenants. Every people has received its own seal and sign of supernatural designation, communicated to its heroes and daily proved in the lives and experiences of its folk. And though many who bow with closed eyes in the sanctuaries of their own tradition rationally scrutinize and disqualify the sacraments of others, an honest comparison immediately reveals that all have been built from the one fund of mythological motifs, variously selected, organized, interpreted, and ritualized according to local need, but revered by every people on earth.

A fascinating psychological as well as historical problem is thus presented to us by our science. Man, apparently, cannot maintain himself in the universe without belief in some arrangement of the general inheritance of myth. In fact, the fullness of his life would even seem to stand in a direct ratio to the depth and range, not of his rational thought, but of his local mythology. Whence the force of these unsubstantial themes, by which they are empowered to galvanize populations, creating of them civilizations, each with a beauty and self-compelling destiny of its own? And why should it be that whenever men have looked for something solid on which to found their lives, they have chosen, not the facts in which the world abounds, but the myths of an immemorial imagination—preferring even to make life a hell for themselves and their neighbors in the name of some violent god, rather than to accept gracefully the bounty the world affords?

Are the modern civilizations to remain spiritually locked from each other in their local notions of the sense of the general tradition? Or can we not now break through to some more profoundly based point and counterpoint of human understanding? For it is a fact that the myths of our several cultures work upon us, whether consciously or unconsciously, as energy-releasing, life-motivating, and directing agents; so that even though our rational minds may be in agreement, the myths by which we are living, or by which our fathers lived, can be driving us, at that very moment, diametrically apart.

No one, as far as I know, has yet tried to compose into a single picture the new perspectives that have been opened in the fields of comparative symbolism, religion, mythology, and philosophy by the scholarship of recent years. The richly rewarded archaeological researches of the past few decades; astonishing clarifications, simplifications, and coordinations achieved by intensive studies in the spheres of philology, ethnology, philosophy, art history, folklore, and religion; fresh insights in psychological research; and the many priceless contributions to our science by the scholars, monks, and literary men of Asia—all have combined to suggest a new image of the fundamental unity of the spiritual history of mankind. Without straining beyond the treasuries of evidence already on hand in these widely scattered departments of our subject, therefore, but simply gathering from them the *membra disjuncta* of a unitary mythological science, I shall attempt in the following pages the first sketch of a natural history of the gods and heroes, such as in its final form should include in its purview all divine beings—just as zoology does all animals, and botany all plants—not regarding any as sacrosanct or beyond its scientific domain. For, just as in the visible world of the vegetable and animal kingdoms, so also in the visionary world of the gods; there has been a history, an evolution, a series of mutations, governed by laws. To show forth such laws is the proper aim of science.

Moreover, just as our science of biology came to maturity only when it dared to reckon man among the beasts, so will that of mythology only when God is reckoned among the gods. It is true that the ultimate nature and being of what has been called God are beyond all human knowledge and consequently beyond science; but so also are the ultimate nature and being of the gods—and of the bees and flowers. Books have been written, however, not only about God, but also about his commandments, program for mankind, and arrangements for eternity; thrones and altars have been fixed upon the tablets of his law; services instituted in his name. It is to such historical curiosities that our science will be addressed, leaving the ineffable unnamed.

Like the aim of Bacon's *Advancement of Learning*, that of our work will be "to point out what part of knowledge has been already labored and perfected, and what portions left unfinished or entirely neglected." To that end the subject can be conveniently divided into four parts: The Psychology and Archaeology of Myth; Oriental Mythology; Occidental Mythology; and Poetic Mythology.

The Psychology and Archaeology of Myth

"Very deep," wrote Thomas Mann at the opening of his mythological tetralogy, *Joseph and His Brothers,* "very deep is the well of the past. Should we not call it bottomless?"

The question points to the problem of the relationship of history to psychology. Is the psyche a function of history, or vice versa? Shall we find, in tracing our mythological themes to their points of origin, that these can be identified in discoverable strata of the well of history? Or shall we find, rather, when the bottom of the deep well has been reached and even broached, that the origin or ground of myth will not have been attained? If the latter, then we shall be justified in asserting that at least some of the archetypes on which the wonder tales and religions of mankind have been founded derive not from any fund of human experience in time but from some structuring principle antecedent to history—or even the cause of history; namely, the form of the psyche itself, as a function of the biology of the human body.

"The deeper we sound," wrote Thomas Mann, "the further down into the lower world of the past we probe and press, the more do we find that the earliest foundations of humanity, its history and culture, reveal themselves unfathomable."

Our initial task must be to ask if this is true. And to this end we shall explore, first, the psychological aspect of our question, to learn whether in the human psychosomatic system there have been found any structures or dynamic tendencies to which the origins of myth and ritual might be referred; turning only then to the archaeological and ethnological evidences, to learn what the earliest discoverable patterns of mythological ideation may have been.

However, as Thomas Mann has already warned, concerning the foundations for which we shall be seeking: "No matter to what hazardous lengths we let out our line they still withdraw, again and further into the depths." The first depth will be the archaeological: that of the beginnings of the high cultures of Mesopotamia, the Nile, Guatemala, and Peru. The second depth will be the paleontological and ethnological: of primitive man, the hunter and early planter. But there will be a third depth even below that, below the ultimate horizon of humanity: for we shall find the ritual dance among the birds, the fishes, the apes, and the bees. And we shall therefore have to ask the evidence whether man, like those other members of the animal kingdom, does not possess any innate tendencies to respond compulsively, in strictly patterned ways, to certain signals flashed by his environment and his own kind.

Oriental Mythology

Having viewed the open question of the origins and earliest patternings of myth through the balanced lenses of archaeology and psychology, we shall find the next natural division of our subject in the highly developed systems of the Orient: the rich yet essentially unified major province represented by the philosophical myths and mythological philosophies of India, Southeast Asia, China, and Japan—to which should be joined the much earlier yet spiritually related mythological cosmologies of archaic Mesopotamia and Egypt. In all of these hieratically organized civilizations will be recognized the basic mythology of a universe not progressing toward any end, but rendering manifest to the contemplative mind, here and now, the radiance of a divine power, which, though transcendent, is yet immanent in all things. Certain aspects of the Greek and even of the pagan Celto-Germanic mythological systems belong to this fundamentally contemplative order of mythopoetic thought. However, the Greeks themselves felt that there was a notable difference between their approach to life and that of the more ancient peoples toward the south and east; and we too generally find it normal to think of the Occident and the Orient under separate heads. The next convenient division of our subject, then, will be:

Occidental Mythology

But the watershed, or dividing line, between the lands of the early Oriental and the more recent Occidental traditions must be drawn—for the field of mythology, at any rate—not at the longitude of the Aegean (with Greece immediately to the west and modern Turkey, or ancient Anatolia, eastward) but through Iran. For the first formulation of the new mythology upon which the Occidental worldview was to be found appeared in the reforms of the Persian prophet Zoroaster (c. 660 B.C.), whose fundamentally progressive concept of history and ethical challenge to the individual to become voluntarily engaged in the furtherance of the Kingdom of God (Ahura Mazda) on earth overcame for the West the earlier mythology of the endless, spontaneously self-generating, cosmic cycle of Eternal Return.

According to the earlier cyclic view, which is the basic view of the great Orient to this day, there was never a time when time was not, nor will there be a time when time will have ceased to be; for the daily round of the sun, the waxing and waning of the moon, the cycle of the year, and the rhythm of birth, death, and new birth in the organic world represent a principle of continuous creation that is fundamental to the nature of the universe. We all know the myth of the four ages—of gold, silver, bronze, and iron—where the world is represented as declining from its golden age, growing ever worse. It will disintegrate, presently, in chaos—only to burst forth again, however, fresh as a flower, and to recommence spontaneously the inevitable course. There is therefore nothing to be gained, either for the universe or for man, through individual originality and effort. Those who have identified themselves with the body and its affections will necessarily find that all is painful, since everything—for them—must end. But for those who have found the still point of eternity, around which all—including themselves—revolves, everything is glorious and wonderful just as it is. The first duty of man, consequently, is to play his given role—as do the sun, the moon, the various animal and plant species, the waters, the rocks, and the stars—without fault; and then, if possible, so to order his mind as to identify it with the inhabiting essence of the whole.

The reform of Zoroaster broke the dreamlike spell of this contemplative, metaphysically oriented tradition, where light and darkness alternated and danced together in a world-creating cosmic shadow play. The first principle of the reform was expressed in Zoroaster's radical separation of light and darkness, together with his assignment to each of an ethical value, the light being pure and good, the darkness foul and evil. Before the creation of the world, he taught, these two were apart. But the violent powers of the dark overwhelmed the light, and a cosmic battle ensued—which was, precisely, the universe. Hence the universe was to be known as a compound of wisdom and violence, light and dark, wherein good and evil were contending fiercely for the victory. And the privilege of man—who, being himself a part of creation, was a compound of good and evil—was to elect, voluntarily, to join the battle in the interest of the light. With the gospel of Zoroaster (announced, it was believed, twelve thousand years following the creation of the world) an epochal turn was given to the conflict in favor of the good; and when he returned (after another twelve millennia) in the person of the messiah Saoshyant, there would take place a mighty battle and cosmic conflagration, through which he would annihilate all darkness, utterly. Whereupon all would be light, there would be no further history, and the Kingdom of God would have been realized forever.

It is obvious, surely, that we have here a potent mythical formula for the reorientation of the human spirit—pitching it forward along the way of time, summoning man to an assumption of responsibility for the reform of the universe in God's name, and thus fostering a new, potentially political philosophy of holy war. The first sociological expression of this new force was in the prodigious Persian empire of Cyrus the Great (d. 529 B.C.) and Darius the Great

(c. 521–486? B.C.), which in a few decades reached from the bounds of India to those of Greece, and under the protection of which the postexilic Hebrews not only rebuilt their temple (Ezra 1:1–11) but also both reconstructed and reinterpreted their ancient Mosaic inheritance. The second formidable sociopolitical expression of the new progressive myth is therefore to be found in the Hebrew application of its message to themselves. The next application appeared in the world mission of Christendom, and the fourth in that of Islam.

"For the children of the desolate one will be more than the children of her that is married, says the Lord. Enlarge the place of your tent, and let the curtains of your habitations be stretched out; hold not back, lengthen your cords and strengthen your stakes. For you will spread abroad to the right and to the left, and your descendants will possess the nations and will people the desolate cities" (Isaiah 54:1–3).

"And this gospel of the kingdom will be preached throughout the whole world as a testimony to all nations; and then the end will come" (Matthew 24:14).

"And slay them wherever you catch them, and turn them out from where they have turned you out; for tumult and oppression are worse than slaughter. . . . And fight them on until there is no more tumult or oppression, and there prevail justice and faith in God; but if they cease, let there be no hostility except to those who practice oppression" (Koran 2:191; 193).

The Greeks, in a measure, participated in this mythos of the war of the Sons of Light with the Sons of Darkness. We find it reflected in some of the later developments of the mythology of Dionysus. Many conflicting earlier and later legends were told of the birth and deeds, death and resurrection of this great deity of the plant world, whose cult of divine ecstasy became the rage in Greece in the seventh century B.C. The ultimate origins of the wild rites are lost in the depths of an unrecorded past: indeed, as we shall see, they are certainly very much older than the history, or even the pre-history, of Greece itself. But we know a good deal concerning the later mutations through which the worship passed before the figure of the great lord of the grain and the vine—of bread and wine, of divine rapture, and of resurrection—became merged with that of Jesus in the sacramental system of the early Church.

According to one important version of his miraculous birth, death, and resurrection, when the great goddess of the operations of agriculture and the fruitful soil, Demeter, came to Sicily from Crete with her daughter Persephone, whom she had conceived of Zeus, she discovered a cave near the spring of Kyane.[2] There she hid the maiden, setting to guard her the two serpents that were normally harnessed to the maiden's chariot. And Persephone there commenced weaving a web of wool, a great robe on which there was to be a beautiful picture of the universe; while her mother, Demeter, contrived that the girl's father, Zeus, should learn of her presence. The god approached his daughter in the form of a serpent, and she conceived of him a son, Dionysus, who was born and nurtured in the cave. The infant's toys were a ball, a top, dice, some golden apples, a bit of wool, and a bull-roarer.[3]

That is the first part of the story of the god Dionysus. The second tells of his death and resurrection. The infant in the cave was given a mirror, and while he was gazing into it, delighted, there approached him stealthily from behind two Titans, who had been sent by the goddess Hera, the jealous wife and queen of Zeus, to slay him. Now the Titans were divine beings of an earlier generation than the gods. They were the children of Sky and Earth, and from two of their number, Kronos and Rhea, the gods themselves, the Olympians, were born. The Titans and their mythology derived from an earlier stratum of thought and religion than the classical pantheon of the Olympians, and the episodes in which they appeared frequently had traits of an extremely primitive tone.

For example, in the present case, the two Titans stealing into the cave were painted with white clay or chalk—like the cannibals, whom we shall presently be meeting, at their feasts of ritual sacrifice. The Titans pounced upon the playing child, tearing him into seven parts, which they boiled in a cauldron supported by a tripod and then roasted on seven spits.[4] But when they had consumed their sacrifice—all except the heart, which had been rescued by the goddess Athene—Zeus, attracted by the odor of the roasting meat, entered the cave, and when he beheld the scene, slew the white-painted cannibal Titans with a bolt of lightning. The goddess Athene thereupon presented the rescued heart in a covered basket to the father, who accomplished the resurrection, according to one version of the miracle, by swallowing the precious relic and himself then giving birth to his son.

The primitive aspects of this myth can be rediscovered, ritually enacted in a gruesome series of rites still practiced among the cannibals of the primitive equatorial regions. But for the present, let us turn our attention to the manner in which the crude inheritance was spiritually transformed and reinterpreted in the image of the concept of man's nature as a battleground of good and evil.

The chief channels through which this mythology was preserved and developed from the sixth century B.C. until about the fourth A.D. were numerous, widely scattered Orphic conventicles, which, as we know, exercised a considerable influence on both the philosophical and the religious speculations of the crucial time. A direct and powerful line leads from the Orphic schools through Pythagoras (c. 582–c. 507 B.C.) and the Eleatic philosophers to Plato (427?–347 B.C.), the Alexandrian mystery cults, and the great Neoplatonic thinkers, not only of the first millennium A.D. but also of the high Middle Ages and the Renaissance.

According to an important Orphic version of the myth of the killed and eaten infant Dionysus, it was from the ashes of the annihilated Titans that mankind arose. Man, therefore, is of mixed origin, containing a divine principle (Dionysus) and a wicked (that of the Titans). The image is analogous to that of the origin of the universe described by Zoroaster, and is actually an expression of the same idea of man's obligation to engage in a struggle of ethical significance, to release the godly substance from the grip of the dark and evil. However, in the Greek version of the problem we do not find any progressive, potentially political mythos of the ultimate salvation of the world. As in the Orient, we hear, rather, of the "cycle of birth or becoming" (*kyklos tēs geneseōs*); and the call to the individual is to save, not the world, but himself: to purge away the wicked portion of his nature and to cultivate the godly, through vegetarianism, asceticism, and assiduous practice of the Orphic rituals through many lives.

We cannot pause at this point to probe the relationships to one another of the Orphic, Zoroastrian, and remoter Eastern traditions. Suffice it to say that, for any basic study of the foundations of Occidental mythology, this is a fundamental question to be faced. And the second question will be that of the interplay of the two contrary themes of the personal (Orphic) and the universal (Zoroastrian) salvation throughout the history of Occidental religion—the first retaining the archaic concept of the never-ending cosmic cycle, but with a view of the world rather as evil than as divine: the second foreseeing, on the other hand, an end to it all and the ultimate realization of the Kingdom of God on earth.

But the Orphic transformation of the Dionysian tradition—which, though it hardly touched the Synagogue, exerted a considerable influence on the Church and for a time even touched the Mosque—was not the only, or even the most important, Greek contribution to the development of mythological thought and practice in the West. For the more typical and more challenging influence was in the sphere, not of religion, but of art; and this we must study according to a completely different set of rules, thoughts, and deep concerns, and under a totally different rubric, namely:

Poetic Mythology

The great Greek Presocratic philosophers, from Thales (c. 640–546 B.C.) to Zeno (336?–264? B.C.), well knew that their mythological inheritance was composed in the language of the past. As F. M. Cornford has observed:

> The Zeus of Aeschylus still bears the name of the polygamous father of the gods
> and men, whose temper made his consort an expert in the arts of wifely deceit; but
> it is clear that Aeschylus did not believe that such a person guided the destinies of
> the world. A great part of the supreme god's biography had to be frankly rejected
> as false, or reinterpreted as allegory, or contemplated with reserve as mysterious
> myth too dark for human understanding. But the very clearness of unmistakable
> detail in the Homeric picture made it a hard task to distort the contents of myth in
> the sense of a revised morality.[5]

We can understand the problem; for we are now facing it ourselves,
twenty-six hundred years later, in our own mythological inheritance of the
Bible and ecclesiastical dogma. The completely unforeseen and still unpre-
dictable findings of modern science have blasted forever the geocentric universe, where a Joshua could have caused the sun to stand at Gibeon and the
moon in the valley of Ajalon, while the Creator assisted him in the slaughter of
his enemies by tossing down great stones upon them from a heaven just above
the clouds (Joshua 10:12-13)—to which, twelve hundred years later, Jesus and
his virgin mother would magically ascend.

By many of the Greeks—as by many of ourselves—the archaic mythopoetic inheritance continued to be revered: its festivals were celebrated and its
gods were addressed in prayer, as though they enjoyed some sort of independent life apart from the human imagination. However, among the poets,
artists, and philosophers, such direct belief in the literal truth of a poetically
conceived mythology was impossible. They knew that, just as they were themselves coining and developing myths, so in the remote past the inherited
mythology had also been composed—under the influence of divine inspiration, no doubt, yet by the hands and labors of functioning poets.

An important distinction must be drawn in our studies of mythology between the attitudes toward divinities represented on the one hand by the priest
and his flock, and on the other by the creative poet, artist, or philosopher. The
former tend to what I should like to call a positivistic reading of the imagery of
their cult. Such readings are fostered by the attitude of prayer, since in prayer it
is extremely difficult to retain the balance between belief and disbelief that is
proper to the contemplation of an image or idea. The poet, artist, and philosopher, on the other hand, being themselves fashioners of images and coiners of
ideas, realize that all representation—whether in the visible matter of stone or
in the mental matter of the word—is necessarily conditioned by the fallibility
of the human organs. Overwhelmed by his own muse, a bad poet may fall into
the posture of a prophet—whose utterances we shall define (for the present) as

"poetry overdone," overinterpreted—whereupon he becomes the founder of a cult and the generator of priests. But so also a gifted priest may find his images deepening, changing form, or even dissolving: whereupon he will possibly become either a prophet or, if more greatly favored, a creative poet.

Three major metamorphoses of the motifs and themes of our subject, therefore, have to be recognized as fundamentally different even though fundamentally related, namely: the true poetry of the poet, the poetry overdone of the prophet, and the poetry done to death of the priest. Whereas the history of religion is largely a record of the latter two, the history of mythology includes all three, and in doing so it brings not only poetry but also religion into a fresh and healthily vivified relationship to the wellsprings of creative thought. For there is a tendency in poetry ("poetry underdone") to rest in the whimsies of personal surprise, joy, or anguish before the realities of life in a universe man never made; whereas in religion the opposite tendency may prevail—that of rendering no personal experience whatsoever, but only clichés.

It was the miracle of the Greeks to have stood for creative thought—that is to say, poetic thought—in a world in which for some four thousand years the same old themes had been worked and reworked, served this way and that; but always in the ways either of prophecy and religion, or, on the other hand, of mere moral instruction or entertainment, as, for example, in the fable or in the wonder tale. The category of art—not as a form of anonymous craftsmanship in the service of either luxury or religion, but as a vehicle of individual insight and experience—the world owes, apparently (or, at least, so far as the evidence at present available suggests), to a certain peculiar circumstance in the character and society of the Greeks, of which they themselves were both aware and proud. And this is the second great distinction to be noted at the heart of our Occidental mythological tradition; the first having been the ethically toned progressive principle, announced in the Zoroastrian mythos of the battle of powers of darkness and powers of light. Once again we may take our lead from F. M. Cornford:

> Greek theology was not formulated by priests nor even by prophets, but by artists, poets, and philosophers. The great civilizations of the East were dominated by a sacerdotal caste, and the temple became for them the center of intellectual, no less than of religious life. In Greece nothing of this sort ever happened. There was no priestly class guarding from innovating influence a sacred tradition enshrined in a sacred book. There were no divines who could successfully claim to dictate the terms of belief from an inexpugnable fortress of authority. One consequence was that the conception of deity could be dissociated from cult, and enlarged to include beings and things which no one ever dreamed of connecting with the obligation of worship.[6]

And so it is that, although in the Far and Middle East a rich tradition of storytelling flourished and, in the later periods, an elegantly turned and polished art of the literary myth, any systematic study of the aesthetic approach to mythology as a fundamental factor in the development of a cultural ideal for man must begin with the Greeks. With Alexander's invasion of India (327 B.C.) and the founding of the brief-lived but highly influential Hellenistic states of Bactria (c. 250–c. 135 B.C.) and the Punjab (c. 200–c. 58 B.C.), a reflection of the Greek humanistic ideal played for a time over the arts of the Oriental courts.[7] But even there, the forces of the priest and the yogi come finally to preponderate—except in China and Japan, where the Confucian poet-scholar and Taoist poet-sage developed a mythologically inspired aesthetic orientation, which in the modern world is the most forceful counterplayer to the poetic tradition of the West.

In the Celto-Germanic mythologies of the high Middle Ages, an extremely sophisticated handling of symbols and aesthetic forms, based rather on bardic than on priestly thought and experience, lets us know that the lesson of the Greeks was never lost in the West. The contemporary poetry and philosophy of Islam also carried a great charge of humanistic inheritance. And then, finally, in the Renaissance, it was the poets, artists, and philosophers of Europe who carried not the west alone, but mankind, into the new chapter of civilization, where every mythological theme of the past that is not transmuted into poetry (poetic truth) is doomed to become simply a provincial relic.

In our natural history of the gods and heroes it will be our task to search for the laws of the alchemy of that transmutation. In the primitive world, where the clues to the origin of mythology must be sought, gods and demons are not conceived in the way of hard and fast, positive realities. The phenomenon of the primitive mask, for example, is a case in point. The mask is revered as an apparition of the mythical being that it represents, yet everyone knows that a man made the mask and that a man is wearing it. The one wearing it, furthermore, is identified with the god during the time of the ritual of which the mask is a part. He does not merely represent the god: he *is* the god. The literal fact that the apparition is composed of (a) a mask, (b) its reference to a mythical being, and (c) a man, is dismissed from the mind, and the presentation is allowed to work without correction upon the sentiments of both the beholder and the actor. In other words, there has been a shift of view from the logic of the normal secular sphere, where things are understood to be distinct from each other, to a theatrical or play-sphere, where they are accepted for what they are *experienced* as being, and the logic is that of "make-believe"—"as if."

We all know the convention, surely! It is a primary, spontaneous device of childhood: a magical device, by which the world can be transformed from banality to magic in a trice. And its inevitability in childhood is one of those universal characteristics of man that unite us in one family. It is a primary datum, consequently, of the science of myth, which is concerned precisely with the phenomenon of self-induced belief.

Leo Frobenius wrote in a celebrated paper on the force of the daemonic world of childhood:

> A professor is writing at his desk and his four-year-old little daughter is running about the room. She has nothing to do and is disturbing him. So he gives her three burnt matches, saying, "Here! Play!" and, sitting on the rug, she begins to play with the matches: Hansel, Gretel, and the witch. A considerable time elapses, during which the professor concentrates upon his task, undisturbed. But then, suddenly, the child shrieks in terror. The father jumps. "What is it? What has happened?" The little girl comes running to him, showing every sign of great fright. "Daddy, Daddy," she cries, "take the witch away! I can't touch the witch any more!"

Frobenius further observes:

> An eruption of emotion is characteristic of the spontaneous shift of an idea from the level of the sentiments (*Gemüt*) to that of sensual consciousness (*sinnliches Bewusstsein*). Furthermore, the appearance of such an eruption obviously means that a certain spiritual process has reached a conclusion. The match is not a witch; nor was it a witch for the child at the beginning of the game. The process, therefore, rests on the fact that the match *has become* a witch on the level of the sentiments and the conclusion of the process coincides with the transfer of this idea to the plane of consciousness. The observation of the process escapes the test of conscious thought since it enters consciousness only after or at the moment of completion. However, in as much as the idea *is,* it must have *become.* The process is creative, in the highest sense of the word; for, as we have seen, in a little girl a match can become a witch. Briefly stated, then: the phase of *becoming* takes place on the level of the sentiments, while that of *being* is on the conscious plane.[8]

We may take this observation as a clue, not only to the origins of myth and of the fabulous rituals by which men and women have allowed themselves to be tortured as by demons, but also to the radical distinction between mythology as read by the Greek poets, artists, and philosophers and mythology as functioning in the primitive sphere.

Three categories are to be distinguished for the mythology proper: daemonic, metaphysical, and humanistic. The first is characteristic of the earliest high civilizations, as well as of all primitive societies and folk cultures; the second achieved its apogee in medieval India, China, and Japan; while the last distinguishes the classical inheritance of the West.

According to the first, the gods and daemons represent something with a life and consciousness of its own, a "something not ourselves" (to quote Cornford's felicitous paraphrase of the Greek term *theos,* "god"), which, though it is rather a force than a shape and works invisibly, yet appears in shapes.[9] It appears in visions, where it works upon the spirit of the individual; and it appears in the paraphernalia of the ritual, to work upon the spirit of the group. Furthermore, many, if not all, rites have taken their rise from individual vision.

The Judeo-Christian-Islamic prophetic inheritance must be regarded (if we are to retain an objective distance) as a powerful variant of this first category of myth, wherein the daemons of Abraham, Jesus, Paul, Mohamet, and the rest have been overinterpreted, not as personal patrons (like the daemon of Socrates) nor even as tribal patrons (like the deities of the Navaho), but as the father-creator of the universe, with a single program for the entire human race, to be administered by the representatives of this special visionary tradition. In fact, we may say that, just as the second of our categories of myth, the metaphysical, reached its apogee in the Far East and South Asia, so did the first, the daemonic, in the variously developed monotheistic theologies of the Synagogue, the Church, and the Mosque.

The second view, the metaphysical, seems to have taken its rise in the hermit groves and philosophically cultivated courts of India, in the eighth and seventh centuries B.C. It developed then, with increasing subtlety and sophistication as well as range of schools and peoples involved, until by the ninth century A.D. the whole of the Orient was a great symphony of metaphysical references.

We read already in the *Brihadāranyaka Upanishad* (eighth to seventh centuries B.C.):

> This or that people say, "Worship this god! Worship that god!"—one god after another! This is his creation, indeed, and he himself is all the gods. . . . He has entered into everything, even the fingernail tips, as a razor would be hidden in a razor case, or fire in a fire holder. Him they see not; for as seen, he is incomplete. When breathing, he is named the breath; when speaking, the voice; when seeing, the eye; when hearing, the ear; when thinking, the mind: these are merely the names of his acts. Whoever worships one or another of these—he knows not; for he is incomplete in one or another of these. One should worship with the thought that he is one's very Self; for therein all these others become one. But that thing, namely, this Self, is itself but the footprint of this All: by it one knows this All, just as, verily, one finds [one's quarry] by a footprint. . . . So, whoever worships another divinity than his Self, thinking "He is one and I another," he knows not. He is like a sacrificial animal for the gods. Verily, indeed, just as many animals can be of service to man, even so each single person is of service to the gods. And if even one animal is taken away, it is not pleasant. What then, if many? Therefore, it is not pleasing to the gods that men should know this.[10]

Much the same insight can be sensed in the sayings of the Greek Xeno-phanes of Colophon (fl. 536 B.C.), the reputed founder of the Eleatic school from which Plato derived certain mythologically colored strains of his philoso-phy. He said:

> There is one God, greatest among gods and men, neither in shape nor in thought like unto mortals. . . . He is all sight, all mind, all ear. . . . He abides ever in the same place motionless, and it befits him not to wander hither and thither. . . . Yet men imagine gods to be born, and to have raiment, voice, and body, like themselves. . . . Even so the gods of the Ethiopians are swarthy and flat-nosed, the gods of the Thracians, fair-haired and blue-eyed. . . . Even so Homer and Hesiod attributed to the gods all that is a shame and a reproach among men—theft, adultery, deceit, and other lawless acts. . . . Even so oxen, lions, and horses, if they had hands wherewith to carve images, would fashion gods after their own shapes and make them bodies like to their own.[11]

Or again, we have the words of Antisthenes (born c. 444 B.C.): "God is not like anything; hence one cannot understand him by means of an image."[12]

In the Orient the tendency of the philosophical development was to retain the atmosphere of myth, employing its symbols and rites as adequate means by which to ready the mind for intuitive insights into the ineffable mystery of the universe:

> There the eye goes not;
> Speech goes not, nor the mind.
> We know not, we understand not
> How one should teach It.
>
> For It is other, indeed, than the known,
> And, moreover, above the unknown![13]

In the Occident, however, the tendency has been progressively toward such a definitively humanistic point of view as that epitomized in Nietzsche's vol-ume of disillusionment, *Human, All Too Human,* where he writes that all—morality and religion, art and prophecy—in spite of their pretensions to supernatural authority, transcendental insight, and ineffable inspiration, are fi-nally "human, all too human," and are to be read, consequently, in terms rather of psychology than of theology or metaphysics. One may, if one likes, regard these two views—the metaphysical and the humanistic, these two poles of phi-losophy in the modern world—as representing a play in the human mind of Niels Bohr's principle of complementarity; as a pair of opposites, or a pair of as-pects, beyond which (as beyond the clashing rocks of the Symplegades) an ulti-mate truth of some sort must abide (awaiting perhaps our heroic arrival). But for the present systematization of the materials available to a natural history of the gods and heroes, the view of Nietzsche will suffice. And we shall have to commence, furthermore, far back of the great period of the differentiation of our cultures into Orient and Occident, with the primitive dancing ground of the gods and the mystery of the primitive mask. What was the attitude toward their deities of the participants in those festivals, and what the background from which their gods must have first appeared?

Frobeniu's example of a child's seizure by a witch while in the act of play may be taken to represent an intense degree of the daemonic mythological experience. However, the attitude of mind represented by the game itself, before the seizure supervened, also belongs within the sphere of our subject. For as J. Huizinga has pointed out in his brilliant study of the play element in culture, the whole point, at the beginning, was the *fun* of play, not the rapture of seizure. "In all the wild imaginings of mythology a fanciful spirit is playing," he writes, "on the border-line between jest and earnest."[14] "As far as I know, ethnologists and anthropologists concur in the opinion that the mental attitude in which the great religious feasts of savages are celebrated and witnessed is not one of complete illusion. There is an underlying consciousness of things 'not being real.'"[15] And he quotes, among others, R. R. Marett, who, in his chapter on "Primitive Credulity" in *The Threshold of Religion,* develops the idea that a certain element of "make-believe" is operative in all primitive religions. "The savage," wrote Marett, "is a good actor who can be quite absorbed in his role, like a child at play; and also, like a child, a good spectator who can be frightened to death by the roaring of something he knows perfectly well to be no 'real' lion."[16]

"By considering the whole sphere of so-called primitive culture as a play-sphere," Huizinga then suggests, in conclusion, "we pave the way to a more direct and more general understanding of its peculiarities than any meticulous psychological or sociological analysis would allow."[17] I concur wholeheartedly with this judgment, only adding that we should extend the consideration to the entire field of our present subject.

In the Roman Catholic mass, when the priest, quoting the words of Christ at the Last Supper, pronounces the formula of consecration, with utmost solemnity, first over the wafer of the host (*Hoc est enim Corpus meum:* "For this is My Body"), then over the chalice of the wine (*Hic est enim Calix Sanguinis mei, novi et aeterni Testamenti: Mysterium fidei: qui pro vobis et pro multis effundetur in remissionem peccatorum:* "For this is the Chalice of My Blood, of the new and the eternal Testament: the Mystery of faith: which shall be shed for you and for many unto the remission of sins"), it is to be supposed that the bread and wine become the body and blood of Christ: that every fragment of the host and every drop of the wine is the actual living Savior of the World. The sacrament, that is to say, is not conceived to be a *reference,* a mere sign or symbol to arouse in us a train of thought, but is God himself, the Creator, Judge, and Savior of the Universe, here come to work upon us directly, to free our soul (created in his image) from the effects of the Fall (the Titan substance).

Comparably, in India it is believed that in response to consecrating formulas, deities will descend graciously to infuse their divine substance into the temple images, which are then called their throne or seat (*piṭha*). It is also possible—and in some Indian sects even expected—that the individual himself should become a seat of deity. In the *Gandharva Tantra* we read, for example: "No one who is not himself divine can successfully worship a divinity." And again: "Having become the divinity, one should offer it sacrifice."[18] Or finally, one may even discover that everything—absolutely everything—has become the body of a god: or rather, reveals the omnipresence of God as the ground of all being.

There is a passage recorded among the conversations of the nineteenth-century Bengalese spiritual master Ramakrishna, in which he described such a vision. "One day," he is reported to have said, "it was suddenly revealed to me that everything is Pure Spirit. The utensils of worship, the altar, the door frame—all Pure Spirit. Men, animals, and other living beings—all Pure Spirit. Then like a madman I began to shower flowers in all directions. Whatever I saw I worshiped."[19]

Belief, or at least a game of belief, is the first step toward such a divine seizure. The chronicles of the saints abound in accounts of their long ordeals of difficult practice, which preceded their moments of being carried away; and we have also the more spontaneous religious games and exercises of the folk (the amateurs) to illustrate for us the principle involved. The spirit of the festival, the holiday, the holy day of the religious ceremonial, requires that the normal attitude toward the cares of the world should have been temporarily set aside in favor of a particular mood of dressing up. The world is hung with banners. Or in the permanent religious sanctuaries—the temples and cathedrals—where an atmosphere of holiness hangs in the air, the logic of cold, hard fact must not be allowed to intrude and spoil the spell. The gentile, the "spoilsport," the positivist who cannot or will not play, must be kept aloof. Hence the guardian figures that stand at either side of the entrances to holy places: lions, bulls, or fearsome warriors with uplifted weapons. They are there to keep out the "spoilsports," the advocates of Aristotelian logic, for whom *A* can never be *B;* for whom the actor is never to be lost in the part; for whom the mask, the image, the consecrated host or tree or animal, cannot become God, but only a reference. Such heavy thinkers are to remain without. For the whole purpose of entering a sanctuary or participating in a festival is that one should be overtaken by the state known in India as "the other mind" (Sanskrit, *anya-manas*: absent-mindedness, possession by a spirit), where one is "beside oneself," spellbound: set apart from one's logic of self-possession and overpowered by the force of a logic of indissociation, wherein *A* is *B*, and *C* also is *B*.

"One day," said Ramakrishna, "while worshipping Shiva, I was about to offer a bel-leaf on the head of the image, when it was revealed to me that this universe itself is Shiva. Another day, I had been plucking flowers when it was revealed to me that each plant was a bouquet adorning the universal form of God. That was the end of my plucking flowers. I look on man in just the same way. When I see a man, I see that it is God himself, who walks on earth, rocking to and fro, as it were, like a pillow floating on the waves."[20]

From such a point of view the universe is the seat (*pīṭha*) of a divinity from whose vision our usual state of consciousness excludes us. But in the playing of the game of the gods we take a step toward that reality, which is ultimately the reality of ourselves. Hence the rapture, the feelings of delight, and the sense of refreshment, harmony, and re-creation! In the case of a saint, the game leads to seizure, as in the case of the little girl to whom the match revealed itself to be a witch. Contact with the orientation of the world may then be lost, the mind remaining rapt in that other state. For such it is impossible to return to this other game, the game of life in the world. They are possessed of God: that is all they know on earth and all they need to know. And they can even infect whole societies so that these, inspired by their seizures, may themselves break contact with the world and spurn it as delusory or as evil. Secular life then may be read as a Fall, a Fall from Grace—Grace being the rapture of the festival of God.

But there is another attitude, more comprehensive, which has given beauty and love to the *two* worlds: that, namely, of the *līlā*, "the play," as it has been termed in the Orient. The world is not condemned and shunned as a Fall, but voluntarily entered as a game or dance, wherein the spirit plays.

Ramakrishna closed his eyes. "Is it only this?" he said. "Does God exist only when the eyes are closed, and disappear when the eyes are opened?" He opened his eyes. "The Play belongs to Him to whom Eternity belongs, and Eternity to Him to whom the Play belongs. . . . Some people climb the seven floors of a building and cannot get down; but some climb up and then, at will, visit the lower floors."[21]

The question then becomes only: how far down or up the ladder can one go without losing the sense of a game? Huizinga, in his work already referred to, points out that in Japanese the verb *asobu*, which refers to play in general—

recreation, relaxation, amusement, trip or jaunt, dissipation, gambling, lying idle, or being unemployed—also means to study at a university or under a teacher; likewise, to engage in a sham fight; and finally, to participate in the very strict formalities of the tea ceremony. He writes:

> The extraordinary earnestness and profound gravity of the Japanese ideal of life is masked by the fashionable fiction that everything is only play. Like the *chevalerie* of the Christian Middle Ages, Japanese *bushido* took shape almost entirely in the play-sphere and was enacted in play-forms. The language still preserves this conception in the *asobase-kotoba* (literally, play-language) or polite speech, the mode of address used in conversation with persons of higher rank. The convention is that the higher classes are merely playing at all they do. The polite form for "you arrive in Tokyo" is, literally, "you play arrival in Tokyo"; and for "I hear that your father is dead," "I hear that your father has played dying." In other words, the revered person is imagined as living in an elevated sphere where only pleasure or condescension moves to action.[22]

From this supremely aristocratic point of view, any state of seizure, whether by life or by the gods, must represent a fall or drop of spiritual *niveau:* a vulgarization of the play. Nobility of spirit is the grace—or ability—to play, whether in heaven or on earth. And this, I take it—this *noblesse oblige,* which has always been the quality of the aristocracy—was precisely the virtue (*aretē*) of the Greek poets, artists, and philosophers, for whom the gods (whether of the Homeric, the Orphic, or the Zoroastrian strains) were true as poetry is true. We may take it also to be the primitive (and proper) mythological point of view, as contrasted with the heavier positivistic; this latter is represented on the one hand by religious experiences of the literal sort, where the impact of a daemon, rising to the plane of consciousness from its place of birth on the level of the sentiments, is taken to be objectively real, and on the other, by science and political economy, for which only measurable facts are objectively real. For if it is true that "God is not like anything: hence no one can understand him by means of an image," or that

It is other, indeed, than the known
And, moreover, above the unknown!

then it must be conceded, as a basic principle of our natural history of the gods and heroes, that whenever a myth has been taken literally its sense has been perverted; but also, reciprocally, that whenever it has been dismissed as a mere priestly fraud or a sign of inferior intelligence, truth has slipped out the other door.

But what, then, is the sense that we are to seek, if it is neither here nor there? The reader will perhaps recall that Immanuel Kant, in his *Prolegomena to*

Every Future System of Metaphysics, states very carefully that all of our thinking about final things can be only by way of *analogy.* "The proper expression for our fallible mode of conception," he says, "would be: that we imagine the world *as if* its being and inner character were derived from a supreme mind."[23]

Such a highly played game of "as if" frees our mind and spirit on the one hand from presumption of theology, which pretends to know the laws of God, and on the other from the bondage of reason, whose laws do not apply beyond the horizon of human experience.

I am willing to accept the word of Kant as the view of the metaphysician. And applying it to the range of festival games and attitudes just reviewed— from the mask to the consecrated host and temple image, transubstantiated worshipper and transubstantiated world—I can see, or believe I can see, that a principle of release operates throughout the series by way of the alchemy of an "as if"; and that, through this, the impact of all so-called "reality" upon the psyche is transubstantiated. The play state and the rapturous seizures sometimes deriving from it represent, therefore, a step toward rather than away from the ineluctable truth; and belief—acquiescence in a belief that is not quite belief— is the first step toward the deepened participation that the festival affords in that general Will to Life which, in its metaphysical aspect, is antecedent to, and the creator of, all of life's laws.

The opaque weight of the world—both of life on earth and of death, heaven and hell—is dissolved, and the spirit freed . . . not *from* anything, for there was nothing from which to be freed except a myth too solidly believed, but *for* something, something fresh and new, a spontaneous act.

From the position of secular man (*Homo sapiens*), then, we are to enter the play-sphere of the festival, acquiescing in a game of belief, where fun, joy, and rapture rule in ascending series. The laws of life in time and space—economics, politics, and even morality—will dissolve. Whereafter, re-created by that return to Paradise before the Fall, before the knowledge of good and evil, right and wrong, true and false, belief and disbelief, we are to carry the point of view and spirit of man the player (*Homo ludens*) back into life: as in the play of children, where, undaunted by the banal actualities of life's meager possibilities, the spontaneous impulse of the spirit to identify itself with something other than itself, for the sheer delight of play, transubstantiates the world—in which, after all, things are not quite as real or permanent, terrible, important, or logical as they seem.

Renewal Myths and Rites
of the Primitive Hunters and Planters

I wonder how many of you know that the earliest *unquestionable* evidence of mythology and ritual has been found precisely in this part of the world: Switzerland and the German Alps.

High in the peaks around St. Galen, Emil Bächler discovered and excavated, from 1903 to 1927, three extremely interesting caves: Wildkirchli, Drachenloch, and Wildmannlisloch.[1] Within these, at a depth of about six feet beneath the present surface of the floor, little walls of stone were encountered, some thirty-two inches high, forming bins or storage areas, within which a number of cave-bear skulls were preserved. Some of these skulls had circles of stones arranged around them; others were set upon stone slabs; one had the leg bones of a cave bear (perhaps its own) placed beneath its snout; another had the leg bones pushed through its eyes. Obviously, in some very early period these relics had been associated with a cult. There were flagstone floorings on the level of the bins, stone benches and worktables, flints of an extremely early, pre-Mousterian type, charcoal (indicating the use of fire) and a number of altars: the earliest altars yet found anywhere in the world, and the earliest evidence of the use of fire yet unearthed in Europe.

For the cave bear has been extinct for the past thirty or forty thousand years—since the close of the last glacial age, the Würm glaciation. Moreover, all of the caves were at such a height that they could not have been entered during the period of the great cold. The first two were about seven thousand feet and the last over eight thousand feet above sea level. During the centuries of the Würm they were completely under ice. Therefore, those cave-bear skulls were stored away *before* the coming of the last ice age: during the earlier, comparatively warm period of the Riss-Würm Interglacial, which is to be dated, approximately, between 75,000 and 200,000 B.C.

The German evidence was investigated independently of the Swiss in central Franconia, near Velden, in a cave called Petershöhle, by Konrad Hörmann, during the years from 1916 to 1922; and here again, the objects preserved were the skulls and leg bones of the cave bear. Five such skulls had been placed in closet-like recesses in the walls, about a hundred thousand years ago.[2]

Nothing earlier in the way of a sacred site has yet been identified anywhere on earth. The period is considerably earlier than that of the great Cro-Magnon caves of southern France and northern Spain, which are definitely post-glacial. Nor had the human race yet evolved to the status of *Homo sapiens*. The hands that stored those skulls away were of an earlier, far less attractive creature known as Neanderthal Man (*Homo neanderthalensis*).

His was an age when the countryside of Europe was not at all as it is today. England and Ireland were part of the mainland and great rivers flowed through the valleys that are now the Irish Sea, the North Sea, and English Channel— rivers to which the Thames, Seine, Garonne, and even the Rhine were but tributaries. And what is now the strait of Gibraltar was then a land bridge connecting Africa and Europe, while Italy and Sicily stretched in a broad, irregular mass to the southern mainland—so that what is now the Mediterranean was then two inland lakes. The elephant, southern mammoth, broad-nosed rhinoceros, and hippopotamus ranged in a landscape more tropical than that of modern Europe. Lions stalked the bison, aurochs, and giant deer. And presently, as the cold of the coming glacial age began to press down from Scandinavia and a sheet of ice, covering the whole Baltic, crept southward to envelop northern Germany while the ice caps of the Alps reached down some 2,000 feet below their present level, over the tundras and cold steppe-lands, the musk ox, woolly mammoth, and woolly rhinoceros appeared; herds of reindeer, also, and the arctic fox. The cave lion, cave leopard, and great cave hyena stalked their prey. Herds of wild horses, cattle, and bison grazed upon a plain that stretched far eastward, into Asia. And the vigorous Neanderthalers, remaining in those dangerous regions, ran down and slaughtered even the woolly mammoth, not with arrows—for the bow and arrow had not yet been invented— but with clubs, heavy rocks, and pointed sticks. They had to press close in for such a kill, and the work required a man's skill and strength as well as courage.[3]

It was therefore the male, and not the female, upon whom the whole life and substance of the little hunting bands depended. Animal food was their staple; animal skins provided warmth; animal sinews were their ropes; animal teeth and claws, their ornaments. There is reason to believe (as we shall see) that the magical energy of woman was utilized in the rituals of that long age of the early hunt; but it was through the male that the life-sustaining benefits finally came, and the male point of view, the male force, the male mode of experiencing life, death, and renewal was the ultimate determinant in the myths and rituals of those primitive votaries of the Great Hunt and the Master Bear.

It is, then, to such an age that these Alpine sanctuaries are to be referred.

And the earliest *human* burials of which we have knowledge are also of that remote age of Neanderthal Man; for example: the skeleton of a youth of about seventeen reposing in a sleeping posture, pillowed on a pile of flint, with a beautiful stone hand-axe at his side and the charred, split bones of wild cattle round about, interred in a cave in southern France;[4] or, in a cave on the coast of Italy, a man's skull surrounded (like some of the bear skulls) with a neat oval of stones, and with receptacles round about full of the bones of slaughtered beasts, indicating an offering and feast.[5]

There can be no doubt that Neanderthal Man observed some sort of cult. Furthermore, the idea of a sanctuary is evident, within which a protective ritual was executed. And by analogy with all that we know of the religious activities of later man, this ceremonialism points to a sense of the holy: that peculiar sentiment which Rudolf Otto identified as the unique, distinctive category of religion. "That mental state," as Rudolf Otto has declared, "is perfectly *sui generis* and irreducible to any other. . . . While it admits of being discussed, it cannot be strictly defined. . . . It cannot, strictly speaking, be taught, it can only be evoked, awakened in the mind; as everything that comes 'of the spirit' must be awakened."[6]

We have to ask, therefore: What was the occasion, the empirical experience, that awakened in man (or even proto-man, if you like) that state of spiritual arrest before the numinous which has been cherished and cultivated ever since as the highest, deepest, and most luminous state of mind of which the human being is capable?

We do not know what death can have meant to the Paleolithic hunter. Nevertheless, some sense of its force can be gained from certain primitive races living in the world today; for incredible though it may seem, the hunting cults of the Paleolithic age survive among many of the tribes of northern Asia and America.

For example, among the Ainus of Japan there is still practiced a bear sacrifice that any visitor with a bit of luck can observe. The Ainu are a puzzling race; for, although their neighbors are Mongolians for thousands of miles around, their skin is white and they have blue eyes, wavy hair, and immense beards. These interesting people have the wonderful idea that the world of men is so much more interesting and beautiful than that of the gods that deities like to come here and pay us visits. On all such occasions they are in disguise, wearing the bodies of animals, birds, fish, or insects. The bear is a visiting mountain god; the owl a village god; the dolphin a god of the sea. But of all these, the most honored divine visitor is the bear.[7]

There is a difficulty, however, that confronts the god on the occasion of his visit; for he cannot quit the animal form that he has assumed and return to his own home until the animal is killed: the god is locked, so to say, in its animal costume. And so the hunter, killing the animal, releases the god—and this, it is believed, is something the deity desires; for although he has come to us on a visit, he does not wish to remain here forever, as a dolphin, as an owl, or as a bear.

One can readily see that for any people whose whole mode of life is that of direct killing—dealing death, hand to hand—such a mythology would be of considerable psychological importance; for although, as Spengler has declared, "man is a beast of prey," man, like no other beast, knows what he is doing when he kills.[8] Like no other beast of prey, he has the knowledge of death and knows, when he kills, that he is, indeed, killing. The first function of myth, therefore, as it would now appear, was to conquer death, that is to say, to overcome the psychological impact of the act and necessity of killing. "For it takes a powerful magic," Leo Frobenius once remarked, "to spill blood and not be overtaken by the blood revenge."[9]

Or perhaps we can even go a step further and say that a certain hint of the Freudian Oedipus complex is here to be identified; for if it is true, as Géza Róheim has said, that *Father* is the first enemy and everything killed is therefore *Father,* then the fear of spilled blood and the compulsion to atone—to wipe out the death—is heavily charged, not only with noumenal, but also with Oedipal dread.[10]

When a bear is killed by an Ainu hunter, the man comes running down from the mountain to his village, shouting that a god is about to pay the people a visit. A number of young men then join him and, in a kind of procession, they carry the dead bear into the man's house by way not of the door but of a hole knocked in the wall—the so-called "god's window." Such an entry is known as a "god's arrival." Furthermore, the fire burning in the center of the house, on the hearth, is a goddess—a mountain goddess, just as the bear is a mountain god; for in Japan volcanic fire is a well-known phenomenon. Fujiyama is an extinct volcano, and it surely is no accident that the Ainu name of their goddess Fire, protectress of the hearth, is Fuji. When the bear is carried in triumph to the house, the fire goddess bids him welcome. He enters by the "god's window" and the two, god and goddess, converse together by the fireside all night, while the people sing and play music to entertain them. The next day, when the bear is slaughtered, cooked, and eaten, offerings of its own meat are made to its head, which is placed in the seat of honor; and when the bear is supposed to have finished eating, the god is given thanks for his visit, praise, and many presents, and, ceremonially dismissed, returns to his mountain home.[11]

When a very young black bear is caught in the mountains it is carried back alive to the village with a great deal of shouting, as a divine little visitor. One of the women adopts it, takes it to nurse at her breast, lets it play about with her children, and treats it with great affection. When it becomes big enough to hurt and scratch, however, it is put into a cage and kept there for about two years. Then comes the time when it is thought proper to release the young bear from its body and send it back to its divine home. This sacrifice is not regarded as a cruel act, but as one of kindness to the visitor. It is called *iyomande,* meaning "to send away," and though a certain cruelty and baiting are involved, the bear is supposed to be extremely happy.

The man who is to give the feast calls out to the people of his village: "I am about to sacrifice the dear little divine thing from among the mountains. Come, my friends, to the feast. Let us enjoy together the pleasures of this 'sending away'!"

A number of prayer-sticks are made. These are called "message bearers." They are from two to five feet long, whittled in such a way as to leave shavings clustered at the top, and they are stuck into the earth, beside the hearth fire, where the fire goddess dwells, after which they are brought to the place where the bear is to be killed.

The men of the village now approach the cage; the women and children follow, dancing and singing. All sit in a circle before the bear, and the leader, sitting very close to the cage, lets the little visiting god know what is going to happen.

"O Divine One," he says to the cub, "you were sent into this world for us to hunt. Precious little divinity, we adore you; pray, hear our prayer. We have nourished and brought you up with a deal of pains and trouble, because we love you so. And now that you have grown big, we are about to send you back to your father and mother. When you come to them, please speak well of us and tell them how kind we have been. Please come to us again and we shall again do you the honor of a sacrifice."

Ladies and gentlemen, please observe: the bear is invited to return. "Come to us again, and we shall again do you the honor of a sacrifice." To these people of the North—these people of the bear sacrifice—there is no such thing as death. There is no such thing as a beginning in birth. For death and birth are simply the passing back and forth of an immortal individual through a veil or curtain. And the function of the rite is to facilitate and celebrate this passage. It is not the reenactment, here and now, of an archetypal event that first took place in the beginning of time, *in illo tempore.* There is no such concept in this mythology. It is simply that the bear is now going home and should carry away no sentiment of ill will; and if it should wish to come again it may be sure that it will be honorably greeted, given a good home, and sent away with gifts.

The young bear, secured with ropes, is made to walk around the circle of people. Blunt little arrows are shot at him and he is teased until he becomes furious. Then he is tied to a decorated stake; six young fellows seize him by the legs, the head and tail; two poles, called "poles for strangling," are held to his neck, above and below; a perfect bowman sends an arrow into his heart in such a way that no blood spills to the earth; the poles are squeezed together, and the little guest is gone.

The bear's head then is removed with the whole hide, feet, and tail attached, carried into the house, and arranged among prayer-sticks and valuable gifts, to share a parting feast. A tasty morsel of its own flesh is placed beneath its snout, along with a helping of dried fish, some millet dumplings, a cup of *sake* or beer, and a bowl of its own stew. Then it is honored with another speech:

"O Little Cub, we give you these prayer-sticks, dumplings, and dried fish; take them to your parents. Go straight to your parents without hanging about on your way, or some devils will snatch away the souvenirs. And when you arrive, say to your parents: 'I have been nourished for a long time by an Ainu father and mother and have been kept from all trouble and harm. Since I am now grown up, I have returned. And I have brought these prayer-sticks, cakes, and dried fish. Please rejoice!' If you say this to them, Little Cub, they will be very happy."

A feast is celebrated, there is dancing, more prayer-sticks are made and placed upon the bear's head, another bowl of its own stew is placed before it, and when time has been allowed for it to finish, the man presiding at the feast calls out: "The little god is finished; come, let us worship!" He takes the bowl, salutes it, and divides the contents among the guests. The other parts of the beast then are eaten also, while some of the men drink the blood for strength and smear a portion upon their clothes. The head of the bear is separated from the rest of the skin and, being set upon a pole called "the pole for sending away," it is placed among a number of other skulls remaining from earlier feasts. And for the next few days the festival continues, until every bit of the little god has been consumed.[12]

"It is perfectly evident," writes Dr. Herbert Kühn in commenting upon these rites and others of their kind, "that the usages and customs of the Interglacial period have been retained up to the very present in these peripheral regions of the earth. . . . The bear skulls still are flayed and preserved in sacred places, offering places. They are covered and set round with slabs of stone. Special ceremonies still are celebrated at the offering places. Even today two vertebrae of the neck are allowed to remain attached to the skull, just as then. And even today we often find that the large molar of the bear has been ground down, precisely as Luther Friedrich Zotz found the case to be in the course of an excavation of a series of caves in the glacial mountain heights of Silesia."[13]

"Such details among the contemporary Asiatic hunters as the grinding down of the tooth of the bear and leaving of two vertebrae attached to the skull, just as in the European Interglacial period, prove that the continuity has actually remained unbroken for tens of thousands of years."[14]

It is to be noted also that in the Alpine Caves remains were found of fire. But Neanderthal Man did not cook his food. Is it then possible that fire was first domesticated, not for any practical use but as a fetish: as the living presence of that mountain goddess whom we have just beheld in conversation with the bear? She is a deity of considerable importance among the Ainu, serving not only as a guardian mother of the house, but also as a guide of souls to the other world.

And so let us attend, now, an Ainu funeral, noting its resemblance to the "sending away" of the bear and then recalling the matter of those two Neanderthal graves.

Among the Ainu, on such an occasion the master of the family becomes the celebrant. "You are a god now," he says to the corpse. "And without hankering for this world, you are to go now to the world of the gods, where your ancestors abide. They will thank you for the presents that you bring. So now go on quickly! Do not pause to look back." He puts a pair of leggings on the voyager's legs, a pair of mittens on his hands. "Take care," he tells him, "not to lose your way. The old goddess of the fire will guide you aright. I have already asked her to do so. Rely on her, and go your way with care. Farewell!"

A rich dinner is prepared for both the spirit of the departed and the people at the wake; and when they are about to carry away the coffin, the celebrant again has a word for their departing friend. "We have made a fine staff to help you on your way. Take hold of it firmly at the top and walk securely, minding your feet, lifting and lowering them as you raise and lower the staff. You have plenty of food and drink as souvenirs. Look neither to right nor to left but go on quickly and delight your ancestors with your presents. Forget your brothers, sisters, and other relatives remaining in this world. They are safe and sound under the care of the old goddess Fire. Do not brood upon them or else the folks where you are going will laugh at you."

The coffin is not carried out through the door, but a part of the side of the house is taken away and repaired before the mourners return. The ghost, then, will not know how to get back in. Or if the one who has died is the mistress of the house, the whole dwelling is burned. Into the grave go jewels, earrings, kitchen knives, pots and ladles, looms, and other such, if the departed was a woman; swords, bows, and quivers, if a man. And when the burial, or "throwing away" as it is called, has been completed, the mourners leave the grave walking backward, lest, turning, they should be possessed by the ghost of the deceased; and they are holding weapons in their hands—the women sticks, the men their swords—which they wave back and forth for their defense.[15]

The sentiment or experience illustrated by this rite is precisely that which Rudolf Otto has termed "daemonic dread." As he declares, this is not equivalent to any natural fear. No natural fear passes over into it merely by being intensified. It is the first, crude, primitive form of the numinous dread of the higher mystical experience.[16]

But in these rites the obvious intention is to ban or block the impact of this dread. A myth has been invented—the myth of no death—to protect the mind from the necessity of adjusting itself to an invasion from that abyss of darkness over which all life rides. "Life," wrote Schopenhauer, "is something that should not have been." The plants do not know this. The animals do not know this. For, as Dr. Neumann observed in his eloquent lecture the first day of this *Tagung*, the animals are rooted in nature. They play their natural roles without anxiety, like the sun, like the moon, like the stars. Man, however, has become alienated from his source and experiences nature with dread, both in its macro-cosmic aspect, as the objective world over against which his consciousness stands as subject, and in its microcosmic aspect, as the spontaneity of his own nature—his unconscious, his joy in being.[17]

The hunter, daily dealing death, is washed in blood—as, indeed, is all of nature. And the first myth of the self-protective ego, defending itself from the necessity of yielding its own blood to be the life of the world, is that of an im-mortal ground underlying the phenomenology of the passing world.

This comforting myth, this protective idea that there is no such thing as death, but only a going away and in birth only a returning, this idea that fun-damentally nothing happens, but all is mere appearance, disappearance and reappearance—a sort of cosmic peek-a-boo game—is one that occurs sponta-neously to children. Jean Piaget, in his volume on *The Child's Conception of the World*, presents a number of examples of the infant's thoughts in this regard:

"Do people turn back into babies when they get very old?" asked a little fel-low, five years of age.

"When you die," asked another, "do you grow up again?"

"And then," said the child of Dr. Melanie Klein, "I'll die, and you too, Mamma, and then we'll come back again."[18]

Such infantile ideas cannot properly be called myths, but they are the ele-ments, the bricks, so to say, out of which mythologies are made.

There is a legend of the Blackfoot Indians of the North American plains that reveals the force of these defensive ideas, not only for the psychological protection of the beast of prey that knows what he is doing when he kills, but also for the moral organization of his community. The Blackfoot Indians of Montana were buffalo hunters and one of their best devices for slaughtering a large herd was to lure the animals over a cliff and butcher them when they fell on the rocks below.

Now the legend of which I speak tells of a time when the hunters, for some reason, could not induce the animals to the fall, so that the people were starving. And so one early morning, when a young woman went to get water and saw a herd of buffalo feeding on the prairie, right at the edge of the cliff above the fall, she cried out, "Oh! If you will only jump into the corral, I shall marry one of you." She was amazed when the animals began to come jumping, falling over the cliff; but when a big bull with a single bound cleared the walls of the corral and approached her, she was terrified.

"Come!" he said, and he took her arm.

"Oh no!" she cried, pulling back.

"But you said that if the buffalo would jump, you would marry one. See! The corral is filled." And without further ado, he led her away onto the prairie.

Now when the people missed the young woman, her father took his bow and set out to find her. Arriving at a buffalo wallow—a place where the buffalo come for water and to lie and roll—he sat down to consider what he should do, and while he was brooding, a beautiful black-and-white bird, a magpie, came and lighted on the ground.

"Ha!" said the man. "You are a handsome bird! Help me! As you fly about, look for my daughter, and if you see her, say: 'Your father is waiting by the wallow!'"

The bird flew to a nearby herd and, seeing a young woman among the bison, lit on the ground not far from her and said quietly, "Your father is waiting by the wallow!"

"Not so loud!" she whispered, frightened, looking around; for her bull-husband was sleeping close by. "Go get me some water."

When the bull woke, he said to his wife, "Go back and tell him to wait."

So she took a horn from his head and hurried to the wallow.[19] "Father!" she cried, "Why did you come? You will surely be killed." And when he urged her to run with him, she refused. "They would pursue and kill us," she said. "We must wait until he sleeps again."

She returned, and the bull drank a swallow from his horn. "Aha!" said he. "There is a person close by!"

"No! No!" she answered.

The bull drank some more, then got up and bellowed. What a terrible sound! Up stood the bulls, raised their short tails and shook them, tossed their great heads, and bellowed back. Then they rushed in all directions and, coming to the wallow, hooked the poor man with their horns and trampled him, so that soon not even a small piece of his body could be seen.

Then his daughter cried, "Oh, my father, my father!"

"Ah-ha!" said the bull. "You are mourning for your father. And so now, perhaps, you can see how it is with us. We have seen our mother, fathers, many of our relatives, hurled over the rock walls and slaughtered by your people. But I shall pity you. If you can bring your father to life again, you and he may go back to your people."

The woman turned to the magpie. "Help me!" she cried. "Go and search in the trampled mud. Try to find some little piece of my father's body."

The bird quickly flew, tore up the mud with his sharp beak, and then, at last, found something white: a joint of the backbone. The young woman placed this particle on the ground and, covering it with her robe, sang a certain song. Removing the robe, she saw her father's body lying there, as though dead. Covering it again, she resumed her song, and when she next took the robe away, her father was breathing; then he stood up. The buffalo were amazed.

"We have seen strange things today," the bull husband said to the others. "The man we trampled into small pieces is alive again. The people's holy power is strong."

He turned to the young woman. "Now," he said, "before you and your father go, we shall teach you our dance and song. You must not forget them."

For this ritual of the buffalo dance was to be the magical means by which the buffalo killed by the people for their food should be restored to life, just as the man killed by the buffalo had been restored.

All the buffalo danced; and as befitted the dance of such great beasts, the song was slow and solemn, the step ponderous and deliberate. And when the dance was over, the bull said, "Now go to your home and do not forget what you have seen. Teach this dance and song to your people. The sacred object of the rite is to be a bull's head and buffalo robe. Likewise all those who dance the bulls are to wear a bull's head and buffalo robe when they perform."

The father and daughter returned to their camp and the chiefs selected a number of young men, who were taught the dance and song of the bulls. That was the way the Blackfoot association of men's societies called All Comrades first was organized. Its function was to regulate the ceremonial life and to punish offenders.[20]

One finds a great many tales of this sort among the North American tribes. Their basic point is that there is a mutual understanding between the human and animal worlds, according to which the game animals give their bodies willingly to be man's food. The animals are willing victims. But there is an understanding, also, that the hunters will perform a ritual of renewal, so that the herds may be restored to life. The resurrection of the dead man was made possible by the finding of a particle of bone. Without this, nothing could have been accomplished, but with it, he returned just as he had been before. We may regard this bone as our token of the hunter's nuclear idea of the miracle of renewal. The bone does not disintegrate in the womb of the earth and germinate into something else, like a planted seed, but is the undestroyed base from which the same individual that was there before becomes magically reconstructed, to pick up life where he left it. The same creature comes back by way of an actual fragment or element of his former body.

Furthermore, this rite was in no sense a reenactment of any archetypal event from the "time of the beginning." The rites of the primitive hunters are not supposed to have descended from an age of mythological ancestors. They are said to have come, for the most part, directly from the animals themselves—from just such Animal Masters, or Master Animals, as the buffalo bull of this legend.[21] And they have been received by such people as dwell in the world today, possessed however of shaman power. The atmosphere of this mythology is not mystical, but magical and shamanistic. The girl, even without knowing it, had shaman power; the great bull, too, had shaman power: he jumped and was not killed like the rest; the magpie was a shaman. According to the view of these people such power exists among shamans and visionaries to this day and it is through them—not from the ancestors of a mythological age—that the people have received their rites.

One more aspect of these shamanistic, hunting mythologies and rites must now be shown, namely the cosmology underlying them; and in order to suggest something of the broad geographical range of this primitive mode of thought, I shall choose my illustration from an African tribe. Many of the African tribes are planters. The pygmies, however, have an ancient tradition of the hunt; and so, when four of these little people—a woman and three men—attached themselves to an expedition conducted by Leo Frobenius in the Congo, he one day asked them if they would supply the company with some antelope meat. They replied that they would have to wait until the next day, because there were some preparations to be made that could be accomplished only at dawn, and Frobenius then kept his eye on them to see what these preparations might be.

Before the sunrise the four little people climbed a nearby hill and, when they had reached the summit, cleared the ground of all bits of growth. One of the men then drew something on the cleared earth while the others pronounced formulae and prayers. As soon as the sun appeared, one of the men, with an arrow in his drawn bow, stepped over to the cleared ground and, when the rays of the sun struck the drawing, the following ritual took place. The woman, lifting her hands as though reaching for the sun, uttered loudly some unintelligible syllables, the man released his arrow, the woman cried again, and the men then dashed into the forest with their weapons. When Frobenius went to see what had been drawn, he found the outline of an antelope with the arrow in its neck.[22]

That afternoon the hunters shot their quarry with an arrow through its neck. And they took from it some hair and a calabash of blood which they carried the next morning to the top of their hill for the second portion of the rite. The hairs and blood they smeared upon the picture and when the sun's rays again struck it, they quickly erased the whole thing and pulled out the arrow.[23]

The crucial point of the ceremony was that the rite should be executed at dawn, the arrow flying into the antelope along the first ray of the sun. For in all hunting mythologies the sun is a great hunter. At dawn his arrows slay the stars. By analogy: the human hunter is to be identified with the sun, his arrow with a ray of the sun, the antelope with a star. Then, just as tomorrow night will see the star return, so will tomorrow the antelope. And the woman, apparently, was the cosmic night itself: the womb of renewal and gate of return.

In the celebrated Cro-Magnon painted grotto of Altamira, which is to be dated approximately from 35,000 to 10,000 B.C., we find the same idea illustrated.[24] For those beautiful bulls, so often reproduced, are painted on the ceiling. They are stars. The cave is the cosmic night and they are the shining, immortal herd of the night sky—the archetypes of those annual herds that appear, as willing victims, to give their bodies and return.

"On earth, as it is in heaven": that is the theme. Man is returned to the innocence of the sun and stars, and of the animal world, which is rooted in nature, by an equation of himself with the sun, the great lion of the heavens, and of his victims with the herds of the night sky. And by concentrating on these, he is able to erase from consciousness the actual threat of the night of annihilation. The reality of nature and himself as nature has been countered by a myth of personal immortality.

"After death," said an Eskimo shaman, Igjugarjuk by name, whom the explorer Dr. Rasmussen met in the arctic of northern Canada, "we do not always remain as we were during life. The souls of men, for instance, may turn into all kinds of animals. Pinga, the guardian spirit of the universe, looks after the souls of animals and does not like to see too many of them killed. Nothing is lost. The blood and entrails must be covered up after a caribou has been killed. So we see that life is endless. Only we do not know in what form we shall reappear."[25]

The rites and myths are childish—as, indeed, all rituals are and all mythologies. The inhabiting idea, however, of the Self transcending death is one that we know from the greatest teachers of mankind: the Lord Krishna's song, for example, or the sages of the Greeks.

"Know that by which all of this is pervaded to be imperishable," we read in the *Bhagavad Gītā*. "Only the bodies, of which this eternal, imperishable, incomprehensible Self is the indweller, can be said to have an end."[26]

And from the Greek sage, Pythagoras:

"All things are changing; nothing dies. The spirit wanders, comes now here, now there, and occupies whatever frame it pleases. From beasts it passes into human bodies, and from our bodies into beasts, but never perishes."[27]

This I would like to call the primary myth of the masculine spirit, summoned into manifestation by the challenge of death: the abyss of the deep night sky, both without and within: the night of being and becoming absolutely nothing.

And I should like to pose, now, in contrast to this, the contrary myth that appears in those parts of our planet in which the plant world, and not the animal, is the dominant factor and determinant of human experience. There the primary symbol, the archetype of experience, is not the bone, which does not dissolve in the earth, but the seed, which indeed does so: dies, so to say, and in death is transformed into something other, which then is the nourishment and very substance of all life. And here, furthermore, it is not upon the work and life feeling of the male that the community depends, but upon the female, who, in her normal functioning as mother and nourisher, participates in the nature of the bearing earth itself and deeply knows, therefore, its secret.

Leo Frobenius was the first to point out the contrast of these two mythological worlds, respectively, of the animal-taught and the plant-taught primitive societies.[28] And it was just ten years ago that Professor Adolf Jensen, Director of the Institute for Culture Morphology in Frankfort, presented in this hall an example of the myth that I wish to bring before you as typical of the latter. We do not know how far back in time these planting myths are to be traced. They are of far more recent origin than those of the Animal Master and the Bear Sacrifice. And yet, their great age is well attested by their prodigious distribution: from the jungles of West Africa eastward to India and Southeast Asia, across the Pacific to equatorial America.[29] Their field, in fact, is that whole vast equatorial belt, where the primary source of man's food is not the hunt, but the cultivation of such nourishing fare as the banana, coconut, breadfruit, and yam. And among the characteristic traits of this zone there is a basic, widely diffused myth that represents our present world of death and birth as having come into being only following an act of murder.

In the beginning, we are told, there was no death; there was no begetting of new beings; and there were no food plants, for there was no need to eat; there was no moon to mark the passages of time; and there was no division of creatures into men and beasts. Nor were the people of that mythological age precisely people: they partook of animal and plant as well as human traits.

According to an Indonesian version of this general myth, the nine first families of mankind emerged from clusters of bananas, and where they settled there were nine dance grounds. A certain man among them, however, killed a pig, and this was the first killing of anything in the world. He found a coconut on the tusk of this pig: the first coconut in the world; and when he planted it—having wrapped it, first, in a piece of cloth bearing the picture of a serpent—a palm tree grew. The man climbed this palm to cut from it a blossom, but cut his own hand while doing so, and from the mixture of blood and palm sap a little girl was born, whom he called Hainuwele, "Leaf of the Cocopalm." She grew very fast and in three days was mature. Then a great dance that was to last nine nights was celebrated on the nine dance grounds. The men danced in a large ninefold spiral and the women sat in the center, reaching betel nut to the dancers, just as they do in the festivals to this day. Hainuwele stood in the center; but instead of passing out betel nut, she gave the men all kinds of wonderful things, valuable objects that had come from her body, such as coral, beautiful dishes, golden earrings, and great gongs. The people pressed about her for more, but presently became jealous of her wealth. And so the men dug a deep hole in the dance area and, while she was passing out these objects, in the course of their slowly cycling movement they pressed her toward the hole and threw her in. A loud song drowned her cry. They quickly covered her with dirt and the dancers trampled this with their steps, dancing till dawn, when the festival ended.

But when Hainuwele failed to come home her father knew that she had been killed. He went to the dance ground, dug up the corpse, cut it into many pieces, and buried these in the area round about. Then the buried portions of the body began to grow, turning into things that up to that time had never existed anywhere on earth, the plants that have been the food of the people ever since.[30]

Thus death came into the world and with it the food by which men live. The world lives on death: that is the insight rendered in this myth. Moreover, as we learn from other mythological fragments in this culture sphere, the sexual organs appeared at that time; for death without reproduction would have been the end, as, likewise, reproduction without death.

We may say, then, that the interdependence of *thanatos* and *eros,* their import as the complementary aspects of a single state of being, and the necessity of killing—killing and eating—for the continuance of this state of being, which is that of man on earth, and of all things on earth, the animals, birds, and fish, as well as man—this deeply moving, emotionally disturbing glimpse of death as the life of the living—is the fundamental motivation supporting the rites around which the social structure of the early planting villages was composed. They place death in the middle of the scene: and not death alone, but killing—as the precondition of life.

The headhunt is practiced in this culture zone as a ritual act preliminary to marriage; for as murder preceded begetting *in illo tempore,* so must it now. Here killing is not an act of heroism, but of religion, rendering here and now the monstrous archetype, so that life may realize the awful depth of its own nature—not with dread, but with surrender.[31]

A typical ritual of this zone has been describe by the Swiss ethnologist Paul Wirz, in his work on the Marind-anim of Dutch South New Guinea.[32] The mythological beings of the age of the beginning appear in the ceremonies of these headhunting cannibals to enact the world-fashioning events of the mythological age to the tireless chant of many voices, the boom of log drums, and the whirring of the bull-roarers, which are the voices of the mythological beings themselves, rising from the earth. Toward the end of the boys' puberty rites, which terminate in a sexual orgy of several days and nights, from which, however, the boys themselves are excluded, a fine young girl, ceremonially painted and costumed, is led into the dancing ground and made to lie beneath a platform of very heavy logs. With her, in open view of the festival, the initiates then cohabit, one after another; and while the youth chosen to be last is embracing her, the supports of the logs are jerked away and the platform drops to a great boom of drums. A howl goes up and the dead girl and boy are dragged from the logs, cut up, roasted, and eaten.[33]

This savage ritual is typical of the culture world of the Great Goddess, who is at once the womb and tomb of the universe. And even where the victims are not boys and girls but animals—pigs, for example, goats, or bulls—the victim is never an offering in the sense of a gift rendered to some god, but is the god itself. Its death is a rendering here and now of the mystery of that one who becomes many in us all by way of a continuous immolation. This divinity is androgyne, as well as both dead and begetting at the same time.

Nor is it possible to miss the echo of this solemn goat-song in the myths and rites of the early agricultural civilizations: the mythologies of Ishtar and Tammuz, Isis and Osiris. In the earliest civilizations of the archaic world the evidence for rites involving the immolation, not simply of such a young couple, but of the entire royal court, is overwhelming.

In the Royal Tombs of the ancient Sumerian city of Ur, Sir Leonard Woolley excavated a number of spectacular group burials. In one he found the chamber of a king and beside it that of his queen (or perhaps these two, as later students have observed, may have been a substituted priest and priestess; for their date, c. 2500 B.C., is a little late for this sort of royal immolation).[34] The members of the king's court had been disposed around his tomb in perfect order; and above these, likewise in perfect order, were the skeletons of the queen's court, which, apparently, had followed. The queen herself had been dressed precisely in the manner in which the goddess Ishtar is described in the Mesopotamian myths of her voluntary descent to the underworld following her spouse, and at the queen's hand there was a golden cup, which had contained her drink of death. Among the rich ornaments in her chamber there lay the silver head of a cow: in the king's chamber, the head of a bull. And there were a number of beautiful little harps among the remains, one still caressed by the skeleton hand of its girl harpist, the sounding box having the form of a bull, with a bull's head of gold, embellished with a lapis lazuli beard.[35]

We know this bull from the myths. It is the moon-bull, Sin, who dies and is resurrected, and the rhythm of whose cycle is the rhythm of the womb.

Hainuwele, the Indonesian sacrifice, not only became the plant world upon which mankind lives, but also, after three days, rose into the sky as the moon. Her animal counterpart, furthermore, was the pig, as the king's, here, is the bull. Her murder followed that of the pig and just as the coconut from which she grew was derived from the pig's death, so were the other plants from hers. Many other mythologies of this planting-culture zone assign the first death to a man-serpent—a sort of *nāga*—whose head then was cut off and planted: and this would seem to have been the earliest pattern of the myth. A vestige appears in the tale of Hainuwele in the serpent painted on the cloth in which the coconut was wrapped before planting. For the growth, then, of the coconut tree, as the first valuable food plant, reproduced in every nut the form of the man-serpent's head. And the headhunt, also, is now well explained as ritual repetition of that decapitation: particularly, since the head is to be opened in a certain way, like a coconut, and the contents consumed.[36]

Another vestige of the serpent as the first sacrifice appears in our own serpent, winding up the tree, addressing Eve in conversation.[37] Eve and the serpent are the archetypal couple through whom death and birth came into the world. They were not murdered during, but cursed following, their mythological act and we have instead of the coconut an apple; nevertheless, all the elements of the primitive planting myth are present.

In the mythology of the primitive planters, death and renewal are not pictured as a curse, but as a monstrous wonder, wherein the divine being whose flesh is meat indeed and whose blood is drink indeed becomes our very flesh and we, in turn, then yield our own flesh in reenactment. The cross of Christ, rising on Calvary, "The Hill of the Skull," Golgotha, where Adam's head is supposed to have been buried, supports and validates our own creative civilization with the force of this terrible image.[38] Growing from the buried head of the First Adam, like a tree, bearing on its boughs the Second Adam, "Fruit of the Tree," Holy Rood has made of man's death the sign of man's rebirth; and it surely is in the spirit of that willing sacrifice that both the Royal Tombs of Ur and the primitive rituals of the early planters must be viewed.

An early Portuguese voyager in South India tells of a certain king whom he saw in Malabar (which to this day is an area with a very strong matriarchal emphasis), who, on a certain day determined by the position of the planet Jupiter in the zodiac, mounted a platform before his people and with some very sharp knives cut off his nose, ears, lips, and other members, and as much of himself as he could, throwing everything away hurriedly until so much of his blood was gone that he began to faint, whereupon he quickly cut his throat.[39]

Or consider the largest of the Royal Tombs of Ur, where the remains of sixty-eight women were found in regular rows, each lying on her side, legs slightly bent and hands brought up to her face, so close together that the heads of those in front rested on the legs of those behind. Twenty-eight had worn hair ribbons of gold, all but one of the rest, hair ribbons of silver; and there were four harpists grouped together about a copper cauldron, which Woolley associates with the manner of their death—a poison, voluntarily drunk, which had carried this multitude through the winged gate. They had met their death in the way of a great game; for all were stars. Their king was the moon: his queen was Ishtar, the planet Venus. An eon had ended, and the whole celestial court dissolved into the night, as prerequisite to renewal: renewal, however, not of the individuals, but of the game—the civilization. For in this tradition there was no such thing, really, as an individual in our sense. All were but organs of the group. And with an attitude of acquiescence in the process, submission, or even—I might say—*amor fati,* their bodies were given to the earth, like seeds, for the renewal and continuous re-creation of the world.

And what of that one young lady who had no ribbon, either of gold or of silver? Actually, she had a ribbon of silver on her person. It was found among the bones of her skeleton at the level of the waist: carried apparently in her pocket, just as she had taken it from her room, done up in a tight coil with the ends brought over to prevent its coming undone. She had been late for the party and had not had time to put it on.[40]

The contrast between these planters' myths and rites and those of the hunters, I should say, could not be greater. They represent the two elementary poles of response to the *mysterium tremendum:* that of defense and that of sur-render.[41] And whereas there is something charmingly boyish about the first, in the second the whole mystery of woman's range of life experience comes into play: the way of experience tellingly rendered in the words of a noble Abyssinian woman quoted by Frobenius in one of his African studies.

"How," this woman asked, "can a man know what a woman's life is? A woman's life is quite different from a man's. God has ordered it so. A man is the same from the time of his circumcision to the time of his withering. He is the same before he has sought out a woman for the first time, and afterwards. But the day when a woman enjoys her first love cuts her in two. She becomes another woman on that day. The man is the same after his first love as he was before. The woman is, from the day of her first love, another. That continues so all through life. The man spends a night by a woman and goes away. His life and body are always the same. The woman conceives. As a mother she is another person than the woman without child. She carries the fruit of the night nine months long in her body. Something grows. Something grows into her life that never again departs from it. She is a mother. She is and remains a mother even though her child die, though all her children die. For at one time she carried the child under her heart. And it does not go out of her heart ever again. Not even when it is dead. All this a man does not know; he knows nothing."[42]

The point is that woman is life, and goes with it in her experience; that life is what there is to know, and nature is transformation.

With this then as our clue to the feminine mystique of the goddess Earth and her child, the plant child who is to be consumed, let us ask now, in conclusion, to what deepest depth of prehistory the earlier, hunter's way of thought can be traced. I have said that the Alpine cave-bear sanctuaries and human burials of Neanderthal Man represent the earliest *unquestionable* evidence of mythology and ritual. Some further clues, however, have recently appeared, which suggest an even greater depth than the Riss-Würm Interglacial.

You have all heard of the bones recently unearthed in South Africa of a series of ape-like creatures, with the brain capacity about of a chimpanzee, but with upright posture. Their date is at the beginning of the Pleistocene: conservatively, about 600,000 B.C. And they have been named both Australopithecus ("the southern ape") and Plesianthropus ("proximate man"); for the question of their humanity is still under debate.[43]

At the Fifth International Congress of Anthropological and Ethnological Sciences, held at the University of Pennsylvania in September 1956, Dr. Raymond Dart, of Witwatersrand University, South Africa, showed a convincing series of slides in which the bone implements of these creatures were illustrated. They included the lower jaws of large antelopes, which had been cut in half to be used as saws and knives; gazelle horns with part of the skull attached, which showed distinct signs of wear and use, possibly as digging tools; and a great number of Plesianthropoid palates with the teeth worn down, which had been used as scrapers. But the really sensational slides were those showing a number of baboon and Plesianthropoid skulls that had been fractured by the blow of a bludgeon. All had been struck by an instrument having two nubs or processes at the hitting end, which Professor Dart and his collaborators have surmised to have been the heavy end of the leg bone of a gazelle. But apes do not slay with weapons. Ergo: our little friend was not an ape, but a man.[44]

The animal remains associated with the bones of these earliest known hominids have been chiefly antelopes, horses, gazelles, hyenas, giraffes, and other beasts of the plain—very swift runners, so that the art of the hunt must have been considerably developed. Professor Dart, furthermore, has found abundant evidence of a practice of removing the heads and tails of the animals killed. From a sorting of about six tons of bone-bearing rock, representing the parts of at least 433 creatures, it was learned that Plesianthropus habitually decapitated the animals that he slew. The head parts of antelopes, the wild horse and ox, baboons, pigs, hyenas and porcupines, giraffes and rhinoceroses were found in great number, far separated from the bodies—and Professor Dart, in a recent paper on this subject, has compared this evidence of a head-cult with the cavebear skulls of the Alpine sanctuaries—some 400,000 years later in date.[45]

Throughout the length of this immense period there is no evidence of any kind suggesting a planter's cult or culture; and so it appears—at least from the evidence now available—that man was a killer from the start, a beast of prey, who knew, however, what he was doing when he killed and sought to protect himself by magic from its effect.

❧❧❧

If an authority on architecture looking at the buildings of New York were to observe, "They are all made of brick"; then viewing the ruins of ancient Mesopotamia remarked, "They are all made of brick"; and finally, visiting the temples of Ceylon, declared: "They are all made of brick"; would you say that this man had an eye for the qualities of architecture? It is true that they are all of brick. It is true, also, that a study might be made of the differences between the bricks of Ceylon, those of ancient Sumer, those, say, of the Roman aqueducts still standing in southern France, and those of the city of New York. However, these observations about brick are not all that we should like to hear about the architecture of the great cities of the world.

Now let me present to you a problem in the architecture of myth.

Early one morning, long ago, two Sioux Indians on the North American plains were out hunting with their bows and arrows; and as they were standing on a hill looking for game, they saw in the distance something coming toward them in a very strange and wonderful manner. When this mysterious thing drew nearer, they perceived that it was a very beautiful woman, dressed in white buckskin and bearing a bundle on her back. One of the men immediately became lustful and told his friend of his desire, but the other rebuked him, warning that this surely was no ordinary woman. She had come close now and, setting down her bundle, asked the first to approach her. When he did so, he and she were suddenly covered by a cloud and when this lifted there was only the woman—with the man, nothing but bones at her feet, being consumed by snakes.

"Behold what you see!" she said to the other. "Now go and tell your people to prepare a large ceremonial lodge for my coming. I wish to announce to them something of great importance."

The young man returned quickly to this camp; and the chief, whose name was Standing Hollow Horn, had several teepees taken down, sewn together, and made into a ceremonial lodge. Such a lodge has twenty-eight poles, of which the central pole, the main support, is compared to the Great Spirit, Wakan Tanka, the supporter of the universe. The others represent aspects of creation; for the lodge itself is a likeness of the universe.

"If you add four sevens," said the old warrior priest Black Elk, from whom this legend was derived, "you get twenty-eight. The moon lives twenty-eight days and we reckon time by the moon. Each day of the lunar month represents something sacred to our people: two of the days represent the Great Spirit, Wakan Tanka, who is our Father and Grandfather; two, the earth, our Mother and Grandmother; four are for the four winds; one is for the spotted eagle; one for the sun, one for the moon, one for the morning star; four are for the four ages; seven for our seven great rites; one is for the buffalo; one for the fire; one for the water; one for the rock; and one is for man. You should know also that the buffalo has twenty-eight ribs, and that in our war bonnets we usually wear twenty-eight feathers. There is a meaning in everything, and these are the things that are good for men to know and to remember."[46]

The priest explained the image of the man consumed by snakes. "Anyone attached to the senses and things of this world," he said, "lives in ignorance and is being consumed by the snakes that represent his own passions."[47]

Are we not reminded here of the Greek myth of the young hunter Actaeon, who, following a forest stream to its source, discovered the goddess Artemis bathing in a pool, perfectly naked? And when she saw that he looked lustfully upon her, she turned him into a stag that was pursued by his own hounds, torn to pieces, and consumed. The two myths are comparable. Black Elk's reading of his own accords with the sense of the Greek also. The two, that is to say, are made of bricks of the same kind.

But do such images take form naturally in the psyche? Can they be expected to appear any place on earth, spontaneously, in mythological systems? Or must we say, on the contrary, that since mythologies serve specific, historically conditioned cultural functions—just as architectural structures do—if two can be shown to be homologous they are historically related? Can the Greeks and the Sioux possibly have received their inheritances from the same source? And are these common themes, therefore, evidence rather of cultural diffusion than of psychological spontaneity and parallel development? Before such questions can be answered, we must know more about the deities involved and their background. Let us continue, therefore, with this legend.

When the people had built a lodge that was symbolically a counterpart of the universe, they gathered within it and were extremely excited, wondering who the mysterious woman might be and what she wished to say. She entered by the door, which was facing east, and walked sunwise around the central pillar: south, west, north, and east. "For is not the south the source of life?" the old teller of the tale explained. "And does not man advance from there toward the setting sun of his life? Does he not then arrive, if he lives, at the source of light and understanding, which is the east? And does he not return to where he began, to his second childhood, there to give back his life to all life, and his flesh to the earth whence it came? The more you think about this," the old Indian said, "the more meaning you will see in it."[48]

Once again, we find that we are on familiar ground. We are recognizing every element. The ceremonial lodge is a temple, and like many of which we have heard during the years of these Eranos lectures, is an image of the universe in the form of a circle. "We have established here the center of the earth," the old Medicine Man explained, "and this center, which in reality is everywhere, is the dwelling place of Wakan Tanka."[49] Can this figure be a counterpart of the circle of Nicholas Cusanus, whose circumference is nowhere and whose center is everywhere, the circle of the spirit? It is amazing to catch an echo of *this* thought from the lips of an old warrior of the Sioux.

Shall we then join our voice to those who write of a great Perennial Philosophy, which has been the one eternally true wisdom of the human race, from time out of mind? Or shall we hold, rather, to the answer of the nineteenth-century anthropologists—Bastian, for example, Tylor, and Frazer—who attributed such parallels to something rather psychological than metaphysically substantial: "the effect," as Frazer formulated the idea, "of similar causes acting alike on the similar constitution of the human mind in different countries and under different skies"?[50]

We note the formula four times seven, giving twenty-eight supports of the universe; the numbers four and seven being standard symbols of totality in the iconographies of both the Orient and the Occident: and this game of sacred numbers itself is a highly significant common trait. One of the twenty-eight is the pivot of the universe. The number surrounding it then is twenty-seven: three times nine: three times three times three. We think of Dr. Jung's numerous discussions of the symbolism of the four and three. We think of the nine choirs of angels, three times three, that surround and celebrate the central throne of the Trinity. The number four recurs in the clockwise circumambulation, now associated not only with the four directions but also with the life stages of the individual, so that the symbolism is being applied both to the macrocosm and to the microcosm: the two being tied by the number twenty-eight to the cycle of the moon, which dies and is resurrected and is therefore the cycle of renewal. Furthermore, the buffalo has twenty-eight ribs and is therefore himself a counterpart of the moon. Do not the buffaloes return every year, miraculously renewed, like the moon? We think of the Moon Bull of the archaic Near East, whose image appeared on the harps in the Royal Tombs of Ur: the animal symbol of the moon god, Sin, after whom Mount Sinai was named, so that it should represent the cosmic mountain at the center of the world. At the foot of that mountain—as we know—the High Priest, Aaron, conducted a festival of the golden calf, which Moses then committed to the fire, ground to bits, mixed with water, and caused the people to drink, in a kind of inverse communion meal—reminding us of the killing, roasting, and eating of the young Marind-anim of which I spoke in the last hour.[51] Only after this sacrifice did Moses receive, on the mountain top, where the heaven god meets the goddess Earth, the full assignment of the law and the promise of the Promised Land—not for himself (for he was now, himself, to be the sacrifice), but for the people. When he came down from the mountain the skin of his face shone like the moon, so that he had to wear a veil when he was before the people, like the archaic kings of the Moon Bull.[52] In the mythology of Christ, three days in the tomb, crucified and resurrected, there is implicit the same lunar symbolism. The Sacrificial Bull: the Sacrificial Lamb: the Cosmic Buffalo! Their symbology is perfectly interpreted by this old Medicine Man of the

Sioux when he declares that the buffalo is symbolic of the universe in its temporal, lunar aspect, dying yet ever renewed, but also, in its twenty-eighth rib, of the Great Spirit, which is eternal.

Chief Standing Hollow Horn was seated at the west of the lodge, the place of honor, because there he faced the door, the east, from which comes the light, representing wisdom, and this illumination a leader must possess. The beautiful woman came before him and, lifting the bundle from her back, said to him: "Behold this bundle and always love it; for it is holy. No impure man should ever see it. Within there is a very holy pipe with which you are to send your voices to your Father and Grandfather."

She drew forth the pipe and with it a round stone, which she placed upon the ground. Lifting the pipe, with its stem to the sky, she said: "With this pipe you will walk upon the earth; for the earth is your Mother and Grandmother. Every step taken upon her should be a prayer. The bowl is of red pipestone; it is of earth. Carved upon it is a buffalo calf, who represents all the quadrupeds living upon your Mother. The pipe stem is of wood, representing all that grows upon the earth. And these twelve feathers, hanging here, where the stem enters the bowl, are feathers of the spotted eagle. They represent that eagle and all the winged things of the air.

"When you smoke this pipe, all these things join you, everything in the universe, and they send their voices to your Father and Grandfather, the Great Spirit. When you pray with this pipe you pray for all things and all pray with you."[53]

The proper use of the pipe, as told by the old Medicine Man, Black Elk, requires that it should be identified with both the universe and oneself. A live coal is taken from the fire and the keeper of the pipe then places upon it a bit of sweet-grass that he has lifted four times to heaven with a prayer. "Within this grass," runs the prayer, "is the earth, this great island. Within it is my Grandmother, my Mother, and all creatures who walk in a holy manner. The fragrance of this grass will cover the universe. O Wakan Tanka, my Grandfather, be merciful to all."

The bowl of the pipe then is held over the burning grass in such a way that the smoke enters it, passing through the stem and coming out the end, which is directed toward heaven. "In this way," explained Black Elk, "Wakan Tanka is the first to smoke and by this act the pipe is purified."[54]

The pipe then is filled with tobacco that has been offered in the six directions: to the west, north, east, and south, then to heaven, then to earth. "In this manner," the old man said, "the whole universe is placed in the pipe."[55] Finally, the man who fills the pipe should identify it with himself. There is a prayer in which this identity is described:

> These people [says the prayer] had a pipe,
> Which they made to be their body.
>
> O my Friend, I have a pipe that I have made to be my body;
> If you also make it to be your body,
> you shall have a body free from all causes of death.
>
> Behold the joint of the neck, they said,
> *That* I have made to be the joint of my own neck.
>
> Behold the mouth of the pipe,
> *That* I have made to be my mouth.
>
> Behold the right side of the pipe,
> *That* I have made to be the right side of my body.
>
> Behold the spine of the pipe,
> *That* I have made to be my own spine.
>
> Behold the left side of the pipe,
> *That* I have made to be the left side of my body.
>
> Behold the hollow of the pipe,
> *That* I have made to be the hollow of my body.
>
> . . . use the pipe as an offering in your supplications,
> And your prayers will be readily granted.[56]

This holy game of purifying the pipe, expanding the pipe to include the universe, identifying oneself with the pipe, and then igniting it in a symbolic sacrifice of the cosmos—macro- and microcosm—is a ritual act of the kind that we know from the Vedic Brahmanic rituals, where the altar and every implement of the sacrifice is allegorically associated both with the universe and with the individual. This ritual of the pipe is in precisely the same spirit.

Moreover, we now learn that the feathers on the pipe are of the spotted eagle, which is the highest flying bird in North America and therefore equivalent to the sun. Its feathers are the solar rays—and their number is twelve, which is the number, exactly, that we too associate with the cycle of the sun in our twelve months of the solar year and signs of the zodiac. There is a verse in one of the sacred songs of the Sioux which says:

> The Spotted Eagle is coming to carry me away.

Do we not think of the Greek myth of Ganymede carried away by Zeus, who came to him in the form of an eagle? "Birds," declares Dr. Jung in one of his dissertations on the process of individuation, "are thoughts and flights of the mind. . . . The eagle denotes the heights . . . it is a well-known alchemistic symbol. Even the *lapis,* the *rebis* (made out of two parts, and thus often herma-phroditic, as a coalescence of Sol and Luna) is frequently represented with wings, in this way standing for premonition—intuition. All these symbols in the last analysis depict the state of affairs that we call the self, in its role of transcending consciousness."[57]

Such a reading certainly accords with the part played by our spotted eagle in the rites of the North American tribes. It explains, also, the wearing of eagle feathers. They are counterparts of the golden rays of a European crown. They are the rays of the spiritual sun, which the warrior, like the hunter, typifies in his life. Furthermore—as we have been told—their number in the war bonnet is twenty-eight, the number of the lunar cycle of temporal death and renewal, so that here Sol and Luna have been joined.

There can be no doubt whatsoever but this legend of the Sioux is fashioned of the same materials, precisely, as the great mythologies of the Old World—Europe, Africa, and Asia. The parallels on every level, both in imagery and in sense, are far too numerous and too subtle to be the consequence of mere accident. And we are not yet finished!

For when the holy woman before chief Standing Hollow Horn had told him how to use the pipe, she touched its bowl to the round stone that she had placed upon the ground. "You will be bound by this pipe," she said, "to your Father and Grandfather, your Mother and Grandmother."

The Great Spirit, the old Medicine Man explained, is our Father and Grandfather; the earth our Mother and Grandmother. As Father and Mother they are the producers of all things, but as Grandfather and Grandmother they are beyond our understanding.[58]

These are the two modes of considering God that Rudolf Otto has termed the "rational" and the "ineffable": the same that are called in India *saguṇa* and *nirguṇa Brahman:* the Absolute with qualities and without.

"This rock," the holy woman continued, "is of the same red stone as the bowl of the pipe; it is the earth—your Mother and Grandmother. It is red; you, too, are red; and the Great Spirit has given you a red road."

The red road is the road of purity and life. The various Indian nations have many names for this road. The Navaho call it the "Pollen Path of Beauty." Its opposite, the black road, is followed by those "who are distracted, ruled by the senses, and live rather for themselves than for their people."[59] This was the road followed by the man at the opening of the story, who was consumed by snakes. And so we notice now that even the ethical polarity that we recognize between the bird and serpent as allegoric of the winged flight of the spirit and the earth-bound commitment of the passions, here too is suggested.

"These seven circles that you see upon the red stone," the woman said, "represent the seven rites in which the pipe will be used. Be good to this gift. With it, your people will increase and there will come to them all that is good." She described the rites and then turned to leave. "I am departing now, but I shall look back upon your people in every age; for, remember, in me there are four ages: and at the end, I shall return."

Passing around the lodge in the sunwise direction, she left, but after walking a little distance, looked back and sat down. When she got up again, the people were amazed to see that she had turned into a young red and brown buffalo calf. The calf walked a little distance, lay down and rolled, looked back at the people, and when she got up was a white buffalo. This buffalo walked a little distance, rolled upon the ground, and when it rose was black. The black buffalo walked away, and when it was far from the people turned, bowed to each of the four directions, and disappeared over the hill.[60]

The wonderful woman thus had been the feminine aspect of the cosmic buffalo itself: the earthly buffalo-calf represented on the red pipe-bowl as well as its mother, the white buffalo, and its grandmother, the black. And she had gone to be resumed in her eternal portion, having rendered to man those sacred visible things and thoughts by which he was to be joined to his own eternity, which is here and now, within him and all things, in the living world. Let us try to follow her to her source.

Let us follow, first, down the well of the past—the deep well of history and prehistory; for actually, a good deal is now known concerning the history of our North American tribes and their mythologies. We know, for example, that the Sioux were not always hunters of the buffalo, dwelling on the great plains. In the sixteenth-century they lived among the lakes and marshes of the upper Mississippi, in the heavily wooded regions of Minnesota and Wisconsin, traveling mainly in bark canoes. They were a tribe of the forest, not of the plains, and knew practically nothing of the buffalo.[61] The White Buffalo woman cannot possibly have been a factor in their mythology at that time.

However, many of the other elements of this myth can have been known to them from of old; for example, the idea of the four ages and the lunar cycle, the ritual of the holy pipe and of the cosmic ceremonial lodge; that is to say, all of those elements that we have been equating with those known to our own tradition, and which belong rather to the world of the plant than to that of the hunt. In fact, to press the problem further, I should say that much of what we have heard in this myth suggests even the more complex, celestially oriented myths of the high civilizations, with their great play upon the numbers 3 and 4, 7, 12, and 28, their ethical themes and developed metaphysics.

We are not surprised, therefore, to learn that before the Sioux reached their northern forest station at the headwaters of the Mississippi, where they paddled their delicate bark canoes on the woodland lakes and rivers of the north, they had inhabited a more southerly sector of the long Mississippi valley, where the inhabitants were by no means merely hunters.[62] For about two thousand years, influences had been entering the Mississippi valley from Mexico, where a high civilization was flourishing, based on agriculture, governing its festival year by an astronomically correct calendar, and possessing cities that amazed the Spaniards when they arrived, comparable in size, grandeur, and sophistication, to the greatest in the Orient.[63] The use of tobacco—which is not a wild, but cultivated plant—in the holy pipe should have let us know that the ritual could not have been originally of hunters. Furthermore, the Sioux themselves were not merely hunters. They planted maize, squash, and lima beans, and these, like tobacco, had come to the Mississippi valley from the south.

Let me name for you a few of the plants cultivated in South and Middle America before the coming of Columbus, so that you may judge of the force there of the agricultural principle and wonder, perhaps, what the Europeans can have been eating at that time besides bread, venison, and wine. For what would French cooking be without the *pomme de terre?* The potato was first developed in Chile, Bolivia, and Peru. What would Italian cooking be without tomato sauce? Tomatoes were developed in Mexico and Guatemala. Think of Spain without chili-peppers, Switzerland without chocolate, Western civilization without rubber, the modern world without tobacco! Tobacco was first brought to Europe in 1558 by Francisco Fernandes, who had been sent by Philip II of Spain to investigate the products of Mexico. The domesticated turkey also was brought to Europe at that time. In all, some fifty or sixty varieties of domesticated plants were first developed in pre-Columbian America, including maize, squash, the lima bean, pineapple, peanut and avocado, kidney bean, pumpkin, watermelon, papaya, and sweet potato.[64]

More astonishing, however, is the fact that as early as 1000 B.C. an Asiatic cotton was being grown in Peru, together with a type of gourd—the bottle gourd—which had also been imported from Southeast Asia by way of a trans-Pacific voyage.[65] Furthermore, as Professor Jensen pointed out in his Eranos lecture of ten years ago, to which I have already alluded, even on the primitive mesolithic level there is abundant evidence of an equatorial cultural continuum, extending all the way from West Africa eastward, through India and Southeast Asia, across the Pacific to America; and I can assure you that from year to year evidence accumulates re-enforcing this hypothesis—which is now practically a proven fact. And one of the characteristic elements of this

Kulturkreis is precisely the myth of the killed and buried plant divinity.[66]

In other words, the basic myth of the planting mythology that we considered in the last hour has been identified in a continuous series of transformations running from the African Ivory Coast to the Amazon. And in each region it has been adjusted to the local vegetation. In primitive Indonesia it is referred to the banana, coconut, and yam; in Mexico to maize; in Brazil to manioc; in ancient Ur it was applied to wheat; in Japan to rice.

Can the legends of the Sioux, then, have been touched by this tradition?

It would be amazing had they not. For at the time of their residence in the central Mississippi valley there was an intensive concentration here of agricultural villages with immense, rectangular temple mounds arranged around central plazas, towns of several hundred souls, crops of maize, squash, and beans, spiritual as well as secular governors, and recondite religious iconographies.[67] This so-called Middle Mississippi Culture had struck its roots, apparently, as early as the fifth century B.C. and culminated in the fifteenth A.D., with extensions eastward to the Atlantic, westward into Arkansas, and north through Illinois.[68] The culture level was about equivalent to that of France at the time of Vercingetorix, the period of Caesar's Gallic Wars. Furthermore, the temple mounds let us know that the influence of Mexico was direct and of considerable force.

But we have evidence today of a direct impact on the nuclear centers of Peru and Middle America from China and Southeast Asia, commencing at least as early as the eighth century B.C., when China was already halfway through its great period of the Chou dynasty, and continuing perhaps to the twelfth century A.D., when the fabulous—but ephemeral—Khmer civilization of Ankor can be shown to have directly influenced the Mayan architecture of Chiapas, Tobasco, Campeche, Piedras Negras, and the Toltec city of the fabled King Quetzalcoatl.[69]

It is entirely possible, therefore, that every one of those elements that have impressed us in the mythology of the Sioux are actually constituents of that same great mythological complex of the agriculturally based high civilizations from which our own mythology is derived and that, consequently, they do not illustrate any generally valid archetypology of the psyche but an archetypology only of the high civilizations—which, as we know from the archaeology of the past few decades, derive, one and all, from the Mesopotamian mother of civilizations, into whose secrets we have glanced in the Royal Tombs of Ur.

On the other hand, the enveloping atmosphere of the legend is very different from that of the myths, either of the primitive planters, or of the higher agricultural civilizations. Compared with the Blackfoot origin legend of the buffalo dance and All Comrades society, it immediately reveals itself to be of the same order. These two tribes, the Blackfeet and the Sioux, were enemies and of very different racial stock—the Blackfeet were Algonquins, the Sioux, Siouan. Yet their legends of the origin of their buffalo rites contain the same motifs. In both cases, the rites are described as having been brought to the tribe from the animals themselves, by the buffalo maid or buffalo wife. In the Blackfoot variant she was a woman of the tribe, in that of the Sioux, the female aspect of the cosmic buffalo itself. Many more variants of this theme have been collected from the tribes of the great plains: and although all of them reveal a strong infusion of planting motifs, the basic stance remains shamanistic. The rites are not, for the most part, referred to a mythological age of mythological ancestors, but were derived from visionary encounters with the Animal Masters or Master Animals.

There is now plenty of evidence to show that on the buffalo plains of North America there survived to the end of the nineteenth century, and even somewhat into the twentieth, a powerful late formation of truly Paleolithic culture forms. There is a variety of North American stone spear point, called the Clovis Point, for which a radiocarbon date of 35,000 B.C. plus has been established, and which is consistently associated with remains of the mammoth. Another, the Folsom Point, belongs to about 8,000 B.C. and is found with the remains of an extinct bison. The Paleolithic grottoes of southern France and northern Spain, you will recall, are dated from c. 35,000 to 10,000 B.C. But points of these kinds continued to be fashioned on the plains of North America well into the first millennium A.D.

It is really an amazing, thrilling experience for anyone acquainted with the customs of the North American tribes to enter one of those French or Spanish grottoes. The caves were not domestic sites, but sanctuaries of the men's rites: rituals of the hunt and of initiation. They are dangerous and absolutely dark. And the pictures on the rocky walls are never near the entrances but always deep within—placed frequently with an amazing sense for dramatic impact. The painted animals, living forever in eternal darkness, beyond the tick of time, are the germinal, deathless herds of the cosmic night, from which those on earth—which appear and disappear in continuous renewal—proceed, and back to which they return. And whenever human forms appear among them, they are shamans, wearing the costumes that Indian shamans wear to this day.[70]

One sees, also, many silhouetted handprints—the hands of the hunters of those times; and from a number of them certain finger joints are missing. Our Indians, too, chopped off their finger joints as offerings to the sun, or to Wakan Tanka—with prayers for power and success.[71]

In a few of the caves, deep and special chambers have been found, where rites of exceptional power must have been celebrated. In the grotto of Trois-Frères, for example, there is a long, very narrow, tube-like passage—a long flume hardly two feet high—through which you have to crawl and wriggle on your belly for about fifty yards, until, at last, you come to a large chamber with animal forms engraved everywhere on the walls, and among them, directly opposite and facing the very difficult passage through which you have painfully arrived, is the celebrated Sorcerer of Trois-Frères: a dancing shaman, with the antlers of a deer, a beard flowing to his chest, two big, round eyes staring at you, the body and front paws of a lion, tail of a wolf, and legs of a man.[72]

At Lascaux, in a kind of crypt or lower chamber, there is the picture of a shaman lying on the ground in a shamanistic trance, wearing the mask and costume of a bird. His shaman staff is beside him, bearing on its top the figure of a bird. And, standing before him, is a great bison bull, struck from behind, mortally, by a lance.[73]

And in the cave Tuc d'Audoubert there is a little chamber entered only by a very small hole, through which a man can scarcely squeeze. Within are two clay statuettes in high relief—unique in Paleolithic art—representing a bison bull and cow, the bull mounting the cow, while on the ground are the footprints of a dancer, who had been dancing on his heels, in imitation of the hoofs of the buffalo, whose song, as we have heard, is slow and solemn, and whose dance step is ponderous and deliberate. And there were also in this chamber a number of phallic forms roughly modeled in clay.[74]

Ladies and gentlemen: I think that we can now presume to say that we have beheld our goddess Buffalo in divine connubium, and know from what far land and time, beyond their ken, the very beautiful woman came whom the two Sioux Indians saw on the North American plain. For there can be no question concerning the land of origin of the hunting tribes of North America. The vast area of the Paleolithic Great Hunt, which stretched in a single sweep from the Pyrenees to Lake Baikal, in Siberia, actually went on to the Mississippi. And the Indians, who came from northern Asia in many waves, brought with them the rites and hunting methods of that world.

These rites and methods, that is to say, were not separately invented in Europe, Asia, and America, but carried from one area to the other. And the *mythogenetic zone,* the primary area of origin of the myths, was certainly the Old World, not the New. North America was, therefore, not a primary zone, but a *zone of diffusion,* an area to which the myths and rites were transferred.[75]

However, a transfer of this kind is never inert. There are two processes of secondary creativity that come into play when mythologies are transferred, and I should like to speak of them briefly, for just a moment.

The first we may term *land-taking.* In the case, for example, of the primitive planting myth that we discussed in the last hour, the mythological being who was sacrificed and now lives again in the food plants is associated in Brazil with manioc, in Japan with rice, and in Mexico with maize. It is everywhere the same myth, the same mystery play, but in each province the local landscape is its theater and the local animals and plants become its actors. Land-taking, then, is the act of taking spiritual possession of a newly entered land with all its elements, by assimilation to a myth already carried in one's heart in the way of a continuing culture. We are not to suppose that in every province of the tropical continuum the one same myth was separately developed.

The second process that I would like to mention is the one that Professor Eliade illustrated in his lecture on the Cargo Cults of Melanesia; namely, *acculturation.* Here, motifs from an alien culture complex are received into a native tradition by a process of syncretistic assimilation. And the rapidity with which such a process can take effect—as we have seen—is amazing. In the Cargo Cults, like a flash fire, the new inspiration reached far beyond the colonial culture zone, far into the bush, into the wild country of men who had never seen a white man.

And so it was of old, also, in America, when the mythologies of Mexico penetrated the Mississippi: the motifs of the higher mythology were syncretistically assimilated by the northern hunters and applied to their own fields of myth and rite. The Sioux and Pawnee, for example, assimilated to their image of the Master Buffalo the Mexican astronomical myth of the Four Ages—the same four cosmic ages that were known to Hesiod as the ages of Gold, Silver, Bronze, and Iron, and to India as the cycle of four *yugas,* during the course of which (it is declared) the cow of virtue lost with each *yuga* one leg—standing first on four legs, then on three legs, then on two, and now, in our own miserable age, on one.

The Pawnee and the Sioux declare that their Cosmic Buffalo, the father and grandfather of the universe, stands at the cosmic gate through which the game animals pour into the world and back through which they go when they are slain, to be reborn. And in the course of the cycle of the four world ages, with the passage of each year, that buffalo sheds one hair, and with the passage of each age, one leg.[76]

The resemblance of this image to that of India is amazing; and the more so when compared with a tale from the *Brahmavaivarta Purāṇa* which Heinrich Zimmer recounts at the opening of his volume on *Myths and Symbols in Indian Art and Civilization.* There, the Lord of the Universe, the god Shiva, whose animal is the white bull Nandi, appears in the form of an old yogi named Hairy, who has on his chest a circular patch of hair from which one hair falls at the end of each cosmic cycle. At the end of a Brahma year of such cosmic cycles all the hairs are gone and the whole universe dissolves into the night sea, the Ocean of Milk, to be renewed.[77]

Who will say by what miracle—whether of history or of psychology—these two homologous images came into being, the one in India and the other in North America? It is possible that one of the paths of diffusion just described may have been followed. However, it is also possible that the two images were developed independently by some process of *convergence,* as an "effect," to use Frazer's words, "of similar causes acting alike on the similar constitution of the human mind in different countries and under different skies"; for in India, too, there was a meeting of animal and plant cultures when the Aryans arrived with their flocks in the Dravidian agricultural zone. Analogous processes may have been set in play—as in two separate alchemical retorts.

So that we must now confess that our tracking down of the goddess Buffalo may have brought us face-to-face with a problem not of history only, but of psychology as well. We have perhaps broken beyond the walls of time and space, and should ask by what psychological as well as historical laws these primitive myths and their counterparts in the higher cultures might have been formed.

There is, however, no such thing as an uncommitted psychology of man *qua* "Man," abstracted from a specific historical field. For, as Dr. Adolf Portmann has pointed out to us in his lectures in this hall, the human infant is born (biologically speaking) a year too soon, completing in the social sphere a development that other species accomplish within the womb; in fact, developing in the social sphere precisely those powers most typically human: upright posture, rational thought, and speech. Man—as "Man"—develops in a manner that is simultaneously biological and social, and this development continues through adolescence—in fact, through life.

Moreover, whereas the instinct system of the animal is relatively inflexible, fixed, stereotyped, according to species, that of man is not so, but open to imprint (*Prägung*) and impression. The Innate Releasing Mechanisms of the human central nervous system, through which man's instincts are triggered to action, respond to Sign Stimuli that are not fixed for all time and general to the species, but vary from culture to culture, century to century, individual to individual, according to imprints indelibly registered during the long course of a sociologically conditioned childhood. And if I have read aright the works of Dr. Portmann and his colleagues: there has not yet been identified a single triggering image, a single Sign Stimulus, that can be firmly verified as innate to the human psyche.[78]

How, then, shall we rest secure in any theory of psychological archetypes based upon our own culturally conditioned mode of responses, or upon a study of the myths and symbols of our own tradition, or even a comparative study of that large complex of primitive planting and higher agricultural traditions, which, as I have just indicated, are both historically and prehistorically related to our own?

We have to realize that the walls have lately been knocked from around all mythologies—every single one of them—by the findings and works of modern scientific discovery. The four ages, the four points of the compass, the four elements! What can those mean to man today, in the light of what we are learning? Today we have ninety-six elements, and the number is still growing. The old soul and the new universe—the old microcosm and the new macrocosm—do not match; and the disproportion is about equivalent to that of four to ninety-six. No wonder if a lot us are nervous! The little tower of Babel, which to some in its day seemed to be threatening God in his heaven, we see now surpassed many times in every major city of the world, and rockets fly where once the angels sang. One cannot *tutoyer* God anymore: the mystery is infinite, both without and within. That is the *tremendum* that our modern mind—this flower of creation—has revealed for us to absorb, and it cannot be willed or walled away by any system of archaic feeling. It will not be screened from us, nor we protected, by any organization of archaic images. There has not yet been identified a single image that can be definitely guaranteed as innate to man.

And so, we are compelled to face our problem of the imagery of myth largely from a historical point of view, after all. That wonderful sentence of Charles Darwin's that Dr. Benz quoted the other day, and which apparently shocked Darwin himself, where it was suggested that the image of God might be only an imprint impressed upon the mind of man through centuries of teaching, fits the case precisely—at least as far as anything but faith can tell us. But faith itself would then be only a reflex of the imprint.

So let us briefly review, in these closing minutes of the hour, a few of those inevitable imprints to which the human individual, no matter where he may have developed, must always have been subject. These we may number, I believe, among the sources of those archetypal images that are found in all mythologies, variously arranged. They supply at least one series of those Sign Stimuli by which our human energies are triggered to action and organized for life as the instincts of the beasts by the Sign Stimuli of their species: those energy-releasing signs by which man is struck and moved, as it were, from within.

The first of such imprintings are, of course, those to which the infant is subjected in its earliest years. These have been extensively discussed in the literature of psychoanalysis, and may be sketchily summarized about as follows:

(1) those of the birth trauma and its emotional effects; (2) those of the mother and father images in their benevolent and malevolent transformations; (3) those associated with the infant's interest in its own excrement and the measures of discipline imposed upon it in relation to this context; (4) those of the child's sexual researches and acquisition of a castration complex (whether in the male or in the female mode); and then, (5) the constellation of these imprints now generally known by the name of Oedipus. There can be little doubt that no matter where in the world an infant may ever have been born, as long as the nuclear unit of human life has been a father, mother, and child, the maturing consciousness has had to come to a knowledge of its world through the medium of this heavily loaded, biologically based triangle of love and aggression, desire and fear, dependency, command, and urge for release.

But now, in every primitive society on earth—whether of the hunting or of the planting order—these inevitable imprints and conceptions of infancy are filled with new associations, rearranged and powerfully re-imprinted, under the most highly emotional circumstances, in the puberty rites, the rites of initiation, to which every young male (and often every female too) is subjected. That long flume in the Paleolithic grotto of Trois-Frères, with the vivid image of the dancing, staring sorcerer in the chamber to which it led, must have been employed in such a rite. A fundamental motif in the puberty rites of many lands is that of death to infancy and rebirth to manhood, and this grotto shows every sign of having been used for just such an effect. Moreover, in these rites, the child's body is painfully altered—through circumcision, subincision, ritual defloration, clitoridectomy, tattooing, scarification, or whatnot; so that there is no childhood to which the child can now return. And through these forceful rearrangements of the references of the father image, mother image, birth idea, etc., the reflex system of the whole psyche is transformed. The infantile system of responses is erased and the energies carried forward, away from childhood, away from the attitude of dependency that is a function of the long infancy characteristic to our species—on to adulthood, engagement in the local tasks of man- and womanhood, to an attitude of adult responsibility and a sense of integration with the local group.

A neurotic, then, can be defined as one in whom this initiation has failed of its effect, so that in him those socially organized Sign Stimuli that carry others on to their adult tasks continue to refer only backward—to the imprint system of the infant. The mother image then is experienced only as a reference to the human mother of one's childhood, not to the life-producing, disciplining, and supporting aspect of the world (which is our Mother and Grandmother), and the father is not Wakan Tanka, but that "undemonstrative relative," as James Joyce terms him, "who settles our hash bill for us." All attempts, therefore, to interpret myths through a study of the imagery of neurotics necessarily run the risk of failing to consider precisely that aspect of mythology which is distinctive, namely, its power to carry people *away* from childhood—from dependency—on to responsibility.

Furthermore, the peculiar interests of adulthood differ radically from one society to another, and since it is a primary function of myth and ritual in traditional societies to shape youngsters into adults and then to hold the adults to their given roles, mythology and ritual, in as far as they serve this local, moral, ethical aim, cannot be called functions of any generally valid human psychology, but only of local history and sociology.

Professor A. R. Radcliffe-Brown of Cambridge University has well discussed this aspect of our subject in his work on the pygmies of the Andaman Islands, where he writes as follows:

> (1) A society depends for its existence on the presence in the minds of its members of a certain system of sentiments by which the conduct of the individual is regulated in conformity with the needs of the society. (2) Every feature of the social system itself and every event or object that in any way affects the well-being or the cohesion of the society becomes an object of this system of sentiments. (3) In human society the sentiments in question are not innate but are developed in the individual by the action of the society upon him. (4) The ceremonial customs of a society are a means by which the sentiments in question are given collective expression on appropriate occasions. (5) The ceremonial (i.e. collective) expression of any sentiment serves both to maintain it at the requisite degree of intensity in the mind of the individual and to transmit it from one generation to another. Without such expression the sentiments involved could not exist.[79]

Mythology, in short, is not a natural, spontaneous production of the individual psyche, but a socially controlled reorganization of the imprints of childhood, so contrived that the Sign Stimuli moving the individual will conduce to the well-being of the local culture, and that local culture alone. What is effective, as well as distinctive, in every mythology, therefore, is its locally ordered architecture, not the bricks (the infantile imprints and their affects) of which this structure is composed: and this architecture, this organization, differs significantly, according to place, time, and culture stage.

However, there is one more aspect and great function of mythology to be noted—and here we find ourselves moving away from the local back to general human terms; for man has not only to be led by myth from the infantile attitude of dependency to the system of sentiments of the local group, but also, in adulthood, to be prepared to face the mystery of death: to absorb the *mysterium tremendum;* since man, like no other animal, not only knows that he is killing when he kills, but also knows that he too will die; and his old age, furthermore, like his infancy, is a lifetime in itself, as long as the whole life span of many a beast.

But this role and function of myth was already treated in the first hour, and so, I shall now add only one remark. I shall observe only that even if the view of the Freudian school is correct and the experience of dread before this *tremendum* is finally but a reflex of the child's Oedipal dread of the father and thus an imprint not of later but of earlier life, nevertheless, it is an imprint of peculiar metaphysical moment. For the susceptibility of the human mind to this experience is what has alienated man from nature and made it necessary for all mythologies to serve the one paramount task, throughout the world, of wooing *das kranke Tier* (to quote Nietzsche) back to life.

It lay beyond the program of the present paper to review in the higher mythologies the interplay of the two primitive stances to this dread that were discussed in the first hour: that of the hunt (negative toward death and positive toward ego) and that of the tropical planters (negative toward ego and positive toward death). Yet, surely, it is apparent, even on first glance, that in the Western, Judeo-Christian phases of the post-Neolithic development of civilization a masculine resistance to the mystery of death and generation has come forcefully into play. For the Messianic idea, which plays such a role here, is nothing if not a refutation of the world as it now stands and a prayer for something better in a timeless time to come, whereas, in the primary primitive planting mythology, the day of the Messiah is now: here and now. The godhead, or godly power, lives already in all things, because dead to itself. It is in us. And we are *It* in as far as we, too, are dead to ego. There is nothing to come. There is nothing to change. This—right here and now—is It.

And throughout the world, wherever the feminine, submissive and mystical, in contrast to the masculine, ego-protective, magical system with its rites of conjuring has prevailed, we find in the myths no comprehension whatsoever of these patriarchal dreams of a happy day some time to come—but rather, a fierce, Dionysian rapture (which to the other side seems no less monstrous than life itself) wherein the cannibal feast of the life that lives on life and is ever-renewed, mightily—utterly careless of the individual: utterly careless of all rules of order—is celebrated with a shout and a howl. The primitive planting myth of life *in* death is subtly transformed, in the late, historical cultures, into one of life *as* death: and again that sense of alienation is returned to us, on the screen of a promise for the future. The primitive renewal, in contrast— whether of the hunters or of the planters—is ever present.

Hence, it is not surprising that in the present historical epoch of cultural death and renewal, nihilism and released spontaneity, when we are all again, like primitive man, feeling our way into a new world, a world as yet unknown (which, however, has come pouring out of our own arts and sciences), there is an appeal that has been felt by many of our creative minds in these primitive myths of a continuing creation, uncircumscribed, as yet, by any zodiac or an Alpha and Omega.

And so one more idea, now, in conclusion:

Some years ago Professor Portmann told us of a certain species of butterfly, the grayling (*Eumenis semele*), the males of which assume the initiative in mating by pursuing a passing female in flight. And those little males generally prefer females of darker hue to lighter—to such a degree that if an artificial model of darker hue is presented than anything known to nature, the sexually motivated grayling male will pursue the work of art in preference to the darkest female of the living species. "Here we find," comments Dr. Portmann, "an 'inclination' that is not satisfied in nature, but which perhaps, one day, if inheritable darker mutations should appear, would play a role in the selection of mating partners. Who knows," he then asks, "whether such anticipations of particular Sign Stimuli . . . may not represent one of the factors in the process of selection that determines the direction of evolution?"[80]

Stimuli of this kind, going beyond the offerings of nature yet triggering innate releasing mechanisms, are known as "supernormal sign stimuli," and, as this amusing little deception of the grayling shows, though nature responds to them, they are produced by art.

I am now suggesting that a mythology is a context of supernormal sign stimuli, produced by art for the government of nature. And these signs, through the ages, have been releasing, progressively—though frequently to our shock—the energies of the deepest secret of our being, which is, of course, the *mysterium tremendum.*

"There is a power called Sila," said an old Eskimo shaman from the remote rim of northernmost Alaska, "but Sila cannot be explained in so many words. It is a strong spirit, the upholder of the universe, of the weather, in fact all life on earth—so mighty that his speech to man comes not through ordinary words, but through storms, snowfall, rain showers, the tempests of the sea, through all the forces that man fears; or through sunshine, calm seas, or small, innocent playing children who understand nothing. When times are good, Sila has nothing to say to mankind. He has disappeared into his infinite nothingness and remains away as long as people do not abuse life but have respect for their daily food. No one has ever seen Sila. His place of sojourn is so mysterious that he is with us and infinitely far away at the same time."[81]

These words from the lips of an old fighter and man killer—who was no saint, let me assure you—I am citing as an envoi, to balance the historical stress of the body of my lecture. For in every time, in every culture, men have been born whose minds have broken past their culture horizon. Among the hunters, these have been the shamans, and their wisdom may, after all, be that of man *qua* Man.

"The only true wisdom," said the shaman Igjugarjuk, of whom I spoke to you in the last hour, "the only true wisdom lives far from mankind, out in the great loneliness, and it can be reached only through suffering. Privation and suffering alone can open the mind of a man to all that is hidden to others."[82]

And what, then, is the wisdom that is learned by the one who shatters within himself the fears that bind the others of his tribe to their little rites? What is the wisdom learned from Sila's voice?

"All that we know," said Najagneq, the shaman from the northern rim of the arctic, "is that the voice is gentle, like a woman's: a voice so fine and gentle that even children cannot become afraid. And what it says is: 'Be not afraid of the universe!'"[83]

How early in the history of mankind revelations of this order were received and recognized, we shall never know.

Johann Jacob Bachofen

It is fitting that the works of Johann Jacob Bachofen (1815–1887) should have been rediscovered for our century, not by historians or anthropologists, but by a circle of creative artists, psychologists, and literary men: a young group around the poet Stefan George, in Munich, in the twenties.[1] For Bachofen has a great deal to say to artists, writers, searchers of the psyche, and, in fact, anyone aware of the enigmatic influence of symbols in the structuring and moving of lives: the lives of individuals, nations, and those larger constellations of destiny, the civilizations that have come and gone, as Bachofen saw, like dreams—unfolding, each, from the seed force of its own primary symbol, or, as he termed such supporting images, "basic insights" (*Grundanschauungen*) or "fundamental thoughts" (*Grundgedanken*). And he himself had such an easy, graceful skill in his interpretation of symbols, unshelling flashes of illumination from all sorts of mythological forms, that many of his most dazzling passages remind one of nothing so much as a marksman exploding with infallible ease little clay figures in a gallery. Read, for example, the brief chapter on the symbolism of the egg! From any page of this passage one can learn more about the grammar of mythology than from a year's study of such an author as, say, Thomas Bulfinch, whose *Age of Fable* appeared just four years before Bachofen's *Mortuary Symbolism*.

Comparing the approach of these two mid-nineteenth-century students of classical mythology, one immediately remarks that, whereas the interest of Bulfinch lay in the anecdotal aspect of his subject, summarizing plots, Bachofen's concern was to go past plots to their symbolized sense, by grouping analogous figures and then reading these as metaphors of a common informing idea. He describes the method in his section on India:

> We must distinguish between the form of the tale and its content or idea. The form lies in the fiction of a single definite event, which takes its course and moves toward its conclusion through a concatenation of circumstances and the intervention of a number of persons. This formal element must be discarded as a fabrication, a fable, a fairy tale, or whatever we may term such products of the free fancy, and excluded from the realm of historical truth. But in respect to the guiding thought, we must apply a different standard. This retains its significance even though the garment in which it is shrouded may merit little regard. In fact, when dissociated from this single incident, it takes on the greater dimension of a general historicity, not bound by specific localities or persons.

We are on the way, here, to Carl G. Jung's "collective unconscious." And it was this informed recognition of an implicit psychological, moral import in all mythology that chiefly recommended Bachofen to the poets.

In his introduction to *Mother Right* Bachofen explains his science further:

> It has been said that myth, like quicksand, can never provide a firm foothold. This reproach applies not to myth itself, but only to the way in which it has been handled. Multiform and shifting in its outward manifestation, myth nevertheless follows fixed laws, and can provide as definite and secure results as any other source of historical knowledge. Product of a cultural period in which life had not yet broken away from the harmony of nature, it shares with nature that unconscious lawfulness which is always lacking in the works of free reflection. Everywhere there is system, everywhere cohesion; in every detail the expression of a great fundamental law whose abundant manifestations demonstrate its inner truth and natural necessity.

Moreover, since, according to this view, mythologies arise from and are governed by the same psychological laws that control our own profoundest sentiments, the surest way to interpret them is not through intellectual ratiocination but the exercise of our psychologically cognate imagination. As Bachofen declared in the retrospective autobiographical sketch that he wrote in 1854 at the request of his former teacher, the great jurist and historian Friedrich Karl von Savigny:

> There are two roads to knowledge—the longer, slower, more arduous road of rational combination and the shorter path of the imagination, traversed with the force and swiftness of electricity. Aroused by direct contact with the ancient remains, the imagination [*Phantasie*] grasps the truth at one stroke, without intermediary links. The knowledge acquired in this second way is infinitely more living and colorful than the products of the understanding [*Verstand*].

To read mythology in this way, however, it is necessary to cast aside one's contemporary, historically conditioned manner of thought and even of life. "It is one of my profoundest convictions," Bachofen told his old preceptor, "that without a thorough transformation of our whole being, without a return to ancient simplicity and health of soul, one cannot gain even the merest intimation of the greatness of those ancient times and their thinking, of those days when the human race had not yet, as it has today, departed from its harmony with creation and the transcendent creator."

One can see why the academicians shuddered—and the poets were delighted. Rainer Maria Rilke was touched; Hugo von Hofmannsthal as well. But there was far more to the reach of Bachofen's work than a poet's grammar of the symbolizing imagination. Implicit in this grammar, and developed in his ample volumes, is the idea of a morphology of history—first, of classical antiquity, but then, by extension, of mankind: an idea of the course and moving principles of our destiny that is becoming, in a most interesting way, increasingly corroborated as archaeologists throughout the world lift forth from the earth, for all to see, the tangible forms that his intangible mythoanalytic method of invisible excavation (pursued at home in his library) had anticipated.

🌢 🌢 🌢

One has to keep reminding oneself, when reading this perceptive scholar, that in his day the sites of Helen's Troy and Pasiphaë's Crete had not yet been excavated—nor any of those early Neolithic villages that have yielded the multitudes of ceramic naked-goddess figurines now filling museum cabinets. Bachofen himself was impressed by the novelty of his findings. "An unknown world," he wrote, "opens before our eyes, and the more we learn of it, the stranger it seems." Indeed, in his student years he had already passed beyond the learning of his century when he noticed that there were customs recognized in Roman law that could never have originated in a patriarchal society; and on his first visit to Rome, with his father in 1842, his intuition of a second pattern of custom was reinforced by his reading of the symbols that he found there on certain tombs.

Inspired, then, by what today would be called an "organic," "holistic," or "functional" theory of culture—believing, that is to say, that whether great or small, sacred or profane, every element of a cultural aggregate must be expressive, ultimately, of the "informing idea" (*Grundanschauung*) of the culture from which it took its rise—the young Bachofen realized that the anomalous features recognized in the Roman legacy would have to be explained either as imports from some alien province or as vestiges of a no less alien period of native Italic culture, antecedent to the classical; and, as he tells in his work on mother right, it was in Herodotus' account of the customs of the Lycians that he found his leading clue.[2] "The Lycians," he read, "take their names from their mother, not from their father"; from which he reasoned that, since a child's derivation from its mother is immediately apparent, but from its father remote, primitive mankind may not have understood the relation of sexual intercourse to birth. Descent from the mother would then have been the only recognized foundation of biological kinship, the men of the tribe representing, on the other hand, a social, moral, and spiritual order into which the child would later be *adopted*, as in primitive puberty rites.

There is an interesting confirmation of this bold hypothesis in the writings of one of the leading anthropologists of our own century, namely Bronislaw Malinowski, whose volume *The Sexual Life of Savages* (based on notes from a four-year expedition to New Guinea, 1914–18) has the following to say of the natives of the Trobriand Islands:

> We find in the Trobriands a matrilineal society, in which descent, kinship, and every social relationship are legally reckoned through the mother only, and in which women have a considerable share in tribal life, even to the taking of a leading

part in economic, ceremonial, and magical activities—a fact which very deeply influences all the customs of erotic life as well as the institutions of marriage. . . .

The idea that it is solely and exclusively the mother who builds up the child's body, the man in no way contributing to this formation, is the most important factor in the legal system of the Trobriands. Their views on the process of procreation, coupled with certain mythological and animistic beliefs, affirm, without doubt or reserve, that the child is of the same substance as its mother, and that between the father and the child there is no bond of physical union whatsoever. . . .

These natives have a well-established institution of marriage, and yet are quite ignorant of the man's share in the begetting of children. At the same time, the term "father" has, for the Trobriand, a clear, though exclusively social definition: it signifies the man married to the mother, who lives in the same house with her and forms part of the household. The father, in all discussions about relationship, was pointedly described to me as *tomakava,* a "stranger," or even more correctly, an "outsider.". . . What does the word *tama* (father) express to the native? "Husband of my mother" would be the answer first given by an intelligent informant. He would go on to say that his *tama* is the man in whose loving and protecting company he has grown up . . . the child learns that he is not of the same clan as his *tama,* that his totemic appellation is different, and that it is identical with that of his mother. At the same time he learns that all sorts of duties, restrictions, and concerns for personal pride unite him to his mother and separate him from his father.[3]

Now, as we know today, it is extremely risky to reason from the circumstances of a contemporary tribe back to earliest mankind: we have learned too much in the past few years concerning the antiquity of our species, which is today being reckoned (largely on the basis of the finds of L.S.B. Leakey in the Olduvai Gorge in Tanganyika) as far back as to circa 1,800,000 B.C. In Bachofen's day the absurdly recent biblical date for the creation not only of mankind but of the world (3760 B.C., according to one manner of reckoning; 4004 by another) was still, in most quarters, accepted as about correct. Adam Sedgwick, Darwin's geology teacher, set down, for example, that "man has been but a few years' dweller on the earth. He was called into being a few thousand years of the days in which we live by a provident contriving power."[4] And so it was that, like most others of his generation, Bachofen could believe that in dealing with the ancients he was searching a tradition "going back," as he more than once averred, "almost to the beginning of things." And his romantic sense of the holiness of his task derived, in part at least, from this illusion.

Bachofen recognized and described two distinct orders of mother right, associating the first with the absolutely primitive, nomadic, hunting, and foraging states of human existence, and the second with the settled agricultural. However, unfortunately for the cogency of his argument, when looking for examples of an absolutely primitive condition, he made the mistake of naming a wild lot of horse and cattle nomads who were not primitive at all (they were barbarous enough, but not primitive); namely, the Massagetae, Nasamones,

Garmantes, etc., whom classical historians had described using their women in common and copulating publicly, without shame. Bachofen termed the primitive socioreligious order that he deduced from this uncertain evidence the premarital "hetaerist-Aphroditic," representing it as governed by the natural law (*ius naturale*) of sex motivated by lust, and with no understanding of the relationship of intercourse to conception. The classical goddess symbolic of such a way of life was Aphrodite; its vegetal symbol for the Greeks and Romans had been the wild, rank vegetation of swamps, in contrast to the ordered vegetation of the planted field; and its animal symbol was the bitch. Its brutal order of justice was the justice of the balance, eye for an eye and tooth for a tooth, retaliation; yet with the mitigating, softening, humanizing principle already at work of mother love.

"Raising her young," Bachofen observed, "the woman learns earlier than the man to extend her loving care beyond the limits of the ego to another creature, and to direct whatever gift of invention she possesses to the preservation and improvement of this other's existence. Woman at this stage is the repository of all culture, of all benevolence, of all devotion, of all concern for the living and grief for the dead."

The second stage in Bachofen's reconstruction, which he associated with agriculture, is better attested by far than the first, and is, in fact, acknowledged by many anthropologists today pretty much as Bachofen described it— though, of course, with greater definition of detail and emphasis on the local variations. Professor W.H.R. Rivers, for example, states in a detailed article on mother right in James Hastings's *Encyclopaedia of Religion and Ethics* (in which, by the way, the name of Bachofen does not occur), both that "there is reason to connect mother-right with a high development of the art of agriculture," and that "it is almost certain that by far the most frequent process throughout the world has been a transition from mother- to father-right."[5]

In Bachofen's usage, the term "mother right"—which Malinowski and Rivers also employ—does not require that the woman should hold political sway; in fact, according to his theory of stages, the normal head of a primitive hetaerist-Aphroditic horde would have been a powerful male tyrant, who through main strength would have been able to make use of whatever women he chose. The force of the principle of mother right would even then have been evident, however, in the family concepts and emotions of kinship and concern, as well as in magic and religion wherever the properly female powers of fruitfulness and nourishment were concerned.

But in reaction to the sexual abuses to which females, under such primitive circumstances, would have been subjected, revolts must have ensued, Bachofen reasoned, and he thought he could point to a number of instances in classical history and legend: the various tribes of the Amazons in both Africa and Asia, and, in particular, the notorious deed of the women of Lemnos. Such revolts and the conditions following them would have been, he believed, transitional, leading away from the earlier communal usages to the later settled, monogamous state of life. And another influence, perhaps equally conducive to monogamy, he supposed, would have been the acceptance by the male of his proper domestic role when, finally, the inevitable recognition of the physical similarities between fathers and their own children would have led to both an understanding of, and a pride in, the relationship of parent and child.

However, the main transforming force Bachofen identified was the rise of agriculture and the coming into being, therewith, of a comparatively gentle, settled mode of existence, favorable to the female. Furthermore, since woman is the living counterpart of the tilled and holy earth, the female acquired new importance in the ritualistic magico-religious sphere wherever agriculture flourished. Bachofen therefore named this second, higher stage of mother right the "matrimonial-Demetrian," or "-Cereal," for the Greek agricultural goddess Demeter and her Roman counterpart Ceres; and the greatest part of his lifework was devoted to researches in the mysteries of this higher, nobler transformation of the *ius naturale*.

Like the lower, it was supported by the force and majesty of sex; but now with the desire for progeny, not merely the urge of lust. Furthermore, the analogy of begetting and birth to the sowing and harvest of the tilled fields gave rise to those great poetic mythologies of the earth goddess and her spouse that have been everywhere the support of the basic rites and mysteries of civilization. Bachofen has filled his pages with the most eloquent celebrations of the beauty and power of these mighty mythologies, the systems of analogy on which they are founded, and the contribution they have made to the humanization of mankind; and no matter what one's final judgment may be as to the value of his reconstruction of the stages of the evolution of society, there can be no doubt concerning the force and value of his readings of that great heritage of mythic symbols which is basic not only to the civilizations of the Occident but to those of the Orient as well—and was even echoed in pre-Columbian America among the Aztecs, the Pawnee, the Zuñi, and the Sioux.

In fact, when it comes to considering the larger, world-historical as opposed to the merely classical, application of Bachofen's theories of the stages of mother right, it is relevant to note that the first field anthropologist to recognize an order of matrilineal descent among primitive peoples—and even to have associated this order with Herodotus' account of the Lycians—was an eighteenth-century missionary among the Indians of Canada, the Reverend Joseph François Lafitau, S.J. (1671–1746); in his *Mœurs des sauvages Améri-quains comparées aux mœurs des premiers temps* (Paris, 1724), at times he launches into eulogies of the spiritual, social, and practical *supériorité des femmes* that even rival those of Bachofen himself.

> C'est dans les femmes que consiste proprement la Nation, la noblesse du sang, l'arbre généalogique, l'ordre des générations et de la conservation des familles. C'est en elles que réside toute l'autorité réelle. . . . Les hommes au contraire sont entièrement isolés et bornés a eux-mêmes, leurs enfants leurs sont étrangers, avec eux tout périt.[6]

Moreover, one of the very first to acknowledge the importance for science of Bachofen's researches and to write to him in appreciation was an American anthropologist, the jurist and ethnologist Lewis Henry Morgan, whose pioneering study of the Iroquois had prepared him to recognize the value and universal reach of Bachofen's revelation.

❦ ❦ ❦

Bachofen's instinctive response to those silent signals from the lost world of "the mothers" that captured his imagination in youth and held him fascinated throughout life has been attributed, possibly with reason, to a lifelong devotion to his own young and beautiful mother. Daughter of a distinguished patrician family of Basel, née Valeria Merian, she was hardly twenty when he was born, in 1815. He remained a bachelor until her death in 1856 and for nearly a decade thereafter, when he married, in 1865, the young and beautiful Louise Elizabeth Burckhardt, who was the age his mother had been when he was born.

Among the bachelors of scholarship, however, there have been many devoted sons, yet none with quite Bachofen's gift; and the awakening—or let us say, rather, in Bachofen's own terms, the fathering and fostering of that gift—must be ascribed to the masters of the great romantic school of historical research with whom he studied, the most influential of whom was the distinguished jurisprudent Friedrich Karl von Savigny, whose lectures he attended and friendship he enjoyed at the University of Berlin from 1835–1837. This was the same inspiring professor of the history of law who, thirty years before, had launched the brothers Grimm on their world-celebrated pioneering careers in Germanic philology, mythology, and folklore.

Bachofen was born December 22, 1815, in Basel, where both his father's family and his mother's had been established and respected since the sixteenth and seventeenth centuries. Burgomasters and city counselors were numbered among his ancestors; art collectors and geologists. Johann Jacob, however, seems to have been the first historian of either line. As a youngster he first attended a private "house school," together with his younger brother Carl, where little Jakob Burckhardt, three years younger than himself, also arrived as a pupil. Then came his boyhood grammar-school years, from which he graduated with honors in 1831. He attended the fine high school in which Nietzsche was later to be a teacher; and after two years there and two semesters at the University of Basel, he went on to Berlin to study law—and to encounter the great man who would become the master of his destiny and mystagogue of his way to wisdom.

Von Savigny was an imposing, gracious scholar with an eye for the genius of a student. As the leading mind of Germany's new "historical school" of jurists, he had himself been a major contributor to the unfolding of that country's romantic thought in its golden age, and something of the atmosphere of those enchanted days must still have hung about him. The family of his wife, Kunigunde Brentano, had been intimates of the Goethe household: her father, a companion of Goethe's youth; and her younger sister, Bettina, that same pretty little elf who, in 1807, threw herself in worship before Goethe's feet in a gesture of such charm that he allowed her to continue to be a cherished nuisance in his life until 1811—when a violent scene between his young admirer and Christiane, his wife, put an end to the whole affair. Clemens Brentano, the colorful brother of these two attractive sisters, had been a member, in those days, of the Heidelberg group of romantics, and in collaboration with Ludwig Achim von Arnim (who was later to marry Bettina) had edited the famous ballad collection *Des Knaben Wunderhorn* (1805–1808), to which the young Grimms, still in their teens, also were contributors.

Kunigunde and Friedrich Karl were married in 1804, and though he then was a youth of but twenty-five, his formidable treatise on *The Law of Property* had already appeared the year before and been recognized as introducing a new approach to the interpretation of law—an organic, holistic, ethnological-historical approach, it might be called today; and in view of its undoubted influence on both the Grimm brothers and Bachofen at the critical, formative moments of their careers, it must be counted among the most influential seminal writings of its time. Briefly, the proposition argued was that, since the laws of a people are part and parcel of their national life, law codes cannot be imposed arbitrarily on alien populations without regard for their past history or present state of civilization: law and language, religious and secular custom, are of a piece.

In 1804, at the time this argument made its impact on the Grimms, it carried for young Germans a special patriotic appeal. The French, who had been ravaging Europe since March 1796 (when Napoleon, addressing the ragged army of a destitute Republic, had issued his famous proclamation: "You are badly fed and all but naked. . . . I am about to lead you into the most fertile plains of the world. Before you are great cities and rich provinces; there we shall find honor, glory, and riches."), were now the absolute masters of Europe, and on the first day of spring, March 21, 1804, their Code civil des Français, later known as the Code Napoléon, had come automatically into force throughout the Empire, without any regard whatsoever either for the past history or for the present state of civilization of any of the numerous peoples involved. Von Savigny's ethnological-historical thesis, consequently, inspired the brothers Grimm to dedicate their learning and their lives to a reconstruction of the old Germanic backgrounds and ideals of their national cultural heritage. Bachofen's case was different: he was not German but Swiss, and in his day the Napoleonic terror was already a nightmare of the past.

Yet inherent in Bachofen's work, as well as in that of the brothers Grimm, was an intense social motivation and a passionate interest in learning that contributed a sense of timeliness and even urgency to his otherwise rather recondite researches. For the period in which he matured was one rather of social and class confusion than of international strife; and, as he viewed the scene from his Alpine vantage point, the whole fabric of European civilization was being torn asunder in the name of principles that were misconceived and by means that could lead, in the end, only to ruin. As he tells in his retrospective sketch, he made his second trip to Rome at the very peak of the fateful year of 1848, and the second day after his arrival, the honorable and admirable Count Pellegrino Rossi, whose lectures he had attended at the University of Paris, was murdered on the steps of the Roman House of Assembly. "The storming of the Quirinal, the flight of the Pope, the Constituent Assembly, the proclamation of the Republic," he writes, "followed in quick succession. . . . And with the arrival of Garibaldi's band and the various patriotic legions from all over Italy, things became even more fantastic."

"It is a mistake of the Progressives to imagine that they will never be surpassed," he wrote twenty years later to his friend the classical historian Heinrich Meyer-Ochsner of Zurich. "Before they know it, they are to be ousted by the 'More-Enlightened.' They have still, as Athens once had too, schoolmasters for their bosses; but at last there will come the porters and the criminals. . . . When every scoundrel counts for as much as an orderly citizen, it's all out with rational government. . . . I begin to believe that for the historians of the twentieth century there will be nothing to write about but America and Russia."[7]

In contrast, therefore, to the young Grimms, for whom the great cause of the hour had been the rescue of the German soul, the cause for the Swiss scholar Bachofen, from his earliest years to the end, was the rescue of all of Europe. "The supreme aim of archaeology," he wrote in his *Mortuary Symbolism*, "... consists, I believe, in communicating the sublimely beautiful ideas of the past to an age that is very much in need of regeneration." And so it was that, whereas von Savigny's learned inspiration had sent his sensitive earlier students searching, for the rescue of their heritage, into its spiritual backgrounds in the northern Indo-Germanic past, so now, one generation later, it sent the young Swiss, Bachofen, off to Rome, to Greece, and beyond, to the realm of "the mothers" of Goethe's *Faust*.

❦ ❦ ❦

Bachofen's dates, 1815–1887, significantly match those of Charles Darwin (1809–1882), and his first important publication, *An Essay on Ancient Mortuary Symbolism*, even appeared in the same year as Darwin's *Origin of Species*— 1859. The significance of these coincidences appears when it is remarked that both men were pursuing independent researches, one in fields of physical, the other of spiritual investigation, just when the scientific concept of a natural evolution of forms was only beginning to supplant the old biblical doctrines of a special creation of fixed species, with man above and apart, and a special revelation of God's law to but one chosen people. Bachofen, like Darwin, was a pioneer, therefore, in the formulation of a scientific approach to a very tender subject, and, like his contemporary in the biological field, he took as the first principles of his thinking two methodological axioms: (1) phenomena are governed by discoverable natural laws; and (2) these laws are continuously operative, uninterrupted by miraculous intervention.

Observing, therefore, that within the field of his concern there was an apparent graduation of forms, from the simpler to the more complex, the less conscious to the more, Bachofen assumed that these must represent the stages of a general course of cultural evolution. And again as in the biological field, so in this of cultural evolution, the representatives of the various periods of development lay scattered over the earth, having undergone in the various provinces of diffusion local adjustments to environment and independent secondary developments and regressions. To reconstruct the master pattern of the general development, consequently, the first requirement had to be a diligent collection of specimens from all quarters; next, meticulous comparison and classification; and finally, imaginative interpretation—proceeding step by step to ever more inclusive insights. In *The Myth of Tanaquil*, published 1870, Bachofen is explicit in this regard:

The scientific approach to history recognizes the stratifications of the spiritual modes that have gradually made their appearance, assigns to each stratum the phenomena that pertain to it, and traces the genesis of ideas. Proceeding thus through all the stages of reality, it leads us to realize what this spirit of ours once was, through the passage of the ages, but is today no more.

Specifically, Bachofen's procedure was, first, to saturate his sight and mind with the primary documents of his subject: Roman legal texts, Etruscan tombs, ceramic wares, etc., regarding each specimen of antiquity as a biologist would a bug, casting from his mind presuppositions, viewing it from all sides, considering its environment, and comparing it with others.

"A historical investigation which must be the first to gather, verify, and collate all its material," he states in one of his most important passages, "must everywhere stress the particular and only gradually progress to comprehensive ideas."

In the biological sciences, specimens gathered from all quarters of the earth are compared, clustered, and classified according to categories of broader and broader scope: variety, species, genus, family, order, class, phylum, and finally, kingdom. So also, in Bachofen's spiritual science:

Our understanding will grow in the course of investigation; gaps will be filled in; initial observations will be confirmed, modified, or amplified by others; our knowledge will gradually be rounded out and gain inner cohesion; higher and higher perspectives will result; and finally they will all be joined in the unity of one supreme idea.

And so we find that, just as in his elucidation of legends he pressed past the anecdotes, so likewise in his interpretation of cultures: religious beliefs, laws and customs, family structures, political practices, philosophies, sciences, crafts and economics, are all viewed as related manifestations of implicit informing ideas, and it is to the recognition and naming of these that his attention is addressed.

Wherever identical, or essentially comparable, constellations of myth and custom are discovered, Bachofen assumes a relationship. "Agreement in idea and form between the mythologies of countries far removed from one another discloses a cultural connection which can be explained only by migration," he declares, for instance, in his study of the myth of Tanaquil; which is a principle, of course, that would be accepted without question by any botanist or zoologist. And since, within the various provinces of a distribution of this kind, all sorts of secondary variations will have occurred—local progressions, regressions, transpositions of emphasis, etc.—the dual task of the researcher, after gathering his specimens and arranging them according to province, will have to be, first, to identify the source and interpret the informing idea of the earliest examples of each complex, and then, to isolate and interpret severally the observed variants.

All attempts at interpretation, however, according to Bachofen's view, must concur with the realization that the mainsprings of mythological thought are not those of a modern rational ideology. Mythological symbols derive from the centers rather of dream than of waking consciousness, and their sense, consequently, cannot be guessed through conscious ratiocination. The meaning of a myth resounds in its evoked associations, and if the scholar is to become aware of these, he must allow their counterparts to arise within himself from those regions of his own nature that he shares still with early man. "If it is true, as Aristotle says," Bachofen wrote in his retrospective sketch, "that like can be grasped only by like, then the divine can be apprehended only by a divine mind, and not by the rationalistic self-conceit that sets itself above history. Abundance of information is not everything, it is not even the essential."

Now of course there is romanticism in this kind of thinking, romanticism and religion: but so had there been romanticism in the sages, prophets, and visionaries who brought forth the early symbols. And it was through his acquiescence in the modes of their experience, thought, and communication that this modern gentleman was enabled to recognize in their messages, collected in his fine patrician home, the accents of a prehistoric world and way of life that was remoter and darker by centuries than the classical civilizations of Rome and Athens: from a deeper vein of the soul, as well as of time, than the classical scholarship of his day had yet suspected to exist. And he was mercilessly massacred, consequently, in the academic journals. One of the learned reviewers of his work on mortuary symbols wrote: "408 closely printed pages, full of the queerest, most adventurous dreams—dreams that in their profundity pass, at times, into realms even of consummate imbecility."[8] The work on mother right, two years later, received more of the same ruthless treatment—and at this point Bachofen seems to have decided that he had had enough. Some twenty years before he had had to endure an earlier round of public humiliation, when a school of newspaper sharks of the political left had taken it upon themselves to protest both his appointment to a professorship in Roman law at the University of Basel and his elevation to a place on the City Council, attributing both honors to family influence. At that time, after waiting a decent interval for the hue and cry to abate, he had quietly resigned both posts; and now, again, he simply walked away. His beloved mother had died five years before, and now his zeal for his career died as well. He packed and took a trip to Spain.

But as fate and his destiny would have it, in his luggage he had brought along for leisure reading Theodor Mommsen's recently published *History of Rome* (1854–56), and as he made his way through its three volumes, this

greatly celebrated work of truly massive scholarship seemed to him to epitomize precisely that "rationalistic self-conceit that sets itself above history"
which he despised from the depth of his soul. It so aroused his ire that he determined, then and there, to refute it by presenting in a work of his own a fundamental problem in classical culture history that could not be handled—and,
indeed, would not even have been recognized—from such a materialistic,
political-economic point of view. Returning to Basel, therefore, he set himself
to work, and eight years later gave forth the final major harvest volume of his
learning, *The Myth of Tanaquil.*

❦ ❦ ❦

It is in this last of Bachofen's major works, *The Myth of Tanaquil,* which appeared in the year 1870, that his view can best be studied of the inward force
of spiritual principles—*Grundanschauungen, Grundgedanken,* as opposed to
merely economic and political, rationally determinable laws—in the shaping
of the destinies of historic civilizations. The profound contrast of the Orient
and the Occident also is confronted here, and in terms, specifically, of a contrast in the motivating spiritual modes of mother and father right.

Both Bachofen's critics and his admirers have frequently remarked his tol-
erance of both the pagan-Oriental and the Christian-Occidental—archaic
matriarchal and progressive patriarchal—strains in our compound modern
heritage. His much shorter-lived Danish contemporary, Sören Kierkegaard
(1813–55), had found it necessary in the name of spiritual integrity to reject
the pagan from his soul in favor of the Christian strain, while his young friend
Friedrich Nietzsche (1844–1900), likewise finding the two together intolerable, had rejected with a vocabulary of moral exaltation no less elevated than
Kierkegaard's, not the pagan, but the Christian. The genial, somewhat portly,
comfortably long-lived Swiss patrician Bachofen, on the other hand, seems to
have found no difficulty whatsoever in remaining a solid Protestant, wholly
committed in his own way of life to what good Protestants take to be the basic
Christian virtues, while yet becoming, with every fiber of his being, the most
inspired interpreter and protagonist in his century of the moral orders—
Aphroditic as well as Demetrian—of the goddess.

It is true that in the past Hegel and Goethe, Petrarch, Erasmus, and many
other Christian humanists had managed to live with both traditions. "Zwei
Seelen wohnen, ach! In meiner Brust," mused Goethe's hero, Faust. However,
the classical soul had been for them largely of the Apollonian, patriarchal order,
while the supernatural claims of the biblical revelation had not yet been dis-
credited by nineteenth-century scholarship and science. They did not have to
abjure their reason in order to be Christians, nor their Christianity to be scions

of the Greeks. Hegel had regarded the two orders, respectively, as the *thesis* and *antithesis* of a single spiritual process, of which his own philosophy announced the *synthesis*. Goethe contrived to wed the two in his marriage of Helen and Faust. But in Bachofen's peaceful soul there seems to have been no sense of disaccord whatsoever. With a perfectly calm, scientific eye—good biologist of the spirit that he was!—he regarded with equal understanding every stage of what he took to be an orderly evolution of human ideals from the early earthbound modes of the Aphroditic and Demetrian, nomadic and early agricultural, stages, to the more elevated and illuminated modes of the higher civilizations: Athenian, Roman, medieval, and humanistic-modern. For him there was alive at the heart of each of these orders of life the vital force of an informing insight, *Grundanschauung, Grundgedanke,* which it was the aim of his science of symbols to identify and elucidate. And what he rejected with whole heart—as Nietzsche rejected Christian "yonder-worldlings" and Kierkegaard, the dialecticians of *this* world—was the sealing away of these wellsprings of inspiration with a pavement of economic and political modern thought—of which violation of the creative spirit Mommsen had become for him the prime example.

However, even the most patient and well-disposed modern reader may feel, on turning to *The Myth of Tanaquil,* that its almost aggressively *un*-modern, moralizing vocabulary so colors the argument as to violate the very principle of objectivity that the sentiments of a romantically inclined Swiss Protestant patrician into the institutions of Rome was an impropriety even less acceptable to modern taste than Mommsen's projection of the psychology of a nineteenth-century history professor.

For we have learned, these days, from a school of romantics of our own, not to evaluate cultures in terms even of "low" and "high," let alone "basely sensuous" and "spiritually pure"; and especially to eschew all such phraseology in relation to the cultural contrasts of Orient and Occident, Africa, Asia, and Europe. The later Professor Robert H. Lowie, of the University of California, evaluating in 1937 the ethnological theories of his nineteenth-century predecessors, wrote, "In his chronology, Bachofen is a typical evolutionist of the old school. Once more a belief in progressive stages appears. . . ."[9] And in the same vein, Professor R. R. Marett, of Exeter College, Oxford, censured not only Bachofen but also his contemporaries Lewis H. Morgan and J. F. McLennan. "Every one of these great thinkers must plead guilty to the charge," he declared, ". . . of definitely committing themselves to a treatment involving the fallacious notion of a unilineal evolution."[10] Yet even as these anti-evolutionary judgments were being pronounced with all the confidence of a young science, the excavations of the archaeologists (from a different department, however, of the university system) were beginning to reveal that there had indeed been a stage-by-stage evolution of human culture from low to high, and even from what, in terms of a nineteenth-century point of view, might well have been described as "basely sensuous" to "spiritually pure."

The essential epoch-making cultural mutations, it now was being shown, had occurred in specific, identifiable centers, from which the effects then had gone out to the ends of the earth, like ripples on a pond from a tossed stone. And wherever those expanding waves had reached, they had combined variously with waves from the earlier centers of mutation, so that all sorts of interesting configurations were discoverable for anthropological monographs. To make the point, one need mention only the epochal invention of the food-producing arts of agriculture and stock-breeding, about the ninth millennium B.C., in the Near East (Asia Minor, Syria, Palestine, northern Iraq, and Iran). From this center a new style of human living spread westward and eastward to the Atlantic and Pacific. Next, a galaxy of small agriculturally based cities (the earliest in the world) appeared in the Tigris-Euphrates valley about 3500 B.C., and within these, writing and mathematics were invented, as well as an astronomically calculated calendar, monumental architecture, kingship, and all the other basic elements of archaic civilizations. The combination then appeared in Egypt c. 2850 B.C., Crete and India c. 2600, China c. 1500, and Middle America between about 1200 and 800. Next, the mastery of the horse, 1800 B.C. or so, in the grasslands of Southeast Europe and Southwest Asia, was followed by the irresistible incursions of the patriarchal, horse-and-cattle-herding, chariot-driving Aryans into the tilled lands of India and the Near East, Greece, Italy, and Western Europe. At about the same time the Hebrews entered Canaan, bringing a unique brand of patriarchal monotheism from which the world-conquering, missionary civilizations of Christianity and Islam arose. And finally there evolved in Rome (first pagan, then Christian) the concept and corpus of civilizing law that in time became the root and stock from which not only every modern constitution derived, but also the universal charter of the United Nations—not to mention those further contributions of Europe to the world, the scientific method of research and the power-driven machine, from which innovations the great sky and ocean liners have emerged that today are bearing from every corner of the earth to the corridors of that same U.N. those graduates of Oxford, Cambridge, Paris, Harvard, and Columbia who bring back to Alma Mater the recirculating spiritual "winds of change" of this amazing twentieth century of ours.

Are we not to name all this an "evolution," "unilinear" and in "progressive stages?"

Moreover, it is difficult to pretend not to notice that all the main creative centers of this development were situated in a zone between 25 and 60 degrees north of the equator, 10 degrees west and 50 east of Greenwich.

This stage-by-stage evolution, which in broad outline Bachofen discerned (though with no idea, of course, of the great length of its backward reach in time), he did not regard as the consequence of a merely physical accumulation of inventions, but treated as a function of psychological mutations: a graded maturation of the mind. And he saw this growth epitomized, stage by stage, in relevant symbolic images, hypostatizing the founding insights (*Grundanschauungen*) of each of the several degrees. Every system of mythology, he states, is the exegesis of such a nuclear symbol: "It unfolds in a series of outwardly connected actions what the symbol embodies in a unity." And the message of the symbol is not a mere thought or idea, but a way of *experience* which can be understood only by responding to its summons.

"The symbol awakens intimations," Bachofen writes; "speech can only explain. The symbol plucks all the strings of the human spirit at once; speech is compelled to take up a single thought at a time. The symbol strikes its roots in the most secret depths of the soul; language skims over the surface of the understanding like a soft breeze. The symbol aims inward; language outward." And in accord with the inward sense of its commanding symbol, Bachofen held, the civilization of each mounting stage brought forth the mythology and creative deeds of its unique destiny—as did Gothic Europe in response to its symbol of the Crucified Redeemer, Israel to the Covenant, Athens to its sky of Apollonian light, and the Lycians to the female earth.

Bachofen envisioned the course of the spiritual maturation of humanity in five capital stages. Two, as we have seen, were dominated by the female point of view; three, thereafter, were dominated by the male. Within the geographic range of his purview, he identified Africa and Asia as the chief seats of development of the earlier stages of this sequence, and Europe—specifically Greece and Rome—of the later.

From the Near East, according to his reading of the evidence (and we now can be reasonably certain that his reading was correct), there came the earliest agricultural village communities of Greece, and of Italy as well. They were characterized, according to his theory, by the religiously enforced moral order of the second stage of mother right, the agricultural telluric-Demetrian. Their mythologies and associated symbolic customs were of a profoundly poetic beauty—recognizing in every significant phase of life the mystery of the female power, symbolized in the mother goddess Earth and present in every wife and mother. It was a world, as he tells, held in form by "that mysterious power which equally permeates all earthly creatures," the love of mothers for their young; and the blood kinship of the matrilineal family was the fundamental structuring principle of the social order.

It is pertinent to remark at this point that in Bachofen's nineteenth century the Hegelian concept of a dialectic of statement and counterstatement, thesis and antithesis, in the rolling tide of history was a commonly accepted thought, inflected variously, however, by the numerous vigorous theorists of that really great period of creative historical thinkers. Karl Marx, for instance (whose dates, 1818–83, match very closely those of our author), saw, wherever he looked, the economic-political conflict of exploiter and exploited. Nietzsche, who came to Basel in 1869 as a young professor of classical philology and for the next half decade was a frequent guest in Bachofen's home (spending Sundays, however, with his idol Richard Wagner in Lucerne, whose dates, 1813–83, again approximately match Bachofen's span of years), saw the dialectic of history, and of individual biography as well, in terms of an unrelenting conflict between the forces of disease, weakness, and life-resentment, on the one hand, and, on the other, courage and determination to build life forward toward a realization of potentials. Bachofen, far more learned in the matter of antiquity than either of these celebrated thinkers, and indeed than Hegel himself, saw the dialectic as of the mothering, feminine, earth-oriented, and the masculine, mastering, idea- and heaven-oriented powers. In his masterwork *Mother Right* he had already written:

> The progress from the maternal to the paternal conception of man forms the most important turning point in the history of the relations between the sexes. The Demetrian and the Aphroditean-hetaeric stages both hold to the primacy of generative motherhood, and it is only the greater or lesser purity of its interpretation that distinguishes the two forms of existence. . . . Maternity pertains to the physical side of man, the only thing he shares with the animals: the paternal-spiritual principle belongs to him alone. Here he breaks through the bonds of tellurism and lifts his eyes to the higher regions of the cosmos.

The first stage in the rise of the masculine principle to supremacy is symbolized, according to Bachofen's view, in the figure of the solar child, the solar hero, born without earthly father from the virgin-mother Dawn: the mythic personification of the rising sun. Here the masculine principle is still subordinated to the female.[11]

The second stage he terms the Dionysian. Its mythologies are of the sun god at the zenith, equidistant from its rising and setting hours, masterfully fertilizing the earth as the phallic power. However, there is a dangerous regressive trend potential in this situation. "The Dionysian father," Bachofen writes, "forever seeks receptive matter in order to arouse it to life." Thus the masculine principle has not yet broken free to the independent sphere of its own *ius natu-rale,* while, as exciter of the female, Bacchus-Dionysus, the god of women and the wine of life, tends to reactivate the primary passions of physical lust, and so to precipitate a regression from the marital-Demetrian to the hetaerist-Aphroditic stage of sexuality. And this, he declares, is the way things went and have remained in Africa and Asia, where "the original matriarchy underwent the most thorough Dionysian transformation."[12]

In Greece the long struggle against the earlier telluric mother-nature pow-ers is documented in the myths and legends of such heroes as Bellerophon, Heracles, Theseus and Perseus, Oedipus and Orestes. There is marked in these an advance to the sky-bright Apollonian stage of masculine spirituality. How-ever, the advance was only temporary; for in the end it was Dionysus and his maenads who again gained the day in Greece. Only in Rome did an essentially masculine spiritual order become effectively established and confirmed—in the tenets and world legacy of Roman civil law.

It is therefore the great argument of Bachofen's *Myth of Tanaquil* that the effort of European man to achieve the proprietorship and rational control of his own destiny, releasing himself from the dominion of cosmic-physical forces and a primitive philosophy of existence, must be recognized as having gained its first enduring victory as the dominant driving force and creative principle of the history of Rome. And it was a victory gained only at the cost of a ruthless suppression and subordination of the claims and allures of the natu-ral world—the more cruel and ruthless, the greater the allure.

"It is no paradox," he states, "but a great truth borne out by all history that human culture advances only through the clash of opposites." And in the case of Rome, the clash was between the Oriental principle represented in the Aphroditic, Demetrian, and Dionysian legacies of the Sabines and Etruscans, Hellenistic Carthage, and finally, Cleopatra's Hellenistic Egypt, and, on the other hand, the austerity of a race inspired to create, under the sign of reason, a world empire of illuminated law.

Bachofen interpreted both Rome's terrible annihilation of Carthage and Virgil's sympathy with that violent work, displayed in the *Aeneid,* as expres-sions, respectively, in act and in sentiment, of the inward necessity of this spir-itual clash; and in demonstration of the fact that it was indeed a clash primarily of *Grundanschauungen,* spiritual ideals, and not of merely economic and polit-ical interests, he analyzed the transformation of the elements of the legend of Queen Tanaquil as they passed from their seat of origin in the Asiatic Near East to European Rome.

They had been the elements there of an obscene fertility festival, an orgy of the type described in Frazer's *Golden Bough,* "to make the crops to grow." The festival queen had been a temple prostitute in the character of the Great Goddess, and her temporary spouse, with whom she was publicly united in accordance with the primal *ius naturale,* was a young lusty in the role of the god, who, following his service, was sacrificed on a pyre; while for a period of five days and nights a general orgy rendered appropriate veneration to the hetaeric divinity of the occasion.

Folk festivals of this sort arrived in Italy from Asia and were particularly evident in the traditions of the Sabines and Etruscans—of which Bachofen cites numerous examples; and Tanaquil's legend was one of these. She was represented as the queenly throne-giver of the last three kings of the Roman Etruscan line: Tarquinius Priscus (the legendary fifth king of Rome, r. 616–578 B.C.), of whom she was supposed to have been the consort and advisor; Servius Tullius (the sixth legendary king, r. 578–534), the son of a slave woman, who married Tanaquil's daughter and by the contrivance of his mother-in-law succeeded to the throne; and finally, Tarquinius Superbus (the seventh and last legendary king of this line, r. 534–510 B.C.), who was supposed to have been Tanaquil's son or, according to other accounts, her spouse. But such a female donor and patroness of royal rule and power is not properly a Roman but an Asiatic figure, derived, along with the concept of kingship itself, from Asia, and of the same symbolic context as the Asiatic goddesses and heroines of legend, Anahita and Mylitta, Dido and Cleopatra. Bachofen's great point is that in Rome her entire character was transformed, and that neither economics nor politics but a spiritual ideal was the force responsible for the change. She lost her "basely sensuous" Aphroditic-venereal traits and became the model matronly patroness of the rights of women in the Roman state, an example of the nobility of the dutiful Roman wife, and a champion of the humanizing principle of love and mercy in a society governed otherwise by sheerly masculine ideals of statecraft. And this transformation accorded, furthermore, with the whole spirit of Roman as opposed to Oriental culture, whether in its religious, economic, political, or aesthetic aspect: for these are all of a piece. They do not derive one from another, but are expressions equally of a common *Grundgedanke,* manifest in the various departments of life; and to read them otherwise is to flatten the whole structure and thus to lose sight of the problem of history itself.

Furthermore, not only was Tanaquil transformed from a goddess of hetaeric type to one of "spiritual purity," but in the course of time a second development ensued, when she was conceived not as a goddess but as a historic queen. Bachofen concludes this remarkable, inexhaustibly suggestive discussion by saying:

We might be tempted to regard this subordination of the divine to a human idea as the last stage in a process of degeneration from an earlier, more sublime standpoint. And indeed, who will deny that beside the cosmic world-spanning ideas of the Bel-Heracles religion, which gave rise to the notion of a woman commanding over life and throne, the humanized Tanaquil of the Roman tradition, adapted as she is to everyday life, seems an impoverished figure, scarcely comparable to the colossal Oriental conception. And yet this regression contains the germ of a very important advance. For every step that liberates our spirit from the paralyzing fetters of a cosmic-physical view of life must be so regarded. . . . Rome's central idea . . . the idea underlying its historical stage and its law, is wholly independent of matter; it is an eminently ethical achievement, the most spiritual of antiquity's bequests to the ensuing age. And here again it is clear that our Western life truly begins with Rome. Roman is the idea through which European mankind prepared to set its own imprint on the entire globe, namely, the idea that no material law but only the free activity of the spirit determines the destinies of peoples.

❦   ❦   ❦

Johann Jacob Bachofen's career falls into three clearly marked stages. The first, his period of preparation, extends to 1851, the year of an inspiring horseback pilgrimage that he took through Greece. The following decade, 1852–61, was the period of labor on his major works. The manuscript of his *Greek Journey* was finished in 1852, but remained unpublished until its rescue, in 1927, by the Munich group. In 1854 he composed his retrospective sketch, in 1859 published the work on *Mortuary Symbolism,* and in 1861, *Mother Right;* after which, as already remarked, he left Basel for a change of air in Spain.

The final period of his career began with the eight years of leisurely, peaceful labor on *The Myth of Tanaquil,* while a new and pleasantly fulfilling transformation of life and home took place around him. In 1865 he married and traveled with his young bride to Rome, the magical mother-city of his learning, from which he had returned in youth with "a new seriousness of soul" and "a more living, positive background" for his studies. A son was born the next year, 1866; and Bachofen retired, then, from a judgeship he had held since 1842. The arrival in Basel, three years later, of Nietzsche brought a new brilliance to the Bachofen domestic circle, and it was about that time that signs began to appear, as well, of a new, significant, and rapidly increasing scientific appreciation of his published works—not, indeed, from the classical circles of academic hardshelled crabs to which he had turned, at first, in vain; but from the unforeseen quarter of a new science, anthropology.

For during the year of Nietzsche's arrival there came into Bachofen's hands a copy of John F. McLennan's *Primitive Marriage* (published in London, 1865), and there he found that his own work not only had been decently recognized, but also was furnishing the basis for an entirely new approach to a totally new scientific topic: the prehistory of marriage. The next year, 1870, Alexis Giraud-Teulon, a young scholar from Geneva, came to Bachofen's door, full of admiration for the great man who had opened to science the world age of mother right; and it was in that same year that Bachofen's interest in his own career was suddenly renewed.

"My task," he wrote on November 10 to his old friend Meyer-Ochsner, "is now to assemble the evidences of the maternal system from all peoples of the earth, to prepare, on the basis of this amplified material, for a second edition of *Mother Right. . . .* Sources of such information are the works of travel. . . . And I am enjoying from these the great advantage of becoming familiar with a world that expands my horizon immensely and brings me into spiritual rapport, moreover, with new peoples, new individuals, and a truly heroic race of voyagers, missionaries and bravely adventurous hunters. We have been brought up in just too limited a classical way. . . ."[13]

And it was very much as though his readings in the expanded field were sending out telepathic calls; for almost immediately letters of encouraging admiration arrived, on the one hand, from that greatest anthropological traveler of all, Professor Adolf Bastian of the University of Berlin, President of the Berlin Anthropological Society, and on the other, from the leading American ethnologist of the period, Lewis Henry Morgan, whose *League of the Iroquois* had appeared some twenty years before (1851). On Christmas Day in 1871 this honorary member of the Hawk clan of the Seneca nation of the Iroquois sat down at his desk in Rochester, New York, and wrote to the distant outcast in the Alps: "My first notice of your investigations was in Prof. Curtius' *History of Greece.*[14] I there found that you were examining a class of facts closely allied to those upon which I had been for some time engaged. I have now your Mother-right. . . ."[15] The correspondence that ensued endured until the year of Morgan's death in 1881, and during the course of it, there appeared one day at Bachofen's door, in further testimony of the regard in which he was held across the sea, shipment of publications on the aborigines of America, which had been sent to him from Washington, D.C., with the compliments of the Government of the United States.

Ironically, Lewis H. Morgan's widely read treatise on the prehistoric stage-by-stage evolution of culture, *Ancient Society,* published 1877, in which Bachofen's achievement is accorded both recognition and due praise, caught the eyes and imagination of Karl Marx and Friedrich Engels, into whose vision of an early communal order of civilization its hypotheses seemed to fit; and so the works of the two learned jurists, respectively of Rochester, N.Y., and of Basel, were admitted to the canon of permitted Marxist readings.[16] In fact, in Engel's own treatise on *The Origin of the Family, Private Property, and the State* (1884), Bachofen's view of the evolution of culture is accorded respectful approbation—though with correction, of course, of the romantic bourgeois thought of a basically spiritual instead of economic-political-exploitational motivation of the procession.

Bachofen did not live to complete or even to initiate the publication of his proposed revised and enlarged version of *Mother Right.* In 1880 and 1886 he produced two volumes of shorter pieces, entitled *Antiquarian Letters, Dealing Chiefly with the Earliest Concepts of the Family.* However, on November 27, 1887, he suffered a stroke and died. His widow and son brought out a posthumous work, *The Lamps of Roman Tombs,* in 1890; it carried an introduction by Alexis Giraud-Teulon, the loyal spiritual son who had been the first to render Bachofen the satisfaction of a gesture of recognition. Giraud-Teulon's own treatise, *Les Origines de la famille, questions sur les antecédents des sociétés patriarchales,* had greeted the master's eyes in 1874. By the time of his death a considerable harvest was beginning to be gathered from those diligent gardens of Academia which Heine, in his *Harzreise,* amusingly describes as consisting of beds of little sticks set up in rows, each bearing a bit of paper with a notation from some book—the work then consisting in transferring notations from older beds to new, in ever-changing arrangement. However, this fame itself became largely responsible, in the end, for the fading of Bachofen's name, when, at the turn of the twentieth century, there was a trend in anthropology away from theoretical reconstructions of the earliest state of man.

For Bachofen's name had finally become associated almost exclusively with the one aspect of his writing that was most open to question—that, namely, which the Marxists had picked up, of the primal Aphroditic-hetaerist stage of communal sexuality. A formidable attack on this view of primitive life appeared in 1902 in a work by the anthropologist Heinrich Schurtz, *Altersklassen und Männerbünde,* where it is argued that "marriage in its beginning goes back as far as the evidences of human society can be followed," and furthermore, that "the alleged vestiges and evidences of a period of sexual promiscuity are nothing but manifestations of the sexual license of the mature but still unmarried young."[17]

We have remarked already the anti-evolutionary schools of social science that arose in the United States and England. On the Continent, also, grandiose total views lost favor as new ethnological information came pouring, in great variety, from all quarters of the earth, and as the great remoteness in time of the earliest Paleolithic, and even pre-Paleolithic past became increasingly apparent and impressive. Bachofen's reputation foundered, along with the reputations of a number of other interesting nineteenth-century pioneers who, in the frame of the brief prehistoric prospect of their period, had supposed themselves to be working closer to the flaming sword of the archangel at the gate of the garden of Eden than was the case.

Ironically again, however, the other aspects of Bachofen's thought were meanwhile becoming increasingly accepted—but over other scholars' names. For example, in Sir James G. Frazer's *The Golden Bough,* which first appeared in 1890 (the year of Bachofen's posthumous *Lamps of Roman Tombs*) and was then reissued in twelve massive volumes between 1907 and 1915, the central problem under investigation is of a piece with those by which Bachofen's interest had been aroused. This was a Roman custom that could not be explained in normal classical terms: the reported tradition of the goddess Diana's sacred grove at Nemi, where the priest—regarded as the husband of an oak tree— gained his office by murdering his predecessor and would lose it when he himself, in turn, was slain. The great British scholar, in his own way, actually completed in this mighty work the last task that Bachofen had set himself, "to assemble the evidences of the maternal system from all peoples of the earth"; and he arrived, as had his predecessor—apparently independently—at the recognition of an age of mother right antecedent to that of the Greek and Roman patriarchal systems.[18]

Following Frazer's work, and in acknowledged dependence upon it, there appeared in 1903 Jane Harrison's richly documented *Prolegomena to the Study of Greek Religion,* which, if Bachofen's name were mentioned anywhere in its pages, might be read from beginning to end as an intentional celebration and verification of his views. In the twenties Sir Arthur Evans excavated the ruins of Cretan Knossos, and in the fifties the young genius Michael Ventris deciphered some of the writings discovered there: and the prominence in this pre-Hellenic treasure trove, both of the Great Goddess and of her son and consort Poseidon (whose name, *Posei-dās,* means "Lord of the Earth"), has now confirmed irrefutably not only Bachofen's intuition of an age of mother right preceding the patriarchal ages, but also his recognition of Syria and Asia Minor as the proximate Asiatic provinces from which the agriculturally based mother right culture complex came to the isles and peninsulas of Greece and Rome.[19]

Furthermore, it may be noted that Bachofen's methodological idea of the *Kulturkreis* as an organically coherent culture province generated and sustained by the force and phenomenology of an informing *Grundanschauung* became the leading inspiration of a number of extremely influential independent ethnological researchers: Leo Frobenius and Adolf Jensen, for instance, and Fathers Wilhelm Schmidt and Wilhelm Koppers.

However, the most important aspect of Bachofen's contribution is not his mere anticipation of archaeological finds nor even his influence on ethnologists who have developed and applied his ideas, but the profundity and lucidity of his reading of mythological symbols—specifically the symbols of the great creative pre-Homeric, pre-Mosaic "age of fable" that now lies open to our eyes. For that was the age from which the founding themes and images of both our classical and our biblical mythologies were derived; which is to say, the *Grundan-schauungen,* the grounding themes and images of an essential part of our cultural heritage and, thereby, of our own culturally conditioned psychology: the creative period, as we now know, of those agriculturally based mother right symbologies that Sigmund Freud, in *Totem and Taboo,* confessed he was unable to explain. "I cannot suggest," Freud wrote in 1912, "at what point in this process of development a place is to be found for the great mother-goddesses, who may perhaps in general have preceded the father-gods."[20]

Bachofen's concentration of his whole mind and being for some fifty years of his life on the reading of the pictorial script of precisely that system of religious imagery—stemming from an age of mythopoetic thought immediately antecedent to both the biblical and the classical patriarchal formations—opened in a magical way a deeper view than any patriarchal mythology or its analysis, not only into our cultural past, but also into our culturally structured souls. That is why the psychologist Ludwig Klages, who was the first member of the Munich circle to be struck by the force of these perceptions, wrote in a statement published in 1925 that Bachofen had been "the greatest literary experience" of his life, determining the whole course of his career.

"In Bachofen," he declared, "we have to recognize perhaps the greatest interpreter of that primordial mentality, in comparison with the cultic and mythic manifestations of which, all later religious beliefs and doctrines appear as mere reductions and distortions."[21]

Leo Frobenius termed the same period of mythopoetic creativity to which Bachofen's whole genius had been dedicated, the period at "the apogee of the mythological curve." Before it extend the millennia of primitive, pre-agricultural hunting and foraging cultures. After it come the flowerings of the great monumental civilizations of Mesopotamia and Egypt, Greece and Rome, India, China, and across the Pacific, Mexico and Peru—the symbologies and mythologies of which are as like to each other as so many descendants of a single house. Sir James G. Frazer likewise points back to that age as the ultimate source of those magical rites and myths "to make the crops to grow" that survive in modified, reinterpreted, and distorted forms in many of our own basic religious practices and beliefs. Bachofen, at that source, was thus indeed at the "time of the beginning"—not of mankind, as he believed, in the short terms of early nineteenth-century science, but of civilization. And so it is that, through the extraordinary ability of his own alert humanity to interpret the mythic forms of that germinal time, we are introduced to the psychological ground of our entire cultural heritage. Nietzsche, as we have said, had to reject the Christian strain of our mixed heritage; Kierkegaard, the pagan. Wise, deep-seeing, sagely Bachofen, on the other hand, could with equal eye regard the whole sweep of what he saw to be an orderly progression in which his own mode of consciousness participated as a member. And it was to this realization of an ultimately unitary *ius naturale* of spiritual exis- tence, made manifest throughout the range of human faith and works, that his life vocation ultimately called him.

"A time inevitably comes," he wrote to his Berlin master, Von Savigny, "when the scholar seriously examines his studies for their relation to the supreme truths. He becomes aware of a desire, an urgent need, to come a little closer to the eternal meaning of things. The husk no longer suffices. The thought of having struggled so long with mere worthless forms becomes a tor- ment. And then one is saved by the realization that even in these things one may discover 'the eternal footprint.'. . . I see more and more that *one* law gov- erns all things."

The Mystery Number of the Goddess

All Things Anew

As prophesied in *The Poetic Edda,*

> Five hundred and forty doors there are,
>   I ween, in Valhall's walls;
> Eight hundred fighters through each door fare
>   When to war with the Wolf they go.[1]

540 × 800 = 432,000, which in the Hindu Purāṇas, or "Chronicles of Ancient Lore," is the number of years reckoned to the Kali Yuga, the present cycle of time, which is to be the last and shortest of four cycles that together compose a "Great Cycle" or Mahāyuga of 4,320,000 years, which is to end in a universal flood.

The Purāṇas date from c. A.D. 400 to 1000; the Eddic verses from c. A.D. 900 to 1100. The obvious question to be asked, therefore, is, By what coincidence can this number have appeared both in India and in Iceland in association with a mythology of recurrent cycles of time? For as told further in the Eddas,

> Now do I see the earth anew
> Rise all green from the waves again;
> The cataracts fall, and the eagle flies,
> And fish he catches beneath the cliffs.
>
> In wondrous beauty once again
> Shall the golden tables stand mid the grass,
> Which the gods owned in days of old.
>
> The fields unsowed bear ripened fruit,
> All ills grow better, and Baldr comes back;
> Baldr and Hoth dwell in Hropt's battle-hall,
> And the mighty gods.[2]

One cannot but think of the prophesied Day of Doom of the New Testament (Mark 13), which, according to Rev. 21:1, is to be followed by "a new heaven and new earth; for the first heaven and the first earth had passed away, and the sea was no more." Can the number 432 have been associated with this biblical cycle as well as with the Hindu cycle and the Norse? We read further in the book of the revelation beheld on the Greek island of Patmos by St. John.

Then came one of the seven angels who had the seven bowls full of the seven last plagues, and spoke to me, saying: "Come, I will show you *the Bride, the wife of the Lamb.*" And in the Spirit he carried me away to a great, high mountain, and showed me the holy city Jerusalem coming down out of heaven from God, having the glory of God, its radiance like a most rare jewel, like a jasper, clear as crystal. It had a great, high wall, with twelve gates, and at the gates twelve angels, and on the gates the names of the twelve tribes of the sons of Israel were inscribed; on the east three gates, on the north three gates, on the south three gates, and on the west three gates. And the wall of the city had twelve foundations, and on them the twelve names of the twelve apostles of the Lamb.

And he who talked with me had a measuring rod of gold to measure the city and its gates and walls. *The city lies foursquare, its length the same as its breadth, and he measured the city with his rod, twelve thousand stadia; its length and breadth and height are equal.* He also measured its wall, a hundred and forty-four cubits by a man's measure, that is, an angel's. The wall was built of jasper, while the city was of pure gold, clear as glass. . . . And the twelve gates were twelve pearls, each of the gates made of a single pearl, and the street of the city was pure gold, transparent as glass. (Rev. 21:9–21, abridged; the italics, of course, are mine.)

12,000 × 12,000 × 12,000 stadia = 1,728 billion cubic stadia, which, when divided by 4, equals 432 billion.[3] Moreover, in Rev. 13:18, it is declared that the number of the name of the "beast rising out of the sea, with ten horns and seven heads, with ten diadems upon its horns and a blasphemous name upon its heads" (Rev. 13:1), is 666; whereas 6 × 6 × 6 = 216, which is half of 432.

The earliest known appearance of this number was in the writings of a Chaldean priest of the god Marduk, Berossos, who, c. 280 B.C., composed in Greek a synopsis of Babylonian myth and history in which it was reported that, between the legendary date of the "descent of kingship" on the early Sumerian city of Kish and the coming of the mythological flood, ten kings ruled in Sumer through a period of 432,000 years. The universal flood there reported is the same as that of Genesis 6–7, of which the earliest known account has been found on a very greatly damaged cuneiform tablet from the ruins of Nippur, of a date c. 2000 B.C.[4] There the ancient tale is told of a pious king Ziusudra, last of the line of ten long-lived antediluvian monarchs of the city of Shuruppak, who, while standing by a wall, heard a voice advising him to build himself an ark.

The . . . place . . .
The people . . .
A rainstorm . . .
At that time [the Goddess] Nintu screamed like a woman in travail.
The pure [Goddess] Inanna wailed because of her people.
[The god] Enki in his heart took counsel.
[The Great Gods] An, Enlil, Enki, and [the Goddess] Ninhursag.
The gods of heaven and earth invoked the names of An and Enlil.

Ziusudra at that time was king, the lustral priest of . . .
He built a huge . . .
Humbly prostrating himself, reverently . . .
Daily and perseveringly standing in attendance . . .
Auguring by dreams, such as never were seen before . . .
Conjuring in the name of heaven and earth . . .

> . . . the gods, a wall . . .
Ziusudra, standing at its side, heard:
> "At the wall, at my left hand stand . . .
> At the wall, I would speak to thee a word.
> O my holy one, open thine ear to me.
>
> "By our hand a rainstorm . . . will be sent,
> To destroy the seed of mankind . . .
> Is the decision, the word of the assembly of the gods,
> The command of An and Enli . . .
> Its kingdom . . . its rule . . ."

All the windstorms of immense power, they all came together.
The rainstorm... raged along with them.
And when for seven days and seven nights
The rainstorm in the land had raged,
The huge boat on the great waters by the windstorm had been carried away.
Utu, the sun came forth, shedding light over heaven and earth.

Ziusudra opened a window of the huge boat.
He let the light of the sun-god, the hero, come into the interior of the huge boat.
Ziusudra, the king,
Prostrated himself before Utu.
The king: he sacrifices an ox, slaughters a sheep.

> "By the soul of heaven, by the soul of earth, do ye conjure him, that he may . . .
>   with you.
> By the soul of heaven, by the soul of earth, O An and Enlil, do ye conjure and
>   he will . . . with you."

Vegetation, coming out of the earth, rises.
Ziusudra, the king,
Before An and Enlil prostrates himself.
Life like that of a god they bestow on him.
An eternal soul like that of a god they create for him.
Whereupon Ziusudra, the king,
Bearing the title, "Preserver of the Seed of Mankind,"
On a . . . mountain, the mountain of Dilmun, they caused to dwell . . .[5]

Returning to the Bible, we find that, in Genesis 5, ten antediluvian patriarchs are named from Adam to Noah; the first, of course, being Adam, who, as

we read, "when he had lived 130 years became the father of a son . . . and named him Seth." Continuing: "When Seth had lived 105 years, he became the father of Enosh. . . ." And likewise: "When Enosh had lived 90 years, he became the father of Kenon . . . When Kenon had lived 70 years, he became the father of Mahalalel," and so on, to, "When Lamech had lived 182 years, he became the father of a son, and called his name Noah. . . ." Following all of which, we learn from Genesis 7:6 that "Noah was 600 years old when the flood of waters came upon the earth."

Comparing this remarkable genealogical fantasy with Berossos's equally bizarre list of the years of reign of the antediluvian kings, and totaling the two sums, we find as follows:

Berossos		Genesis 5 and 7:6	
Antediluvian kings	*Years of reign*	*Antediluvian patriarchs*	*Years to begetting of sons*
1. Aloros	36,000	Adam	130
2. Alaparos	10,800	Seth	105
3. Amelon	46,800	Enosh	90
4. Ammenon	43,200	Kenon	70
5. Megalaros	64,800	Mahalalel	65
6. Daonos	36,000	Jared	162
7. Eudoraches	64,800	Enoch	65
8. Amempsinos	36,000	Methuselah	187
9. Oprates	28,800	Lamech	182
10. Xisuthros	64,800	Noah, yrs. to flood:	600
[= Ziusudra]	432,000		1,656

Between the totals of Berossos and the compilers of Genesis 5–7, there is apparently an irreconcilable difference. However, as demonstrated over a century ago in a paper, "The Dates of Genesis," by the distinguished Jewish Assyriologist Julius Oppert, who in his day was known as the "Nestor of Assyriology," both totals contain 72 as a factor, this being the number of years required in the precession of the equinoxes for an advance of 1 degree along the zodiac.[6] 432,000 divided by 72 = 6,000, while 1656 divided by 72 = 23. So that the relationship is of 6,000 to 23.[7] But in the Jewish calendar, one year is reckoned as of 365 days, which number in 23 years, plus the 5 leap-year days of that period, amounts to 8,400 days, or 1,200 seven-day weeks; which last sum, multiplied by 72, to find *the number of seven-day weeks in 23 × 72 = 1,656 years,* yields 1,200 × 72 = 86,400, which is twice 43,200.

So that in the Book of Genesis two distinct theologies have been now revealed. The first is that of the usually recognized personal Creator-God of Abraham, Isaac, and Jacob, who saw that "the wickedness of man was great in the earth . . . and was sorry that he had made man on the earth, and it grieved him to his heart. So the Lord said, 'I will blot out man whom I have created from the face of the ground, man and beast and creeping things and birds of the air, for I am sorry that I have made them'" (Gen. 6:5–7). Whereas the other, very different theology has been hidden all these years beneath the elaborately disguised number 86,400, which can be only a covert reference to the mathematically governed Gentile cosmology preserved to this day in the Hindu Purāṇas, of an unending series of cycles of world appearances and dissolutions, the latter following inevitably upon the former, not because of any god's disappointment in his creation, but as night follows day.

For the Jews, it will be recalled, had been for fifty years exiled from their own capital to Babylon (586–539 B.C.), and the priestly hands that compiled the genealogical schedule of Genesis, chapter 5—so nicely contrived to join the 600 years of Noah's age at the time of the Flood, as reported in chapter 7, to produce a total exactly of 1,656—were of a postexilic generation and contemporaries approximately of Berossos, the famous Chaldean priest.

The Goddess Universe

But already in the mangled cuneiform Flood text above, quoted from c. 2000 B.C., the signs are discernible of at least two distinct orders of mythology. For in Sumerian terms, that text was very late, and during the course of a preceding culture-history of no less than 1,500 years, the founding cosmological insight represented in the Flood legend had become overlaid by folkloristic layerings of imaginative, anecdotal narrative. Throughout those very greatly troubled times the land of Sumer had been open to both peaceful settlement and violent invasions by Semitic hordes from the Syro-Arabian desert, until finally, c. 2350 B.C., the mighty usurper, Sargon I of Akkad, carved out for himself with great violence and destruction—of which his monuments proudly boast—an empire that extended from the Taurus ranges to the Persian Gulf, which "began," as Samuel Noah Kramer has remarked, "the Semitization of Sumer that finally brought about the end of the Sumerian people, at least as an identifiable political and ethnic entity . . . . His influence made itself felt in one way or another from Egypt to India."[8]

The mutilated Flood text of c. 2000 B.C. is from the ruins of Nippur, which Sargon's grandson, Naram-Sin, sacked and desecrated c. 2230 B.C. The Sargonids themselves were then overpowered, c. 2150 B.C., by a mountain people from the Zagros range, the Guti, who overran the empire and maintained control in Mesopotamia until c. 2050 B.C., when Utuhegel of Erech, a Sumerian, overthrew their king Tirigan and, having caused him to be blinded and brought before his throne, "set his foot upon his neck."[9]

The following century, which is that of our Flood text and known to scholarship as Dynasty III of Ur (c. 2050–1950 B.C.), was an immensely productive season of renewed Sumerian achievement in the arts, in temple building, religious reconstruction, and text recording. Indeed, practically all that we now know of the literature, mythology, and culture of this remarkable, first literate people in the history of civilization dates from the monuments of this one brief but very precious Sumerian century.[10] A resurgent, reconstructed civilization, however, is not the same as an originating, form-envisioning culture; 350 years of alien domination cannot be written away. As Kramer has described the condition of the material of which he has been the leading modern translator:

> Intellectually speaking, the Sumerian myths reveal a rather mature and sophisticated approach to the gods and their divine activities; behind them can be recognized considerable cosmological and theological reflection. By and large, however, the Sumerian mythographers were the direct heirs of the illiterate minstrels and bards of earlier days, and their first aim was to compose narrative poems about the gods that would be appealing, inspiring, and entertaining. Their main literary tools were not logic and reason but imagination and fantasy. In telling their stories they did not hesitate to invent motives and incidents patterned on human action that could not possibly have any basis in rational and speculative thought. Nor did they hesitate to adopt legendary and folkloristic motifs that had nothing to do with cosmological inquiry and inference.
>
> As yet, no Sumerian myths have been recovered dealing directly and explicitly with the creation of the universe; what little is known about the Sumerian cosmogonic ideas has been inferred from laconic statements scattered throughout the literary documents. But we do have a number of myths concerned with the organization of the universe and its cultural processes, the creation of man, and the establishment of civilization.[11]

Prehistorically, the Sumerians were not aboriginal to Mesopotamia. Their native hearth is unknown. Speaking an agglutinative tongue showing affinities, on one hand, with the Uralo-Altaic languages (Balto-Finnish, Hungarian, Volgaic, Uralien, Samoyuedic, Turkish, Mongolian, and Eskimo) and, on the other hand, with the Dravidian tongues of India, the Pelasgian of pre-Homeric Greece, Georgian of the Caucasus, and Basque of the Pyrenees, they had arrived apparently c. 3500 B.C. to find the river lands already occupied by an advanced Neolithic, farming and cattle-raising population known to science as the Ubaidian (also, Proto-Euphratean), who, as Kramer tells, were "the first important civilizing force in ancient Sumer, its first farmers, cultivators, cattle-raisers, and fishermen; its first weavers, leather-workers, carpenters, smiths, potters, and masons."[12] The culture stage represented was that of Marija Gimbutas's *The Goddesses and Gods of Old Europe, 7000-3500 B.C.,* where the paramount divinity of eastern Europe in that period is shown to have been (to quote Gimbutas's characterization) "the Great Goddess of Life, Death, and Regeneration in anthropomorphic form with a projection of her powers through insects and animals."[13] "As a supreme Creator who creates from her own substance," states Gimbutas, "she is the primary goddess of the old European pantheon." And further: "Because her main function was to regenerate life forces, the goddess was flanked by male animals noted for their physical strength.... The European Great Goddess, like the Sumerian Ninhursag, gave life to the dead."[14]

The elegance of the grade of civilization represented in the remains of this Mother Goddess culture-stratum in all of its appearances, whether in the Old Europe of Marija Gimbutas's revelations, the late Neolithic and Chalcolithic sites of Anatolia and the Near East, or in the pre-Harappan strata of Neolithic northwest India, gives evidence to the bold suggestion of Alain Daniélou in his recently published comparative study of the religions of Shiva and Dionysus, of a single "great cultural movement extending from India to Portugal," dating from the sixth millennium B.C., and documented, not in scripture (since there was no writing at that time), but in the grace and clarity of its visual arts.[15] For the ambiance is strongly female: exemplary of a profoundly felt, inward knowledge of the transpersonal imperatives and quality of life, to which expression is given in visual art as a cosmetic or accenting adornment, not only of the person, but of anything of significance to life in the culture.

It is this joy in the beautification of life that especially marks the monuments of this earliest agricultural stage; and everywhere its paramount divinity is that metaphoric apparition of the life that outlives death who became in later centuries venerated as the Goddess of Many Names. "I am she," she declared, for example, upon appearing as Queen Isis before her devotee Lucius Apuleius at the conclusion of the ordeal described in his allegorical picaresque novel, *The Golden Ass* (second century A.D.):

> I am she that is the natural mother of all things, mistress and governess of all the elements, the initial progeny of worlds, chief of the powers divine, queen of all that are in hell, the principal of them that dwell in heaven, manifested alone and under one form of all the gods and goddesses.[16] At my will the planets of the sky, the wholesome winds of the seas, and the lamentable silences of hell are disposed; my name, my divinity is adored throughout the world, in divers manners, in variable customs, and by many names.
>
> For the Phrygians that are the first of all men call me the Mother of the gods of Pessinus; the Athenians, which are sprung from their own soil, Cecropian Minerva; the Cyprians, which are girt about by the sea, Paphian Venus; the Cretans, which bear arrows, Dictynian Diana; the Sicilians, which speak three tongues, infernal Proserpine; the Eleusinians, their ancient goddess Ceres; some Juno, others

Fig. 1. Goddess of the World Mountain. Design from a gold signet ring. Knossos, Crete, c. 1500 B.C. From Sir Arthur Evans, *The Palace of Minos,* 4 vols. (1921–36).

> Bellona, others Hecate, others Ramnusiee, and principally both sort of Ethiopians, which dwell in the Orient and are enlightened by the morning rays of the sun; and the Egyptians, which are excellent in all kind of ancient doctrine, and by their proper ceremonies accustomed to worship me, do call me by my true name, Queen Isis.
>
> Behold I am come to take pity on thy fortune and tribulation; behold I am present to favor and aid thee; leave off thy weeping and lamentation, put away all thy sorrow, for behold the healthful day which is ordained by my providence.[17]

On a gold signet ring from Minoan Crete, c. 2000–1500 B.C., the goddess appears standing in majesty on a mountaintop, holding in her extended hand the staff or scepter of authority. Her equivalent form in Sumer at that time was Ninhursag, named in the Flood legend quoted above. "Her name," as Samuel Kramer remarks, "may originally have been Ki '(mother) Earth,' and she was probably taken to be the consort of An, 'Heaven'—An and Ki thus may have been conceived as the parents of all the gods. She was also known as Nintu, 'the lady who gave birth.'"[18]

In a celestial manifestation, the Goddess was known to the Sumerians in the person also of the pure and lovely Inanna (likewise named in the Flood text), who from heaven descended through seven gates to the netherworld to bring the dead to eternal life.[19] In later Semitic myths, she is Ishtar, descending to the underworld to restore life to her beloved Tammuz, and in the Hellenized-

Semitic Christian heritage her part is played by Christ in the episode, following the Crucifixion, of his "Harrowing of Hell," when, shattering the infernal gates, he "descended into hell," there to rescue to eternal life the prophets and justified of the Old Testament (leaving, however, the Greeks and Romans, Socrates, Plato, Aristotle, Virgil, Cato, Horace, and the rest, in the devil's keep).

There were many variants of the adventure represented in the vast amalgam of analogous mythologies brought together and compounded during the period immediately following the conquests of Alexander: Egyptian Isis searching to resurrect the remains of Osiris, her dismembered lord; Eleusinian Demeter seeking to recover her abducted child, Persephone; Aphrodite and Adonis; Babylonian Ishtar and Tammuz.[20] In India, the model was the bride of Shiva, Satī (pronounced Suttee), whose role was to be enacted, until forbidden by British law in 1829, by every widowed wife following in death her deceased lord, whether (if low caste) buried alive with his corpse or (if high caste) consumed alive with him on his funeral pyre, so that, as one together in death, the two should be brought as one to eternal life: the wife becoming thus the sacramental counterpart of Christ Crucified in the Christian image, as Savior unto eternity of her spouse in the house of death.[21]

And the celestial sign of the efficacy of such "death following" was recognized, both in India and throughout the Near East, in the celestial exemplar of the planet Venus, first as Evening, then as Morning Star: first, following her lord, the Sun, into night and then leading him forth to renewed day. As Venus, Ishtar, Satī, Isis, Inanna, and the rest, the Goddess of Many Names functioned and was revered universally as the source and being, not only of all temporal life, but also of life eternal. In Sumer, as Ninhursag, we see her in the first role and, as Inanna, in the second, while in daily life she was to be perceived in every woman. For as expressed by the nineteenth-century Hindu saint Ramakrishna, "All women (according to this way of thought) are the embodiments of Sakti. It is the Primal Power that has become women and appears in the form of women."[22]

Māyā-Śakti-Devī

The earliest and richest aggregate of testimonials to the character and functionality of this all-embracing and supporting, universal divinity in the earliest period and theater of her preeminency is that illustrated and expounded in Marija Gimbutas's unprecedented exposition. And the fundamental original trait of the Goddess there represented at the opening of her historic career is that she was at that time bisexual, absolute, and single in her generative role. "As a supreme Creator who creates from her own substance, she is the primary goddess," Gimbutas declares, "of the Old European pantheon. In this she contrasts with the Indo-European Earth Mother, who is the impalpable sacred earth-spirit and is not in herself a creative principle; only through the interaction of the sky god does she become pregnant."[23]

The idea is equivalent to that which in India is implicit in the compound noun *māyā-śakti-devī,* the "goddess" (*devī*), as at once the "moving energy" (*śakti*) and the "illusion" (*māyā*) of phenomenality. For according to this nondualistic type of cosmogonic metaphor, the universe as *māyā* is *Brahman,* the Imperishable, as perceived. It is thus its own sole cause as well as substance. The analogy is given in the *Muṇḍaka Upanishad* of a spider and its web. "As the spider brings forth and takes back its thread . . . so creation springs from the Imperishable."[24] And further, in the *Vedāntasāra:* "As from its own standpoint the spider is the efficient cause of its web, from the point of view of its body it is also its material cause."[25]

In distinct contrast to the Creation attributed some six millennia later to the male Creator God, who in Genesis 1:7 is declared to have

> formed man of dust from the ground and breathed into his nostrils the breath of life, the creation and creatures of the all-creating Goddess are of her own substance. The dust itself is of her body; not inert but alive. Nor was there, at any time, an unformed "chaos" to which form had to be given by a god's intention. Form, in this nondual view, is of the essence of the cosmogonic process throughout space, which is of her body, and through time, which is equally of her nature.

An outstanding characteristic of many of the artworks illustrated in Gimbutas's volume is the abstract formality of their symbolically adorned and proportioned form. In Gimbutas's words,

> While the Cycladic figurines of the third millennium B.C. are the most extremely geometricised, rigid constraint of this kind, though less marked, characterizes most of the groups of Old European Neolithic and Chalcolithic figures. . . . Supernatural powers were conceived as an explanatory device to induce an ordered experience of nature's irregularities. These powers were given form as masks, hybrid figures and animals, producing a symbolic, conceptual art not given to physical naturalism.[26]

Painted or inscribed upon these symbolically composed little revelations of powers intuited as informing and moving the whole spectacle of nature were a number of characteristic conventionalized signs or ideograms, which, as recognized by Gimbutas, were of

> two basic categories: those related to water and rain, the snake and the bird; and those associated with the moon, the vegetal life cycle, the rotation of seasons, the birth and growth essential to the perpetuation of life. The first category consists of

symbols with simple parallel lines, V's, zigzags, chevrons and meanders, and spirals. The second group includes the cross, the encircled cross and more complex derivations of this basic motif which symbolically connects the four corners of the world, the crescent, horn, caterpillar, egg and fish.[27]

Statuettes of the Goddess in many forms (we have no knowledge of her names at that time) identify her with every one of these tokens of the structuring force of a universe of which she (like the spider at the center of its structured web) is at once the source and the substance. As summarized in Gimbutas's words:

> Female snake, bird, egg, and fish played parts in creation myths, and the female goddess was the creative principle. The Snake Goddess and Bird Goddess create the world, charge it with energy, and nourish the earth and its creatures with the life-giving element conceived as water. The waters of heaven and earth are under their control. The Great Goddess emerges miraculously out of death, out of the sacrificial bull, and in her body the new life begins.[28]

Compare the New Jerusalem, 4×432 billion cubic stadia in volume, like a radiant jewel coming down from God following the sacrifice of the Savior; the Eddic "earth anew from the waves again," following the immolation of 432,000 gods; or the periodic renewals, following the terrible dissolutions every 4,320,000 years, of the Indian Mahāyuga; likewise, the glorious *anodos* of the Virgin, Koré, of the Greek mysteries, following the *kathodos* of her sorrowful descent into the netherworld, in the very way of Inanna, Ishtar, and celestial Venus, first as Evening, then as Morning Star. Compare, also, the predictable reappearances of the vanished moon every 29 days, 12 hours, 44 minutes, and 2.8 seconds, following 3 nights of absence from a starlit sky.[29]

The Pulse of Being

At what period and in what part of the archaic world did the number 432,000 become attached to the system of signs symbolic of the predictable renewals after periodic dissolutions of a living universe which in the iconography of Old Europe had been imaged as the body of its Creator? The datings recognized by Gimbutas for the relevant regions of the Old European Neolithic are as follows:[30]

I. *The Aegean and Central Balkan Area*
    Neolithic, c. 7000–5500 B.C.
    Chalcolithic, c. 5500–3500 B.C.
II. *The Adriatic Area*
    Neolithic, c. 7000–5500 B.C.
    Advanced Neolithic–Chalcolithic, c. 5500–3500 B.C.

III. *The Middle Danube Basin*
      Neolithic, c. 5500–4500 B.C.
      Advanced Neolithic and Chalcolithic, c. 5000–3500 B.C.
IV.   *The East Balkan Area*
      Neolithic, c. 6500–5000 B.C.
      Chalcolithic, c. 5000–3500 B.C.
V.   *The Moldavian-West Ukranian Area*
      Neolithic, c. 6500–5000 B.C.
      Chalcolithic, c. 5000–3500 B.C.

7000–3500 B.C. are then the bounding dates of this epoch in the chronology of the evolution of consciousness in Old Europe. Engraved signs which have been interpreted as giving evidence of a "linear Old European script" have been identified on as many as one out of every hundred of the Chalcolithic statuettes, as well as upon numerous plaques, dishes, spindle-whorls, and other objects devoted, from c. 5500 B.C., as votive offerings to the Goddess.[31] No signs have yet been reported, however, of a knowledge at that time of any such order of mathematical symbolics as the recognition of cycles of 43,200 or 432,000 years would have required.

The earliest recognizable mathematical documents known to archaeology are from Sumer, third millennium B.C., and their system of numeration is sexagesimal (base 60). As interpreted by Kramer:

> The mathematical school texts which have come down to us are of two types: tables and problems. The former include tabulations of reciprocals, multiplications, squares and square roots, cubes and cube roots, the sums of squares and cubes needed for the numerical solution of certain types of equations, exponential functions, coefficients giving numbers for practical computation (like the approximate value of the square root of 2), and numerous metrological calculations giving areas of rectangles, circles, etc. The problem texts deal with Pythagorean numbers, cubic roots, equations, and such practical matters as excavating or enlarging canals, counting bricks, and so on. As of today, almost all problem texts are Akkadian, although they must go back in large part to Sumerian prototypes since nearly all the technical terms used are Sumerian.[32]

Indeed, a Sumerian tablet of about 2500 B.C. from the ruins of Shuruppak, home city of the Flood hero Ziusudra, already contains a table for the calculation in sexagesimal terms of the surfaces of square-shaped fields.[33]

In what period this method of mathematical calculation was first applied to measurement of the movements of the celestial lights, no one has yet determined. However, as a moment's attention to a calculator will demonstrate, $60 \times 60 \times 60 \times 2 = 432,000$, while $60 \times 60 \times 60 \times 60 \times 2 = 25,920,000$; 25,920 being the number of years required in the precession of the equinoxes for the completion of one full circuit of the Zodiac, since, as already remarked in discussion of Julius Oppert's observations touching the relevance of the biblical sum of 1656 years to Berossos's 432,000, the advance of the equinoctial points along the Zodiacal celestial way proceeds at the rate of 1 degree in 72 years. And 360 degrees × 72 years = 25,920 years, for one completion of a Zodiacal round, which period has for centuries been known as a Great or Platonic Year. But 25,920 divided by 60 equals 432. And so again this number appears, now, however, in exact relation to a scientifically verifiable cosmological eon or cycle of time.

Moreover, as I learned some years ago from a popular handbook on physical fitness, a man in perfect condition, at rest, has normally a heart rate of approximately 1 beat per second: 60 beats a minute; 3,600 beats an hour; in 12 hours 43,200 beats and in 24 hours 86,400. So we hold this measure in our hearts, as well as in the manufactured watches on our wrists. Can it be that the Old Sumerians, c. 2500 B.C., might already have had some notion of the relevance of their sexagesimal system to the mathematics of any such macro-micro-meso-cosmic coordination?[34]

From an authoritative work on Indian tantra yoga I learn that, according to the *Dhyanābindu* and other related *Upanishads,* all living beings inhale and exhale 21,600 times a day, this being in evidence of their spiritual as well as physical identity in the nature of the universal *māyā-śakti-devī,* the Great Goddess who in India is celebrated in a litany of her 108 names. 21,600 × 2 = 43,200.[35] But 108 × 2 = 216, while 108 × 4 = 432, and 432 × 60 = 25,920.

It was H. V. Hilprecht in Philadelphia at the University Museum in 1905, poring over literally thousands of cuneiform clay fragments upon which mathematical reckonings were inscribed, who first recognized this last figure, which is of the Great or Platonic Year, among remains of such early date. In his report, published 1906, he wrote, "All the multiplication and division tables from the temple libraries of Nippur and Sippar and from the library of Ashurbanipal are based upon 12,960,000." And as he there pointed out, 12,960 × 2 = 25,920.[36] Alfred Jeremias was inclined to accept this discovery as indicating the likelihood of a recognition of the precession in Mesopotamia as early as the third or perhaps even fourth millennium B.C. "If this interpretation is correct and the figure really does refer to the precession," he wrote, "then it proves that before Hipparchus an exact reckoning of the precession had been achieved, which later was forgotten."[37] And he wrote again, "It is, in fact, incredible that the Babylonians, experienced as they were in the observation of the heavens, should not have deduced from the difference between earlier and later observations a shift of the equinoctial point. . . . As soon as the position of the sun at the time of the spring equinox became a point of observation, the precession during centuries *must* have been noticed. . . . Indeed in the course of one year it comes to 50 seconds, and during longer periods cannot possibly have been ignored."[38]

It is generally held that an Asiatic Greek, Hipparchus of Bithynia (fl. 146–128 B.C.), in a treatise entitled "On the Displacement of the Solstitial and Equinoctial Signs," was the first to have recognized the precession of the equinoxes and that it was not until A.D. 1526 that the exact reading was announced of 1 degree every 72 years. Yet the Chaldean priest Berossos, a century and a half before Hipparchus's time, had already taken seriously the number 432,000, as had, also at that time, the compilers of Genesis 5–7, whose antediluvian cycle of exactly 1,656 years shared as a factor with Berossos the critical precessional term 72. The still earlier possibility suggested by Hilprecht and Jeremias of a Sumerian anticipation of all this in the third or fourth millennium B.C. has not, as far as I know, been further examined or even seriously discussed.[39]

So that, although it is reasonably certain that it was in Sumer, c. 3500–2500 B.C., that the figure 25,920 divided by 60 equals 432 first became associated with the order of a universe, which in the Neolithic period had been revered as the body of a goddess, we know little or nothing of the stages and processes by which these two distinct traditions—the earlier of mythology, folklore, mysticism, and legend; the later of mathematical logic, cosmological inquiry, rational and speculative thought—were brought together and conjoined. All that can be confidently said is that by the sixth century B.C. at the very latest, in the mathematically formulated speculations of the mystical, secretive brotherhood founded by the Samian sage Pythagoras (born on the island of Samos in the Aegean, c. 580 B.C.; died in Metapontum, Italy, c. 500 B.C.)—whose fundamental dictum, "all is number," had opened the way to a systematic study of the mathematics of form and harmony which united, as of one transcendent science epitomized in music, the laws at once of outer space (cosmology), inner space (psychology), and the arts (aesthetics)—the two, apparently contrary approaches of the visionary and the empiricist were brought and held together as substantially in accord.

Reconstruction of the scientistic mythos of Pythagoras has been rendered for scholars problematic by the fact that the master himself (like the Buddha, his Oriental contemporary, c. 563–483 B.C.) left no writings. Furthermore, the mystical brotherhood that he founded in southern Italy not only was governed by rules of secrecy, but in the middle of the fifth century B.C. was forcibly disbanded and its membership dispersed. Sources purporting to represent the movement go back at best to fourth-century sources, which are already uncritical in character and often amalgams of Pythagorean, Orphic, and Neo-Platonic information.[40] Hence, it is impossible to determine how much of what has come down to us can be attributed to Pythagoras himself, how much may have been derived by him from the general body of mystic lore already shared by the numerous gurus of his day throughout the Near, Middle, and Far East, or how much of this esoteric learning may have become assimilated to the movement centuries later.

The idea, for example, of sound (Sanskrit *śabda*) as generator of the perceived universe is fundamental to the Vedas and all later Hindu thought. Alain Daniélou, in his *Introduction to the Study of Musical Scales,* quotes from a commentary on a Sivaite Sutra:

> The initiating point (*bindu*), desirous to manifest the thought which it holds of all things, vibrates, transformed into a primordial sound of the nature of a cry (*nāda*). *It shouts out the universe, which is not distinct from itself.* That is to say, it thinks it. Hence the term, *śabda,* "word." Meditation is the supreme "word": it "sounds," that is to say, "vibrates," submitting all things to the fragmentation of life. This is how it is *nāda,* "vibration." This is what is meant by the saying: "Sound (*śabda*), which is of the nature of *nāda,* resides in all living beings."[41]

Likewise, in the Chinese "Book of Rites," *Li Chi,* which, as Daniélou reminds us, was edited by Confucius (c. 551–478 B.C., again a contemporary of Pythagoras), we are told,

> Music makes for common union. Rites make for difference and distinction. From common union comes mutual affection; from difference, mutual respect. . . . Music comes from within; rites act from without. Coming from within, music produces serenity of mind. Acting from without, rites produce the finished elegance of manner. Great music must be easy. Great rites must be simple. Let music achieve its full results, and there will be no resentments. Let rites achieve their full results, and there will be no contentions. The reason why bowings and courtesies could set the world in order is that there are music and rites.[42]

Tung Chung-shu, a later Confucian scholar, second century B.C., expanded upon these thoughts:

> Tuned to the tone of Heaven and Earth, the vital spirits of man express all the tremors of Heaven and Earth, exactly as several citharas, all tuned on *Kung* (the tonic), all vibrate when the note *Kung* resounds. The fact of the harmony between Heaven and Earth and Man does not come from a physical union, from a direct action, it comes from a tuning on the same note producing vibrations in unison. . . . In the Universe there is no hazard, there is no spontaneity; all is influence and harmony, accord answering accord.[43]

A characteristic Pythagorean symbolic diagram cited by all authorities as in some way epigrammatical of an essential doctrine of the movement is the so-

called *tetraktys*, or "triangle of fourness," which can be viewed either as an equi-
- lateral triangle of 9 points composed around a single central point or
- as a pyramid of 10 points arranged in 3 expanding stages of descent,
- respectively of 2, 3, and 4 (= 9) points, unfurling from a single
- point at the summit.[44] The Pythagoreans, by all accounts, regarded even numbers (2, 4, 6, and so on) as female; uneven (3, 5, 7, and so on), as
male; interpreting 1 as neither even nor odd but germinal of both series, corresponding thus to the Indian tantric *bindu*, "desirous to manifest the thought
which it holds of all things." As *nāda*, vibrating, transformed into primordial
sound, this initiating impulse "shouts out the universe, which is not distinct
from itself"; that creative "shout" being in modern terms the Big Bang of creation, whence from a single point of inconceivable intensity this entire expanding universe exploded, flying into distances that are still receding.

In Indian mystical utterances, this universal Sound is announced as OM.
In Oriental modal music, it is represented in the tonic in relation to which the
melody is heard. And in Pythagorean thought it was identified with *Proslambanomene*, the supporting ground tone, A, which thereby was considered to
have 432 vibrations (whereas the pitch in modern tunings is raised to around
440). Musically, as Daniélou points out, the primal sound given measure yields
first its octave (2/1), after which a third tone, the fifth (3/2), is heard, in relation to which the others then find place.[45] And in this regard he cites a verse
from the *Tao Te Ching:* "The Tao produced One; One produced Two; Two produced Three; Three produced all things."[46]

In Indian thought the first characteristic of *māyā* (from the verbal root *mā*,
"to measure") is duality; and for the Pythagoreans, likewise, the world-process
was a complex of dualities sprung from the imposition of "limitation" or "measure" (= *māyā*) upon the "unlimited" (*Brahman*); the "unlimited" and its "limitation" then being the first of a series of nine further pairs of opposites: odd and
even, light and dark, and so on, essentially the Chinese *yang* and *yin*.

Out of the stress of such a context of universal polarization, the Indian
(*Sānkhya*) philosophers recognized as arising three "qualities or characteristics" (*guṇas*), through the interrelation of which all of "nature" (*prakṛiti*) was
seen as motivated; namely, "inertia, mass, or heaviness" (*tamas*); "energy and
vitality" (*rajas*); and the "harmony or clarity" (*sattva*) of any balanced relationship of the opposed two.[47] In Pythagorean terms, the same three would correspond, respectively, to (1) the "unlimited," (2) the "limiting," and (3) the
"harmony" or "fitting together" (*harmonia*) of any "beautiful order of things"
(*kosmos*), whether as a macrocosm (the universe), microcosm (an individual),
or mesocosm (ideal society or work of art). And the number representative

in that system of such a visible order is 4.

And so now, counting the number of points of the Pythagorean *tetraktys*, from the base upward to the creative *bindu* (beyond number) at the top, the sum of their sequence, 4–3–2, is of course 9; as is that, also, of 2–1–6 (which is half of 432); as well as of 1–0–8 (half of 216); which last is the number of her names recited in worship of the Indian Great Goddess, Kālī, Durgā, Umā, Sitā, Satī, and Pārvatī ("Daughter of the Mountain"). Moreover, the total 9 is implicit, also, in the sum of years of the biblical 10 patriarchs, from the day of Adam's creation to that of the end of the antediluvian age in Noah's Flood, since $1 + 6 + 5 + 6 = 18$, while $1 + 8 = 9$. And finally, most remarkably, in the course of the precession of the equinoxes the number of years required for the completion of one circuit of the Zodiac at the rate of 1 degree in 72 years (noting that $7 + 2 = 9$), is $2 + 5 + 9 + 2 + 0 = 18$, where again, $1 + 8 = 9$.

Creatress and Redemptress

"Nine times now, since my birth," wrote Dante at the opening of his early book of poems, *La Vita Nuova,*

> the heaven of light had turned almost to the same point in its own gyration, when the glorious Lady of my mind, who was called Beatrice by many who knew not what to call her, first appeared before my eyes. She had already been in this life so long that in its course the starry heaven had moved toward the region of the East one of the twelve parts of a degree; so that at the beginning of her ninth year she appeared to me, and I near the end of my ninth year saw her. She appeared to me clothed in a most noble color, a modest and becoming crimson, and she was girt and adorned in such wise as befitted her very youthful age. At that instant, I say truly that the spirit of life, which dwells in the most secret chamber of the heart, began to tremble with such violence that it appeared fearfully in the least pulses, and, trembling, said these words: *Ecce deus fortior me, qui veniens dominabitur mihi* [Behold a god stronger than I, who coming shall rule over me]. . . .

And further:

> When so many days had passed that nine years were exactly complete since the above described apparition of this most gentle lady, on the last of these days it happened that this admirable lady appeared to me, clothed in purest white, between two gentle ladies who were of greater age; and, passing along a street, turned her eyes toward that place where I stood very timidly; and by her ineffable courtesy, which is today rewarded in the eternal world, saluted me with such virtue that it seemed to me then that I saw all the bounds of bliss. The hour when her most sweet salutation reached me was precisely the ninth of that day. . . .

At the age of twenty-four, June 8, 1290, Beatrice Portinare died, and the whole universe for Dante became so filled thereafter with the radiance of her angelic grace that in thought of her alone his heart was lifted to her place in heaven, in the sight of God. Writing of the mystery of the cosmic measure of her glory he wrote:

> I say that, according to the mode of reckoning in Arabia, her most noble soul de-
> parted in the first hour of the ninth day of the month; and, according to the reck-
> oning in Syria, she departed in the ninth month of the year, since the first month
> there is Tisrin, which with us is October. And according to our reckoning, she de-
> parted in that year of our indiction, that is, of the years of the Lord, in which the
> perfect number was completed for the ninth time in that century in which she
> had been set in this world; and she was of the Christians of the thirteenth century.
>
> One reason why this number was so friendly to her may be this: since, accord-
> ing to Ptolemy and according to the Christian truth, there are nine heavens which
> move, and, according to the common astrological opinion, the said heavens work
> effects here below according to their respective positions, this number was her
> friend to the end that it might be understood that at her generation all the nine
> movable heavens were in most perfect relation. This is one reason thereof; but
> considering more subtly and according to the infallible truth, this number was
> she herself; I mean by similitude, and I intend it thus: the number three is the root
> of nine, for without any other number, multiplied by itself it makes nine, as we see
> plainly that three times three make nine. Therefore, since three is the factor by it-
> self of nine, and the Author of miracles by himself is three, namely, Father, Son,
> and Holy Spirit, who are three and one, this lady was accompanied by the number
> nine, that it might be understood that she was a nine, that is, a miracle, whose
> only root is the marvelous Trinity. . . .[48]

The Pythagorean *tetraktys,* viewed as an upward-pointing triangle built of
9 points with a tenth, as *bindu,* in the center, suggests an Indian tantric diagram (*yantra*) symbolic of the female power in its spiritually alluring role recognized by Goethe in the last two lines of his *Faust: Das Ewig-Weibliche / Zieht
uns hinan!*

Gimbutas, writing of the geometric diagrams engraved on the statuettes of
Old Europe, c. 7000–3500 B.C., gives special attention to the lozenge with a
dot in the center. "The dot, representing seed, and the lozenge, symbolizing
the sown field," she writes, "appear on the sculptures of an enthroned pregnant
goddess and are also incised or painted on totally schematized figurines. . . . A
lozenge is often the most prominent feature, the rest of the female body serving
only as a background to the ideographic concept."[49]

Among the best known of those Indian tantric diagrams known as *yantras,*
designed to inspire and support meditation, that of the *downward* pointing triangle with a dot in its center is an explicit symbol of female energy in its generative role.[50] This triangle is an adaptation of the prominent genital triangle of
the typical Neolithic female statuette. The dot is known as the *bindu,* the
"drop" (which, like a drop of oil in water, expands), and the triangle as the *yoni*
(womb, vagina, vulva; place of origin, birth, and rest).[51] As contemplated by
the *śakti* worshiper, the whole sign is of the Goddess, alone, as *māyā-śakti-devī,*

in the sense of those earliest Neolithic figurines, recognized and interpreted by Gimbutas, of the Goddess "absolute and single in her generative role," at once the cause and the substance (like the spider in its web) of this living universe and its life.

In those *yantras* where the dot or "drop" is unfolded, however, it is represented in India as a phallos, a *lingam;* so that, whereas in the dot/triangle symbol the connotation might have been appropriately read either as of the Goddess alone or as of a goddess and god in union, here, although the "seed" and "field" are still together *within* the Goddess, the image is now explicitly of the male and female organs joined. The earlier, nondualistic image has been turned, that is to say, into a dualistic symbol, transferring from the female to the male the initiating moment and impulse of creation.

This radically distinct construction must represent and have closely followed upon the critical historic turn, dated by Gimbutas to c. 3500 B.C., from the earlier Neolithic and Chalcolithic concept of the Goddess as sole cause and very substance of the body of this universe to an Indo-European or Semitic, dualistic manner of symbolization, where she is no longer in herself and alone "Great" but the consort of a "Great" God.

There is in Hesiod's *Theogony* an unmistakable hint of this change, where Gaia, the earth, is represented as the mother of the heaven-god, her spouse. "First of all there came Chaos and after him," we read, "came Gaia of the broad breast, to be the unshakable foundation of all the immortals.... But Gaia's first born was one who matched her in every dimension, Ouranos, the starry sky, to cover her all over. . . . She lay with Ouranos and bore him deep-swirling Okeanos. . . ."[52]

Likewise in the Old Testament, Proverbs 8, the Great Goddess in her character as "Wisdom" reveals herself as having been from the beginning with Yahweh as cocreator.

> The Lord created me [Hebrew, *ganani,* in other versions translated as "possessed me" or "acquired me"] at the beginning of his work, the first of his acts of old.[53] Ages ago, I was set up, at the first, before the beginning of the earth. When there were no depths I was brought forth, when there were no springs abounding with water. Before the mountains had been shaped, before the hills, I was brought forth; before he had made the earth with its fields, or the first of the dust of the world. When he established the heavens I was there, I was there, when he drew a circle on the face of the deep, when he made firm the skies above, when he established the foundations of the deep, when he assigned to the sea its limit, so that the water might not transgress his command, when he marked out the foundations of the earth, then I was beside him, like a master workman; and I was daily his delight, rejoicing before him always, rejoicing in his inhabited world and delighting in the sons of men.

And now, my sons, listen to me: happy are those who keep my ways. . . . (Prov. 8:22–32)

The *upward* pointing triangle, both of the Indian *yantras* and of the Pythagorean *tetraktys*, like its downward pointing counterpart, is susceptible of two readings, whether as of the Goddess alone or as of the Goddess in union with a male of her own birth, who may even (as in both the Bible and the Koran) finally usurp her role and character as sole creator—not of a universe identical with himself, however, but of a cosmological artifact, distinct from and subordinate to his unique, unnatural, and finally irrelevant divinity.

There is from India an astonishing tantric image known as *cinna masta* (pronounced chinna masta, of the "severed head"), which is of the Goddess cutting off her own head to release her devotees or children from the bondage of her *māyā*. The Greek figure of beheaded Medusa, from the stump of whose neck the winged steed Pegasus flies to become a constellation, is a counterpart of this symbolic form. In later classical times, the winged steed in soaring flight was interpreted as allegorical of the soul released from the body to immortality, and by the masters of the Renaissance the same ascending flight was read as of poetic inspiration—which cannot come to birth until the obstacle of the rationalizing head is removed.

In medieval Christian thought, the two contrary forces symbolized in the downward and upward pointing triangles were personified, respectively, in Eve and the Virgin Mary, through the second of whom the effects of her predecessor's Original Sin were reversed. The idea is aptly rendered in the Latin pun of a popular Catholic hymn still sung to the Virgin as "Star of the Sea," *Ave Maris Stella*, where the upward turn is suggested simply by reversing Eva's name to Ave:

ave maris stella	Hail, O Star of ocean,
Dei Mater alma,	God's own Mother blest,
Atque semper Virgo,	Ever sinless Virgin,
Felix coeli porta.	Gate of heav'nly rest.
Sumens illud Ave	Taking that sweet Ave
Gabrielis ore,	Which from Gabriel came,
Funda nos in pace,	Peace confirm within us,
Mutans hevae nomen.	Changing Eva's name.[54]

The Muses Nine

In the "year of our Lord" 1439, an ecumenical council of the Roman Catholic church which had been assembled in Ferrara to attempt to resolve the delicate *filioque* argument, that in 1054 had separated the Greek and Latin churches, was transferred to Cosimo de' Medici's Florence when a plague hit the earlier city. A large and distinguished Greek delegation was in attendance, and the Medici was so inspired with admiration for their Platonic, Neoplatonic, and Pythagorean learning that he determined forthwith to establish on his own estate at Careggi an academy on the model of Plato's in Athens (which in A.D. 529, along with all the other pagan institutions of that time, had been closed by order of the Emperor Justinian).

With the fall of Constantinople in 1453 to the Turks and the subsequent appearances in the Latin West of Greek manuscripts from Byzantium brought by refugee priests and monks, the historic moment arrived for Cosimo to begin reassembling in his villa as much as might be ever retrieved of the vestiges of classical learning. The University of Florence—likewise alerted by the council—had in 1439 resumed the teaching of the Greek language, which, except in the monasteries and abbeys of Ireland, had been lost to the Latin West for more than seven hundred years. The young Marsilio Ficino (1433–99), an ardent student of both Greek and Latin, had become the Medici's chief translator and advisor, and with the willing cooperation of the victorious sultan Mehmed II himself, Cosimo initiated and organized a thoroughgoing, systematic search for manuscripts that in good time yielded the founding core of an incomparable library, which was later named, after Cosimo's grandson, the Lorentian (Laurenziana).

In this way, through the enterprise of a single inspired individual, the vast catastrophe to the intelligence of Europe which had followed upon the deliberate destruction in A.D. 391 of the irreplaceable Alexandrian library, research center, and museum (Greek, *Mouseion*, from *Mouseios,* "of the Muses") was in some measure redressed. Reputed to have contained no less than 500,000 volumes burned to extinction by Christian zealots, the *Mouseion* had been a center, not only of Hellenistic, Neoplatonic, and Pythagorean learning, but also of Semitic. The Septuagint translation into Greek of the Old Testament had been made there. And that there were influences from India as well cannot be doubted since already as early as the fourth century B.C. the Buddhist emperor Asoka (as reported in his rock-carved edicts) had sent teachers of the Buddhist Dharma, not only to the court of Ptolemy II of Egypt (the Ptolemies were the founders of the *Mouseion*), but also to Antiochus II of Syria, Magas of Cyrene, Antigonas Gonatus of Macedonia, and Alexander II of Epirus.[55] Plotinus, the founder of Neoplatonism, born A.D. 205 in Egypt, commenced his career in Alexandria. Theon, the fourth-century mathematician to whose recension of

Euclid's *Elements* we owe our knowledge of that work, was also a contributor to the dignity of that culminating Hellenistic center of universal learning. His extraordinary daughter Hypatia, the first notable woman in mathematics and the recognized head of the Alexandrian Neoplatonist school of her day, born A.D. 370, was in March 415 mob-murdered by a mass of monks and general Christian fanatics spiritually inflamed by contagion of their recently installed, vigorously antipagan bishop, now canonized, St. Cyril of Alexandria. Whereafter, submerged beneath an increasing tide of "barbarism and religion" (to use Edward Gibbon's phrase), magnificent Alexandria sank to historical insignificance, only the flotsam and jetsam of its invaluable treasury to be ever retrieved.

However, the galaxy of inspired artists—sculptors, architects, and painters—who appeared as by magic around the philosophical oasis of Cosimo's reconstituted academy and library was amazing. And that his harvest of antiquity, translated from Greek into Latin largely by Marsilio Ficino, had indeed revived the inspiration of late classic spirituality is evident in every detail of the works of art of that moment of Europe's reawakening to its native heritage. It was as though the Muses had themselves awakened and found voice. For among the sculptors of that company were Donatello and Ghiberti; among the architects, Brunelleschi and Michelozzo; painters, Fra Angelico, Andrea del Castagno, and Benozzo Gozzoli; while of the second generation—of the period of Cosimo's grandson Lorenzo the Magnificent (1449–92), whose teacher had been Ficino—we read of Verrocchio and his pupils Leonardo da Vinci, Botticelli, and Michelangelo; the last named having begun his career at the age of fifteen as a pupil in the sculpture school in Lorenzo's garden.

Pico della Mirandola (1463–94) was another inspired associate of this incredible academy, who, having studied not only Latin and Greek but Arabic, Hebrew, and Aramaic as well, was the first Christian philosopher to apply Cabbalistic learning to the support of Christian theological propositions. In 1486, he arranged for a pan-European assemblage in Rome before which he would announce and defend nine hundred theses drawn from Latin, Greek, Hebrew, and Arabic sources. Thirteen of his theses were declared heretical, however, and the assembly was forbidden by the pope.

Yet the depth and range of his learning, reaching back to those centuries of syncretic, transcultural philosophical formulations which had followed upon Alexander the Great's "marriage of East and West" (out of which, indeed, the dogmas of the Latin church had themselves evolved), survived the papal ban. For his bold comparative insights, interpreting Egyptian, Hebrew, Greek, and Christian mythic and symbolic forms as culturally distinguished metaphors of a single, universally consistent *poetica theologica,* perfectly represented the expanding spirit and world horizon through which Renaissance art and thought were being released in his day from the inbred, tight little fold of the Middle Ages. At the Medici Villa di Careggi, sculpture, architecture, painting, and philosophy were of one accord in the representation of *all* names and forms, whether of the mind or the world beheld, as equally radiant of some universal mystery.

In the allegorical diagram of the "Music of the Spheres" that was published in 1496 as the frontispiece of Francinus Gafurius's *Practica musice,* this idea of a mystery partly revealed is suggested by the clothing of the Muses, whose forms appear in descending series at the left of the composition.[56]

Their number, like that which Dante associated with Beatrice, is 9; for their root, too, is a trinity. However, the trinity here is not of three male divinities with the Virgin then as a feminine fourth but of the classical three Graces with Apollo as a masculine fourth. And as the Muses are here clothed, so the Graces, performing their round-dance on the noumenal plane beyond and above the visible sky, directly in the presence of Apollo, are unclothed. They are the triune personifications of the Aristotelian *primum mobile,* or "first moving thing," which is of the tenth or highest celestial sphere and derives its circular motion directly from God, the "unmoved mover." Here the image of God, as Apollo, is clothed, since the "unmoved being" of such a "first cause" transcends envision-ment (i.e. all names and forms); whereas the Graces are movement itself. As stated in the Latin of the inscribed scroll overhead: "The energy or virtue (*vis*) of the Apollonian mind moves or inspires (*movet*) everywhere the Muses."

Both the names and the postures of the Graces tell of the qualities of their influence: (1) Thalia ("Blooming, Abundance") unites and relates her opposed companions; (2) Euphrosyne ("Mirth, Festivity, Good Cheer") moves away from the God to the descent, ninefold, of the Muses; while (3) Aglaia ("Splen-dor, Beauty, Triumph, Adornment") confronts him, returning to source.

Pico and Ficino revered these three as an exemplary triad archetypal of all the others of classical myth. In Pico's words, "He that understands profoundly and clearly how the unity of Venus is unfolded in the trinity of the Graces, and the unity of Necessity in the trinity of the Fates, and the unity of Saturn in the trinity of Jupiter, Neptune, and Pluto, knows the proper way of proceeding in Orphic theology."[57] For as Edgar Wind points out in comment on this pas-sage, "it was an axiom of Platonic theology that every god exerts his power in a traidic rhythm."[58]

"The bounty bestowed by the gods upon lower beings," states Wind, con-tinuing, "was conceived by the Neoplatonists as a kind of overflowing (*emana-tio*), which produced a vivifying rapture or conversion (called by Ficino

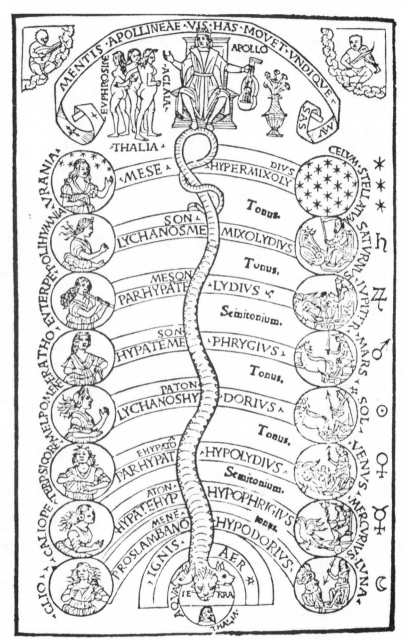

Fig. 2. The Music of the Spheres. Francinus Gafurius, *Practica Musice* (Florence, 1496).

conversio, rapto, or vivificatio) whereby the lower beings were drawn back to heaven and rejoined the gods (*remeatio*)." Moreover: "The munificence of the gods having thus been unfolded in the triple rhythm of *emanatio, rapto,* and *remeatio,* it was possible to recognize in this sequence the divine model of what Seneca had defined as the circle of grace: giving, accepting, and returning. . . . But in Proclus, *Elements of Theology,* prop. 35 (Dodds, 1933, pp. 38f.), the sequence reads: (1) inheritance in the cause, (2) procession from the cause, (3) reversion to the cause; and that is the original Neoplatonic scheme."[59]

Translated into Christian trinitarian terms, this triadic revelation of divine grace would appear as (1) the Father, (2) the Son, and (3) the Holy Spirit, three hypostases or "persons" in one godhead with the idea of the "godhead" represented in Gafurius's design by the clothed Apollo and that of the "persons" or hypostases by the Graces, who in Indian tantric terms are exactly *māyā-śakti-devī,* or in the *Sāṅkhya* view (as noticed above), *prakṛiti,* of three *guṇas* or "characteristics," *sattva, rajas,* and *tamas.*

The serpentine, triple-headed form flowing down the center of the composition is Gafurius's adaptation to his design of a symbolic figure that in Alexandria had been associated with an image of the composite Egypto-Greco-Roman God Serapis. "In the great temple of Serapis at Alexandria," states Wind, from whose *Pagan Mysteries in the Renaissance* I have reproduced this chart,

> the image of the Egypto-Hellenic god was attended by a triple-headed Monster resembling Cerberus [the watchdog at the gate to Hades] but with this difference that the three heads of the [Alexandrian] beast were distinguished as wolf, lion, and dog. The most informative ancient text on this attribute . . . is Macrobius, *Saturnalia* I, xx, where the three heads are explained as signifying the three parts of Time: facing left, the voracious wolf represents the vanished past; the hopefully sniffing dog looks to the right, anticipating the future; while the present, in the middle, is embodied in the majestic lion seen full-face. Petrarch's *Africa* III, 162ff., gives a splendid description of the three heads, followed by a concise statement of the allegory: *fugientia tempora signant.*[60]

Dante, it will be recalled at the opening of *Inferno* I, 28–68, tells of three beasts that in a savage wood confronted him, barring his way to Salvation: a lion, signifying Pride; a leopard, luxurious Desire; and a she-wolf, Violence and Fear. Dante's leopard is equivalent to Gafurius's hopefully sniffing, Alexandrian dog, and the triad of obstructive sentiments named is exactly of those three temptations that were overcome by the Buddha in yoga at the foot of the Bodhi-tree: "desire" (*kāma*), fear of "death" (*māra*), and attachment to temporal social ideals (*dharma*).

There is an immediately evident and more than coincidental likeness of Gafurius's serpent descending through a graded universe to the Indian idea of a yogic "serpent channel" descending from the crown of the head, down the spinal column to a "lotus center" located between the anus and genitalia that is known as "Root Support" (*mūlādhāra*), where the spiritual energy (*śakti*) of the unawakened individual sleeps, coiled on itself like a dormant snake (Sanskrit *kuṇḍalinī*, "coiled serpent"), which is to be aroused through yoga and brought, uncoiling, up the spinal channel to a radiant lotus at the crown of the head called "Thousand Petaled" (*sahasrāra*).

"Gafurius's serpent," Edgar Wind points out,

> is distinguished by a particularly engaging trait. While plunging head-downward into the universe, it curls the end of its tail into a loop on which Apollo ceremoniously sets his feet. A serpent's tail turning back on itself is an image of eternity or perfection (commonly illustrated by a serpent biting its own tail . . .). Gafurius thus makes it diagrammatically clear that Time issues from Eternity, the linear progression of the serpent depends on its attachment to the topmost sphere where its tail coils into a circle."[61]

In Gafurius's design, the circle at the base of the composition, labeled TERRA, corresponds to the yogic "Root Support" where the coiled serpent sleeps. (Serpents shedding their skins to be, as it were, reborn suggest the power of life to cast off death, even to the gaining of eternal life.) The whole upper half of Gafurius's earthly sphere is filled by the vision of those three hovering heads, while below the baseline of the composition, as though hiding below ground, is the first of the nine Muses, whose name, we note, is the same as that of the central member of the unclothed triad of the Graces, namely, Thalia, "Blooming, Abundance." "That the 'descent' of a spiritual force," states Wind, "is compatible with its continuous presence in the 'supercelestial heaven' was a basic tenet of Neoplatonism."

The down-coming of the motivating energy or virtue (*vis*) of the Apollonian mind is here represented as having devolved from the celestial *primum mobile,* represented in the Graces, through their reflexes in the Muses, each of which is shown associated with a planetary sphere, in the pre-Copernican, geocentric, ptolemaic sequence: first, the heaven of fixed stars; next, Saturn, Jupiter, Mars, and the Sun; then, the shadowed spheres of Venus, Mercury, and the Moon; until, finally, wrapped in its increasingly weighty elemental envelopes of Fire (*ignis*), Air (*aer*), and Water (*aqua*), this Earth (*terra*) is entered, where its Muse, unheard, underground, is known as *Surda* ("Silent") Thalia, and is a Muse of Nocturnal Silence.[62]

For her voice of the bounty of nature is by her intended poet unheard, whose whole mind is so obsessed by its vision of the hovering monster, *fugientia tempora signant,* that, terrified of his life and of the life also of the world, he has no ear for the gentle whisper of the supportive universe—which is there nevertheless to be heard behind the tricephalous tumult of the beast.

What is therefore required of him, if he is ever to hear that supportive voice, is to forget the passing of time, "regard the lilies of the field . . . and not be anxious" (Matt. 6:28 and 31): place his head, that is to say, together with all its desires and fears for the good of himself and his world directly into the lion's mouth of HERE AND NOW.

In Genesis 3:22–24, we read that when Yahweh drove Adam and Eve from the garden so that they should not "take of the tree of life, and eat, and live forever . . . at the east of the garden of Eden he placed the cherubim, and a flaming sword which turned every way, to guard the way to the tree of life." That sword of flame is the counterpart of the lion's face of Gafurius's monster, while the guarding cherubim correspond to the heads at either side. An essential feature of temple arts generally, whether of Antiquity or the Orient, is such a threshold feature: two guardians (either in human or in animal form) with a portal between to some sacred precinct.

For example, at Nara (Japan), before the Todaiji Temple with its immense bronze image of "The Great Sun Buddha," Mahavairochana (weight, 452 tons; height, 53 feet, 6 inches; date A.D. 749), there is a large, detached south gate where two imposing giants (26 feet, 6 inches high) stand guard with threatening weapons.[63] The mouth of one is open; that of the other, closed. Fear of death and desire for life would be the immediate sentiments that such an actual pair would excite in any visitor—which are the sentiments to be left behind by anyone passing through, not simply physically as a tourist but for an experience within the sanctuary of release from the pressure of the consciousness of mortality. They correspond to the wolf and leopard of Dante's vision, attending the lion of his pride. So that from this point of view, what is excluding man from the knowledge of his immortality is not the wrath of some external god, but the maladjustment of his own mind. Within the sacred precinct of the Buddhist temple, therefore, seated on a fully opened lotus before the wish-fulfilling "Tree of 'Awakening'" (*bodhi*), the Great Sun Buddha, with his right hand raised in *abhaya-mudrā*, the "fear not posture," and his left extended in the "boon-bestowing posture" *varada-mudrā*, gives freely to all who approach, the gift of his light.

Whereas in contrast (and here is the difference), our biblical Yahweh appears in his unilluminated legend as the archetypal mythic "Hoarder," holding to himself the gift of his grace, and his mythology, consequently, is of man's exile to an earth of dust (Gen. 3:17–19) and of spiritual silence, where no whisper may be heard of Goddess or Muse—except as in that one extraordinary instance, where King Solomon overheard the voice of the Lord God's own Beatrice and Muse, Sophia (Proverbs, *passim*, as above).

No one can possibly function, either as poet or as artist, in any such a desacralized environment. The repudiated and absconded Muse of the living earth, Surda Thalia, must first be invoked and recalled. And that this may occur, "the cherub with his flaming sword is hereby commanded," as William Blake has declared in *The Marriage of Heaven and Hell,*

> to leave his guard of the tree of life, and when he does, the whole creation will be consumed, and appear infinite, and holy, whereas it now appears finite and corrupt. This will come to pass by an improvement of sensual enjoyment.
>
> But first the notion that man has a body distinct from his soul has to be expunged . . . melting apparent surfaces away, and displaying the infinite which was hid.
>
> If the doors of perception were cleansed every thing would appear to man as it is, infinite. For man has closed himself up, till he sees all things thro' the narrow chinks of his cavern.

From the *mūlādhāra,* where the *kuṇḍalinī* sleeps, three portals open upward, those to right and to left leading to subtle channels bearing the breaths, respectively, of the left and right nostrils; only the portal between opening to the subtle "serpent channel," *sushumnā* ("most gracious, rich in happiness"), leads to the cranial lotus "Thousand Petaled" (*sahasrāra*), "replete with every form of bliss, and Pure Knowledge itself."[64]

The channel descending from the left nostril is known as *iḍā* ("nectarous draft, refreshment"); that from the right, as *piṅgalā* ("fiery, tawny red"); the former conducting breath (*prāṇa*) of "lunar" consciousness, and the latter, of "solar": "solar" consciousness being of eternity, hence threatening to temporal life (poisonous, fiery, destructive), whereas "lunar" (which is to say, earthly) is restorative and refreshing. Their two portals in the *mūlādhāra,* flanking that of the *sushumnā,* are likened to the guardians at the entrance to a temple and thus correspond in both position and sense to the wolf and the dog of Gafurius's tricephalous monster.

Now, it can be hardly by coincidence that those overhanging three heads of Gafurius's Renaissance design, based on ideas derived from Hellenistic Alexandria, should match in both placement and function the openings upward from the Indian *mūlādhāra.* As understood in yogic terms: so long as the two breaths, left and right, are regarded in a dualistic way as separate and distinct from each other (as "spirit" and "nature," for example, understood as in opposition), the central portal is closed and locked. However, the yogi practicing "breath control" (*prāṇāyāma*), breathing deeply, first in through one nostril, out the other, then in through the second, out through the first, ensuring each time that the *prāṇa,* the breath, goes all the way down to the *mūlādhāra,* is transforming the opposed breaths into each other as they enter and leave that chamber of the dormant Serpent Power. Untiring, he continues the exercise,

Fig. 3. Seven Lotus Centers of the Kuṇḍalinī. Drawing by Mark Hasserlriis.

until, of a sudden, in the *mūlādhāra,* the two breaths blend to a single fire, which like a blast ascends, together with the awakened Serpent, into the suddenly unlocked *sushumnā.*

In Gafurius's design, the symbolized stages of the transformations of consciousness that follow upon the poet's yielding of his head to the lion's mouth (on having muzzled, so to say, the wolf and the dog, or as Blake has described the change of mind, dismissed the cherub with his flaming sword) are represented metaphorically as under inspiration of the Muses graded in relation to the hierarchy of the ptolemaic order of the spheres. Immediately with his recognition of the instant HERE AND NOW, the hidden Muse, Surda Thalia, wakes. Her voice is heard. And what until then had been the nocturnal silence of a wasteland of dust and toil becomes eloquent of a universal joy.

For, awake and singing, Thalia, "Blooming and Abundance," is the Muse of bucolic poetry, telling of the innocence and blooming of a living earth. And in this function, her inspiration marks the first stage of the opening of any artist's senses to knowledge of the universal body of which his own is a part. The next Muse of ascent is Clio (*Kleio,* "Acclaim"), the Muse of history, associated with the earth-shadowed sphere of the Moon; and the following, Calliope (*Kalliope,* "of the Beautiful Voice," once chief and leader of the nine), is of epic poetry and the earth-shadowed sphere of Mercury (= Hermes, guide of souls from the knowledge of time to that of eternity). These first three of the Muses, representing states of mind overshadowed still by concerns of this earth, correspond in the Indian series to the "dispositions of energy" (*śaktis*) of the first three centers of the *sushumnā,* which are namely, *mūlādhāra* (already discussed), *svādhishthāna* (spinal center of the region of the genitals), and *manipūra* (spinal center of the region of the navel), which are endowed, respectively, with the qualities of the elements earth, water, and fire.

The next three Muses together mark the transformation of consciousness that is in yoga associated with the fourth center, *anāhata,* at the level of the heart, and of the element air (breath, *prāna, spiritus*). They are (1) Terpsichore, "Joy of the Dance," assigned to the earth-shadowed sphere of Venus; (2) Melpomene, the "Singer," Muse of tragedy and of the fiery sun or "Sun Door" of an opening of the heart to compassion by way of an Aristotelian *katharsis,* or purging of egoity through an access of egoless pity and metaphysical terror; to which (3) Erato, "The Lovely One," attuned to Mars, the first unshadowed sphere, adds lyric poetry.

The Muses of the topmost stages are then of arts suggesting raptures such as yogis at the highest centers of their discipline may know: *viśuddha* ("purified," center of the region of the larynx), *ājñā* ("authority, absolute power": of the inner eye, between the brows), and the *sahasrāra.* The related Muses are Euterpe, "Well Pleasing," Muse of the sphere of Jupiter and dulcet music of the flute; Polyhymnia, "Sacred Choral Song," of the austere sphere of Saturn; and finally, "The Celestial One," Ourania, of the science of astronomy and sphere of the fixed stars.

On Gafurius's chart, the voices of these sisters, born (as Hesiod tells) of Zeus and "Memory" (*Mnemosyne*), are identified with the ascending tones of the Pythagorean conjoint tetrachord (ABCDEFGA: the A minor scale), upon which are established the Greek modes: Hypodorian, Hypophrygian, Hypolydian, Dorian, Phrygian, Lydian, Mixolydian, and for good measure, to match the number of the Muses, Hypomixolydian, which is equivalent to Dorian.

The Graces then are pictured above as embodiments of the *primum mobile,* "first moving thing," moved by the energy (*vis*) of the Apollonian mind. However, in what certainly was a much earlier construction, what those Three embodied were aspects of the energy (Sanskrit, *śakti*), not of Apollo, but of the goddess Aphrodite of the fluttering eyelids. Neoplatonically interpreted (as already noticed from Proclus), the three have been allegorized as (1) inheritance in the cause, (2) procession from the cause, and (3) reversion to the cause.[65] Pico and Ficino wrote of them, however, as (1) procession from the cause, (2) rapture by the cause, and (3) return to the cause, in which case the reading is from left to right with the central figure not facing forward, as in Gafurius's design, but with back to the viewer, as in the frequently reproduced Pompeian fresco of the Graces that is now in the Museo Nationale, Naples.[66] Another reading by Ficino of this version of the arrangement was of the triad as allegorical of "Pulchritudo, Amor, and Voluptas," the first issuing from God as a kind of beacon, the second, within the world, moving it to rapture, and the third, returning in a state of joy to its source.[67] There have been, of course, other readings. However, the matter of essential interest here is not of such identifications and allegories, but of the number 3 itself. Aristotle in *De caelo* (1.268a) writes of it as follows:

> The science which has to do with nature clearly concerns itself for the most part with bodies and magnitudes and their properties and movements, but also with the principles of this sort of substance, as many as they may be. For of things constituted by nature some are bodies and magnitudes, some possess body and magnitude, and some are principles of things which possess these. Now a continuum is that which is divisible into parts always capable of subdivision, and a body is that which is every way divisible. A magnitude if divisible one way is a line, if two ways a surface, and if three a body. Beyond these there is no other magnitude, because the three dimensions are all that there are, and that which is divisible in three directions is divisible in all. For, as Pythagoreans say, the universe and all that is in it is determined by the number three, since beginning and middle and end give the number of the universe, and the number they give is the triad. And so, having taken these three from nature as (so to speak) laws of it, we make further use of the number three in the worship of the Gods.[68]

Plato in *Timaeus* (37d–38b) identifies the number with time, which, as he declares, "imitates eternity and revolves according to a law of number."

"The past and future," he writes,

> are created species of time, which we unconsciously but wrongly transfer to eternal being, for we say that it "was" or "is" or "will be," but the truth is that "is" alone is properly attributed to it, and that "was" and "will be" are only to be spoken of becoming in time, for they are notions, but that which is immovably the same forever cannot become older or younger by time, nor can it be said that it came into being in the past, or has come into being now, or will come into being in the future, nor is it subject at all to any of those states which affect moving and sensible

things and of which generation is the cause. These are the forms of time, which imitates eternity and revolves according to a law of number. Moreover, when we say that what has become *is* become and what becomes *is* becoming, and that what will become *is* about to become and that the nonexistent *is* nonexistent—all these are inaccurate modes of expression.[69]

So that, whether viewed thus by Aristotle as the nature of things in space or by Plato as of their becoming in time, the number 3 must be recognized as constitutive of phenomenality, which is to say in mythological terms, the body of the Goddess. In Gafurius's design, the number is represented as permeating the universe, from the triad of Graces to the trinity of heads of the monster whose unfolded coil threads the world—which is an idea consistent with the Neoplatonic axiom that in this universe, as a macrocosm, the whole is repeated in every part, as a microcosm.

Wind calls attention to St. Augustine's recognition of an *imago trinitatis in re alia,* as well as of what he interpreted as pagan "vestiges of the trinity" in all the mythologies of his time (supposing the *trinitas* of his own tradition to be, not simply one of many, but the original of all). In the Indian Vedanta, the ultimate triad of names connotative within the field of *māyā* of the universally immanent, metaphysically transcendent *brahmātman* is *sat-cid-ānanda,* namely, "Being" (*sat*), "Consciousness" (*cit*), and "Bliss or Rapture" (*ānanda*), which in anthropomorphic Occidental terms would be, approximately, Father, Son, and Holy Spirit; Neoplatonically, (1) inheritance in the cause, (2) procession from the cause, and (3) reversion to the cause; and in Greek poetic imagery, the Graces.

In sum then, we may think of 3 as the liminal term of things apprehended in the field of space, time, and causality; what James Joyce in *Ulysses* (part 1, chapter 3, opening phrase) defines as the "Ineluctable modality of the visible: at least that if no more. . . ." Augustine discerned the imprint of the Trinity in all things, regarding, however, the one essential Trinity as male, whereas the Greeks had a number of essential female trinities, for example, the Graces, the Hours, the Fates, and the Furies, as well as the great triad of the "Judgment of Paris," Aphrodite, Hera, and Athene.

Unquestionably, female triads long predated the historical appearance of Augustine's *trinitas* of three male personalities in one divine substance; for the mythologies of the great Neolithic goddesses—as the publications of Marija Gimbutas demonstrate—date back to the eighth millennium B.C.—at least! with antecedents even in the Paleolithic. Gimbutas calls attention, for example, to the late Paleolithic "Venus of Laussel" of c. 20,000–18,000 B.C.[70] In a posture and with a gesture eloquent of some legend, the knowledge of which is irretrievably lost, this impressive little figure, carved in high relief on a limestone block discovered in a rock shelter from the period of the great painted caves of southern France and northern Spain, is of a corpulent, naked female, holding elevated in her raised right hand a bison horn on which thirteen vertical stokes are engraved, while caressing with her left hand her pregnant belly.[71] The figure must have represented some mythic personage so well known to the period that the reference of the elevated horn would have been as well known as, say, in India today, a lotus in the hand of the goddess Śrī Lakshmī. Alexander Marshack in *The Roots of Civilization* remarks that "the count of thirteen is the number of crescent 'horns' that may make up an observational lunar year; it is also the number of days from the birth of the first crescent to just before the days of the mature full moon."[72] Filling the whole back wall of a shallow Paleolithic cave from c. 13,000 to c. 11,000 B.C., at Angles-sur-Anglin (Vienne), there looms a large rock-carved composition of great bellies, massive loins, and upper thighs of three colossal female presences, sexual triangles strongly marked, hovering as an immense triad above the horned head of a bull.[73] And some ten thousand years later, on a stone Gallo-Roman altar excavated from the site of the present Notre Dame de Paris and preserved in the basements of the nearby Musée de Cluny, there is carved the image of a bull beneath a tree upon which three cranes are to be seen. The inscription reads *Tarvos Triagaranus,* "Bull with the Three Cranes," the crane being a bird symbolic at that time of the Celtic Triple Goddess.[74] "The sacredness of the bull," remarks Gimbutas in a discussion of Neolithic symbolic forms, "is expressed in particular through the emphasis on horns. They are sometimes as large as the whole animal figurine. Replete with a mysterious power of growth, the horns have become a lunar symbol, which is presumed to have come into being in the Upper Paleolithic Aurignacian when reliefs of naked women holding a horn begin to appear."[75]

The magnificent female triad at Angles-sur-Anglin (Vienne), hovering above the horned head (or mask) of a bull, in what surely was a holy grotto, is (I believe) the earliest known representation of a triad of any kind in the history of art. The date, c. 13,000–11,000 B.C., is some ten thousand years later than that of the Venus of Laussel, the Woman with the Horn. Another five thousand years and in Asia Minor, among the numerous shrines unearthed at Çatal Hüyuk, a Neolithic town site elegantly published and illustrated by James Mellaart, there are a number of female figures represented as giving birth to bulls; also, walls ornamented with triads of bull heads, as well as arrays of bulls' horns, and an evident association, furthermore, of the symbol of the bull's head with the human cranium.[76] Still another five thousand years, and at the island site in the river Seine of Notre Dame de Paris, that Gallo-Roman altar appeared of three cranes perched in a tree above the figure of a large standing bull.

The evidence is thus consistent, extensive, and unmistakable, of a prehistoric continuity of no less than twenty thousand years for a mythology of the female body as the matrix of what Plato in *Timaeus* referred to as "those states which affect moving and sensible things and of which generation is the cause . . . the forms of time, which imitates eternity and revolves according to a law of number."

Already in the figure of the Venus of Laussel there is evidence of an interest in number; number associated, moreover, with the cycle of the moon, and the crescent moon associated with the horn or horns of a bull. The figure's left hand held to the belly suggests that a relationship had been already recognized between the female menstrual cycle and the waxing and waning of the moon—which in turn implies a dawning of the recognition of an identity of some kind, coordinating earthly and celestial numbers.

Marshack in *The Roots of Civilization* has demonstrated for the Upper Paleolithic an interest in day counts. Examining with a microscope the rows of notches carved in series along staves of horn, ivory, or bone, he found that in every case the successive notches had been carved by different instruments, presumably at different times, and he termed such artifacts "time factored." Moreover, since a significant number showed counts that matched lunar cycles, the possible inference followed of women keeping tally of their menstrual cycles in observation of the phases of the moon.

The phases of the moon are four: three visible (waxing, full, and waning) and one invisible (three nights dark). Persephone, ravished to the netherworld by Hades/Pluto, became—while there invisible to the living—queen of a netherworld of death and regeneration. Such an identification of the mystery of generation with death and sacrifice is, by analogy, in lunar imagery, associated with the fourth, the invisible phase, of the lunar cycle, which in the Eleusinian legend is equated with the night of the marriage of Persephone and Pluto. Classical representations of the triad of goddesses, Athene, Hera, and Aphrodite, at the scene of the Judgment of Paris show them attended by Hermes as a fourth, who, in fact, is the one who summons Paris to the confrontation.[77] The two mythic episodes are of the same mythological vocabulary. And in both, the designation of a male-female *conjunctio* is related, one way or the other, to an association with the idea of a fourth in relation to a three.

The Angles-sur-Anglin triad, in association with the bull as a fourth, is a Paleolithic counterpart of the classical triad attended by Hermes. For as Marija Gimbutas points out, "The male god's principal epiphany was in the form of a bull." And as she remarks further, "A human head grafted onto a bull's body reaches a culmination of power through symbiosis: the wisdom and passions of man merged with the physical strength and potency of the bull."[78] "The bull god was alive," she reminds us,

> in many areas of Greece and particularly in Macedonia in the time of Euripides whose *Bacchae* abounds in bull epiphanies:
>
> > *A Horned God was found*
> > *And a God with serpents crowned*
> > (Euripides, *Bacchae*, 99)
>
> In the Orphic mystery, the worshipper ate the raw flesh of the bull before he be- came "Bacchos." The ritual of Dionysus in Thrace included "bull-voiced" mimes who bellowed to the god. The scholiast on Lychophron's *Alexandra* says that the women who worshipped Dionysus Laphystion wore horns themselves, in imita- tion of the god, for he was imagined to be bull-headed and is so represented in art. . . . Dionysus also manifested himself as the bull Zagreus, in which guise he was torn to pieces by the Titans.[79]

The art of the Upper Paleolithic is the earliest art of which we have knowl- edge, providing our earliest pictorial evidence of mankind's mythic themes and actual ritual practices. The animal paintings in the stupendous temple caves had evidently to do with ceremonials of the hunt; probably also with the initia- tion of adolescents to manhood. The human figures represented are few and ex- clusively male, masked or semi-animal in form. The sculptural art of the numerous female figurines, on the other hand, is related generally to dwelling sites, and whereas in the caves the human figures are in action, performing cere- monials of one kind of another, the figurines are simply presentations in the nude of the female form.[80] The little figures usually have no feet. A few have been found set standing upright in the earth of household shrines. Further- more, in contrast to the shamanic figures in the caves, which seem to be always in the performance of their social functions, the female statuettes are not in ac- tion of any kind.[81] They are simply there, in being, little presences in them- selves, representations and reminders (for contemplation) of the mystery of the female body itself, which is, in fact, the sole source of the life and well-being of the very dwelling site in which the little figure will have been set standing.

In the exceptional example, from c. 20,000 B.C., of the Woman with the Horn, discovered at one end of a long limestone ledge at Laussel, the essential features of the lunar mythology of which the figurines are expressions are un- mistakably brought to view. And in the great triad at Angles-sur-Anglin (Vienne) the further mythological implications of these essential features are unfolded.

Normally, of course, it would be improper to suggest attributions to the figures from the twelfth millennium B.C. of ideas that become clear to us only from the first. However when the vocabularies of two pictorial documents are visibly identical, it becomes difficult to argue that the artists in the first instance cannot have known what they were saying. Three female forms in association with a bull as the fourth! Three major goddesses in association with Hermes as a fourth! Three Graces ("the first moving thing") in association with Apollo as a fourth! Three visible phases of the waxing, full, and waning moon with the moon of the nights invisible as a fourth: the nights invisible being of the moon's apparent death and, then, resurrection! There is plenty of evidence that the people of the Upper Paleolithic understood very well the relationship of sexual intercourse to pregnancy. In the same site at Laussel at which the Woman with the Horn was found, there was also a sculptured representation of a couple in sexual union.[82] Since the elevated horn bearing thirteen strokes may be interpreted (as Marshack has suggested) as symbolic of the visibly waxing moon, while the woman's hand on her belly relates the phenomenon to that of the pregnant womb, there is surely an intention to be recognized in the appearance *in the same sanctuary* of a representation of what Freud and his school have called the "primal scene," which in terms of a lunar symbolic schedule is of the mystery of the fourth, the invisible phase.

Considering further the interesting triad at Angles-sur-Anglin, one cannot but notice that the sexual triangles are, all three, very well defined and that the mesial grooves are conspicuous. The triangles, furthermore, are distinctly equilateral, like the Pythagorean *tetraktys,* with the grooves then suggesting the point at the tetraktian apex as connoting the invisible source from which the visible form has proceeded—which is perhaps pressing the interpretation a bit too far; and yet, the analogy is impossible to miss. The triangle, furthermore, is the same as that which in Indian Tantric iconography is taken to connote the energy of the womb as identical with that of *māyā.*

In the Paleolithic pictogram, the 3 triangles of 3 sides each announce, moreover, the number 9, which is that of the Muses manifesting in the field of space-time the energy (*vis*) of the Apollonian mind as mediated through the Graces—which is again, perhaps, pressing an interpretation too far; yet the number is conspicuously represented as of 3 mighty females hovering over the mask or head of a bull as a fourth—or, in relation to the 9, as a tenth. In relation to the Graces, Apollo appears as a fourth, and in relation to the Muses, as a tenth.

Now, whether allegorical thoughts of this kind can have been present in any way in the minds responsible for this masterwork—whether consciously, half-consciously, or unconsciously—who shall say? Many artists whom I know today are willing, even eager, to impute such mythological implications to their profoundly inspired productions when they learn of them from such scholars as myself. Psychoanalysts with their pudendascopes (James Joyce's word) readily discern intentions in works of art that no artist would have recognized. The method of mythology is analogy, and that the artists of the Paleolithic age were competent in analogy is surely evident in the statement of the Woman with the Horn, where a triple analogy is rendered of the (1) growing horns of a bull, (2) waxing crescent of the moon, and (3) growing child, *en ventre sa mère.*

The imagery of this art is derived, not only from accurate observation, but also from an unconditioned identification with the natural order. And the mythologies originating from that primal age were of the same disposition. The two modes, of art and of myth, therefore, not only supplemented each other, but also remained in accord with the root-being of phenomenal life, self-validated through the sense that they inspired of fulfillment.

By what coincidence of nature, however, can the numerology of the Paleolithic and Neolithic lunar reckoning of 3 + 3 + 3, as the visible body of the universal Great Goddess, have been carried on, only amplified, in the Old Sumerian numerological reading of 4 + 3 + 2, to accord with an actual "Great," or "Platonic" Zodiacal cycle of 25,920 solar years, where 2 + 5 + 9 + 2 + 0 = 18, and 1 + 8 = 9, whose root, as Dante saw, is a trinity?

Of Harmony and of Discord

In what has been called by some "The Heroic Age," of those centuries of barbaric invasions and wiping out of cities that we find celebrated in the Indo-European Iliad and Mahābhārata, as well as throughout the Old Testament, there were brought onto the historic stage two sorts of nomadic, herding and fighting peoples bearing analogous, though significantly differing, sociologically oriented systems of mythology inspired by notions of morality wherein the high concern was not of harmony with the universe in its mystery but of the aggrandizement and justification of some local, historical tribe or cult. The whole character, as well as function, of mythology was thereby transformed; and since the myths, ideals, and rites of the new orders of justified violence overlay wherever they fell the earlier of an essential peace at the heart of the universe, the history of mythology in a great quarter of the world for the past three thousand years has been of a double-layered continuum. In some parts, notably India, the mythology of the Goddess returned in time to the surface and even became dominant. Already at the conclusion of the *Kena Upanishad* (seventh century B.C., or so) there is described a notable and amusing scene, where the Indo-European Vedic gods are found powerless and introduced to the knowledge of *Brahman* by "a woman exceedingly beautiful, Umā, Daughter of the Mountain Himavat."[83] Also in Greece, the Great Goddess returned to power in many forms, most notably in the mysteries of Eleusis; and in the Near East as well, where a constant biblical refrain became of kings "who did evil in the sight of the Lord," as Solomon, for instance who "went after Ashtoreth the goddess of the Sidonians, and after Milcom the abomination of the Ammonites . . . built a high place for Chemosh the abomination of Moab, and for Moloch the abomination of the Ammonites, on the mountain east of Jerusalem. And so he did for all his foreign wives, who burned incense and sacrifices to their gods" (1 Kings 11:5–8).

Read again the mad account of the rampage of the very good King Josiah of Judah (c. 640–609 B.C.), when he

> deposed the idolatrous priests whom the kings of Judah had ordained to burn incense in the high places at the cities of Judah and round about Jerusalem; those also who burned incense to Ba'al, to the sun, and the moon, and the constellations, and all the host of the heavens. And he brought out the Asherah from the house of the Lord, outside Jerusalem, to the brook Kidron, and beat it to dust and cast the dust of it upon the graves of the common people. And he broke down the houses of the cult prostitutes which were in the house of the Lord, where the women wove hangings for the Asherah. And he brought all the priests out of the cities of Judah, and defiled the high places where the priests had burned incense, from Geba to Beersheba; and he broke down the high places of the gates that were at the entrance of the gate of Joshua the governor of the city, which were on one's left of the gate of the city. However, the priests of the high places did not come up to the altar of the Lord in Jerusalem, but they ate unleavened bread among their brethren. . . ." (2 Kings 23:5–9)

Thus the force of the underlying layer, even where officially suppressed or apparently forgotten, worked its influence, often in subtle ways; as for example, in the instance already recognized, of the number 86,400 concealed in the length of years of the biblical antediluvian age.

From as early as the fourth millennium B.C., the Indo-European, cattle-herding, patriarchal warrior tribes were overrunning and transforming the civilization of Europe.[84] Through centuries, waves of invasion followed waves, and with each there was carried into the field of world history another inflection of what Georges Dumézil has in many volumes represented as the prototypical structure of an Indo-European mythology, reflecting the tripartite class structure of a social order of farmers and cattle breeders under a leadership of battle-eager warrior-chiefs and magician-priests.[85]

In the Near East, very much the same was happening, as patriarchal, goat- and sheep-herding Semitic tribes from the Syro-Arabian desert, under the leadership likewise of warrior-chiefs and magician-priests, were in the names of their gods consummating devastating victories over such long-established cities of the region as, for instance, Jericho (Joshua 6).[86] So that, as a consequence of all of this truly unspeakable violence and barbarity over an immense part of the already civilized portion of Europe and Asia (only Egypt on its desert- and god-protected Nile remained through those millennia unbroken), what the historian of mythologies everywhere uncovers, from the British Isles to the Gangetic Plain, is a consistent pattern (retained in religions even to the present day) of two completely contrary orders of mythic thought and symbolization flung together, imperfectly fused, and represented as though of one meaning.

The elder of the two, by far, was of the Neolithic Great Goddess, of whom the earliest known images, as recognized by Gimbutas, are of Old Europe, c. 7000–3500 B.C., with antecedents, however, in the Upper Paleolithic period, going back to some 20,000, or more, B.C. And the critical point to be made here is that the interest of the earlier order of myth was emphatically in nature, and in the nature, specifically, of the female body as the giver of life and thus of one constitution with the universe. As bird, as fish, as duck, as deer, as frog, even as water, the Great Goddess appears: in many forms, if not already also of many names.

At which point it becomes perhaps appropriate to remark that in every lifetime there is indeed a period when the mother, and specifically the mother's female body, is, in fact, the universe. Indeed, it would be possible even to argue that the infant's initial experience of the mother as universe, transformed in later life into a sense of the universe as mother, should be recognized as the primal impulse of all mythological symbolization whatsoever.

In any case, in the art and arts of the Neolithic stage, not only of Old Europe but of the whole range known to us of peoples of the world, the *mysterium tremendum and fascinans* of life itself as motherhood and as birth, as growth and as transformation terminating in a return to the mother in death, out of which source appears new life, is universally, at this stage of civilization, the all-engrossing, first and last concern. I see no evidence anywhere among the remains of peoples at this stage of the development of civilization anything like the compulsion recognized by Dumézil in Indo-European mythology, to project upon the universe the conditions of their own social order. On the contrary, the compulsion is, rather, to adapt society to the conditions dictated by as much as can be understood of the universe.

And in the succeeding epoch of this biologically instructed, mother-goddess–dominated tradition of mythological symbolization (that, namely, of the early Sumerian recognition, third millennium B.C. or so, of a mathematically controlled universal order of cycling eons of 43,200—432,000—or 4,320,000 years) the high concern was still to bring the now comparatively complex sociology of a constellation of agriculturally supported city-states into conformity with the order of the universe.

Ragnarök

The voice of the prophetess Völva, summoned by Othin to rise from the earth and discourse of the doom of the gods:

> On a hill there sat, and smote on his harp,
> Eggther the Joyous, the giants' warder;
> Above him the cock in the bird-wood crowed,
> Fair and red did Fjalar stand.

> Then to the gods crowed Gollinkambi,
> He wakes the heroes in Othin's hall;
> And beneath the earth does another crow,
> The rust-red bird at the bars of Hel.

> Now Garm howls loud before Gnipahellir,
> The fetters will burst, and the wolf run free;
> Much do I know and more can see
> Of the fate of the gods, the mighty in fight.

> Brothers shall fight and fell each other,
> And sisters' sons shall kinship stain;
> Hard is it on earth, with mighty whoredom;
> Axe-time, sword-time, shields are sundered,
> Wind-time, wolf-time, ere the world falls;
> Nor ever shall men each other spare.

> Fast move the sons of Mim, and fate
> Is heard in the note of the Gjallarhorn;
> Loud blows Heimdall, the horn is aloft,
> In fear quake all who on Hel's roads are.

> Yggdrasil shakes, and shiver on high
> The ancient limbs, and the giant is loose;
> To the head of Mim does Othin give heed,
> But the kinsmen of Surt shall slay him soon.

> How fare the gods? How fare the elves?
> All Jotunheim groans, the gods are at council;
> Loud roar the dwarfs by the doors of stone,
> Masters of the rocks, would you know yet more?

Now Garm howls loud before Gnipahellir,
The fetters will burst and the wolf run free;
Much do I know, and more can see
Of the fate of the gods, the mighty in fight.[87]

The dissolution at the end of time of the shadow-play of the pairs-of-opposites: Armageddon, the biblical version of that day, of which Jesus also prophesied, when "brother will deliver up brother to death, and the father his child, and the children will rise against parents and have them put to death" (Mark 13:12 et al.). Even the crowing of the cock, thrice, which Peter heard to his shame . . . (Matt. 26:73–75; Mark 14:66–72, et al.).

On that day, the wolf Fenrir is to swallow the sun and with gaping mouth advance on the land, his lower jaw against the earth and upper against heaven. The World Ash, Yggdrasil, will tremble, trees shatter, crags fall to ruin. The sea will gush upon the land, and the ship Naglfar (made of dead men's nails) steer landward, bearing Loki aboard and the Rime-Giants. The Midgard Serpent that surrounds the earth will be at Fenrir's side, blowing venom, with all the champions of Hel following. And the heaven will be cloven in their din.

Then Heimdall, who sits at heaven's end guarding Bifrost, the Rainbow Bridge (he sees equally well by night and by day, hears the grass grow on earth and the wool on sheep, needs less sleep than a bird, and sits snug in his hall, drinking gladly of good mead), will sound mightily the Gjallarhorn; when the gods, all waking, will in council meet, don war weeds, and venturing, 800 through each of Valhall's doors, 432,000 join the fiends of Hel in a festival of mutual slaughter.[88]

"My hypothesis proposes," states the Icelander Einar Pálsson, of his treatment in seven volumes of *The Roots of Icelandic Culture,* "that the world picture of pagan Iceland—the universe of the Vikings—was the SAME as that of the Romans and the Greeks, modified by time, a Nordic language and Christian currents. . . . What I have NOT found during 35 years of study into the roots of Icelandic culture is anything which points to a separate 'Nordic' or even 'Germanic' religion in the sense that it is different from that of the cultures of Sumer, Egypt, Greece, and Rome."[89]

The Nordic settlement of the island during the six decades A.D. 830–890 was by Viking families of two separate strains: a Celtic Christian from the British Isles and a pagan directly from Norway. Pálsson's recognition of a context of late classical (Neoplatonic) ideas in the Celtic Christianity of Iceland has been recently corroborated archaeologically, by the sensational discovery at Dagvertharnes, in the west of Iceland, on the shores of the Breithafjördur, of remains that have been described as "strongly reminiscent of Celtic dwellings excavated in Britain," together with "ten carved stones . . . including a pyramidal stone [a tetrahedron] and what seems to be a stone cross."[90] The excavation was conducted by the archaeologist Thorvaldur Fridriksson of the University of Gothenburgh at a site that had been already identified by Pálsson as having the significance of the tetrahedron in Celtic Christian ideology, namely, as connoting a hallowing in the settlement of land. The date as first announced was nearly two centuries too early but as corrected is in perfect accord with Pálsson's, after A.D. 870.

The Celtic Christianity which had been thus carried to Iceland was a direct continuation of the Mission of St. Patrick, the traditional date of whose arrival in the British Isles is A.D. 432(!). The year before that date, at the Byzantine church council at Ephesus (the most important Near Eastern temple-city at that time of the Great Goddess of Many Names), Mary had been declared to be, indeed, *Theotokós*, the "Mother of God." And within half a century of that epochal date the Christian Roman Empire collapsed; all of Europe except Ireland was overrun by pagan Germanic tribes (Britain's invaders were the English); and for the next three to four centuries the task of re-Christianizing Britain and the Continent was the high concern of Irish monks. St. Columba's founding on the island of Iona, in the Inner Hebrides, A.D. 563, of a church and monastery dedicated to the pursuit of the work in Scotland, and the ambitious mission to Switzerland, Burgundy, and Italy of St. Columbanus with twelve companions, c. 598–614, are the two best known of these undertakings. Two centuries later, at the courts of Charles the Bald, near Laon, the Irish monk John Scotus Erigena (c. 810-877) was translating out of Greek the writings of pseudo-Dionysius the Areopagite, St. Gregory of Nyasa, St. Epiphanius, and St. Maximus the Confessor, besides composing two philosophical treatises of his own: *De predestinatione* (in 851) and *De divisione naturae* (862–866), both of which were promptly condemned for implications, not only of pantheism, but also of reincarnation.[91]

For the church of St. Peter, in Rome, had meanwhile recovered authority, and already in the year 664, at the Synod of Whitby in Northumbria, the Irish monks with their Neoplatonic theology based on the Book of Revelation and Gospel According to John, supported by their own mystical experiences in a tradition of meditation unmatched for severity save in India, had been required to retire from England, yielding to the Roman party the field which they there had tilled. Erigena's works, therefore, composed two centuries later, in the period just preceding the settlement of Iceland, were of a tradition which on the Continent had already gone underground, to be represented covertly in the symbolic language of alchemy and, most notably during the twelfth and early thirteenth centuries, in the Manichaean (Albigensian) heresy and the fundamentally Celtic legend of the Holy Grail. Not until Cosimo de' Medici's founding of his academy in Florence would the Greek language, bearing its heritage of Neoplatonic and Pythagorean thought, return to recognition in the Latin West.

What Erigena had proposed in his *De divisione naturae* was a reconciliation of the Christian doctrine of creation by a personal Creator-God with the Neoplatonic doctrine of emanation; a syncretization elegantly epitomized in his definition of four cosmogonic principles:

1. The uncreated creating
2. The created creating
3. The created uncreating
4. The uncreated uncreating

whereby the first and last are of God, as beginning and end, while the second and third are of the two modes of existence of created beings: the intelligible and the sensible.[92] For man, according to this Gnostic view, is a microcosm of the universe: with his senses perceiving the sensible world, with reason examining its intelligible causes, and with the intellect knowing God. Through sin, the animal sensual nature predominates. With release from sin, the return to God begins; and with physical death, reunion with the uncreated.

Among the first of Erigena's Celtic Christian contemporaries to arrive in Iceland (as chronicled in the *Landnámabók,* "Book of the Claiming of the Land") were two brothers and a sister, who, sailing presumably from the Hebrides, put to shore along the south coast in the delta area now known as Landeyjar, "Land Islands," where there is a triple hill called Bergthórshvoll, which they evidently regarded as a holy spot. An earlier, pagan settler, Ketill hoengr by name, had already recognized, "claimed," and settled this whole part of the island.

In the western quarter, meanwhile, a second Christian company put to land in the neighborhood of Dagverthanes, where there have now been found the remains of what appears to have been a Celtic monastery. The leader of that group was Authr djúpúthga, widowed queen of King Oleifr the White of Dublinshire, a daughter of Ketill flatnefr, a chieftain of the Hebrides. Four of her brothers and sisters are named also as leading settlers of Iceland: Helgi bjólan (at Kjalarnes, near Reykjavík), Björn austraeni (at Snaefellsnes, in the middle west), Thórunn hyrna (at Eyjafjörthur, in the north), and Jórunn mannivitsbrekka (in the southeast, at Kirkjuber, where the *Landnáma* states Christian Celtic hermits had lived before the advent of the Norsemen). Örlygr Hrappsson, a nephew of this family, brought up by a Bishop Patrick in the Hebrides, had been told by his bishop to settle where he would find "three stones raised upright," which suggests that Bishop Patrick must have had in mind a lithic monument already known from accounts of earlier Celtic Christians.[93]

The appearance anywhere on the landscape of a suggestion of the number 3—in particular 3 rocks—was for these people a feature of significance, betokening a holy and appropriate site for Christian settlement. For the sense of the term *landnám,* "land claiming," was of a spiritual claiming as well as physical occupation of a newly discovered land. By recognizing in its natural conformations features symbolically suggestive, the settlers were enabled to inlay upon a *visible* landscape the outlines of an intelligible, otherwise invisible one, reminiscent of the mythology that they had brought with them in their heads; so that when the work was done, the whole of their settlement would have become for them an icon of the New Jerusalem.

And so we learn that some thirty miles inland, northeastward of the Landeyjar, there is a mountain showing 3 peaks, which was revered in the earliest period as a holy mountain by analogy with Golgotha and its 3 crosses: each cross to be associated with the 5 wounds of Christ, and the $5 \times 3 = 15$ wounds, with the 15 mysteries of his Virgin Mother Mary: 5 joyous mysteries (the Annunciation, Visitation, Nativity, Presentation in the Temple, and Finding of the Child Teaching in the Temple); 5 sorrowful mysteries (the Agony in the Garden of Gethsemane, Scourging, Crowning with Thorns, Carrying of the Cross, and the Crucifixion); 5 glorious mysteries (of the Resurrection, Ascension, Pentecostal Descent of the Holy Ghost upon the Apostles, Assumption of the Virgin Mary to Heaven, and her Coronation there by her Son).

The name, Thríhyrningur, of the holy mountain, means "Three Horn," which, according to Pálsson, may be understood also to mean "triangle." Most modern Icelanders, " he adds, "have taken it for granted that the name meant 'three peaks.'"[94] "Three Horn" suggests a lunar association, which in the earlier Celtic pagan period would have carried a reference to the great Celtic triple goddess of innumerable forms and names—Danu/Anu/Ana; Morrighan/Badhbh/Macha; and so on—who in folklore is known as Queen Mab of the ubiquitous Fairy Hills.

The Celtic imagination readily associates the silence of hills with the mystery of eternity (Erigena's "uncreated creating" and "uncreated uncreating"), out of which arise and appear the ephemera of space-time and back into which they disappear. A number of the best-known legends of the Middle Ages are of adventures into mountain fastnesses, those of Tannhauser in the *Venusberg,* for example, or of Parzival at the mountain-castle of the Grail. Pálsson points to an association of Mount Thríhyrningur with the Grail keeper and Grail legend.[95]

Mythologically, such holy mountains have served as images symbolic of the *axis mundi,* that universal still point around which movement originates, and in every part of the ancient world they have been associated in this function with the being and presence of one or another of the forms of the Great Goddess: the mighty Cretan Goddess on her mountaintop; Ki and Ninhursag of most ancient Sumer; Pārvatī in India, as the bride of Shiva and daughter of the snow-topped Himalaya. The image of the upward-pointing triangle is implicit in such a prominence, and this in turn suggests an association with the Pythagorean *tetraktys* and the upward-pointing tantric *yantra* symbolic of the triad out of which the 9 unfolds, with a tenth point, the *bindu,* at the center.[96]

The original abode of Ketill hoengr, the first *pagan* settler of the southern area, was at a site named Hof, meaning "Temple," which became then a point from which symbolic measurements of the land were counted. A line drawn northeast-southwest through Hof, toward the point, northeast, of midsummer sunrise (June 22, summer solstice), and the opposite point, southwest, of midwinter sunset (December 22, winter solstice, Yule or Christmas), extends northeast to a place called Ströng, the "Pole," "Stick," or "Staff," and southwest, across and beyond the triple hill Bergthórshvoll, out to sea to a triple rock, Thrídrangar, uprising from a volcanic shelf that is still active and associated mythologically with the gate or portal to the timeless sphere of the *primum mobile,* or ninth heaven.[97]

Now from Bergthórshvoll to Stöng, the distance measured in Roman feet (as Pálsson has found) is 216,000 feet, or half of 432,000 (1 Roman foot = 29.69 centimeters: 216,000 Roman feet = approximately 64 kilometers, or 40 miles). At the center of this span is Steinkross, where presumably there was at one time a stone cross around which an immense geographical circle was envisioned, 216,000 Roman feet in diameter, as an earthly replica of the heavens. Steinkross in the center was thus a counterpart of the pole star, the hub of the universe, while the circle itself, as a counterpart of the Zodiac, was divided in 12 "houses."

Known as the Wheel of Rangárhverfi, this schematic reflection of the heavens supplied the model for the spiritually grounded social organization that is represented in the original Icelandic constitution of A.D. 930, whereby a body of 36 "priest-kings," or Gothar, 3 to each of the 12 "houses," governed the island as at once its secular and spiritual authority. Kingship, in this view, had "a sacral character," as Pálsson declares, "it was part of the total universe . . . it reached unto the hidden depths of nature and the powers that rule nature. It was the king's function to 'maintain the harmony' of the integration between Man and the Cosmos."[98] Which, as we have already found, was the whole sense of the old Sumerian, as well as later Pythagorean, attention to the ordering mysteries of number.

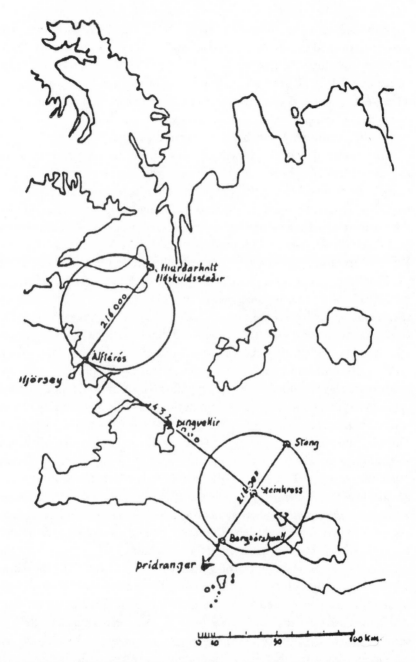

Fig. 4. Ketill hoengr's "Measuring Tree of the Universe," uniting the two original Icelandic settlements, south and west, showing Thingvellir between Steinkross and Álftárós, midway of a line of 432,000 Roman feet. Ninth century. Reconstruction by Einar Pálsson, *Raetur íislenzkrar menningar,* 7 vols. (1969–85).

From Steinkross, accordingly, a line projected 432,000 Roman feet north-westward touched the rim of a second symbolic circle, 216,000 Roman feet in diameter, by which the region was enclosed of the original, western, Celtic Christian settlement. And precisely midway of this symbolic line, there is Thingvellir (a magnificent setting of volcanic landscape and adjacent plain), where the central place of assembly was fixed of the Althingi, the governing body politic of the whole inhabited quarter of the island.

The historical source of this concept of a society as a mesocosmic coordi-nating force attuning human life to a natural order mathematically structured is not to be sought for in any of the primal Indo-European tribal pantheons, where, as Georges Dumézil has demonstrated, mythology and religion reflect the tripartite structural pattern of the basic Indo-European social hierarchy of (1) priests, (2) warriors, and (3) producers (cattle breeders and agriculturists). What we here find, in contrast, is not a mythology reflecting the social order of a nomadic tribe, but a social order reflecting the Pythagorean concept of a mathematically structured macrocosm. For over a century and a half, Ger-manic scholarship has been arguing the opposed claims of those who interpret Germanic myth as a creation sui generis and those who view it as significantly influenced by Hellenistic and even early Christian models. Einar Pálsson's un-covering in ninth- and tenth-century Iceland of the indubitable signs of a mathematically structured Pythagorean philosophical ground that was identi-cal in all essentials with that of Cosimo de' Medici's fifteenth-century Floren-tine academy confirms the case, once and for all, of those who—with Alfons Dopsch, *Wirtschaftliche und soziale Grundlagen der europäischen Kulturent-wicklung aus der Zeit von Caesar bis auf Karl den Grossen* (2 vols. [Vienna, 1918–20; 2d ed., 1923–24]), and Franz Rolf Schröder, *Germanentum und Hellenismus* (Heidelberg, 1924), *Die Parzivalfrage* (München, 1928), *Altger-manische Kulturprobleme* (Berlin, Leipzig, 1929)—had recognized that for centuries the Germans had been profoundly in touch with and influenced by the civilizations of Greece, Rome, and the Near East.

Specifically, the chief centers of contact were in the west, along the Rhine, where, from the period of Caesar's conquest of Gaul, continuous Gallo-Roman influences, first pagan, then Christian, played into the German culture-field, and in the East, the north shore of the Black Sea, where, from no later than the second century A.D., the Goths were sharing with Iranians and Greeks the rich heritage of Hellenistic art, science, philosophy, and religion. By the fourth cen-tury A.D., until shattered c. 370 by the Huns, a Gothic empire extended from the Black Sea to the Baltic. Ulfila's fourth-century translation of the Bible into Gothic was made for the Visigoths along the lower Danube. There exist frag-ments of a Gothic commentary on the John Gospel, as well as of an exchange of letters concerning textual interpretations between Gothic Christians (who were of the Arian heresy) and Hieronymus (St. Jerome, c. 347–419). Schröder calls attention, also, to a discovery in the Egyptian desert of a bilingual (Gothic/Latin) page from the Bible, possibly of a Gothic officer in the Roman army; or if later, in the period of the Christian empire, either an Arian heretic in exile or some Gothic monk who had retired in meditation to the desert.

Even earlier than the Gothic East, the Christian mission had flourished in the Rhineland. There were established sees in Treves, Metz, and Cologne already in the third century. Moreover, nearly all of the pagan, classical, and Oriental mystery religions had been by that time long established and flourishing in both the Gallo-Roman and Germano-Roman zones. Egyptian Isis and Serapis, Syrian Attis and Cybele, Persian Mithra, Thracian Sabazius, Orpheus, Jupiter, Dolichenus, and many others were represented. Entire communities had exchanged their native deities for these, in whose worship they experienced profounder satisfactions. And the native cults themselves had meanwhile been gradually transformed by influences from these sources.[99]

> I ween that I hung on the windy tree,
>   Hung there for nights full nine;
> With spear I was wounded, and offered I was
>   To Othin, myself to myself,
> On the tree that none may ever know
>   What root beneath it runs.
>
> None made me happy with loaf or horn,
>   And there below I looked;
> I took up the runes, shrieking I took them,
>   And forthwith back I fell.
>
> Then began I to thrive, and wisdom to get,
>   I grew and well I was;
> Each word led me on to another word,
>   Each deed to another deed.[100]

What has been described as the "Christian-Pagan Syncretism" of the earlier Middle Ages—antecedent to (or, as in Iceland, beyond the ban of) the intolerant creedal edict of Theodosius I the Great (issued February 28, 380; confirmed 381, at the second ecumenical council, ten years before the burning of the Alexandrian *Mouseion*)—is explicit in this image of Othin, hung 9 nights on the "windy tree" of the World Ash Yggdrasil (Christ, 3 hours on Holy Rood); a sacrifice, himself to himself (the Son to his consubstantial Father); pierced by the Lance (of Longinus). Identified with Mercury, Othin (Wodan) was named as tutelary of the fourth day of the Alexandrian planetary week, in the series, Sol, Luna, Mars, Mercurius (= Wednesday: Wodan's day), Jupiter, Venus, and

Saturn, and was thus identified, not only with the crucified Christ, but also with Hermes/Mercury/Thoth, Hellenistic Hermes Trismegistus (patron of the hermetic sciences, alchemy, and the like) as well as with a celestial sphere.

Similarly, in the Irish Book of Kells (late eighth to early ninth century), the symbolically illuminated, so-called *Tunc* page, bearing the text of Matthew 27:38 (*Tunc crucifixerant XRI cum eo duos latrones,* "Then there were crucified with him two thieves"), adds to the idea of the crucified Christ a number of mythological themes of a distinctly pagan, Neoplatonic, and perhaps even Oriental tantric cast.[101] The "ornamental animal style" of the illumination itself is identical, for example, with that of the pagan Norse, which in turn is but the northern reflex of an Old Germanic development of a Sarmatian-Scythian animal style of the Gothic Black Sea domain, the origins of which have been traced, on one hand, through Assyria back to Sumer and, on the other hand, into Turkestan, whence carried eastward, it evolved into the animal style of Shang China.[102] It is therefore not by coincidence (or by what anthropologists call "convergence") that the same dual and triple yin-yang symbols that appear on the heads of two drums flanking the altar in Tokyo of the Shinto Yasukuni Shrine (dedicated to the Japanese war-dead) also appear on certain pages of the Book of Kells.

The all-enclosing, feline-headed serpent of the *Tunc* page, shown swallowing fire from its own tail, is a counterpart of the Norse Midgard Serpent as the bounding power of the macrocosm, both as space (water) and as time (fire). Plato, in *Timaeus,* in his bewildering discussion of the four elements, identifies fire with the form of the tetrahedral pyramid (*Timaeus* 55b) and writes of fire as the beginning and end of creation. So we find it here represented as at the beginning and end of an eon. The discovery in Iceland of a stone pyramid among the remains of what appears to have been a Celtic-Christian monastery confirms what Pálsson had already predicted as a likely symbolic form to be found associated with such a site, signifying creation by fire, destruction by fire, the end of one era, the beginning of another, and the hallowing by fire of the land.

The all-enclosing serpent's folds support 3 panels containing 5 persons each, recalling the $3 \times 5 = 15$ crosses that are in Iceland associated with the 3 summits of Mount Thríhyrningur and the 5 joyous, 5 sorrowful, and 5 glorious mysteries of the Virgin; while the convoluted animal at the head of the page, representing Christ as a microcosm, matching the macrocosmic uroboros, appears to be either swallowing or disgorging two animal-headed snakes, one with the head of a fox, the other, of a cat. In color, one is blue, the other, red. Can these possibly correspond to the *iḍā* and *piṅgalā* nerves of the tantric lunar and solar breaths?

Fig. 5. *Tunc* page of the Book of Kells: *Tunc crucifixerant XRI cum eo duos latrones* (Matt. 27:38). Ireland, ninth century. Trinity College Library, Dublin. Drawing by John Mackay.

In Monasterboice (county Louth) there is a monumental Irish stone cross known as the Cross of the Abbot Muirdach (who died in 844), which bears on one side a caduceus-like engraving of two serpents, one upward-turned, the other downward, whose interlacing coils enframe three human heads (such as might refer to Chakras 4, 5, and 6), and with a large human right hand above, reaching up to rest upon a halo.[103] Known as *Dextra Dei,* "the Right Hand of God," such an ornament appearing on the cross of Christ Crucified cannot have been without meaning. But who shall now say what the meaning might have been?

Othin hung 9 days on the "windy tree," by virtue of which sacrifice he gained knowledge of the runes: Christ, 3 hours on Holy Rood, by virtue of which sacrifice he gained for mankind redemption from the mortal effects of the sin of Adam and Eve. Elaine Pagels, in her illuminated and illuminating book *The Gnostic Gospels,* interpreting a body of Jewish and Christian Gnostic texts recently discovered in a ceramic jar unearthed from the Egyptian desert (where it had been buried for preservation, apparently, about the time of the destruction of the Alexandrian *Mouseion*), points out that the gospel of the Gnostic Jesus, like that of Gautama Buddha, had to do, not with sin and redemption, but with illusion and enlightenment (*māyā* and *bodhi*).[104]

Othin sacrificed one eye for knowledge of the runes. One socket ever thereafter gazed inward, the other, ever outward, held to the world of phenomenality. The two interlacing snakes, red and blue, of the *Tunc* page of the Book of Kells are evidently of like meaning: one, of the knowledge inward of eternal life, the other, outward, of temporality; in tantric terms, respectively, "solar" consciousness (the nerve *piṅgalā*) and the "lunar" consciousness (the nerve *iḍā*), the "still point" and the "turning world," *nirvāna* and *saṃsāra,* which are to be known in the way of one "released while living" (*jīvan mukta*) as one and the same, *nirdvandva,* nondual.

This is the mystery symbolized in its simplest geometrical form as a dot in the center of a circle; also, as a dot in the center of a triangle; or, as Gimbutas found in her Neolithic goddess figurines, a dot within a lozenge of four angles. The Christian designation in the year 431 of Mary as *Theotókos,* the very Mother of God, represents the continuation into a later, patriarchal context of this same idea of a nondual goddess-creator of the gods and all things, "bisexual, absolute and single in her generative role," creating (like the spider its web) her world from her own substance. The idea is represented in Indian (Jaina) art in the image of the universe as of a woman's form, with the earthly plane at the level of her waist, heavens in series to the crown of her head, and purgatories to the soles of her feet.[105]

Fig. 6. *Dextra Dei*. Cross of Muirdach, Monasterboice, Ireland, tenth century.

In the Musée de Cluny, in Paris, there is a lovely little *Vierge Ouvrante* of the young mother seated with the Christ Child on her arm.[106] Her body can be opened as a cabinet to reveal a vision within, not only of her son already crucified, but also of the visage of God the Father, as well as God the Holy Ghost as a dove, together with the heavenly choir of saints and angels. And from the same period, in the late-medieval (Marseilles) Tarot deck (of which the earliest preserved examples are from an elegant deck prepared about 1392 by the artist Jacquemin Gringonneur for King Charles VI of France), the culminating symbolic image, displayed on trump card number 21, is of "The World," *Le Monde,* as a dancing nude female (the alchemical female androgyne), framed in a mandorla of 3 colors, yellow, red, and blue (Father, Son, and Holy Ghost), and showing in each of the card's 4 corners one of the Zodiacal signs of the 4 Evangelists.[107] Compare the twelfth-century west portal of Chartres cathedral, where, however, it is not the dancing Goddess Universe who thus appears as the culminating spiritual symbol but Christ of the Second Coming, at the end of time.[108]

Two contrary points of view are represented in this contrast: that of the eye and mind of phenomenality and temporality, anticipating the end of the world as a historical event, and that of the Gnostic transformation of consciousness, whereby the world as normally perceived dissolves in the way of Blake's realization announced in *The Marriage of Heaven and Hell:* "If the doors of perception were cleansed every thing would appear to man as it is, infinite." We find a similar statement of Jesus in the Gnostic Gospel According to Thomas (which, like a jinni of the Arabian Nights, has come out of that buried Egyptian jar): "His disciples said to him: When will the Kingdom come? Jesus said: It will not come by expectation; they will not say: 'See, here,' or 'See, there.' But the Kingdom of the Father is spread upon the earth and men do not see it" (Logion 113). And again: "For the Kingdom is within you and it is without you" (Logion 3).[109]

Othin, by virtue of his sacrifice of one eye, therefore, was enabled to summon from the earth an apparition of the prophetess, from whom he learned not only of the end of his eon of 432,000 years but also of the whereabouts of both the Gjallarhorn (by whose sounding the moment of dissolution was to be announced) and the eye that he had given in pledge to Mimir, spirit of the waters, for the gift of insight.

> I know the horn of Heimdallr, hidden
> Under the high-reaching holy tree;
> On it there pours from Valfather's pledge
> A mighty stream: would you know yet more?

Othin, I know where thine eye is hidden,
Deep in the wide-famed well of Mimir;
Mead from the pledge of Othin each morn
Does Mimir drink: would you know yet more?[110]

The sounding of the Gjallarhorn is to be understood in Gnostic/Pythagorean terms as the harbinger of an awakening, and Heimdallr, from whose breath the tone proceeds, is the Awakener. "He is called the White God," says Snorri. "He is great and holy; 9 maids, all sisters, bore him for a son [compare the 9 Muses with Apollo as a 10th]. He is called also Hallinskidi [the "Ram"] and Gullintanni ["Golden Teeth"]; his teeth were of gold; his horse's name is Gold-top; and he dwells hard by Bifrost [the rainbow bridge from earth to Valhall], in the place called Himinbjorg [Heaven-mount]."[111]

He is, in other words, the Nordic Anthropos. Schröder likens him to Mithra, the Iranian lord of the victory of light, born the night of the winter solstice from a virgin mother rock.[112] One may liken him also to Christ, the "Sacrificial Lamb" or "Ram," born that same night of his virgin mother in a cave. The implied association of Heimdallr as Ram is with the first sign, Aries, of the Zodiac and the spring equinox, namely, Easter. Pálsson makes the point, quoting as authority Ernest G. McClain in *The Myth of Invariance*, that Claudius Ptolemaeus (fl. in Alexandria, A.D. 127–148), correlated the 12 signs of the zodiac with the 15 tones of the Greek 2-octave "Greater Perfect System" in such a way that the Ram (Aries) stood for the ground tone, *Proslambanomene* (see Gafurius's chart, fig. 2), as well as the "limiting tone," *Nete hyperbolaion,* two octaves higher.[113]

Now, in the Pythagorean reckoning, the number of vibrations of Middle-A, *Proslambanomene,* is 432 (modern tunings are generally higher). One octave lower is 216; two octaves lower 108. These are all numbers of the Great Goddess, born, so to say, out of 9.

"At the end and presumably at the beginning of the world," states Pálsson, "Heimdallr blows his horn. . . . The sybil knows where the sound of Heimdallr is hidden:"

Under the high-reaching tree.
The sound of Heimdallr is hidden under the measuring rod of the universe . . .
the Ash Yggdrasil . . .
Voluspa clearly gives one to understand that the sound
resounds in the old tree:
Yggdrasil shakes, and shiver on high
The ancient limbs.

"It would seem the ancients knew," Pálsson continues, "that a certain note causes a thing to resound through the same number of vibrations in an object. If so, it would give a perfect answer to the question why the Ash resounds ("ymr") when Heimdallr blows his horn. It is the resonance of the numbers 108–216–432 which defines the physical world from beginning to end."[114]

Let us here recall the idea already noted from the Indian Vedas of sound, *śabda,* as generator of the perceived universe. "It shouts out the universe, which is not distinct from itself. . . . This is how it is *nāda,* 'vibration.' This is what is meant by the saying: 'Sound (*śabda*), which is of the nature of *nāda,* resides in all living beings.'" And from the Confucian philosopher Tung Chung-shu: "Tuned to the tone of Heaven and Earth, the vital spirits of man express all the tremors of Heaven and Earth, exactly as several citharas, all tuned on *Kung* [the tonic], all vibrate when the note *Kung* resounds. The fact of the harmony between Heaven and Earth and Man does not come from a physical union, from a direct action, it comes from a tuning on the same note producing vibrations in unison. . . . In the universe there is no hazard, there is no spontaneity; all is influence and harmony, accord answering accord."[115] Which is exactly what in the West is known as the Harmony of the Spheres, as represented in Gafurius's design by the lute held extended in Apollo's left hand while his right points to the Graces.

And so we find, indeed, as Pálsson has claimed, that "the world picture of pagan Iceland—the universe of the Vikings—was the SAME as that of the Romans and the Greeks." It was the same as that of India and China as well: a world picture of harmony and accord in the living body of a Mother Universe, who, as Marija Gimbutas's work has shown, was represented in the earliest Neolithic arts of Old Europe, 7000–3500 B.C., as the one "Great Goddess of Life, Death, and Regeneration."

The recognition of a mathematical regularity of $60 \times 432 = 25{,}920$ years in the pulse throughout the body of this universal being (as it were, the great diastole and systole of her heart), which appears to have been first registered in Sumer, c. 3500 B.C., had by 1500 B.C. given rise, from the Nile and Tigris-Euphrates to the Indus and Huang-ho, to four structurally homologous, monumental civilizations, shaped to mythologies metaphorical of a sublime indwelling life informing all things; which in the sixth century B.C. became associated by Pythagoras (a Greek contemporary of the Buddha) with the mathematical laws at once of music, geometry, astronomy, and meditation.

Both the pagan Nordic and early Celtic-Christian theologies of Europe were informed by the scientist insights of this fundamentally Gnostic, Pythogorean way of understanding and symbolization, which elsewhere in the

Latin West was systematically and most viciously suppressed by the champions of a historical institution that James Joyce has somewhere characterized as a "conspiracy of morbid bachelors." Irrepressibly, notwithstanding, the larger view from time to time broke through—in the Celtic, Pelagian heresy, Scotus Erigena's ruminations, Arthurian romance, the Grail legend, even the fortune-telling Tarot deck. In Dante's *Divina Commedia* it is boldly represented, and in the Neoplatonic Florentine academy of the Medicis it gained the field—simply by way of a recognition that all the forms of theological discourse are metaphorical of spiritual values, not to be understood as things-in-themselves.

"Man's last and highest leave-taking," declared the mystic Meister Eckhart, "is leaving God for God," leaving the historically conditioned idea of the God of one's faith for "that [to quote the *Upanishad*] to which speech goes not, nor the mind" (Kena 1.3).[116] Within the field of mythic thought, however, both metaphorically (as one's nature knows) and historically (as Gimbutas shows) the God beyond God is God's Mother.

Mythology and the Arts

Creativity

This business of creativity was greatly illuminated for me by a letter that Schiller wrote to a young poet who was having writer's block.[1] Schiller said to him, "Your problem is that you bring the critical factor down, before you have allowed the lyric to make its statement." Now, every creative act is going to be unprepared for, and consequently it is going to break rules. Any person in any of the arts must learn how to deal with this problem of knowing how a thing ought to be, and how it turns out as you bring it forth. You spend years studying the rules of art, that is, how it ought to be, according to certain essential laws for the development of a cogent form, but what comes out is not in that form. When you are in the act of creating, there is an implicit form that is going to ask to be brought forth, and you have to know how to recognize it. So, they say, you are to learn all the rules—and then you must forget them. As the lyric factor is beginning to move you, the mind is supposed to watch for the emergent form, because anything that comes out of the proper ground of inspiration is formed already. There is an implicit form intrinsic in it, and your job is to recognize it.

This personal creative act is related to the realm of myth, the realm of the muses, because myth is the homeland of the inspiration of the arts. The muses are the children of the goddess of memory, which is not the memory from up there, from the head; it is the memory from down here, from the heart. It is the memory of the organic laws of human existence that sends forth your inspirations. One can help oneself to know something about these laws by studying myths, particularly comparative mythologies. Each mythological system develops in a way that is different from that of another. By comparing the ways, one can see what archetypal form is being applied to this, that, or another mode of what might be called "life-prejudices," that is, what one thinks life ought to be, as the prejudices begin to take over and shape things.

I have become increasingly aware of the fact that there are two entirely different types of mythologies in the world. There are mythologies that emphasize, with more or less force, the sociological situation to which the myth is to be applied. These are socially based mythologies, and they insist on the laws of that social order as being *the* laws. We find this kind of mythology in the Bible. I imagine two thirds of the Old Testament is the statement of rules. Moses goes into the tent of the meeting and Yahweh gives him a set of rules, and then he goes the next day and there is another set, and this goes on and on and on. If you are going to live according to the rules, not of nature but of society, you have to have them written out for you. And again, throughout the Book of Kings, the kings are always making sacrifices on the mountaintops, but the text says that Yahweh did not approve of one or the other king because he neglected some set of rules. What was the worship on the mountaintops? It was the worship of the goddess Nature, that is what it was! So then, when you are studying mythology to find what the rules of nature are, avoid the Bible.

The nature rules live in the heart. The society rules and gods are always "out there." But the source of the lyric is in here, in the heart. And that is the sense of the inward-turned meditation. There is where the god is that is dictating to you. There is where the muses live, in your own heart, not out there in some book.

The classic example of this mythology is the Dionysian system. I was in San Francisco recently where I, John Perry (a Jungian analyst), and Mickey Hart (the drummer for the Grateful Dead), together with Jerry Garcia put on a program. Mickey Hart had composed a piece that he called "The African Queen Meets the Holy Ghost" especially for that conference, the name of which was "Ritual and Rapture from Dionysus to the Grateful Dead." It was my idea. I had had my first rock and roll experience at a performance of the Grateful Dead in Oakland six months earlier. Rock music had always seemed a bore to me, but I can tell you, at that concert, I found eight thousand people standing in mild rapture for five hours while these boys let loose everything on the stage. The place was just a mansion of dance. And I thought, "Holy God! Everyone has just lost themselves in everybody else here!" The principal theme of my talk was the wonderful innocence and the marvel of life when it recognizes itself in harmony with all the others. Everyone is somehow or other at one with everybody else. And my final theme was that this is the world's only answer to the atom bomb. The atom bomb is based on differentiation: I-and-not-that-guy-over-there. Divisiveness is socially based. It has nothing to do with nature at all. It is a contrivance and here, suddenly, it fell apart.

The socially oriented people, the church leaders, political leaders, and so forth, always get nervous when Dionysus gets going. The descriptions of the Dionysian movement that we get from the Greeks and Romans are from the point of view of people who do not like Dionysus.[2] You have the case of Pentheus, the Man of Sorrows, who is torn apart.[3] Well, Pentheus is exactly Christ being torn apart. He is the one that comes out of love and says, "Yes, of course you are torn apart. Your individual will and your individual enclosure in yourself is broken, and all the rules are gone."

Following rules is precisely the theme of T. S. Eliot's *The Waste Land*. Eliot got the title for the poem from the Waste Land theme in the twelfth- and thirteenth-century Grail romances. When Parzival, in the Grail castle, saw the wounded king before him, he was moved to ask, "What ails you, Uncle?" but there was a rule that a knight does not ask unnecessary questions. Here is an example where following rules inhibits spontaneity and the emotion of compassion, which is the only emotion that counts in the realm of religious experience. The awakening of compassion, "com-passion," *"Mit-leid,"* "suffering-with," enveloping that person's pain in your skin, so that you are suffering with him or her equally, this is the awakening of the heart. That is what it is all about, and that is what the lyric moment is: the awakening of the heart.

Years ago, when computers were beginning to come into their own, it is said that Eisenhower went into a room full of computers, and he put a question to them: "Is there a god?" So the computers started twinkling and doing the things computers do, and after about ten or fifteen minutes of this mysterious performance, a voice was heard, and the voice said, "Now there is."

When I bought my computer—anyone who has tried to work a computer knows what my experience was—I thought, well, I wonder what god it is that is in there? Being somewhat an expert on gods, I lived with this computer for a couple of months, and then I recognized the god. It was Yahweh of the Old Testament: a lot of rules and no mercy! But then, when you get to know the rules and your fingers obey them, it is fabulous what that thing can do!

This is the way it is with the rules in art. You have to learn to know them, and if it is a proper, up-to-date local art, the rules will have something to do with the life of people here and now, not a big smoochy general thing about life, but how it is here and now, what our problems and our mysteries are, here and now. You have to know your own day. You have to know your own relation to your own day, and then forget it! Let the thing build into you, the way my knowledge of my computer is built into me now. And then each of you can sing.

One of the big problems for young artists today—and I think I know a lot about them, because I have been living with artists ever since I graduated from college, a long time ago—is that they are all terribly frustrated in the bringing forth of their art, primarily because they have studied sociology. They always think there is a moral to be pointed out, something to be communicated.

Artists are not very good at telling you how it is that they got to be good, but there is one artist that I know of who did, and that was James Joyce. In *A Portrait of the Artist as a Young Man* he gives the best clue that I know of on how to create a work of art. In the last chapter, Stephen Dedalus explains to his friend Lynch the essential points of the artist's work. He tells him that there are two kinds of art. There is proper and improper art. Improper art is kinetic. Improper art moves you either with desire to possess the object or with loathing and fear to resist it and avoid it. Art that excites desire for the object he calls "pornographic." All advertising is pornographic art. Art that excites loathing and criticism of the object he calls "didactic," and so much of our writing, particularly in the first half of this century, has been didactic writing, what I call the work of "didactic pornographers."

Proper art is static. It holds you in ecstatic arrest—arrest at what? Joyce brings up Aquinas at this point, who says that in the art moment, the first experience is *integritas,* the beholding of one object set apart from all objects in the world. This is a thing, and within that thing what is important is the relation of part to part, and part to the whole, the rhythm, the rhythm of beauty. And this is the key of all art. This is the key of form. The rhythm is implicit in your own body. It is implicit in your expression. And when the rhythm is properly, fortunately achieved, the result is radiance, rapture, beholding it. Why? Because the rhythm before you is the rhythm of nature. It is the rhythm of *your* nature. Cezanne says somewhere, "Art is a harmony parallel to nature." Art is the rendition of the interface between your inner nature and the nature out there.

The natural mythologies are also art in that sense. They are modes, they are rhythms, in which everything is an expression of nature. When I was a student in Paris, back in the 1920s, I knew a sculptor, a very great sculptor, Antoine Bourdelle, who used to say, "L'art fait ressortir les grandes lignes de la nature" (art brings out the great lines of nature). And that is all it does. And why is it that you are held in aesthetic arrest? It is because the nature you are looking at is *your* nature. There is an accord between you and the object, and that is why you say, "Aha!"

In one of the *Upanishads* it says, when the glow of a sunset holds you and you say "Aha," that is the recognition of divinity. And when you say "Aha," to an art object, that is the recognition of divinity. And what divinity is it? It is *your* divinity, which is the only divinity there is. We are all phenomenal manifestations of a divine will to live, and that will and the consciousness of life is one in all of us, and that is what the artwork expresses.

Now this is what is meant by an archetype of the unconscious. An archetype of the unconscious is a recognized form, but the problem with it, when you begin to talk about it, is that it is not recognized at all; it is talked about. The thing gets to be a cliché, and it is no good any more. This is another great difficulty in the creative life. If you know exactly what it is you are creating, it is not going to work. You have turned it into a sign or a concept instead of a thing in itself. It has to come out beyond speech, as life does.

My great friend Heinrich Zimmer had a saying: "The best things cannot be told; the second best are misunderstood." The second best are misunderstood because they talk about what cannot be told and one thinks one knows what they are saying. This is the way religion is. The idea of God is an idea that is metaphoric of something that cannot be told, and yet we say that God is good, God is merciful, God is just, and God loves these people and not those, etc., etc. We are not talking about God at all. We are talking about our *idea* of

God. Meister Eckhart, in the thirteenth century, said, "The ultimate leave-taking is leaving God for God." The word that is missing is the other word. The European languages lack that very important word. Monotheism is idolatry in that it imagines its god to be the God for which you leave this one. The Hindus have the word *Brahman* or *ātman*. No Hindu, nobody east of Suez, would mistake god for God, mistake a god for *Brahman*. Gods are all metaphors of this ultimate mystery, the mystery of your own being. So God is not "out there"; God is in here. This is the source of the lyric, and what you are writing about is the word of God that is coming out. That is what is meant by inspiration. That is what is meant by the "Word of God." That life that is of your essence is talking through your inspirations. So let the mind up here relax and listen, not dictate, and recognize the implication of the word.

The Interpretation of Symbolic Forms

I was walking the other day in Washington Square, New York, and heard a little girl say to her father, "Daddy, why do all the churches have plus signs on top?" This I offer as an egregious misinterpretation of a symbolic form; but also as an occasion for asking how we should ourselves interpret the symbolic form of the Cross.

Actually, there are a couple of churches just to the south of Washington Square, one with a tall tower, the other not so tall, and each displays a cross. Interpreted in the simplest way in relation to that circumstance, the meaning of the cross would be: "This is a church." A post office, in that way of signaling, would have been flying an American flag; and in that sense the device is an emblem, sign, token, or signal, letting us know that this is a building of a certain kind. Or if one were driving along a highway and saw a yellow sign showing a black cross, one would know that there was a crossroad ahead. The signal is interpreted according to a context of conventional associations. The cross appears as a plus sign in mathematical equations, along highways as a warning, and over churches as an invitation to prayer.

But why, we now may ask, has this particular sign become the mark of a Christian church? Let us ask somebody who knows: a member, say, of the congregation. His reply will very likely be that the sign is a reference to a historical event: the historical crucifixion of Jesus, who was the founder of the religion represented in the building that is here displaying a cross on its top. That is another way of reading symbolic forms, as references to significant historical events.

But why—or in what way—significant? What was it that was so significant about this particular historical event: the nailing to a cross of this historical personage, condemned to death by his community for the sin of blasphemy? Crucifixion was a common form of punishment in those days. What was it about this particular case that transformed its sign from one betokening shame and disgrace to one befitting the designation of a church? As a knowledgeable informant would tell us, there is a great mythology associated with this particular crucifixion, namely, that of the redemption of mankind from the mortal effects of a calamitous event that occurred—according to report—long ago in a very distant period, when a serpent talked. The first man—the first example of the species *Homo sapiens*—had been forbidden by his creator to eat the fruit of a certain tree. Satan in the form of a snake tempted him (or rather his wife, who had been lately fashioned from one of his ribs) to eat of the forbidden tree. The couple ate, and thereupon both they and their progeny, the whole of the human race, were taken by the Devil in pawn. They could gain redemption only by the miracle of God himself in the person of his eternal son, Second Person of the Blessed Trinity, becoming incarnate in the person of that earthly Jesus who was crucified—not for blasphemy, finally then, but in order to redeem mankind from the Devil; or, according to another reading, to palliate the Creator's wrath by atoning through death for the heinous offense of that primal human act of disobedience.[1]

Clearly, the historical reading of the emblem has here become anomalous, not to say even bizarre, what with a talking serpent, a devil, and an incarnate god entering into the action. Such are not the characters of a readily credible history. And the question becomes further complicated once we notice, and take into account, the fact that in the jungles of Guatemala there is a Mayan temple known as the "Temple of the Cross," at Palenque, where there is a shrine exhibiting for worship a cross that is mythologically associated with a savior figure, named by the Mayans Kukulcan, and by the Aztecs, Quetzalcoatl: a name that is translated "Feathered Serpent," and suggests the mystery of a personage uniting in himself the opposed principles represented in the earthbound serpent and the released free flight of a bird.[2] Moreover, as the Scriptures related to this figure tell us, he was born of a virgin; died and was resurrected; and is revered as some sort of savior, who will return, as in a Second Coming. All this adds another, very troublesome, dimension to our problem of interpreting the symbolic form of the cross, since it must now be recognized, not simply or singly as a reference within one tradition to one historical event, but as a sign symbolically recognized in other traditions as well, and in significant association, moreover, with a number of related symbolic themes.

The figure of the Feathered Serpent linked with the Cross, for example, immediately suggests our own biblical Eden/Calvary continuity. Furthermore, on top of the Mayan cross there is a bird sitting, the quetzal bird, and at the base there is a curious mask, a kind of death mask. Now a number of paintings of the Crucifixion from late medieval times and the early Renaissance period show the Holy Ghost above, in the form of a dove, and beneath the foot of the cross, a skull.[3] The name of the hill of the Crucifixion, as we all know, was in Aramaic, Golgotha, and in Latin, Calvary, both of which words mean "skull." We do not know what interpretation the Mayans gave to their death mask; but in medieval Christian legend, the skull out of which the cross appeared to have grown, as a tree from its seed, was said to be Adam's: so that when the blood of the crucified Savior fell upon it from his pierced hands and feet, the First Man was, so to say, retroactively baptized, and with him the whole human race. Had there been no Tree of the Fall, there would have been no Tree of Redemption— no Holy Rood, as the Cross was called in the Middle Ages. The answer, therefore, to our question as to why the crucifixion of Jesus holds for Christians such importance implies a complex of essential associations that are not historical at all, but mythological. For, in fact, there was never any garden of Eden or serpent who could talk, nor solitary pre-Pithecanthropoid "First Man" or dreamlike "Mother Eve" conjured from his rib. Mythology is not history, although myths like that of Eden have been frequently misread as such and although mythological interpretations have been joined to events that may well have been factual, like the crucifixion of Jesus.

Let us, therefore, examine further the mythological aspect of this symbolic form, which the little girl in Washington Square interpreted as a plus sign on top of churches.

Those familiar with Germanic myth and folklore will recall that in the Icelandic Eddas (specifically, in Hovamol, verses 139–40 and 142) it is told that All-Father Othin, to acquire the Wisdom of the Runes, hung himself for nine days on the world tree, Yggdrasil.

> I ween that I hung on the windy tree,
>   Hung there for nights full nine;
> With the spear I was wounded, and offered I was
>   To Othin, myself to myself,
> On the tree that none may ever know
>   What root beneath it runs.
>
> None made me happy with loaf or horn,
>   And there below I looked;
> I took up the runes, shrieking I took them,
> And forthwith back I fell.
>
> Then began I to thrive, and wisdom to get,
>   I grew and well I was;
> Each word led me on to another word,
>   Each deed to another deed.[4]

No one can miss the parallels here to the Gospel themes of Jesus' three hours on the Cross ($3 \times 3 = 9$), the spear in his side, his death and resurrection, and the boon of redemption thereby obtained. The phrase, "and offered I was/To Othin, myself to myself," is interesting in the light of the Christian dogma of Christ and the Father as One.

Moreover, on top of Yggdrasil, this "Holy Rood" of Othin's suffering, an eagle is perched, like the quetzal bird on the top of the cross at Palenque; while at its roots a "worm" or dragon gnaws, Nithogg by name, who corresponds there to the earthbound serpent aspect of Quetzalcoatl, the Savior. And there is, further, a wonderful squirrel named Ratatosk ("Swift-Tusked"), who is continually running up and down the trunk, reporting to the eagle above the unpleasant things that the dragon is saying about him, and to the dragon below the abusive sayings of the eagle—which in a humorous way suggests to me a psychological process that C. G. Jung has termed "the circulation of the light," from below to above and above to below: the point of view of the unconscious conveyed to consciousness, and of consciousness to the unconscious. And there are, still further, four deer perpetually rotating around Yggdrasil, nibbling its leaves with necks bent back, like the four seasons of the year around the everliving Tree of Time, eating it away; and yet it continually grows. Yggdrasil, like that tree, is ever dying and simultaneously increasing. It is the pivotal tree of the universe, from which the four directions radiate, revolving as spokes of a wheel. And so, too, Christ's Cross has been represented symbolically as at the center of a mandala; just as in the Old Testament image of Genesis 2:8–14, Eden is described as with "the tree of life in the midst of the garden, and the tree of the knowledge of good and evil," and with a river, moreover, that divides and becomes four rivers, flowing in the four directions.

Mandala symbolism (with which, I take it, we are all, these days, fairly familiar) has been interpreted by Jung as grounded in what he identified as the four basic psychological functions by virtue of which we apprehend and evaluate all experience, namely, sensation and intuition, which are the apprehending functions, and thinking and feeling, which are those of judgment and evaluation.[5] A life governed by prudent forethought may be undone by an upsurge of feeling, just as one swayed by feeling may, for a lack of prudent forethought, be carried, one day, to disaster ("Never go out with strangers!"). The cruciform diagram below makes it evident that in this view of Jung's "four functions" we are dealing with the claims and forces of two pairs of opposites; for as feeling and thinking are opposed, so too are sensation and intuition.

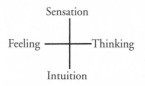

People aware only of the information of their senses, the most obvious actualities immediately present, may be disappointed or undone by unrecognized implications; whereas others, intuitive always of possibilities and implications, may be knocked down by a hard and present fact. In Jung's view, based on his work with patients, each of us tends to favor in the shaping of his life but one of the two functions of each pair—sensation and thinking, for example, which would leave intuition and feeling undeveloped; and any activation of the unattended functions tends to be experienced as threatening and is resisted. Moreover, since the resisted functions are undeveloped—"inferior," as Jung terms them—they are alien to the subject's understanding both of himself and of his world, and whenever they do break through, they overthrow controls and with compulsive force take over: the individual is "beside himself," out of control.

It is evident, then, that in our daily living we are but half men and that all societies actually favor and foster such a fractioning through their moral assignments of men's thoughts, words, and deeds either to the vice side or to the virtue side of their ledgers. Thus in the Christian system of symbolic forms, where the Cross is central, Heaven is above, to which the good go, and Hell below, to which the wicked are assigned; but on Calvary the cross of Jesus stood *between* those of the good thief and the bad, the first of whom would be taken up to Heaven, and the latter sent down to Hell. Jesus himself would descend into Hell before ascending to Heaven since, in his character as total man, eternal as well as historical, and transcendent thus of all pairs-of-opposites (male and female no less than good and evil, as was Adam before the Fall and before Eve had been taken from his rib), he transcends in his being all terms of conflict whatsoever, even that of God and Man. For, as Paul declared to the Philippians (Phil. 2:6–11): "though in the form of God, he did not count equality with God a thing to be grasped [or "held to"], but emptied himself, taking the form of a servant, being born in the likeness of men. And being found in human form he humbled himself and became obedient unto death, even death on a cross. Therefore God has highly exalted him and bestowed on him the name which is above every name, that at the name of Jesus every knee should bow, in heaven and on earth and under the earth, and every tongue confess that Jesus Christ is Lord, to the glory of God the Father."

In this beautiful passage an interpretation is given of the Savior as one uniting, as True God and True Man, eternal and temporal terms, transcending both (not "grasping"), yet to be known as both: as Christ, Second Person of the Trinity, and as Jesus, a once-living man, who was born and died in Palestine. Nailed to the cross, as a living historical man being put to death, he transcends death as he transcends life. The symbolism is obvious: to his left and right are the opposed thieves; himself, in the middle, will descend with one and with the other ascend to that height from which he has already come down. Thus Christ is bound to neither of the opposed terms, neither to the vertical nor to the horizontal beam of his cross, though historically he is indeed bound, even crucified—as we all are in our own lives. We, however, through faith in his image, are unbound and "saved."

If we read this metaphor of crucifixion in the psychological terms suggested by Jung's designation of sensation and intuition, feeling and thinking, then we recognize that in our living—in our temporal, historical living—we are bound either to one or to the other of the opposed terms of each pair, and hence to a knowledge or idea of good and evil that commits us to living as but part men. It follows that to be released from this limitation one must in some sense die to the law of virtue and sin under which one lives in this world and judges, opening oneself to a circulation of energy and light through all four of the functions, while remaining centered in the middle, so to say, like the Tree of Life in the garden, where the rivers flow to the four directions; or like the point of crossing of the two beams of the cross, behind the head of the Savior, crowned with a crown of thorns. "Our old self," states Paul, "was crucified with him so that the sinful body might be destroyed. . . . For sin will have no dominion over you, since you are not under law but under grace" (Rom. 6:6 and 14).

The horizontal beam of the specifically Christian cross, by the way, is fixed, not at the middle of the vertical beam, but higher, at the level of the Savior's head. At the middle it would have crossed at the genitals and have thereby represented a phallic centering—like that of Yahweh's Old Testament law for those circumcised in the Covenant, where the religion is of race; whereas the Christian is of faith, belief, the mind and heart, to which members of any race whatsoever may be joined.

Hinduism, like Judaism, is an ancient religion of race, caste, or birth, and there, too, a phallic symbolism is recognized, the *lingam* and *yoni* (symbolized male and female organs) appearing in the central sanctuaries of temples; whereas in Buddhism, which, like Christianity, is a creedal religion of belief and faith, not of birth and race, the central symbol is that of the Savior with the accent on his illuminated head.

❦ ❦ ❦

In mandala symbolism generally, the sign or figure at the center of the quadrated circle is crucial, in every sense of the word. Like the hub of a turning wheel, it is at the point where opposites come together: East and West, North and South, right and left, up and down; also, motion and rest, time and eternity; as in the words of T. S. Eliot in "Burnt Norton":

> At the still point of the turning world. Neither flesh nor fleshless;
> Neither from nor towards; at the still point, there the dance is,
> But neither arrest nor movement. And do not call it fixity,
> Where past and future are gathered. Neither movement from nor towards,
> Neither ascent nor decline. Except for the point, the still point,
> There would be no dance, and there is only the dance.
> I can only say, *there* we have been: but I cannot say where.
> And I cannot say, how long, for that is to place it in time.[6]

The ancient cities of Sumer, Akkad, and Babylon, from whose mythological systems much biblical myth was derived, were organized roughly in quarters, with a towering temple of the presiding god at the center. This "height" or "ziggurat," as it was called, at the summit of which heaven and earth came to-gether, was symbolic of the *axis mundi,* the world center, where the vitalizing energy of eternity entered the revolving sphere of space-time—as known from the revolving night-sky.

In Buddhist iconography, the Lord Buddha is represented as seated at the foot of a tree, that Bodhi-tree, or "Tree of Awakening," where he achieved illu-mination and thus release from the bondages of the senses, delusion, or, in Sanskrit, *māyā,* which is a word referring to the way in which we generally ex-perience life in the world. It is well defined as *a partial interpretation of a partial experience of the universe:* a misinterpretation of the totality of being, and the living of one's life. On the basis of that fractional glimpse, we are beset by fears and desires that are irrelevant to reality and only intensify the falsification. The Buddha's Tree of Awakening, known as the Immovable Point, is symbolic of that psychological state in which such desires and fears are quelled absolutely, and the mind, so cleared, comes to a knowledge of its own transcendence of all temporal terms and forms.

Plainly, we have a counterpart here to the Christian idea of salvation from sin, and the two historical saviors, Gautama the Buddha (563–483 B.C.) and Jesus the Christ (c. 3 B.C.–A.D. 28?), are in similar roles. The Bodhi-tree of the Buddha and Holy Rood of the Christ are thus in some way homologous in their world-saving roles, even though the vocabularies of the two great religions dif-fer significantly.[7] The Christian is phrased in terms of sin and redemption, or atonement; the Buddhist, in terms of ignorance and enlightenment, or awak-ening. An essential question to be asked, therefore, in relation to the problem of interpreting these symbolic forms, is that of distinguishing the "vehicle" from the "tenor" of their arguments. We must ask if an essential identical message ("tenor") is not implicit in the two, one that underlies the differences in the vo-cabularies ("vehicles"). Are *ignorance* and *sin,* finally, two words for the same condition? Are *enlightenment* and *redemption* two ways of pointing to the same spiritual or psychological crisis? If so, then which vocabulary is the more ex-plicit? If not, what are the essential differences in doctrine?

We are coming very close to some pretty serious questions of religious be-lief, touching the origins of mythological forms, as well as to a number of rather obscure historical and psychological problems.

What is sin? According to the *Catechism of Christian Doctrine* that I learned to quote by heart in primary school: "Sin is an offense against the law of God," and is of three kinds: venial, mortal, and original. "What," we were asked, "is venial sin?" "Venial sin is a slight offense against the law of God in matters of less importance; or in matters of great importance it is an offense committed without sufficient reflection or full consent of the will." "And what is mortal sin?" "Mortal sin is a grievous offense against the law of God." To make such an offense mortal, three things are necessary: "a grievous matter, sufficient reflection, and full consent of the will." "Why is this sin called mortal?" "This sin is called mortal because it deprives us of spiritual life, which is sanctifying grace, and brings everlasting death and damnation on the soul." "So what, then, is original sin?" "Original sin," runs the answer, "is the sin that comes down to us from our first parents; we are brought into the world with its guilt on our soul." "And what is the effect of this guilt?" "Our nature was corrupted by the sin of our first parents, which darkened our understanding, weakened our will, and left in us a strong inclination to evil."[8]

But are not this darkened understanding, weakened will, and inclination to evil exactly what the Buddhists mean by ignorance, fear, and desire; namely, *māyā?* And is it really necessary, or even useful, to interpret these well-known effects of our normally deluded psychological condition as having been historically *caused* by the "sinful" act of an originally undeluded first parent of the human race? At what stage in the entire course of the evolution of our species are we to postulate the appearance of such a first parent? Indeed, is not the whole problem of our release from the "cloud of unknowing" in which we live only confounded and rendered the more dark by the literal acceptance of the imagery of such a symbolic tale as a chronicle of fact?

The crucial point of my argument is that the imagery of religions—whether of the high religions, or of the simpler nonliterate, primitive forms—is gravely misinterpreted, or rather, is interpreted misleadingly when it is understood to apply primarily to historical events. Such a mythologem, for example, as the Virgin Birth: Was that a historical event? If so, it presents a biological, medical problem, far indeed from anything that might properly be regarded as of spiritual interest. It cannot have referred originally to any specific historical event because we find it in mythologies throughout the world. It is a prominent motif in the mythologies of mankind, and many examples antedate by millennia that of the Christian legend. The symbology of religion is, in many of its most essential elements, common to the whole of the human race; so that, no matter to what religion you may turn, you will—if you look long enough—find a precise and often illuminating counterpart to whatever motif of your own tradition you may wish to have explained. Consequently, the reference of these symbols must be to something that is antecedent to any historical events to which they may have become locally applied. Mythological symbols come from the psyche and speak to the psyche; they do not spring from or refer to historical events. They are not to be read as newspaper reports of things that, once upon a time, actually happened.

So let us return to our consideration of the cross in relation to its mythological prelude, the fairy tale of the serpent who could talk, and the Fall of Man in the garden—which supplies the upbeat to the downbeat of our story of man's need for redemption. We all well know the amusing tale as recounted—without any sense, however, of its fun—in the second chapter of Genesis. It is based on a folktale-type known to folklorists as "the one forbidden thing"—of which "Bluebeard" is a good example ("You may open all the doors in my castle but one!"). It commences with a scene of pre-dawn peace, quiet, and wondrous solitude, as do many of the world's delightful early tales of the Earth-Shaper and his giving of life to creatures of his imagination.

In this version, God had a garden, and what he required for it was a gardener; and so he created a man of dust, breathed into his nostrils the breath of life, and there he was, alive, All-Father Adam, God's gardener. But, alone as he was, he was bored. God had formed out of the ground every beast of the field and every bird of the air, and now God brought them to Adam for his entertainment, but all he could think of to do with them was to name them—after which they went off to nibble grass or to eat each other somewhere else—as is the wont of beasts of the field. In any case, Adam still was bored. And so God—working this thing out as he went along—had a big idea. He put Adam to sleep, took out one of his ribs, and fashioned of it the first girl in the world, whom Joyce in *Finnegans Wake* calls "the cutletsized consort," All-Mother Eve. But now there *she* was with nothing to do, and now it was *she* who was bored. For there was Adam, after the first couple of hours of mutual surprise, back at his steady job of cutting the grass, watering trees, and taking care of the garden, while she simply stood around, watching for a while, possibly with some interest, but then, sitting, dreaming, eating candy perhaps. Then, as always occurs in such circumstances, along came this snake, the most subtle, we are told, of all God's wild creatures. The gardener having been warned by God not to eat the fruit of that one tree, of the knowledge of good and evil (this is the "one forbidden thing"), the serpent, seeing Eve idle, seduced her into doing just that. "God told my husband," she said to him, "'You shall not eat of the fruit of that tree, neither shall you touch it, lest you die.'" But the serpent said to her, "You will not die. Rather, when you eat, your eyes will be opened and you will be like God." That was enough. Seeing that the tree was good for food and, moreover, a delight to the eyes, she plucked and ate and her eyes opened. Adam arrived when his work was done, and there she was, already wiser than he, and she gave him to bite, and he ate, and his eyes were opened too; and he realized what she must already have observed, namely, that both of them were naked. And so (for some reason that I can't figure out, but that must be known to the clergy), they sewed fig leaves together and made aprons for themselves. When God walked in the garden in the cool of day and saw them, he asked, "Who told you that you were naked? You have leaves on! Have you eaten of that tree?" Adam blamed Eve, Eve blamed the serpent, and the upshot of it all was that this god—who was, as he later explained, "a jealous god" (Exod. 20:5)—became fearful, because, as he told the angels, "the man has become like one of us, knowing good and evil; and now, lest he put forth his hand and take also of the tree of life, and eat, and live for ever; Therefore," as our Scripture says, "the Lord God sent him forth from the garden of Eden, to till the ground from which he was taken. He drove out the man; and at the east of the garden of Eden he placed the cherubim, and a flaming sword which turned every way, to guard the way to the tree of life" (Gen. 3:22–24).

A likely tale! Yet this is the famous story of the Fall, on which is founded the idea of our need for atonement with an offended God, and on this, then, the Christian religion. In fact, this is the authorized answer to the little girl's question in Washington Square, as to why all the churches have plus signs on top. Until only a few years ago, a person could be put to death for openly questioning the validity of this fairy tale as *the* authorized, eyewitness account of an actual historical, or prehistorical, misadventure: the eyewitness, of course, being God himself, and this Word of God being revealed to the only people in the world who know what God is and how he should be worshiped. By this account, the gods of the Gentiles—of the Greeks and Romans, Germans, Hindus, and the rest—are, if not devils, then mere figments of man's misguided imagination, as Yahweh and the serpent in the garden are not.

What does this signify? Is the Christian religion founded on nothing more respectable than this museum piece of a misinterpreted folktale? If we accept such a position, do we have to jettison the whole shipload of symbols that have been the spiritual cargo of our passage in the Western World through the seas of two thousand years? Let us see if something can be made of this bit of nonsense by interpreting it, not as history, but as poetry, mythology: not by *de*mythologizing the Bible (as one school of theologians would have it, the book has already been demythologized enough through its interpretation as fact), but by *re*mythologizing it as symbolic of the spirit. The documents of religion—any religion, all religions—are to be read, not as early editions of the *New York Times,* but as poetry. Do we ask if the Ancient Mariner of Coleridge actually lived? or if there was a historical Huckleberry Finn? And if there was not, is the sense of the imagery lost? Popular religion, by and large, is a misinterpretation of great poetry, and the corollary of this statement is that the poet is the prophet and that the great poets of today are our prophets for today—not every little versifier, but those poets who in vision or experience have penetrated the mysteries of the veils of time to a knowledge transcending the foreground view of life that rules in the marketplace.

One of the most effective ways to rediscover in any myth or legend the spiritual "tenor" of its symbolic "vehicles" is to compare it, across the reaches of space, or of time, with homologous forms from other, even greatly differing traditions.[9] The underlying core then is readily unshelled from its local, historically conditioned provincial inflections, applications, or tendentious secondary interpretations, and a shared psychological, or spiritual, ground is opened, transcending the conditions of space and time, and of history. For a tradition such as our own, where so much official emphasis has gone into insisting on the local historicity of the generally inherited symbols, such an opening of the eyes to wider horizons and other traditions may work as a marvelous restoration to life and sense of the apparently moribund forms.

Let us go to Nara, the holy city of Japan, where there is a prodigious image of the mythical Buddha known as Mahavairochana, "Great Sun Buddha" (in Japanese, Dainichi Nyorai). The statue is an image of bronze, fifty-three-and-a-half feet high, cast and installed in A.D. 749.[10] What it represents is not the historical Buddha Gautama, who lived and taught in India and Nepal, 563–483 B.C. but a purely and frankly visionary figure, symbolic, in human form, of the light of unclouded consciousness. The counterpart in Christian thought is the Beatific Vision described by Dante at the end of *La Divina Commedia*. Gautama, the historical Buddha, is understood to be an incarnation of the consciousness here envisioned as transcendent; but so, according to Buddhist thought, are we all, only unawakened. The word *buddha* means "awakened." And Gautama's awakening to his Buddhahood at the foot of the "Tree of Awakening"—that "still point of the turning world"—Buddhists regard as a model for us all to follow, toward the realization of our own transcendence-in-truth of the nightmare of our lives in time. Wrote our own poet, Wordsworth: "Our birth is but a sleep and a forgetting"; and Shakespeare, in *The Tempest:*

> We are such stuff
> As dreams are made on, and our little life
> Is rounded with a sleep.

And then we have William Blake: "If the doors of perception were cleansed every thing would appear to man as it is, infinite."[11] Thus we have the message in our own tradition, where it is known, however, as poetry, not religion, while our religion, actually, as I have already said, is being radically misinterpreted because it is read differently from a poem or enacted play.

So let us return for a moment to the poetry of that Japanese temple in Nara of the Buddha Mahavairochana. The approach from the south is guarded by an imposing gate, with a guardian standing at either side in the form of a large wooden statue, twenty-six-and-a-half feet high. The statues stand in threatening attitude, bearing weapons. The mouth of one is open, the mouth of the other is closed. Their look is frightening. They are known as "Thunderbolt Warriors"; in Sanskrit, *Vajrapani;* in Japanese, *Kongōrikishi.*[12] They are the counterparts, in the Buddhist mythic image, of the cherubim placed by Yahweh at the gate of Eden to guard "the way to the tree of life." I recall seeing in a New York newspaper, during the war with Japan, a picture of one of these imposing images, with a caption that read: "The Japanese worship gods like this"—a piece of information, no doubt derived from what in journalese is known as a "reliable source," and published, of course, with high regard for the American public's "right to know." But I had a wicked, uncooperative thought. "No," I thought, "not they but we! It is we who worship a god like that." For in the Buddhist world the worshiper is instructed to walk right between those two gate guardians and approach the tree without fear; whereas, as told in the Book of Genesis, our own Lord God put his cherubim there to keep the whole human race *out.* The Buddha sits with his right hand raised in the "fear not" posture and his left in that of "boon bestowing." One is not to be intimidated by the death threat of those guardians, but to cast aside the fear of death and come through to the knowledge of one's own Buddhahood—or, as that thought would be rephrased, in biblical terms: one's own Godhood, as Yahweh himself recognized when, in Genesis 3:22, he expressed the fear to his angels that man might "become like one of us . . . take of the fruit, and eat, and live forever."

The tree, the gate, and the cherubim: it is a shared symbolic image that the two religions have inherited. But their interpretations differ. Let us ask, specifically, in what way. And let us begin by considering in Buddhist terms the force or meaning of the two cherubim, those "Thunderbolt Holders," at the gate.

First, the mouth of one is closed, and of the other, open. They are thus a pair of opposites. Good and evil are a pair of opposites; so, also, male and female—as Adam and Eve realized when, having eaten of the fruit of the tree, they saw that they were naked. The exile followed this discovery of duality, opposition, separation: it was then that they became separated from God. Approaching the imposing gate of the Buddhist temple at Nara, we too are separated, being not yet within, but outside, the garden. Its two giant guardians are threatening; if they were not of wood, but alive, we should indeed be terrified on beholding them. We should become aware of another pair of opposites, our own fear of death and desire for life: fear and desire. But these, in the Buddhist legend of Gautama's achievement of enlightenment, were exactly the two chief temptations that he overcame while sitting on the "Immovable Spot" beneath the axial tree, at the "still point of the turning world." The god whose name is "Lust (Kama) and Death (Mara)" approached and, to unsettle him, displayed, in his character as the Lord of Lust, his three voluptuous daughters. Had Gautama, sitting there, had any thought of "I," he would have thought "They," and there would have been a response; but there was none; the temptation failed. Transforming himself, therefore, into his character as the Lord of Death, the Antagonist hurled an army of ogres against the one there sitting; but again there was no identification with ego; no sense of fear was evoked, and the temptation failed.

Likewise in ourselves, if our attachment to ego has not been conquered, so that the fear of death and a desire for continued life are still the governing principles of our experience and action, we are unfit psychologically to pass through the guarded gate to the Immovable Spot, where the Buddha sits. Physically we may go through the gate and walk along the broad path into the temple, there to stand taking pictures, or in prayer; but we shall not by that physical act have made the passage psychologically. Or we can even go to India, on pilgrimage to Bodh Gaya, where the tree still stands under which Gautama achieved illumination: we can view that tree, take pictures of it, worship it, and yet not be viewing the same tree at all under which the Buddha sat. For the Bodhi-tree is not geographically situated—as Eden was once thought to be—but is within us, and to be found there; and what is keeping us away from it is attachment to our separate lives as egos—to *ahamkara,* as the Indians say, "the making of the sound, *I.*"

In other words: it is our own attachment to our temporal lives that is keeping us out of the garden. Could we get rid of this, we should walk in truth through what has been called, in a Japanese Zen Buddhist work, "The Gateless Gate," *Mu-mon,* since nothing is there, no cherub at either hand, only our own misidentification of ourselves with our mortal part.

In all mystical lore, a passage through the door of death leads to immortal life; not our merely physical, historical dying (that is the popular reading of the mystery), but a psychological dying to the fear of death. This means that one's center of self-identification has to be shifted from the temporal personality to that, within, which neither was born nor will die, but is eternal. And the whole sense of Buddhism, accordingly, asserts that only when our thirst for life and the life-chilling fear of death are quenched can we know that, within, which has always been there, antecedent to and transcendent of the limitations of the mortal personality. And in this knowledge, all categories, whether of experience, of thought, or of feeling, are transcended; all names and forms, all pairs of opposites, whether of I and Thou, good and evil, yes and no, life and death, or even being and nonbeing, God and the soul.

But returning from this Eastern, Buddhist sojourn for one more glance into our Western book of conundrums—not into its Old, however, but into its New Testament: is it not evident that Jesus, crucified on the Tree of Eternal Life, Holy Rood—that second tree of Eden, the way to which was guarded by Yahweh's cherubim and flaming sword—must have passed through the guarded gate to the Tree and thus opened the gate to ourselves? Indeed, is that not precisely the sense of the term "*New* Testament?" Fearless of death, and clinging neither to life nor (as we have read in Paul to the Philippians) to the form of God, he emptied himself altogether of both temporal and eternal categories, whether of experience, of thought, or of feeling.

"And at the ninth hour [Othin's ninth day!] Jesus cried with a loud voice, '*Éloi, Éloi, láma sabachtháni?*' which means, 'My God, my God, why hast thou forsaken me?'" (Mark 15:34). For he had himself just broken past the bounds, the categories, within which gods and their laws, justices and mercies, operate; sprung like an arrow from its bow into the void, where Father and Son, all opposites, vanish. "And the curtain of the temple was torn in two, from top to bottom" (Mark 15:38).

"I am the door of the sheep," he is reported to have said, in the second-century Gospel According to John. "I am the door; if any one enters by me, he will be saved, and will go in and out and find pasture. . . . I lay down my life, that I may take it again. No one takes it from me, but I lay it down of my own accord. I have power to lay it down, and I have power to take it again; this charge I have received from my Father" (John 10:7, 9:17–18).

But now, who was the Father so named? Yahweh? He who had blocked the road, and the veil of whose temple was rent? Throughout the early Christian centuries this question was in sharp dispute, and the answer that those called Gnostics gave was, to Yahweh, a definite "No!" The Father of the Savior was of another mythology entirely, of eternal light and grace, not of history and the law. "For Christ is the end of the law" (Rom. 10:4). The Greek word *gnosis,* "a knowing, knowledge," and especially "higher knowledge, deeper wisdom," is precisely a counterpart of the Sanskrit *bodhi.* Gnostics, or *gnostikos,* in their various sects, interpreted salvation as did the Buddhists, as the opening of an inward, intuitive eye, or door to illumination. In the second-century Gospel According to Thomas, for example, the following words are attributed to Jesus, when asked by his disciples, "When will the Kingdom come?" Jesus said, "It will not come by expectation; they will not say: 'See, here,' or: 'See, there.' But the Kingdom of the Father is spread upon the earth and men do not see it" (Logion 113).[13] We are not, that is to say, locked out of the garden: it is here, over all the earth, and requires only a change in vision to be recognized. Moreover, this is the change of vision symbolized in the figure of Jesus on the cross: the crucifixion there of the temporal personality, but simultaneously also of the form of God, which was not held to, but was "humbled," becoming "obedient unto death." In other words, we have here, already in the Christian sphere, a spiritual, or psychological, nonhistorical interpretation of the mythic image, altogether in contrast to that which later gained supremacy with the victory in the fourth and fifth centuries of Byzantine orthodoxy. With that victory the opposition between the symbols of the Fall in Eden and redemption on Golgotha, of which Paul had made so much, was interpreted historically, first, as an original offense against God; second, as a subsequent act of atonement; and third, as an ultimate, general coming of the Kingdom at the end of time. The psychologically oriented Gnostic view, on the other hand, is in accord, not only with the Buddhist interpretation of symbolic forms, but also with the Greek, of the mystery cults—indeed, with the ways of all *poetic* approaches to life in its finally ineffable wonder. And since there are many grades, stages, or inflections, of insight recognized and recognizable in these nonhistorical, nondogmatic approaches to the mystery, let me now bring this discussion to a close by reviewing, in the briefest terms, one of the most illuminating systematizations of the graded orders of spiritual realization that has yet been given to the world. It will serve to show us that mythic images should be interpreted poetically, not literally or historically.

I refer to the Indian system of *Kuṇḍalinī,* or unfoldment of the so-called Serpent Power, which is an interpretation, in terms of seven steps, of the transformations of human insight by the vitalizing energies of the psyche rising from states conditioned by fear and desire to those of rapture and transcendent light.[14] The Sanskrit noun itself, *Kuṇḍalinī,* suggests a serpent coiled like a rope (*kuṇḍala,* the coil of a rope). It is a feminine noun and a feminine snake, since in India the moving energy of the psyche and body is symbolized as female. Pictured as coiled, asleep, within a "lotus" (*padma*) or "circle" (*chakra*) at the base or root of the body, situated between the anus and sex organs, this shining female serpent, fine as the fiber of a lotus stalk, is, through yoga, roused and caused to ascend, uncoiling, up the interior of the spine to the crown of the head, where it unites in ecstasy with the radiance of a thousand-petaled lotus known as *Sahasrāra*, "Thousand Sectioned."

In this ancient system of symbology, which comes down apparently from Old Bronze Age times, 2000 B.C. or so, the human spine is represented as equivalent, in the individual body, or microcosm, to the axial tree or mountain of the universe, the macrocosm—the same mythical *axis mundi* symbolized both in the tree of Eden and in the towering ziggurats in the centers of ancient Mesopotamian cities. It may be recognized, also, in the Dantean Mount Purgatory, where the seven ascending stages represent steps in the purification of the soul on its way to the light of the Beatific Vision. The stages of the ascending *Kuṇḍalinī* also are seven, there being between the root base and crown five intermediate lotuses; and as each is touched and stirred by the rising serpent energy, the psychology of the yogi is transformed.

Now what I propose to do is to follow this ascent in its seven stages. My interest, particularly, will be to suggest something of the attendant transformations, not only in psychology, but also in the very ways of interpreting symbolic forms. The reader, if he likes, may try to identify the stations of his own manner of life—his own way of producing *māyā* for himself—in the sequence of these archetypal steps in the amplification of human consciousness. However, the manner of my own discussion is to be neither hortatory nor moralistic, but—at least as far as I can make it so, enwrapped as I am in my own *māyā*—objective, descriptive, and (to use the word rather loosely) scientific.

For this is an old, old, tried-and-true construction of insights that have been gained from centuries of inward, yogic explorations of a landscape that is interior to us all, and as real and actual to an inward view as are the landscapes of the external world to our outward-gazing eyes. Moreover, since each of us, from the point of view of others (and even of ourselves when we are looking into a mirror), is but a particle or feature of nature, so our inwardness in its transpersonal, archetypal, generically human character must be a portion of nature too. When we adventure into our own depths, we are adventuring into nature's depths, and the landscapes here disclosed are interior, not only to ourselves, but also to everything seen as outside. I have myself been interested for many years in the psychological formulations of this yoga, and am now completely convinced of its relevance to the interpretation of the symbolic forms, not only of all Oriental, but also of our own Occidental arts and religions.

To begin, then: the first station, circle, or lotus of the *Kuṇḍalinī*, which, as already told, is at the root or base of the body, is called, appropriately, *Mūlādhāra*, the "Root Base." One's spiritual energy on this level is without any impulse toward or zeal for life. One is simply gripping, hanging on. I think, when considering this chakra, of the character of dragons. We know a great deal about dragons. Their biology and sociology have been studied for thousands of years and described in legends from every part of the world. What dragons do is guard things. The typical situation is that each dragon has a cave, where it diligently guards captured things. These are, most usually, a beautiful virgin girl and a heap of gold (the symbolic values, namely, of the next two chakras up the line); but the dragon has no idea what to do with either. It simply hangs on, guarding. It experiences none of the joys of life generally associated with these two precious things. There are people like this; they just hang on; we call them "creeps." They have no impulse to adventure. They are not properly actors, but re-actors, responding unimaginatively to sheer stimuli. The system of psychology most appropriate to their state of consciousness is Behaviorism: the science of man as worm, and the art favored by such a person—if he has any taste for art at all—will be sentimental naturalism. His attitude toward living will be that which Nietzsche has called a groveling before "hard facts."

The first goal of any shining hero seeking to release the values of the spirit from the guardianship of such unimaginative worms must be to lance them, like a knight, and break the hold of their dragon grip. Accordingly the yogi, by deep and measured breathing, appropriate meditations, controlled body postures, hand postures, the recitation of stirring syllables, and so on, will strive to wake the torpid serpent of his spiritual life from its lethargy, its sleep, its unadventurous dream, to better things; lifting it, in its full, unfolding length, up the long spinal course to the crown, and rousing on its way all the other lotuses of our human potential to their flowering.

And so now, following him in this enterprise, we arrive with our own *kundalinīs* at Lotus Two, the name of which, *Svadhishthana,* means approximately "Her Favorite Resort." It is the lotus of sexual zeal, desire, at the level of the genitals. At last we have a sense of excitement. We are no longer mere reactors, but originators of action; not grovelers before hard facts, for love, as they say, is blind. The facts, indeed, hardly matter; and when finally they do show through, we may find ourselves disillusioned. That is one of the standard crises of marriage. But in the meantime, this lout of a boy and goose of a girl shine for each other like gods. They are on Cloud Nine. They walk, a little on air. Or, described from another point of view, they may be said to have recognized, in their desire for each other, something of the godliness that is actually ingenerate in us all, but is normally encoiled in dragon brawn. One's psychology is, in any case, Freudian at this level. The whole view of life is sexually inspired: one's joys and frustrations are of sex; one's sublimations are of sexual zeal (Freud's libido); and though the frustrations are unremitting and the sublimations viable, a lot of distracting work gets done, and therein is the origin and meaning of civilization: one writes a Ph.D. dissertation, for example, say on Sexual Intercourse; and at the age of forty-five one gets the Ph.D., at the age of twenty having lost the girl.

Chakra Three is at the level of the navel and is known as *Manipura,* "The City of the Shining Jewel." The desire at this level is to consume things, to convert them into oneself or into one's own. The psychology is that of the conqueror, the winner, the master—or, if negatively aspected, the loser, the toady, or the seeker of revenge. In short, the psychology here is of Adler: the will to power.

We must recognize that mankind shares the modes of these three lower Chakras with the animals, for they too hold on to life, no matter how dull it may be; they too have sexual zeal; and they too know the drive to conquer and to overcome. People living with these interests are fundamentally outward turned; their goals are outside, their happiness and fulfillments; and they have to be controlled by law and by inculcated ethical principles, lest they become wolves unto each other. In the main, therefore, it is to mankind on these three levels that the secular laws and institutions of a society are addressed.

But now we come to something else, something specifically human, at the Fourth Chakra, the lotus of the heart: an awakening of the spiritual life. For those aware only of the values of the first three levels of experience, the conditions of their own physical birth are what determine and govern their destinies. But when the rising *Kuṇḍalinī* reaches the level of the heart, the spiritual birth occurs, a new inward life, specifically human; and this is symbolized in the mythological image of the Virgin Birth. The Savior so born— not in the natural way—is *symbolic* of the release of our own spirit from the bondages of unilluminated animality; and he is to be so born in each of us. For as the mystic Meister Eckhart phrased the argument in a beautiful sermon on this mystery: "It is more worth to God his being brought forth ghostly in the individual virgin or good soul than that he was born of Mary bodily."[15] The symbolical attribution of such a birth physically to an actual historical personage, accordingly, is not to be taken literally, but in its teaching sense, as representing the *meaning* of his life to us: the spirituality of his life, which is to become the inspiration and model of our own.

Reading such an upward-leading symbol downward, to the physical plane from which its imagery is meant to release us, only breaks the force of its effectuality—and this whether the physical misreading is of the Pope in Rome or of Dr. Freud. For the interpretation of mythic symbols is to be (using Eckhart's vocabulary) "ghostly," not "bodily"; their entire justification lies in their representation to our senses of an intuitable mystery-dimension that is metaphysical to physical things. However, the power or, rather, the willingness of the physically oriented intellect to waken to the ghostly metaphors and to follow them is a function of its own transformation—or in churchly terms, conversion—at the level of Chakra Four, prior to which crucial event the "Word behind words" cannot even be heard. Hence the oft-quoted saying of the ghostly born, historical Jesus: "Do not give dogs what is holy; and do not throw your pearls before swine, lest they trample them underfoot and turn to attack you" (Matt. 7:6).

In Sanskrit the name of the lotus-station of awakening, where (once again to use Eckhart's words) "God is born in the soul, and the soul reborn in God," is *Anahata,* a name that says, literally, "Not Hit," meaning specifically, "the sound that is not made by any two things striking together." Every sound that our physical ears can hear is made by two things striking together. The sound of my voice, for instance, is of the breath vibrating the vocal cords. The sound that is *not* made by any two things striking together is a sound of the energy of the universe, the interior of the atom, which is antecedent to things and of which all things are manifestations. And what this means is that beyond the range and ranges of all our scientific hypotheses of cause and effect and so on, there is an ultimate, irreducible mystery of being and becoming, which underlies the whole grandiose night-sky display of the galaxies and their suns. Moreover, the mystery of all-being is also the mystery of our own being. Becoming aware of the wonder of this mystery and of its fascination, like that of the sound of a seashell held to the ear, we are hearing, so to say, the sound *Anahata,* "Not Hit," which in the Indian tradition is described as OM. When pronounced, of course, the sound OM is made by two things striking together. However, its pronunciation supplies a directional clue for the inner ear, toward the sound to be secretly heard. And there is an allegorical extrapolation of the import of OM for the guidance of the mind, which has been provided in a brief but substantial piece of Scripture known as the *Mandukya Upanishad.* It will be instructive, at this point, to review this explanation.

First, then, the sound OM may be written, alternatively, as AUM, since O is interpreted in Sanskrit as an amalgam of A and U. So pronounced, it is known as the four-element sound: A-U-M and a fourth, the fourth being the Silence out of which the sound emerges, back into which it will go, and which supports it throughout as a ground against which the A, U, and M are heard.

In the pronunciation of AUM, the beginning is with A, sounding at the back of an open mouth; U then fills the mouth cavity; and M closes at the lips. The whole mouth has thus been filled with the sound, so that all words are but particles of AUM, and their meanings but particles of its whole—much as we, in our limited temporal forms, are but particles or inflections of that Form of forms which is the Lord and our proper end.

Allegorically, as expounded in the *Upanishad,* A is associated with the world of Waking Consciousness, where things are seen as separate from each other; *a* is not *not-a;* an Aristotelian logic prevails: I see You, You see Me; Subject and Object are separate from each other. Further, the objects seen are of gross matter, weighty and not self-luminous, the only self-luminous objects here being fire, lightning, and the sun and stars, which are accordingly regarded as openings, gates, or doors to a higher, self-luminous sphere. And it is this higher sphere, represented in U, that is of Dream Consciousness. Here everything beheld is of a subtle self-luminous substance, wonderfully fluid and quick to change, weightless and fascinating. Furthermore, you the subject beholding them are at the same time they themselves; for dreams are of your own substance or energy, your own will. So that in this sphere, although Subject and Object appear to be different, they are the same.

Now comes the big point: the deities of vision are of this sphere and of the same luminous stuff as dream. Accordingly the vision and the visionary, though apparently separate, are one; and all the heavens, all the hells, all the gods and demons, all the figures of the mythic worlds, are within us as portions of ourselves—portions, that is to say, that are of our deepest, primary nature, and thus of our share in nature. They are out there as well as in here, yet, in this field of consciousness, without separation. Our personal dreams are our personal guides, therefore, to the ranges of myth and of the gods. Dreams are our personal myths; myths, the general dream. By heeding, interpreting, and following dreams we are led to the large, transpersonal fields of archetypal vision—provided, of course, that rational interpretations are not binding us back continually to our own Chakras One, Two, and Three. As the Hindus say, "To worship a god, one must become a god"; that is, one must find that part within that is the deity's equivalent. This is why (in mythological language) God the Son, Knower of the Father, has to become in each of us ghostly born before we can know, as He does, the Father, and say with Him, in knowledge and in truth, "I and my Father are One" (John 10:30); or with Paul, "It is no longer I who live, but Christ who lives in me" (Gal. 2:20).

Passing on to M: the reference here is to the condition of Deep Dreamless Sleep: no dreams, just darkness. There is consciousness, however, beneath the darkness, hidden, of no specific thing or things, whether of waking or of dream; undifferentiated; whole; sheer light. The ultimate goal of yoga is to enter that field awake; coming there to full union with that light. The experience is ineffable, beyond words, since words refer to objects and their relationships, whether of waking or of dream. Hence—Silence, the fourth part of the syllable AUM.

But now, just one more word about AUM and the states of consciousness to which its elements are referred. As the *Upanishad* points out: the objects known to Waking Consciousness are of the past; having already become, they are apprehended an instant later (or, if very far away, like stars, it will be light-years before they are perceived). Consequently, our sciences and statistical analyses, dealing as they must with what is past, are telling us only of what has already occurred, projecting perhaps into the future, but on the basis only of a known past. No real novelty, no really new thing or event can be thus foreknown to science. But the forms beheld in Dream are of the present. Apprehended immediately in the moment of their life, our life, they are of our own becoming, right now, and of the powers that are moving us. Our effective myth, that is to say, is what is moving us as dream. However, this effective myth may not be the same as that which, in our waking state, we think we believe in, and to which we pay our worship on Sundays, in that building with the plus sign on top. A very important exercise should be that of getting our two mythologies—that professed and that actual—together in our present. And as for our future: that is what is hidden in the darkness of Deep Dreamless Sleep.

The hearing of the syllable OM occurs as the rising *Kuṇḍalinī* reaches the level of the heart and wakens the lotus, *Anahata,* of Chakra Four, and it marks the beginning of our life as truly Man, aware of the mystery dimension of things. At this Moment our relationship to things changes. They are no longer simply objects of our lust or aggression, but vehicles of the syllable OM. We hear it everywhere, out there, in here. We are no longer desirous but in bliss, and the Indian Tantric saying, *iti iti,* "It is here! It is here!" is the Good News of our life. "The Kingdom of the Father is spread upon the earth."

However, a new zeal, a new yearning, may now arise in us, to know and to hear that sound directly, not through things, but unmediated—the zeal, that is to say, of the religious quest. And to this end one may abandon the world, as hermits do, and as Jesus did in his retreat to the desert, from which he returned only to teach. "Let the dead bury their dead" (Matt. 8:22). "Sell what you possess and give to the poor, and come, follow me" (Matt. 19:21).

I was reading some time ago (I forget just where) a list, published by the late Dr. Abraham Maslow, of the values for which men and women in our culture commonly live. They were: 1. survival, 2. security, 3. prestige, 4. personal relationships, and 5. personal development. And I thought, when I considered this list: "Well, those, precisely, are the values that are blown sky-high when anyone becomes infected—not only with a religious zeal, but with any life-purpose at all." To which point we have another saying from the Gospels: "He who loses his life for my sake will find it" (Matt. 10:39). This, precisely, is the message of the next Chakra, number Five, the name of which, *Vishuddha*, means "Purification, Purgation": the cleansing and release of consciousness from its worldly infatuation in the passing features and forms of temporal experience. The seat of this center of transformation is at the level of the larynx, the organ of speech and the word. No animal, though it may bark or howl, can formulate by way of speech a concept, an idea representing the meaning of a universal term. We have entered the province of the human mind, the wonderful ornament of our species. The work to be achieved here is that of penetrating appearances to their source, their life, which is recognized with rapture as our own source and life, transcendent of our temporal birth and death. The function of art, according to this way of thinking, is to reveal through temporal forms the radiance of that unconditioned state; the supporting Silence of AUM. Or, to quote to the same point the words of the playwright Gerhart Hauptmann: "Poetizing consists in letting the Word be heard behind words" (*Dichten heisst, hinter Worten das Urwort erklingen lassen*).

And so we pass from Chakra Five to Six, at that point just above and between the eyes which is represented in Indian images by a third eye, the inward eye, which opens to an inward view of the vision of God. Simultaneously the inward ear opens to the sound of AUM directly, in its full force; for the radiance of God is not only of light but of sound. And the name of this center is Ajna, meaning "Command," or "Authority in Knowledge." It is the counterpart, in our tradition, of the heavenly rose of Dante's empyrean, where the soul beholds in eternal rapture the Beatific Vision.

There was a great Indian saint of the last century, Ramakrishna (1836–86), a consummate master of yoga, who, when describing to his disciples the rapture of this sixth center of the *Kuṇḍalinī*, declared that it was as though there were no more than a pane of glass there separating the visionary from his Beloved. Thus the experience is dualistic: that of a subject beholding an object; whereas the ultimate aim of the devotee is to be as one with the Beloved. The great Sufi mystic Hallaj (d. A.D. 922), compared the situation to that of a moth at night seeing a light shining in a lantern.[16] Its zeal is to be one with the flame; but the glass, against which it batters its wings, prevents it from gaining that goal. And when morning comes it returns to its friends, to tell them of the wonderful thing it saw. "You don't look the better for it," they say on seeing its battered wings. (That is the condition and look of the ascetic.) But the next night, returning to its lamp, it manages to get into it and its passion is achieved, its love fulfilled. It becomes its Beloved, and is itself, for one vivid instant, aflame.

Hallaj was executed in Baghdad for having confessed, *Ana il-Haqq*, "I am God," just as in Jerusalem Jesus had been for declaring, "I and the Father are one" (John 10:30). Such talk is heard as blasphemy wherever God and man are experienced as separate. And when Hallaj was brought to be crucified and beheld the cross and the nails, he uttered a prayer of thanks to God, and for mercy to those, who, to win God's favor, now were about to slay him: "For verily if Thou hadst revealed to them that which Thou hast revealed to me, they would not have done what they have done: and if Thou hadst hidden from me that which Thou hast hidden from them, I should not have suffered this tribulation. Glory unto Thee in whatsoever Thou doest, and glory unto Thee in whatsoever Thou willest!"[17] The orthodox community was giving him actually what he yearned for: union with his Beloved; so that it might perhaps be said that the highest religious function of an orthodox community is to give the mystic, in this cruel way, his ultimate release from that separation from God in which they have their pride.

In any case, we have now, in our own ascent of the lotus ladder, to mount beyond the level of Lotus Six to that at the crown of the head, *Sahasrāra*, "Thousand Petaled," where dualism is transcended. The yogis speak of the experience of heaven as the last barrier to fulfillment: the rapture of the Beatific Vision of God—in whatever form He appears—so holds us to "the tasting of the juice of bliss" that we refuse to move on. In Meister Eckhart's words, "Man's last and highest leavetaking is leaving God for God."[18] Or we may think once again of those last words on the Cross: "My God, my God, why hast thou forsaken me?" The passage may be experienced either as the Self taking leave of God or as God taking leave of the Self; either way, duality is transcended and both the soul and its God—both Subject and Object—disappear.

That is the ultimate reading, I would say, of the plus sign on top of churches. Essential to the idea, however, is its realization by a willing victim, not in the fulfillment merely of some duty, but in love. For, once again to cite Meister Eckhart: "It is not the suffering that counts, it is the virtue. I say, to him who suffers not for love, to suffer is suffering and is hard to bear. But one who suffers for love suffers not and his suffering is fruitful in God's sight."[19] Moreover, the suffering of the cross of life is without end, as long as this beatifying crucifixion—which is our lifetime—lasts.

ۿ   ۿ   ۿ

And so, now, to summarize and conclude. What I have myself learned concerning the interpretation of symbolic forms from this Indian model of the lotus ladder of the *Kuṇḍalinī* is chiefly this: that since one's way of experiencing—and so, of interpreting—phenomenality cannot but be a function of one's own level or state of consciousness, there can be no one true way of interpreting and evaluating life, symbolic forms, or anything else. The various psychological systems of our own competing Western schools are themselves committed—as I have tried to suggest—to one plane or another, and their interpretations, accordingly, commit all those who hold to them. Mythological symbols—when alive and working—are energy-evoking and directing signs, "affect symbols," like art; and where they grab you will depend on where you live. A symbol, for example, that in a person fixed at Chakra Two would evoke erotically toned fantasies, might for one moving toward Six lead to the opening of a mystical realization—as the sight of Beatrice did for Dante. For anyone of the first type to insist that *his* manner of experience is that from which the other must be interpreted is, from a larger view, unacceptable, as would be also that of any chap at Chakra Six who disparaged the dignity and values of a life lived at Chakra Two. There are values to be known at all levels, and the master of life is at home in all, responding appropriately to symbols in their context. Moreover, and here is another sobering thought: for the theologian at Chakra Six to anathematize, slay, or even cry down the mystic at Seven, is, from the larger view, intolerable. The Indian saint Ramakrishna used to ask those coming to talk with him: "How do you like to talk about God, with form or without?" Or perhaps you would like to think of God as one who will help you to pass an examination, or will give you the strength to fight and to win, and support you against your foes. "Arise, O Lord! Deliver me, O my God! For thou dost smite all my enemies on the cheek, thou dost break the teeth of the wicked" (Ps. 3:7). Well, you know where you are there; you are at Chakra Three.

And now, with that, just one more word. When all the symbols of religion are interpreted—as by Freud—as referring to Chakra Two, or—as by Adler— to Three, we are dissociated by such readings from the entire history of the human spirit; for the whole sense of specifically religious signs has always been to transport the mind *past* the ordinary One, Two, Three references of their images, onward to an experience of higher, more specifically human insights. And since all such imagery has to be drawn from the contents of normal experience, it is obvious that inferior readings should be possible, and, in fact, that neurotics fixed in one or another of the lower centers should inevitably read the signs to accord. But, as Jung has somewhere remarked—and with this remark I close: "The problem of the neurotic is that everything reminds him of sex. If it also reminds the physician only of sex. . . ."

Amen!

Mythological Themes
in Creative Literature and Art

The Four Functions of Mythology

Traditional mythologies serve, normally, four functions, the first of which might be described as the reconciliation of consciousness with the preconditions of its own existence. In the long course of our biological prehistory, living creatures had been consuming each other for hundreds of millions of years before eyes opened to the terrible scene, and millions more elapsed before the level of human consciousness was attained. Analogously, as individuals, we are born, we live and grow, on the impulse of organs that are moved independently of reason to aims antecedent to thought—like beasts: until, one day, the crisis occurs that has separated mankind from the beasts: the realization of the monstrous nature of this terrible game that is life, and our consciousness recoils. In mythological terms: we have tasted the fruit of the wonder-tree of the knowledge of good and evil, and have lost our animal innocence. Schopenhauer's scorching phrase represents the motto of this fallen state: "Life is something that should not have been!" Hamlet's state of indecision is the melancholy consequence: "To be, or not to be!" And, in fact, in the long and varied course of the evolution of the mythologies of mankind, there have been many addressed to the aims of an absolute negation of the world, a condemnation of life, and a backing out. These I have termed the mythologies of "The Great Reversal."[1] They have flourished most prominently in India, particularly since the Buddha's time (sixth century B.C.), whose First Noble Truth, "All life is sorrowful," derives from the same insight as Schopenhauer's rueful dictum. However, more general, and certainly much earlier in the great course of human history, have been the mythologies and associated rites of redemption through affirmation. Throughout the primitive world, where direct confrontations with the brutal bloody facts of life are inescapable and unremitting, the initiation ceremonies to which growing youngsters are subjected are frequently horrendous, confronting them in the most appalling, vivid terms, with experiences—both optically and otherwise—of this monstrous thing that is life: and always with the requirement of a "yea," with no sense of either personal or collective guilt, but gratitude and exhilaration.

For there have been, finally, but three attitudes taken toward the awesome mystery in the great mythological traditions; namely, the first, of a "yea"; the second, of a "nay"; and the last, of a "nay," but with a contingent "yea," as in the great complex of messianic cults of the late Levant: Zoroastrianism, Judaism, Christianity, and Islam. In these last, the well-known basic myth has been, of an originally good creation corrupted by a fall, with, however, the subsequent establishment of a supernaturally endowed society, through the ultimate world dominion of which a restoration of the pristine state of the good creation is to be attained. So that, not in nature but in the social order, and not in all societies, but in this, the one and only, is there health and truth and light, integrity and the prospect of perfection. The "yea" here is contingent therefore on the ultimate world victory of this order.

The second of the four functions served by traditional mythologies—beyond this of redeeming human consciousness from its sense of guilt in life—is that of formulating and rendering an image of the universe, a cosmological image in keeping with the science of the time and of such kind that, within its range, all things should be recognized as parts of a single great holy picture, an icon as it were: the trees, the rocks, the animals, sun, moon, and stars, all opening back to mystery, and thus serving as agents of the first function, as vehicles and messengers of the teaching.

The third traditional function, then, has been ever that of validating and maintaining some specific social order, authorizing its moral code as a construct beyond criticism or human emendation. In the Bible, for example, where the notion is of a personal god through whose act the world was created, that same god is regarded as the author of the Tablets of the Law; and in India, where the basic idea of creation is not of the act of a personal god, but rather of a universe that has been in being and will be in being forever (only waxing and waning, appearing and disappearing, in cycles ever renewed), the social order of caste has been traditionally regarded as of a piece with the order of nature. Man is not free, according to either of these mythic views, to establish for himself the social aims of his life and to work, then, toward these through institutions of his own devising; but rather, the moral, like the natural order, is fixed for all time, and if times have changed (as indeed they have, these past six hundred years), so that to live according to the ancient law and to believe according to the ancient faith have become equally impossible, so much the worse for these times.

The first function served by a traditional mythology, I would term, then, the mystical, or metaphysical, the second, the cosmological, and the third, the sociological. The fourth, which lies at the root of all three as their base and final support, is the psychological: that, namely, of shaping individuals to the aims and ideals of their various social groups, bearing them on from birth to death through the course of a human life. And whereas the cosmological and sociological orders have varied greatly over the centuries and in various quarters of the globe, there have nevertheless been certain irreducible psychological problems inherent in the very biology of our species, which have remained constant, and have, consequently, so tended to control and structure the myths and rites in their service that, in spite of all the differences that have been recognized, analyzed, and stressed by sociologists and historians, there run through the myths of all mankind the common strains of a single symphony of the soul. Let us pause, therefore, to review briefly in sequence the order of these irreducible psychological problems.

The first to be faced derives from the fact that human beings are born some fourteen years too soon. No other animal endures such a long period of dependency on its parents. And then, suddenly, at a certain point in life, which varies, according to the culture, from, say, twelve to about twenty years of age, the child is expected to become an adult, and his whole psychological system, which has been tuned and trained to dependency, is now required to respond to the challenges of life in the way of responsibility. Stimuli are no longer to produce responses either of appeal for help or of submission to parental discipline, but of responsible social action appropriate to one's social role. In primitive societies the function of the cruel puberty rites has been everywhere and always to effect and confirm this transformation. And glancing now at our own modern world, deprived of such initiations and becoming yearly more and more intimidated by its own intransigent young, we may diagnose a neurotic as simply an adult who has failed to cross this threshold to responsibility: one whose response to every challenging situation is, first, "What would Daddy say? Where's Mother?" and only then comes to realize, "Why gosh! *I'm* Daddy, I'm forty years old! Mother is now my wife! It is *I* who must do this thing!" Nor have traditional societies ever exhibited much sympathy for those unable or unwilling to assume the roles required. Among the Australian aborigines, if a boy in the course of his initiation seriously misbehaves, he is killed and eaten— which is an efficient way, of course, to get rid of juvenile delinquents, but deprives the community, on the other hand, of the gifts of original thought.[2] As the late Professor A. R. Radcliffe-Brown of Trinity College, Cambridge, observed in his important study of the Andaman Island pygmies: "A society depends for its existence on the presence in the minds of its members of a certain system of sentiments by which the conduct of the individual is regulated in conformity with the needs of the society. . . . The sentiments in question are not innate but are developed in the individual by the action of the society upon him."[3] In other words: the entrance into adulthood from the long career of infancy is not, like the opening of a blossom, to a state of naturally unfolding potentialities, but to the assumption of a social role, a mask or "persona," with which one is to identify. In the famous lines of the poet Wordsworth:

Shades of the prison-house begin to close
   Upon the growing Boy.[4]

A second birth, as it is called, a social birth, is effected, and, as the first had been of Mother Nature, so this one is of the Fathers, Society, and the new body, the new mind, are not of mankind in general but of a tribe, a caste, a certain school, or a nation.

Whereafter, inevitably, in due time, there comes a day when the decrees of nature again break forth. That fateful moment at the noon of life arrives when, as Carl Jung reminds us, the powers that in youth were in ascent have arrived at their apogee and the return to earth begins. The claims, the aims, even the interests of society, begin to fall away and, again as in the lines of Wordsworth:

Our noisy years seem moments in the being
Of the eternal Silence: truths that wake,
   To perish never:
Which neither listlessness, nor mad endeavour,
   Nor Man nor Boy,
Nor all that is at enmity with joy,
Can utterly abolish or destroy!

Hence in a season of calm weather
   Though inland far we be,
Our Souls have sight of that immortal sea
   Which brought us hither,
Can in a moment travel thither,
And see the Children sport upon the shore,
And hear the mighty waters rolling evermore.[5]

Both the great and the lesser mythologies of mankind have, up to the present, always served simultaneously, both to lead the young from their estate in nature, and to bear the aging back to nature and on through the last dark door. And while doing all this, they have served, also, to render an image of the world of nature a cosmological image as I have called it, that should seem to support the claims and aims of the local social group; so that through every feature of the experienced world the sense of an ideal harmony resting on a dark dimension of wonder should be communicated. One can only marvel at the integrating, life-structuring force of even the simplest traditional organization of mythic symbols.

Traditional and Creative Thought

And so what, then of the situation today?

As already noted in relation to the four functions traditionally served—the mystical, cosmological, social, and psychological—the spheres of the two that in the course of time have most radically changed are the second and third, the cosmological and social; for with every new advance in technology, man's knowledge and control of the powers of earth and nature alter, old cosmologies lose their hold and new come into being. To be effective, a mythology (to state the matter bluntly) must be up-to-date scientifically, based on a concept of the universe that is current, accepted, and convincing. And in this respect, of course, it is immediately apparent that our own traditions are in deep trouble; for the leading claims of both the Old Testament and the New are founded in a cosmological image from the second millennium B.C. which was already out of date when the Bible was put together in the last centuries B.C. and first A.D. The Alexandrian Greeks had already left the old Sumero-Babylonian, three-layered "heaven above, earth below, and waters beneath the earth," centuries behind, and in A.D. 1543 Copernicus carried us still further. In the modern universe of galaxies, millions beyond millions, spiraling light-years apart in the reaches of space-time, the once believable kindergarten tales of the Tower of Babel threatening God, Joshua stopping the sun, Elijah, Christ and his Virgin Mother ascending physically to heaven, simply are impossible, no matter how glossed and revised. Moreover, the marvels of our universe, and even of man's works today, are infinitely greater both in wonder and in magnitude than any-thing reported from the years B.C. of Yahweh; so that legends that even in the recent past might have produced in reverent readers some *sense* at least—if not *experience*—of a *mysterium tremendum* in Levantine masquerade, can today be read only as documents of the childhood of our race. And when compared with certain of their primitive, ancient, and Oriental counterparts, they are not even very interesting myths.

Moreover, with respect, next, to the moral value of this heritage, with its emphasis on the privilege of race and its concept of an eternally valid moral law, divinely delivered to the privileged race from the summit of Mount Sinai, it can be asked whether in the modern world with its infinite mixture of contributing peoples any such racism can be longer regarded as either edifying, or even toler-able; and further, whether with all the conditions of life in flux (so that, in fact, what only yesterday were virtues are today, in many cases, social evils), anyone has a right to pretend to a knowledge of eternal laws and of a general moral order for the good of all mankind. Just as in science there is no such thing today as a fixed and final "found truth," but only working hypotheses that in the next mo-ment may require revision in the light of a newly found fact, so also in the moral sphere, there is no longer any fixed foundation, Rock of Ages, on which the man of moral principles can safely take his stand. Life, in both its knowing and its doing, has become today a "free fall," so to say, into the next minute, into the future. So that, whereas, formerly, those not wishing to hazard the adventure of an individual life could rest within the pale of a comfortably guaranteed social order, today all the walls have burst. It is not left to us to *choose* to hazard the adventure of an unprecedented life: adventure is upon us, like a tidal wave.

And this brings me to my next point, which is, that not only in the cosmological and sociological, but also in the psychological dimension of our lives, there is dawning today a realization of the relativism of all measures. In the human brain alone there are some 18,000 million nerve cells; so that, as one great physiologist notes: "If nature cannot reproduce the same simple pattern in any two fingers, how much more impossible is it for her to reproduce the same pattern in any two brains!"[6] No two human beings are alike: each is an unprecedented wonder. Hence, who is to tell either you or me what our gift to the world is to be, or what in the world should be good for us? Already in thirteenth-century Europe, when the prestige of an enforced Levantine religion-for-all was at its height, there had dawned the realization that every individual is unique, and every life adventure equally unique. In the Old French prose version of the Grail adventure known as the *Queste del Saint Graal,* for example, there is a line that makes this point with the greatest clarity. The Holy Grail, hovering in air but covered with samite cloth, had appeared before the assembled knights in the dining hall of King Arthur and then, again, disappeared. Whereupon Arthur's nephew, Gawain, arose and proposed to all a vow, namely, to depart next day on a general quest, to behold the Grail unveiled. And indeed, next morning they departed. But here, then, comes the line. "They thought it would be a disgrace," we read, "to ride forth in a group. But each entered the forest at one point or another, there where he saw it to be thickest and there was no way or path."[7] For where you are following a way or path, you are following the way or destiny of another. Your own, which is as yet unknown, is in seed (as it were) within you, as your intelligible character, pressing to become manifest in the unique earned character of an individual life.[8] And it is just this sense of a personal potential to be realized that has given to the greatest Occidental biographies and creative works their character of yearning toward an undefined unknown. Each in his lifetime is in the process of bringing forth a specimen of humanity such as never before was made visible upon this earth, and the way to this achievement is not along anyone else's path who ever lived. In the later episodes of the old French *Queste,* whenever a knight, in the "forest adventurous" of his questing, comes on the trail of another and seeks to follow, he goes astray.

And so we stand now, in the modern West, before an irreducible challenge.

The Grail, so to say, has been shown to us, of the individual quest, the individual life adventured in the realization of one's own inborn potential, and yet, the main sense of our great Occidental heritage of mythological, theological, and philosophical orthodoxies—whether of the biblical or of the classical strain— is of certain norms to be realized, beliefs to be held, and aims toward which to strive. In all traditional systems, whether of the Orient or of the Occident, the authorized mythological forms are presented in rites to which the individual is expected to respond with an experience of commitment and belief. But suppose he fails to do so? Suppose the entire inheritance of mythological, theological, and philosophical forms fails to wake in him any authentic response of this kind? How then is he to behave? The normal way is to fake it, to feel oneself to be inadequate, to pretend to believe, to strive to believe, and to live, in the imitation of others, an inauthentic life. The authentic creative way, on the other hand, which I would term the way of art as opposed to religion, is, rather, to reverse this authoritative order. The priest presents for consideration a compound of inherited forms with the expectation (or, at times, even, requirement) that one should interpret and experience them in a certain authorized way, whereas the artist first has an experience of his own, which he then seeks to interpret and communicate through effective forms. Not the forms first and then the experience, but the experience first and then forms!

Who, however, will be touched by these forms and be moved by them to an experience of his own? By what magic can a personal experience be communicated to another? And who is going to listen?—particularly in a world in which everyone is attuned only to authorized clichés, so that many hardly know what an inward experience might be!

The Problem of Communication

How is it possible to waken new life in words or in mythic forms that in their common use have become confirmed in a context of unwanted associations? Let us take, for example, the word "God." Normally, when this monosyllable is heard we associate it, one way or another, with the idea of "God" in the Bible. Pronounced in India, however, it would not normally carry such associations. We use the same word for a Greek god, a Navaho god, a Babylonian god—all of which are, in fact, so different from each other that the word, employed in this rough and ready way, has no meaning at all. A meaning has somehow to be given to it anew, every time it is used. And indeed, even referred to the Bible, is it the "God" of Genesis 1 or 2, the prophets, Jesus, Paul, St. Patrick, Innocent III, or Luther?

And what about the carriage of communicated experience—or even of ideas—across the great cultural divide between East and West? One cannot directly translate into English any basic Sanskrit religious term. There is no counterpart for the noun *ātman* or for *Brahman, śakti,* or *jīva,* all of which are fundamental. To be rendered, they must be couched in settings of explanation. But they *can* be so rendered: at least well enough to produce in those with a will and readiness to understand, something like their intended effects. And so too, as every poet knows, old words, old themes, old images, can be rearranged and renewed, to communicate sentiments never expressed before; as, for example, in the words and images of Keats in his "Ode on a Grecian Urn."

I am interested in rehearsing, in illustration of this problem, three inflections of a single mythological image that has been used in three greatly differing traditions to communicate altogether differing ideas and manners of experiencing the mystery dimension of man's being.

The first is from the Indian *Bṛihadāraṇyaka Upanishad,* a work of about the eighth century B.C. It tells of that original Being, beyond the categories of being and nonbeing, antecedent to being (that is to say), who had been, and yet had not been, for eternity. (You see! we are already in great trouble here, already at the start! We have no words!) . . . That Being who was no being, at a certain time before time had come into being, said "I."

But in what language did he say that, before languages were known? Well, he said it, we are told, in Sanskrit, which, like Hebrew (the language that Yahweh spoke when he was at work at this same timeless time, performing the same task) is supposed to be an eternal language, the very sounds of which are the structuring tones of the universe. This Being that was no being said, therefore, not "I" exactly, but *ahaṁ,* and as soon as he had said that, he became conscious of himself (we note that he is being spoken of as a *he,* though, as will appear, that designation of gender is inexact). And when he had become conscious of himself, fear overcame him; but he reasoned: "Since there is no one here but myself, what is there to be feared?" The fear departed and a second thought arose: "I wish that I were not alone."

For wherever there is ego-consciousness, according to the Indian view, there is fear, the fear of death, and there is yearning. We all know what comes of yearning. That one, now yearning, became inflated, swelled, split in half—and there she was. He united with her, and she thought: "How can he unite with me, who have been produced from himself?" She turned into a cow, he into a bull, and united with her; she, into a mare, he, a stallion; and so on, down to the ants. And when the whole world with all its beings had been thus begotten by that pair, he looked around himself and mused: "I am creation; I have gushed this forth: it is I."[9]

Let us turn, now, a little westward, to the work of that other Creator of approximately the same date, whose *logoi* were in Hebrew. Here we find this curious little fellow, Adam, fashioned (we are told) of dust (which, however, is simply another way of saying that he had been born of the goddess Earth). He had been made to tend a garden, but he was lonesome; and his Maker, thinking, "Let me find some toys for this boy," formed every beast of the field and bird of the air (also out of dust), and brought them before his melancholy lad, to be named; but none satisfied. Whereupon, a really great thought dawned in the mind of this experimenting god (where it came from, we are not told). He put his problem child to sleep and, as James Joyce says in *Finnegans Wake,* "brought on the scene the cutletsized consort"—the Rib, to wit: and there she was. And Adam said, "At last!"

And here, today, are we.[10]

Let us turn a little further westward, to Greece and the version in Plato's *Symposium,* where, as recounted by Aristophanes: "in the beginning we were nothing like what we are now.

"For one thing, the race was divided into three; that is to say, besides the two sexes, male and female, which we have at present, there was a third which partook of the nature of both. . . . And secondly, each of these beings was globular in shape, with rounded back and sides, four arms and four legs, and two faces, both the same, on a cylindrical neck, and one head, with one face one side and one the other, and four ears, and two lots of privates, and all the other parts to match. They walked erect, as we do ourselves, backward or forward, whichever they pleased, but when they broke into a run they simply stuck their legs straight out and went whirling round and round like a clown turning cartwheels."

The males were descended from the sun, the females from the earth, the hermaphrodites from the moon; and such were their strength and energy that they actually tried—as Aristophanes told—"to scale the heights of heaven and to set upon the gods." Whereupon Zeus, perceiving how powerful and arrogant they were, sliced them each in half, "as one might slice an egg."

But Zeus, it must be understood, had not created these creatures. They had been born, as we have just heard, of the sun, the earth, and the moon, whereas the Olympians—Zeus, Poseidon, and the rest—were not creators, but had themselves been born of the great Cretan Mother Goddess Rhea. Zeus, having sliced the people in half, then called Apollo, son of Leto, to help him heal the whole thing up: who "turned their faces back to front, and, pulling in the skin all the way round, stretched it over what we now call the belly—like those bags you pull together with a string—and tied up the one remaining opening so as to form what we call the navel.

"But now," as we read, continuing, "when the work of bisection was done, it left each half with a desperate yearning for the other, and they ran together and flung their arms around each other's necks, and asked for nothing better than to be rolled into one." Wherefore Zeus, perceiving that the work of the world would never get done this way, and that all these immobilized beings, furthermore, would be dead soon of starvation, scattered mankind abroad, so that each of us, to this day, is born apart from his other half. But lovers, having found each other, wish for nothing more than to be welded again into one. "And so you see, gentlemen," as Aristophanes remarked in conclusion to his friends, "how far back we can trace our innate love for one another."[11]

From Greece, from Palestine, and from India: three variants, obviously, of a single mythic theme, inflected to represent three modes of experience—significantly different—of the mystic dimension of man's being. In the Indian myth, it is the god himself who splits in half, becoming then the world substance; so that for the Indian saint the ultimate religious realization must be of his own essential identity with that Being of beings: "I am that divine Ground." Whereas in both the Greek and the biblical versions of the mythology, the god is a kind of medicine man, operating on his victim from outside. Moreover, in the Bible, the godly figure is represented as the Universal Creator. He stands, therefore, in a position of unchallengeable authority, and the ultimate loyalty of the Bible, therefore, is not to mankind but to God ("What is man, O Lord, that thou shouldst regard him?" Job 7:17; 15:14; Ps. 8:4), whereas the sympathy of the Greeks, finally, is for man; and the respect of the Greeks, for man's reason. We call this latter the humanistic position, and the Hebrew, in contrast, the religious or theological. And our own tradition, unhappily, is mixed marvelously of both. Monday, Tuesday, Wednesday, Thursday, Friday, and Saturday, we are humanists with the Greeks; Sunday, for half an hour, Levantines, with the Prophets; and the following Monday, groaning on some equally troubled psychotherapist's couch.

In the Orient, in the Indian sphere, such a conflict of spiritual terms would be laughed at as delusory, since, according to the teaching there, a man's god is but his own conceptualization of the ground of his own being. As stated in the *Bṛihadāraṇyaka Upanishad:* "Whoever realizes, 'I am *Brahman*,' becomes this All, and not even the gods can prevent him from becoming this; for he becomes thereby their own Self. So whoever worships another divinity than this Self, thinking, 'He is one, I another,' knows not."[12]

Obviously, the term *god* is hardly fit to be used without explanation if it is to serve as a designation of the mythic beings of all three of these traditions;

and particularly, since, in the biblical sense, the god is regarded as in some way an actual being, a sort of supernatural fact, whereas in both the Greek and the Indian versions of the myth, the personages and episodes are neither regarded nor presented as historic, or proto-historic, but as symbolic: they do not refer to actual events supposed once to have occurred, but to metaphysical or psychological mysteries, i.e. an inward, backward dimension of ourselves, right here and now. And in the same way, the closely related image of the Fall can be regarded either in orthodox biblical terms, as a prehistoric fact, or in the pagan way, as a metaphysical-metapsychological symbol.

The biblical version of the Fall in the Garden is readily recalled. No sooner had Eve been formed of Adam's rib than her eyes began to rove. And they fell upon the serpent, who, in the earlier mythologies of that same Levant, had been symbolic of the creative energy and living substance of the universe. Fig-

Figure 1

ure 1 is a representation of this serpent, split, like the Indian creative Self, in two, and generating the universe—as depicted, c. 2000 B.C., on the famous libation vase of King Gudea of Lagash. Figure 2 is another scene of approximately the same date, but with the female power in human form and the male serpent behind her, the Tree of Life before, and beyond that, a male personage wearing the horned headdress of a god who has evidently come to partake of the fruit of the wonderful tree. A number of scholars have recognized in this scene something analogous to the episode in Eden, a full thousand years before Yahweh's day however, and when the figure rendered in the Bible as a mere creature, Eve, would have been recognized as a goddess, the great mother goddess Earth, with the primal self-renewing serpent, symbolic of the informing energy of creation and created things, her spouse. In any case, Master Adam, who had been told and seems to have thought that he had given birth to Eve (though, as we all know today, it is not men who give birth to women, but women who give birth to men), became aware, at length, of the conversation in progress, over by the tree; and he approached. Eve was already chewing. "Have a bite!" she said. "It's good. It will open your eyes to something." But then God,

Figure 2

who walks in the cool of the day, strolling by, was amazed. "What's this!" he thundered. "You have leaves on!" For, having eaten of the knowledge of good and evil (duality) they were egos, moved, like the Indian god, by desire and fear. Their eyes having opened to the nature of life, their shocked consciousness had recoiled. And the Lord, lest they should eat, next, the fruit of a second tree (or perhaps from the other side of the same), the Tree of Immortal Life, expelled the unfortunate pair from the garden: "drove out the man," as we read, "and at the east of the garden of Eden placed the cherubim, and a flaming sword which turned every way, to guard the way to the tree of life."[13]

Now a number of years ago (and this is not to change the subject), during the course of our war with Japan, I chanced to see in one of our New York newspapers a photo of one of those two giant temple guardians that flank the outer gate of the great Todaiji temple at Nara, in Japan: a huge warrior figure with lifted sword and wearing a rather frightening scowl—beneath which I read the legend: "The Japanese worship gods like this." I was at first simply disgusted. But then a strange thought occurred to me: "Not they, but we, are the worshippers of a god like that." For the Japanese do not stop at the gate to worship its door guardians, but walk between them, through the gate, and on into the temple, where an immense bronze image of the Solar Buddha is to be seen seated beneath the Tree of Immortal Life, holding his right hand in the gesture meaning "fear not"; whereas it is we who have been taught to worship the god of the turning flaming sword who would keep mankind from entering the garden of the knowledge of immortal life.[14]

Where, however, is that garden? Where that tree? And what, furthermore, is the meaning or function of those two guardians of its gate?

Some there have been who have actually searched the earth for the Garden of Eden. St. Thomas Aquinas, for instance, declares that it surely must be somewhere on this physical earth, shut off from us by mountains or beyond the uncrossed seas.[15] We have crossed the seas, however, and have crossed the mountains. No earthly paradise has been found. Yet we need not have searched so far; for it is the garden of man's soul. As pictured in the Bible tale, with its four mysterious rivers flowing in the four directions from a common source at the center, it is exactly what C. G. Jung has called an "archetypal image": a psychological symbol, spontaneously produced, which appears universally, both in dreams and in myths and rites. Figure 3 is from an Aztec codex.

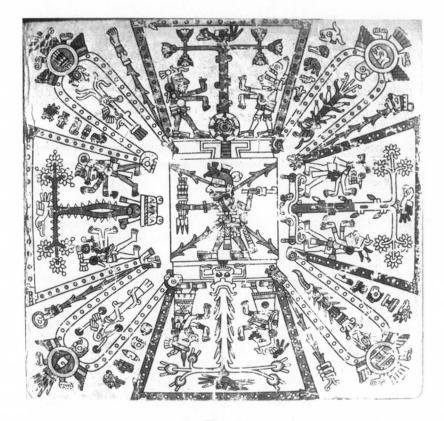

Figure 3

Like the image of a deity, the quadrated garden with the life source at its center is a figment of the psyche, not a product of gross elements, and the one who seeks without for it, gets lost.

But let us look, once more, at those two guardians at the Nara gate. One has his great mouth open; the other, his mouth tightly closed. The mouth open is of desire; the mouth closed, of determined aggression. Those are the two deluding powers that keep one from the garden, the same two that overcame the Father of Creatures when he conceived and pronounced the word "I," *aham*. They are the same two deluding emotions, furthermore, that were overcome by the Buddha when he sat beneath the Bo tree on what is known as "The Immovable Spot" and was tempted, to no avail, first to lust and then to fear, by the prime mover of all beings. According, therefore, to the Buddhist way of interpreting the two cherubim or guardians at the archetypal gate, it is no angry god who has put them there, but our own deluding psychology of ego-centered desires and fears.

The mythological image of the Fall, that is to say, which in the biblical tradition has been represented in pseudohistorical, penological terms, as the consequence of a prehistoric act of disobedience, the Orient reads otherwise, namely in psychological terms, as an effect of our own present anxieties. Hence, in contrast to the great Christian theme of the reconciliation of an offended god through the infinite merits of his true and only son crucified, the Buddhist concept of redemption involves no atonement of any outside power, no atonement theme at all, but the experience within of a psychological transformation—not vicariously wrought by the Savior, furthermore, but inspired by the image and radiance of his life. Like the differing readings of the one word, "god," so the various interpretations of the mythological tree configurate greatly differing theologies, sociologies, and psychologies; and yet, the Bo tree, Holy Rood, and the Tree of Immortal Life in the center of Yahweh's garden, actually are but local inflections of a single mythological archetype, and the image itself was long known, moreover, before any of these cultic readings: as, for example, in the old Sumerian scene of Figure 2, a full thousand years before Eden. Like life itself, such mythological archetypes simply *are*. Meanings can be read into them; meanings can be read out of them. But in themselves they are antecedent to meaning. Like ourselves, like trees, like dreams, they are "thus come" (Sanskrit, *tathāgata*). The Buddha is known as "The One Thus Come," the Tathāgata, because transcendent of meaning; and in understanding him as such, we are thrown back on our own sheer "suchness" (*tathātva*), to which words do not reach.

The Miracle of Art: Aesthetic Arrest

The folk proverb speaks of throwing out the baby with the bath: an archetypal mythological image is not to be thrown away along with the archaic definitions of its meaning. On the contrary, such images—which, in a magical way, immediately touch and waken centers within us of life—are to be retained, washed clean of "meanings," to be reexperienced (and not reinterpreted) as art.[16]

But what is art?

Let me summarize, briefly, the answer to this question given by the greatest artist of the present century, James Joyce, in the last chapter of his first novel, *A Portrait of the Artist as a Young Man,* where he distinguishes between "proper" and "improper" art. Proper art is "static"; improper, "kinetic," by which last Joyce means an art that moves one either to loathe or to desire the object represented. For example, the aim of an advertisement is to excite desire for the object; the aim of a novel of social criticism, to excite loathing for injustices, inequities, and the rest, and to inspire thereby a zeal for reform. "Desire," states Joyce's hero, Stephen Dedalus, "urges us to possess, to go to something; loathing urges us to abandon, to go from something. The arts which excite them, pornographical or didactic, are therefore improper arts. The esthetic emotion . . . is static. The mind is arrested and raised above desire and loathing." And he proceeds, then, to elucidate the psychology of aesthetic arrest by interpreting three terms drawn from the *Summa Theologica* of St. Thomas Aquinas: *integritas, consonantia,* and *claritas.*

Integritas ("wholeness"). Let us take for example any conglomeration of objects. Imagine a frame around a portion of them. The area within that frame is to be viewed now, not as a conglomeration of disparate things, but as one thing: *integritas.* If the objects are on a table of which the frame cuts off a part, the part cut off, then, is "other," and the part within the frame has become a component of that "one thing" of which all the other included objects also are parts.

Consonantia ("harmony"). The self-enclosed "one thing" having been established, what is now of concern to the artist is the rhythm, the relationship, the harmony of its parts: the relation of part to part, of each part to the whole, and of the whole to each of its parts: whether detail *x,* for example, is just *here,* let us say, or a quarter inch to the left, or to the right.

Claritas ("radiance"). When the miracle has been achieved of what Joyce calls the "rhythm of beauty," the object so composed becomes fascinating *in itself.* One is held, struck still, absorbed, with everything else wiped away; or, as Stephen Dedalus tells in his interpretation of this "enchantment of the heart": "You see that it is that thing which it is and no other thing." It is regarded not as a reference to something else (say, as the portrait of some personage whose likeness gives it value), or as a communication of meaning (of the value, say, of some cause), but as a thing in itself, *tathāgata,* "thus come."

But let us now suppose that we are to include within the frame of our work, not indifferent objects only (flowerpots, lemons, apples, tables, chairs), but also human beings; or suppose we are composing a play with people and situations that might well excite loathing and desire: how is our experience of these to be controlled? Joyce speaks of the tragic and comic emotions.[17]

The tragic emotions named, but not defined, by Aristotle, he reminds us, are pity and terror. Joyce defines these: "Pity is the feeling which arrests the mind in the presence of whatsoever is grave and constant in human sufferings and unites it with the human sufferer. Terror is the feeling which arrests the mind in the presence of whatsoever is grave and constant in human sufferings and unites it with the secret cause."[18] The key phrases in these definitions are "grave and constant" and "*arrests* the mind." For what is to be shown is what cannot be changed: those constants inevitable in life, in the world, in the nature of man, in the very processes of being and becoming, to which I have already alluded in my opening definition of the first function of mythology: not the variables, the "correctibles," to which social criticism and ameliorative science can be reasonably addressed, but exactly what I termed there, "the preconditions of existence."

Let us suppose that in our tragic play a Mr. A has shot a Mr. B. What is the "secret cause" of B's death? The evident cause, the instrumental cause, is the bullet by which his body is supposed to have been penetrated. Is that what our play is about: how bullets may cause death? Are we arguing for tighter gun laws, or for not walking in the woods in the fall without wearing a red hat? Or perhaps, the evident cause, the instrumental cause, to which our attention is being addressed is the politics of Mr. A, who is a Fascist, whereas B, God love him, is an "intellectual." Is that, then, what our play is to be about: Fascism and its works? Communism, Fascism, and their likes, may be grave—as indeed they are in the politics of the hour—but in the long view of human affairs, of history and prehistory, they are not (thank heaven) constant.

What, then, is both grave and constant, irreducible, inevitable, in this scene of conflict and death?

Obviously, as in all scenes whatsoever of conflict, whether in nature, in history, or in biography and domestic life, there is in play here a basic law of existence, the polarization of opposites: of positives and negatives, of aims, loyalties, commitments, and delusions in collision. I think of the words of James Joyce in comment on the "male-female" and "brother-battle" themes of his tragicomical masterwork, *Finnegans Wake:* the contenders "cumjustled . . . as were they, *isce et ille,* equals of opposites, evolved by a onesame power of nature or of spirit, *iste,* as the sole condition and means of its himundher manifestation and polarized for reunion by the symphysis of their antipathies."[19] Or I think of the words of the medieval Grail poet Wolfram von Eschenbach, in comment on the epic battle of the Christian Parzival with his unrecognized Muslim half-brother Feirefiz: "One could say that *they* were fighting if one wished to speak of two. They were, however, one. 'My brother and I' is one body—like good man and good wife. . . . The purity of loyal-heartedness is what is battling here: great loyalty with loyalty."[20] When such a point of view on conflict is rendered without partisanship ("Judge not, that you may not be judged"), the secret truth of conflict as a function of being, the very song of life in this "vale of tears," will begin to be heard and felt resounding through all the passages of time—to which awesome mystery, furthermore, we are to become, in the tragic work of art, not merely reconciled, but *united.*[21] One thinks of the dictum of Heraclitus: "We must know that War is common to all, that Strife is

Justice, and that all things come into being by Strife." And again: "To God all things are fair and good and right; but men hold some things wrong and some right." "Good and evil are one."[22] The songs of the bowstring and the lyre equally are of a tension of opposites.[23] And what gives poignancy—that strange life-sweet tone of tragic terror to all revelations of this kind—is the realization that, though poles apart, the antagonists are brothers, in Wolfram's words: "of one flesh and one blood, battling from loyalty of heart, and doing each other much harm."[24]

The "secret cause," then, of the death of Mr. B is what is to be heard in the tick of time, death delivered through life, the *mysterium tremendum* of the ultimate nonexistence of existences: which, in the work of tragic art, is to be experienced and affirmed as the wonder of life. Accordingly, where partisanship, criticism, or propaganda enters into an artwork, the aim and effect of aesthetic arrest is irretrievably lost. Ego-shattering, truly tragic pity unites us with the *human*—not with the Communist, Fascist, Muslim, or Christian—sufferer. Moreover, this pity, as experienced through art, is in the way of a yea, not a nay; for inherently, art is an affirmation, not negation, of phenomenality. In contrast to the message, then, of what I have called "The Great Reversal" (Ah! But see with what ills this terrestrial life is wrought, where moth and rust consume and where thieves break in and steal! Let us lay up our treasure in heaven—or in extinction!), the lesson of proper art is of the radiance of this earth and its beings, where tragedy is of the essence and not to be gainsaid.[25] And this yea itself is the released energy that bears us beyond loathing and desire, breaks the barriers of rational judgment and unites us with our own deep ground: the "secret cause."

In other words, what I am saying here is that the first function of art is exactly that which I have already named as the first function of mythology: to transport the mind in experience past the guardians—desire and fear—of the paradisal gate to the tree within of illuminated life. In the words of the poet Blake, in *The Marriage of Heaven and Hell:* "If the doors of perception were cleansed, everything would appear to man as it is, infinite." But the cleansing of the doors, the wiping away of the guardians, those cherubim with their flaming sword, is the first effect of art, where the second, simultaneously, is the rapture of recognizing in a single hair "a thousand golden lions."

The Fashioning of Living Myths

In Joyce's *A Portrait of the Artist as a Young Man* there is represented, stage by stage, the process of an escape from a traditional and the fashioning of a personal myth, adequate to the shaping of an individuated life. From the first page, attention is focused on the feelings and associated thoughts of a growing boy in response to the sights, sensations, teachings, personages, and ideals of his Irish-Catholic environment, his home, his schools, and his city. The key to the progress of the novel lies in its stress on what is inward. The outward occasions of the inward feeling-judgments are thereby emptied of intrinsic force, while their echoes in the boy's—then the youth's—interior become enriched and recombined in a growing context of conscientiously observed subjective associations. Steadily, a system of sentiments, separate and increasingly distant from that of his fellows, takes form, which he has the courage to respect and ultimately to follow. And since these guiding value judgments are conceived in relation, not only to the accidental details of life in late nineteenth-century Dublin, but also both to the "grave and constant" in human sufferings and to the dogmas and iconography of the Roman Catholic Church—together with the school classics of the Western world, from Homer to his own day—the inward life and journey is by no means an isolating, merely idiosyncratic adventure, but in the best sense a mystery-flight from the little bounds of a personal life to the great domain of universals. The novel is introduced, on the title page, by a line from Ovid's *Metamorphoses* (Book VIII, line 188): *Et ignotas animum dimittit in artes,* "And he turns his mind to unknown arts." The reference in Ovid is to the Greek master craftsman Daedalus, who, when he had built the labyrinth to house the monster Minotaur, was in danger of being retained in Crete by King Minos; but turning his mind to unknown arts, he fashioned wings for himself and for Icarus, his son; then warned the boy:

> Remember
> To fly midway, for if you dip too low
> The waves will weight your wings with thick saltwater,
> And if you fly too high the flames of heaven
> Will burn them from your sides. Then take your flight
> Between the two.[26]

Icarus, however, disobeyed; flew too high and fell into the sea. But Daedalus reached the mainland. And so Joyce would fly on wings of art from provincial Ireland to the cosmopolitan Mainland; from Catholicism to the universal mythic heritage of which Christianity is but an inflection; and through mythology, on wings of art, to his own induplicable immortality.

Thomas Mann, likewise, in his early novelette, *Tonio Kröger,* tells of a youth, who, guided by the inward compass of his own magnetic pole, dissociates his destiny, first, from his family—in this case, German Protestant—but then, also, from "those haughty, frigid ones," as he calls them, the literary monsters of his day, "who," as he discovers, "adventure along the path of great, demonic beauty and despise 'mankind.'" He consequently stands "between two worlds, at home in neither," where it is darkest, so to say, and there is no way or path; or like Daedalus, in flight between sea and sky.

In his masterwork, *The Magic Mountain,* which appeared shortly after World War I, Mann turned this mythological theme of the inwardly guided passage between opposites to the representation of the psychological metamorphosis, not of an artist this time, but of an ingenuous though attractive young marine engineer, Hans Castorp, who had come for a brief visit to a Land of No Return—the timeless playground of Aphrodite and King Death (an Alpine tuberculosis sanatorium)—where he remained to undergo a sort of alchemical transmutation, for a span of exactly seven years. Mann extended the import of this adventure, to suggest the ordeal of contemporary Germany between worlds: between the rational, positivistic West and the semiconscious, metaphysical East; between *eros* and *thanatos,* liberal individualism and socialistic despotism; between music and politics, science and the Middle Ages, progress and extinction. The noble engraving by Dürer of "A Knight Between Death and the Devil," might stand as the emblem of Mann's thesis in this work. He expands the image further to signify Man, "life's delicate child," walking the beveled edge between spirit and matter, married in his thinking to both, yet in his Being and Becoming, something else—not to be captured in a definition. Then in the biblical tetralogy of *Joseph and His Brothers,* Mann passes altogether into the sphere of mythological archetypes, sounding once more, but now *fortissimo,* his life-song of the Man of God, *Homo Dei,* in adventurous passage between the poles of birth and death, from nowhere to nowhere, as it were. And as in the novels of James Joyce—from the autobiographical *Portrait,* through *Ulysses,* to the cycling mythologic nightmare ("whirled without end") of *Finnegans Wake*—so in those of Thomas Mann, from the life-adventure of his Tonio, through that of his unassuming yet gifted Hans, to the unashamedly self-serving, cheating yet imposing and beloved heroes of his tales of Jacob and Joseph, we may follow, stage by stage, the flight of a highly conscious, learned, and superbly competent artist, out of the "Crete" (so to say) of the naturalistic imagery of his accidental birthplace, to the "Mainland" of the grave and constant mythological archetypes of his own inward being as Man.

As in the novels of Joyce, so in those of Mann, the key to the progression lies in the stress on what is inward. The outward occasions represent, however, substantial external contexts of their own, of historical, sociopolitical, and economic relationships—to which, in fact, the intellects of the minor characters of these novels are generally addressed. And that such relationships have force, and even make claims on the loyalties of the protagonists, not only is recognized, but is fundamental to the arguments of the adventures. In the words of Joyce's hero: "When the soul of a man is born in this country there are nets flung at it to hold it back from flight. You talk to me of nationality, language, religion. I shall try to fly by those nets." Obviously, an outward-directed intellect, recognizing only such historical ends and claims, would be very much in danger of losing touch with its natural base, becoming involved wholly in the realization of "meanings" parochial to its local time and place. But on the other hand, anyone hearkening only inward, to the dispositions of feeling, would be in equal danger of losing touch with the only world in which he would ever have the possibility of living as a human being. It is an important characteristic of both James Joyce and Thomas Mann, that, in developing their epic works, they remained attentive equally to the facts and contexts of the outward, and the feeling systems of the inward, hemispheres of the volume of experiences they were documenting. They were both immensely learned, furthermore, in the scholarship and sciences of their day. And they were able, consequently, to extend and enrich in balanced correlation the outward and the inward ranges of their characters' spheres of experience, progressing in such a way from the purely personal to the larger, collective orders of outward experience and inward sense of import that in their culminating masterworks they achieved actually the status, the majesty, and validity, of contemporary myth.

Carl Jung, in his analysis of the structure of the psyche, has distinguished four psychological functions that link us to the outer world. These are sensation, thinking, feeling, and intuition. Sensation, he states, is the function that tells us that something *exists;* thinking, the function that tells us *what* it is; feeling, the function that evaluates its *worth* to us; and intuition, the function that enables us to estimate the *possibilities* inherent in the object or its situation.[27] Feeling, thus, is the inward guide to value; but its judgments are related normally to outward, empirical circumstance. However, it is to be noted that Jung distinguishes, also, four psychological functions that unlock, progressively, the depth chambers of our nature. These are (1) memory, (2) the subjective components of our conscious functions, (3) affects and emotions, and (4) invasions or possessions, where components of the unconscious break into the conscious field and take over.[28] The area of the unconscious," he writes, "is enormous and always continuous, while the area of consciousness is a restricted field of momentary vision."[29] This restricted field, however, is the field of historical life and not to be lost.

Jung distinguishes two orders or depths of the unconscious, the personal and the collective. The Personal Unconscious, according to his view, is composed largely of personal acquisitions, potentials and dispositions, forgotten or repressed contents derived from one's own experience, etc. The Collective Unconscious, on the other hand, is a function rather of biology than of biography: its contents are of the instincts, not the accidents of personal experience but the processes of nature as invested in the anatomy of *Homo sapiens* and consequently common to the human race. Moreover, where the consciousness may go astray and in the interest of an ideal or an idea do violence to the order of nature, the instincts, disordered, will irresistibly protest; for, like a body in disease, so the diseased psyche undertakes to resist and expel infection: and the force of its protest will be expressed in madness, or in lesser cases, morbid anxieties, troubled sleep, and terrible dreams. When the imagery of the warning visions rises from the Personal Unconscious, its sense can be interpreted through personal associations, recollections, and reflections; when, however, it stems from the Collective, the signals cannot be decoded in this way. They will be of the order, rather, of myth; in many cases even identical with the imagery of myths of which the visionary or dreamer will never have heard. (The evidence for this in the literature of psychiatry seems to me now to be beyond question.) They will thus be actually presentations of *the archetypes of mythology* in a relation of significance to some context of contemporary life, and consequently will be decipherable only by comparison with the patterns, motifs, and semantology of mythology in general.[30]

Now it is of the greatest interest to remark, that, during the period immediately following World War I, there appeared a spectacular series of historical, anthropological, literary, and psychological works, in which the archetypes of myth were recognized, not as merely irrational vestiges of archaic thought, but as fundamental to the structuring of human life and, in that sense, prophetic of the future as well as remedial of the present and eloquent of the past. T. S. Eliot's poem *The Waste Land,* Carl Jung's *Psychological Types,* and Leo Frobenius's *Paideuma* appeared in 1921; James Joyce's *Ulysses* in 1922; Oswald Spengler's *Decline of the West* in 1923; and Thomas Mann's *The Magic Mountain* in 1924. It was very much as though, at a crucial juncture in the course of the growth of our civilization, a company of sages, masters of the wisdom that arises from the depths of being, had spoken from their hermitages to give warning and redirection. However, what men of deeds have ever listened to sages? For these, to think is to act, and one thought is enough. Furthermore, the more readily communicable to the masses their driving thought may be, the better—and the more effective. Thus the nations learn in sweat, blood, and tears what might have been taught them in peace, and as Joyce's hero in *A Portrait* states, what those so-called thoughts and their protagonists represent are not the ways and guides to freedom, but the very nets, and the wielders of those nets, by which the seeker of freedom is snared, entrapped, and hauled back into the labyrinth. For their appeal is precisely to those sentiments of desire and fear by which the gate to the paradise of the spirit is barred. Didacticism and pornography are the qualities of the arts that they inspire (their hacks I would term very simply, a bunch of didactic pornographers!), and their heroes are rather the monsters to be overcome than the boon-bringers to be praised.

And so, I come to my last point.

There are (and, apparently, there have always been) two orders of mythology, that of the Village and that of the Forest of Adventure. The imposing guardians of the village rites are those cherubim of the garden gate, their Lordships Fear and Desire, with however another to support them, the Lord Duty, and a fourth, her holiness, Faith: and the aims of their fashionable cults are mainly health, abundance of progeny, long life, wealth, victories in war, and the grace of a painless death. The ways of the Forest Adventurous, on the other hand, are not entered until these guardians have been passed; and the way to pass them is to recognize their apparent power as a figment merely of the restricted field of one's own ego-centered consciousness: not confronting them as "realities" without (for when slain "out there," their power only passes to another vehicle), but shifting the center of one's own horizon of concern. As Joyce's hero, tapping his brow, muses in *Ulysses:* "In here it is I must kill the priest and the king."[31]

Meanwhile, those under the ban of those powers are, as it were, under enchantment: that is the meaning of the Waste Land theme in T. S. Eliot's celebrated poem, as it was also in the source from which he derived it, the Grail legend of the twelfth- and thirteenth-century Middle Ages. That was a period when all had been compelled to profess beliefs that many did not share, and which were enforced, furthermore, by a clergy whose morals were the scandal of the age. As witnessed by the Pope himself, Innocent III (himself no saint): "Nothing is more common than for even monks and regular canons to cast aside their attire, take to gambling and hunting, consort with concubines, and turn jugglers or medical quacks."[32] The Grail King of the legend was one who had not earned through his life and character his role as guardian of the supreme symbol of the spirit, but had inherited and had simply been anointed in the part; and when riding forth, one day, on a youthful adventure of *amor* (which was appropriate enough for a youthful knight, but not for a king of the Grail), he became engaged in combat with a pagan knight whom he slew, but whose lance simultaneously unmanned him; and, magically, his whole kingdom thereupon fell under an enchantment of sterility, from which it would be released only by a noble youth with the courage to be governed not by the social and clerical dogmas of his day but by the dictates of a loyal compassionate heart. Significantly, in the leading version of the tale, by the poet Wolfram von Eschenbach, every time the hero Parzival behaved as he had been taught to behave, the case of the world became worse, and it was only when he had learned, at last, to follow the lead of his own noble nature that he was found eligible to supplant and even to heal the anointed king, lifting thereby from Christendom the enchantment of a mythology and order of life derived not from experience and virtue, but authority and tradition.

In T. S. Eliot's modern poem a similar point is made, referring, however, to a modern Waste Land of secular, not religious, patterns of inauthentic living:

> Unreal City,
> Under the brown fog of a winter dawn,
> A crowd flowed over London Bridge, so many,
> I had not thought death had undone so many.[33]

And again, the answer to the spell of death is understood to be psychological, a radical shift in the conscious center of concern. Eliot turns for a sign to India, to the same *Bṛihadāraṇyaka Upanishad,* by the way, from which my figure came of the primal being who said "I" and brought forth the universe. That same Prajāpati, "Father of Creatures," speaks here with a voice of thunder, DA—which sound is variously heard by his three classes of children: the gods, mankind, and the demons. The gods hear *damyata,* "control yourselves"; mankind hears *datta,* "give"; and the demons hear *dayadhvam,* "be compassionate."[34] In the *Upanishad* this lesson is declared to epitomize the sum of that sacred teaching by which the binding and deluding spell of egoity is undone, and in the modern poem equally, it is again pronounced as a thunder voice, releasing a rain of enlivening grace from beyond the hells and heavens of egoity. Joyce, also, in *Ulysses,* invokes a thunderclap (which then resounds through every chapter of his next work, *Finnegans Wake*) to break the self-defensive mask of his young hero, Stephen Dedalus, whose heart thereafter is open through compassion to an experience of "consubstantiality" with another suffering creature, Leopold Bloom. And finally—to close this sample series of timely modern works renewing timeless mythological themes—Thomas Mann's hero Hans, on the Magic Mountain, his spirit set in motion by the same two powers by which the Buddha had been tempted—namely, Death and Desire—follows courageously, unimpressed by all warnings of danger, the interests of his heart, and so, learns to act out of a center of life within, or, to use Nietzsche's phrase, as "a wheel rolling from its own center" (*ein aus sich rollendes Rad*). Whereupon, once again, there is heard a "thunderclap," the *Donner-*

schlag, as Mann calls it, of the cannon-roar of World War I, and the same young man who formerly had found an office job too much for him has the heart to enter voluntarily the battlefields of his century and to return thus to life.

For what to the young soul are nets, "flung at it to hold it back from flight," can become for the one who has found his own center the garment, freely chosen, of his further adventure.

To conclude, then, let me simply cite the brief poem "Natural Music" of the Californian poet Robinson Jeffers, where the whole sense of my argument will be found epitomized, and the way once again disclosed between the two Billikins of the garden gate to a realization of that joy at the still point of this turning world that is the informing will of all things. Joy, states James Joyce, is the proper emotion of comedy, and in Dante's *Divine Comedy* true beatitude is discovered only in the contemplation of that radiant Love by which all the pains of hell, toils of purgatory, and rapturous states of heaven are sustained: joyful wonder in the marvel of things, being, finally, the gift immortal of myth.

And so, to Jeffers (in reading whose lines, it will help to recall that the grassy Californian hills are in summertime yellow and in winter green):

Natural Music

The old voice of the ocean, the bird-chatter of little rivers,
(Winter has given them gold for silver
To stain their water and bladed green for brown to line their banks)
From different throats intone one language.
So I believe if we were strong enough to listen without
Divisions of desire and terror
To the storm of the sick nations, the rage of the hunger-smitten cities,
Those voices also would be found
Clean as a child's; or like some girl's breathing who dances alone
By the ocean-shore, dreaming of lovers.[35]

The Occult in Myth and Literature

There is a wonderful essay by Schopenhauer, "On the Foundations of Morality," in which he asks the following question: "Why is it, how is it, that a human being can so experience and participate in the danger and pain of another, that, forgetting his own safety, he will fly spontaneously to that other's rescue?" "How is it," Schopenhauer asks, "that what we think of as the first law of nature, namely, self-preservation, can be thus suspended, and another law immediately take over?"

When I was in Hawaii, some three summers ago, an extraordinary event occurred. Those of you who know Oahu will surely recall the Pali: the great ridge that cuts across the center of the island, where the prevailing wind beating through from the north produces a great gale. People go up there just to get blown about: an easy way to become excited. And another thing people go there for is to commit suicide.

Well, on the occasion of which I am speaking, there was a police car driving up the Pali road, and on the edge of the cliff, ready to jump, was a man. The car stopped, and the officer on the right side, springing out and reaching over the guardrail that separated the road from the cliff, grabbed the man just as he jumped; and of course the weight and impulse were enough to pull the policeman over; so that he, too, was going, until the second officer, just in time, got around there to catch him and to pull the two of them back.

When this story came out in the papers and the first officer was asked why he hadn't let the man go, he replied: "I couldn't. Had I let that man go, I could not have lived another day." He had actually given his life to a man who was altogether unknown to him, and it had been by no more than a split second of chance that he himself had been rescued. And then a pretty scene took place. The chap who had been rescued was pleased to have been saved—as suicides frequently are, I am told. One doesn't have to go through with such an act to experience the sense of it. Or as C. G. Jung says somewhere: "Don't get caught in a symbolic situation!" The policeman who had saved the man gave him his handkerchief to wipe the sweat off his face, and when the fellow was about to return it, said to him: "No, you can keep that, to remind you of something."

What a beautiful man! And when I read of that event in the newspaper, Schopenhauer's question jumped to my mind. How *is* it, and why is it, that a human being should do such a thing: so forget himself, so lose himself in another, that he gives that other his life?

Now Schopenhauer's answer was that this enigmatic impulse is of a metaphysical order, a metaphysical realization. It is an impulse rising from below the plane or threshold of our conscious living and judging, springing from our knowledge of a deep truth: namely, that I and that other *are* one, that the whole field of our experience of separateness is a secondary field, and that, beneath it, beyond it, there is a deep, first level, which is of unity.

But this, of course, is an idea that was already implicit, for Schopenhauer, in Kant's *Critique of Pure Reason,* Part 1, "Transcendental Aesthetic," where it is shown that the "forms of sensibility," time and space, condition all of our perceptions, and that it is within this field of time and space that what Nietzsche then termed the *principium individuationis,* the principle of individuation, is experienced. Whence it follows that whatever may underlie or be antecedent to our experiences within this field must be unity, a "primordial unity," or perhaps, indeed, something even more mysterious than unity, beyond all of our categories of thinking whatsoever—categories such as of unity and multiplicity being but forms, finally, of our thinking.

Underlying this field of multiplicity, then, there is mystery. And this is the mystery of our being, the mystery of the being of the universe, the mystery of the being of all things. It is hidden. And the word for "hidden" is "occult."

Now all experiences of the occult, no matter how interpreted, tend to suggest, at least to our feelings, if not also to our intellect, that behind the veil of this temporal-spatial experience-field of ours there is a deeper, truer field, which now and then may reveal itself to us, or into which we may drop; and in such a moment of self giving one may have the sense of being overwhelmed by an impulse from the center of one's own being. As we read in the *Katha Upanishad:*

> Though it is hidden in all things,
> That True Self shines not forth.
> Yet it is seen by subtle seers
> Of superior, subtle intellect.

The old mythologies of the primary stages of human development generally regard this "hidden" depth or power as immanent, actually resident *within* the field of phenomenal experience. A basic myth of many of the primitive peoples of the world tells of a time in which there was no time—the timeless "mythological age" of the ancestors. There was no differentiation there between male and female, or even between man and beast. Those were undifferentiated, semi-human, semi-animal beings, and for them there was no death. But then, one way or another in that timeless time—differing from one version of this mythos to another—a murder was committed; one of those beings was killed. And with that killing, death came into the world, and with death, time. Moreover, with that killing, sexual differentiation became explicit: male and female were separated from each other, and birth came into the world to balance death, as the poles of our temporal existence. The being that had been killed was chopped up, and the fragments, then buried, gave rise to food plants; so that what is eaten to sustain men's lives is in fact the flesh and blood of that sacrifice. That is the hidden truth of our lives, made known to us through a mythic image. And this is a basic myth, found throughout Oceania for example, and in all those tropical zones of Southeast Asia where the earliest planting cultures now seem to have developed. The idea is that the food that we eat is the substance of an ancestral, divine being that has given of itself, either willingly or unknowingly (in many of the legends, willingly), and that the precondition of our separate lives in time is the one life given of that one being on whose death we all subsist.[1]

For actually, the first fact of life is that life consumes life, eats life; and the image of the uroboric serpent biting its own tail is a representation of this mystery. But another mystery of the serpent is indicated when it sheds its skin to be born again. So that along with the idea of death as the precondition of life comes this other idea of an involved power in life, within this phenomenal field of time and space, which puts on bodies and puts them off (as we read in the *Bhagavad-Gita*) as a man puts on and puts off clothing.

With the end, that is to say, of the mythological age, the mythological age did not actually end. It retired, so to say, behind the screen of time and space. And there are those—"of superior, subtle intellect," as we read in the *Upanishad*—who can penetrate that screen and break into that timeless zone. The notion, the basic notion, is of a timeless primordial "time" succeeded by this actual time with its apparent births and deaths; but then, on the outskirts, as it were, all around the margins of this temporal world, there is the continuation—hidden—of the mythological age. And one can break into that, as one breaks into a space of dream on falling asleep.

For indeed, between the worlds of myth and dream there are many instructive analogies. When we leave the field of our waking lives—where we become young, mature, or aged, in the course of our separate passages through the corridor of time—we descend into a timeless realm of the unconscious. Salvador Dali has captured the quality of this realm in his painting "The Persistence of Memory, or Wet Watches," picturing a sort of bending of time in the space of the unconscious. For one can have experiences, even in one's very old age, on passing into realms of dream, of returning to early childhood, or to adolescence. Those possibilities live on and seem to be still there.

Moreover, as in myth, the figures are mixed, compound. James Joyce deals with this area of experience in *Finnegans Wake,* and his language there is itself a kind of "wet watch" language, with multiple implications in each word. Moreover, not only do we all drop into that space in our dreams, but there are festivals and places where the dream time, or mythological age, persists. The very essence of all rituals of an authentically mythological sort is that time, in them, is suspended. For example, in the Roman Catholic Mass: this ritual, as understood traditionally, is not simply a "commemoration" of the Crucifixion; it is *the* Crucifixion. Time and space have been, as it were, dissolved in the rite. And the Host itself *is* the body and blood of the Crucified—that Willing Victim— entire. A traditional mythological law has there suspended all the principles of phenomenal time and space, the *principium individuationis* and all these separate parts. Just as all of us, separately, are one, so in the host to be consumed there is one body, one divine mystery being. And it is out of the impulse of that body, that mystery being, that one acts—as Schopenhauer saw—when performing such a deed as the one that I described in the first moments of this talk.

Now this metaphysical notion of the immanence within all things, behind or within the veil of space-time, of something hidden, or occult, is the very essence of the message of early mythologies. And with the rise in Mesopotamia of the earliest city-states, about the middle of the fourth millennium (3500 B.C. or so), there was added to this idea a new dimension. For it was at that time that a completely new type of social order came into being. The earlier societies, whether of ranging hunters and foragers, or of settled planters dwelling in villages, had been comparatively small. They had been societies of equivalent adults, where everyone had knowledge of the total cultural heritage. However, with the rise in Mesopotamia of those earliest city-states—Ur, Uruk, Lagash, Nippur, Shuruppak, and the rest—a new sort of differentiated society arose. There were professional priests, professional governors, trading people, tillers of the soil, and so forth—people of greatly differing trainings and ideals. And these had to be held together in the way of a single body, as, for example, in the ancient Indian caste system, where the members of the priestly caste, the Brahmins, are compared to the head of the social body; those of the governing caste, the Kṣatriyas, to the shoulders, chest, and arms; the merchants, Vaiśyas, to the belly; and the toiling servants, Śūdras, to the legs. The whole society, in that way, was conceived as a single unit: a *man,* duplicating in its form and nature the form and nature of the universe, which, too, was pictured in the likeness of a great human form—most frequently, the form of a mighty female, the World Mother, within whose body we all have our being.

And now, it was precisely in that first period of professionalism that the priestly caste invented the art of writing—about 3200 B.C., the period known as Uruk B; and not only writing, but mathematics, using mainly the sexagesimal system (calculating by sixties), as we do to this day when measuring circles, circles of time or circles of space: sixty seconds, sixty minutes, 360 degrees. Writing, mathematics, priestly orders, kingship, taxation, and monumental symbolic architecture: all came into being together at that one historic moment in Mesopotamia, about 3200 B.C., whence the idea passed to Egypt, appearing with the first dynasty, now usually dated about 2850 B.C. It appeared in Crete and in the Indus Valley about 2500 B.C.; in China, with the Shang dynasty, 1500 B.C.; and in Mexico, with the Olmecs, about 1200 B.C. Underlying all of these appearances was the same fundamental notion that had emerged first in the minds of the priestly watchers of the skies in Mesopotamia. Observing the passage of the planets, recording meticulously their positions, year after year, those first systematic astronomers presently realized that the planets were moving at mathematically determinable rates through the fixed constellations. And the concept then arose—which had never existed in the world before—of a cosmic order, mathematically controlled. Together with this the notion arose, also, of a society based on the imitation of this order, which is a notion that we honor to this day in our festivals—spring festivals, fall festivals, midsummer and midwinter festivals—marking those great "junctions" (*Sandhyas,* they are called in Sanskrit) where darkness and light come together.

And there is what appears to me to be an extremely significant mathematical formula, which acquires great meaning in this context and which I think it would be well for me now to present to you. It has to do with the number of years assigned to a cycle of time in the Indian Puranic writings, the number of years in a Kali Yuga, namely, 432,000. When I was one day reading in the Norse Eddas, I noticed that in the *Grímnismál* it is stated that in Othin's warrior hall there are 540 doors, and that on the "Day of the Wolf," at the end of the aeon (here is implied the idea again of a cycle of time), there will pass through each door 800 warriors, to give battle to the anti-gods in a great world-concluding conflict. But 800 times 540, I realize, comes to 432,000, the same number, that is to say, that we know from India. So I asked myself, "How come?"

The date of the putting together of the *Poetic Edda* was approximately A.D. 1200, and that of the composition of the *Grímnismál,* possibly 900 to 1050. The Indian Puranic writings are more difficult to date, but the *Mahābhārata,* which is the greatest of them all, has been reasonably assigned to a development between the fourth century B.C. and fourth A.D. Was I to conclude that the Indian work had somehow influenced the Icelandic? I was baffled until, a few years later, reading of the work of a Babylonian priest named Berossos who wrote in Greek about 280 B.C., I learned that he had stated that in Babylonian mythology the number of years assigned to the period between the rise of the first city-state, Kish, and the coming of the mythological flood, was 432,000. Well, there we had it. The Babylonian tradition—in the middle, between India and Iceland—was older than either. Furthermore, it was exactly of the region of the earliest mathematically organized astronomical thinking. Apparently, the one seed-idea had been diffused in the two directions, westward into Europe, where it reappeared in the Eddas, and eastward to the Indian world.

But there was another, associated, mythic idea recorded in the Babylonian text, namely, of ten kings who reigned during that whole long spell of 432,000 years. Well, I thought, ten kings, they must have had very long lives. Where else had I read of such long lives? How about Methuselah: the Old Testament! So I turned to the Book of Genesis, to learn how many patriarchs could be counted from Adam to Noah. And of course there were ten. For how many years? Well, So-and-So was of such an age when he begat old So-and-So, and so on, and it came to 1656 years. Well, I am no mathematician, and so spent some two weeks trying to relate the number 1656 somehow to 432,000, with no success, when one day the idea occurred to me: "Some German has worked this out." Who, then, would it have been? I thought of one of my old heroes, Alfred Jeremias, and began reviewing some of his writings. There I began to get the smell of it, and when he cited in a footnote a paper read by a distinguished Jewish Assyriologist, Julius Oppert by name, in 1876, before the Göttingen Society for the Sciences, I knew that I had found my man. His title was "The Dates of Genesis," and there it all was. What he had found was that in 1656 years there are 86,400 seven-day weeks, which is just twice 43,200. So this number is to be found, not only in the sacred lore of India, but also, curiously hidden, in both the *Torah* and Icelandic ballads.

Next, I asked myself how many years there are in one full solar round of the zodiac, through the precession of the equinoxes. We are moving into the Aquarian age and are at present in the Piscean; before this, it was the Arien, and before that the Taurian. How long would it take for the equinox to proceed through the whole cycle? The answer is 25,920 years; and if we divide that sum by sixty, we get 432. There is, then, an obvious relationship between the number of years in these mythological cycles of which we have been speaking and the actual, mathematically numerable astronomical cycle. Moreover, this is not a number that could have arisen spontaneously out of the psyche, in the way, let us say, of a Jungian archetype. It is a number that could have been arrived at only through a systematic observation of the heavens. And the first people able to do this were the ancient Mesopotamians: the Sumerians, Babylonians, and Chaldeans. —So when did St. Patrick Christianize Ireland? The date officially given is 432 A.D. which is not likely to be the actual date, but a mythological date representing the beginning of a new aeon, the aeon of the Christian religion in Ireland.

Well, there's just one more detail left, to be added to this picture. Some years ago I was given by a friend a very useful little book concerned with the art of keeping oneself in physical shape. Its name is *Aerobics,* and its author, Major Kenneth Cooper. It tells how far and how fast you must run, each day, in order to keep alive; or how far to swim, how many tennis games to play, and all that kind of thing. Well, I was reading along with great interest, when, on page 101, I came upon this statement: "A conditioned man, who exercises regularly, will have a resting heart rate of about sixty beats per minute or less. . . . Sixty per minute, times sixty minutes, equals 3600 beats per hour. Times twenty-four hours, equals 86,400 beats per day." Or, in twelve hours, 43,200! The number is right here on our watches. This mystical, magical number! And right here in our hearts! And the final lesson of all this—the whole sense and lesson of all of the great Bronze Age mythologies—is that the organism of the human being and the organism of the universe are, respectively, the small and the large mediums of the one-same rhythmic order; and that in our articulation of the year, the counting of our months and days, and even the timing of our seconds, we are touching upon a formal principle that is of the essence both of the universe and of ourselves. Moreover, this same idea of a great macro-microcosmic order is what is made visible in the symbologies of traditional civilizations, where the social order is conceived of as a "mesocosm," by putting oneself in tune with which, one is put in tune, not only with one's own essential nature, but also, simultaneously, with the nature of the universe. And this is the hidden, the occult, secret of the universe, society, ourselves, and all things, and its number is 432, the number and prime sign of the occult.

But now, if you add four, three, and two, you get nine; and the digits of 1656 add up to eighteen, which is twice nine; while the sum of eight plus one is again nine. The number nine becomes in this way another signal of the order of the cosmos, the secret hidden order. And how many Muses are there? Nine! These open our inward eyes and ears to the hidden messages of the various orders of nature and human experience; the orders celebrated in bucolic poetry, history, epic poetry, the dance, tragedy, love poetry, flute song, sacred choral song, and astronomy. When Dante first beheld Beatrice, she was nine years old, he tells us; and when next he saw her, eighteen. Beatrice is a nine, he states, because her root is in the Trinity. And it was in the experience of awe before the beauty of Beatrice that his eyes and ears were opened to the song of God's love and grace in the world. This number is the number, moreover, of the great goddess Aphrodite, as the personification of love, and of whom the nine Muses and three graces are the specialized manifestations. There is a beautiful harmony to be recognized in these mythological images; and this harmony is a reference to the hidden, the occult, which sits within the universe and all things.

Now it was in India, where this old Bronze Age mythology has been maintained intact to the present, that a wonderful new stage of interpretation and understanding developed in the period of the *Upanishads,* when it was recognized that all deities and demons are visionary projections of what sits within the human heart itself. They are thus manifestations of the psychological potentialities of mankind, manifestations of what is hidden within ourselves. So that we may search for this hidden either outwardly or inwardly and, either way, will be coming to the same place.

Tat tvam asi! Consider this statement of the *Chhandogya Upanishad*, which dates from 800 B.C. or so: "You are It"; you yourself are that which you are seeking to know. Not, however, the you with which you identify yourself, which came into being in time and will go out of being in time. Not that, not that, not that! You are to identify yourself, rather, with the witness of that temporal self. I see and know my body. I am not my body; I am the witness of that body. I know my thoughts, my feelings. I am not my thoughts, my feelings. I am the witness of those thoughts and feelings. Then the Buddha comes along and tells us that we are not the witness, either. With that, we have been driven, so to say, out back of the wall, becoming identified, as it were, with that which transcends our individuated spatial and temporal personalities; and we have come to something like the metaphysical realization to which Schopenhauer was pointing in that first question that I mentioned. And this way of interpreting and understanding the occult, as immanent within oneself and all things, is the way of what I would like to call the "primary" mythologies of the world, whether primitive, archaic, or Oriental.

In our Western world, on the other hand, starting already in the Levant, the Near East, a radically different style of thought has taken over. I divide the mythological world-map with a vertical line drawn through Persia. Eastward of Persia there are two great, creative high-culture centers: one is India, the other, China. And in both of these we discover this all-pervading sense of the immanence of the occult: in India, in the idea of *Brahman*, and in China, in the Tao. Westward of the Great Divide, we again have two great creative high-culture centers: one, the Near East, where the high civilizations first emerged, and the other, Europe; and these two have been for centuries in very close play with each other, closely connected both historically and geographically, whereas the two great Eastern centers are situated widely apart, in comparative isolation, and so have been for centuries extremely conservative in their styles.

Now there were two extremely important innovations that transformed the mythologies of the Levant and that then very soon affected Europe. One came along with the rise of Zoroastrianism, where the principles of light and darkness are separated from each other absolutely and the idea is developed of two contending creative deities, one good, the other evil. Nietzsche, in his *Thus Spake Zarathustra,* treats of this as having been at one time a useful thought, but now outgrown: absolute good and absolute evil. There is in the earlier traditions no such dualistic separation of powers, and we in our own thinking have inherited something of this dualism of Good and Evil, God and Devil, from the Persians.

The second great, transforming innovation was that which came with the historic rise to power of the Semitic races and their especial concept of deity. In all other Oriental traditions, and in all of our own earlier Indo-European traditions, the principal deities were understood philosophically as visionary personifications of the powers of nature, representing the occult in this great universe and in the motivations of our lives. The various local, tribal "ancestral" deities are in such systems secondary, subordinate to the primary nature gods, and themselves little more than the guardian spirits and teachers of their respective local groups. In many of the most important Semitic mythologies, however, whether of the Amorites, the Babylonians, Assyrians, or Akkadians, the principal god was the tribal deity. But now, just consider: when your gods are nature gods, you can go from one place to another and say, "He whom you call Indra, we know as Zeus." For example, in Caesar's *Gallic Wars,* chapter six, one finds the author describing the deities of the Celts, but he gives them the related Roman names, Mercury, Apollo, Mars, Jupiter, and Minerva, so that we hardly know of which Celtic gods he is treating. And such syncretism is characteristic of all peoples of the world, except the Semites. Imagine any Hebrew saying: "He whom we call Yahweh, you call Indra." No indeed! This one is ours and special; and His law is the social law of our group, the Law of God that we are taught in school, and He is not to be compared in any way to anything like your mere nature deities. Moreover, He is the One God who is truly GOD.

There is in this way envisioned a radical separation between what is regarded as the Ultimate God, a supernatural deity set apart from nature, and the powers by which this world of nature is moved. What the Old Testament, read as history, tells, is the very violent story of the conflict between Yahweh and the nature gods of Canaan. The kings are forever going over to the nature gods, sacrificing on the hilltops, "doing what was evil in the sight of the Lord"; and the mighty Goddess, she of many names, who is the true and ultimate deity of nature and of the muses, who brings forth and nourishes all life, and of whom the gods are the agents, is known there as "the Abomination" (2 Kings 23:13).

And so, with all of this we have a totally new kind of occult, a kind of two-way occult: on the one hand, the approved occult, which is the worship of our own tribal deity, who is supernatural, transcendent of nature, good, and not to be known through the study of nature, but only through "Revelation"; and on the other hand, in absolute contrast, the diabolical occult of the powers of the nature religions, who are in some contexts described as independent enemies of Yahweh, but in the Christian tradition, generally, as a devil who can act only with the permission of the one true and only God.

In this mythological context the idea of the occult, as black magic, becomes associated with all of the religious arts of the traditional pagan world, and the very symbols of such gods as Shiva and Poseidon, for example, become symbolic of the devil.[2] The trident of Shiva and Poseidon and the pitchfork of our devil are the same. Moreover, there now begins to become associated with the occult a new tone, one of fearful danger, diabolical possession, and so forth, and what formerly was demonic possession—possession by a god such as Dionysus—becomes evil: a new mythology of warlocks and witches, pacts with the devil, and so forth, comes into being. But there is an earlier mythological law that tells that when a deity is suppressed and misinterpreted in this way, not recognized as a deity, he indeed may become a devil. When the natural impulses of one's life are repressed, they become increasingly threatening, violent, terrible, and there is a furious fever of possession that then may overtake people; and many of the horrors of our European Christian history may be interpreted as the results of this natural law. Also, the violence of which one reads throughout the body of the Old Testament, the bloodbaths of Elijah's wrath, the relish of the prophets in the foreseen destruction of great cities—these may be interpreted similarly; and how all this should be read as a religious text is something that I have found difficult to explain to my Indian friends.

What we have here to note, therefore, is the fact that in our European Christian heritage we have had two completely contrary mythologies of the occult to assimilate: the Semitic, Levantine, of a supernatural god, absolutely in opposition to the pagan powers of nature, and then, against this, the view, inherited from the Greeks and Romans, of Dionysus, that prefigurement of the very devil himself, as a deity to be brought somehow into balance and accord with the god of light of the classical Apollonian world.

And there is even one more difficulty to be noticed; for, whereas officially, by the end of the Middle Ages, we had left behind the old idea of the immanence of the occult and were dealing, instead, with two transcendent occults: that of the one true good God and that of all the bad devils, true worship over here and black worship over there, the Mass and then the Black Mass—that sort of separation—there was one more great crisis still to arise, namely that so elegantly discussed by Ortega y Gasset in his *Meditations on Quixote,* where he points out that when Galileo with his telescope, in the early seventeenth century, recognized in the movements of the planets the laws of an *earthly* science, there came into play in human consciousness a new order of belief: that of the fact, the hard, crude fact, which in that century became more potent than it ever had been before.[3]

For whereas in the myths, and even in medieval chivalric legend, the world of the hero's adventure had been a reflection of his own readiness for exactly the adventure that arose, the world had now become hard. Don Quixote rides out, as knights of the past had ridden; but when knights of the past had been ready for the Grail adventure, the Grail castle had appeared. Don Quixote was ready for an adventure with great giants, but what did he run into? Windmills![4]

As Ortega points out, with this scientifically enforced hardening of the fact world, the possibility of adventure has been destroyed—because adventure is the quality of a life lived in terms of its own inward dynamic, inward imagination, inward expectation, and that, precisely, is what this hard world of fact opposes. Moreover, this hard world of fact became harder, harder, and harder, as the centuries proceeded, until, by the middle of the nineteenth, what people were reading were novels, not of individual adventure, but of the environment and of how this determines the nature of the individual. As he summarizes the case: with Darwinism, the hero was swept right off the earth. And yet, Don Quixote had been able to say: "Although some sorcerer out there may be turning all my giants into windmills, he cannot destroy my courage, nor my will to continue in this adventure."

And so the situation in which we now discover ourselves, of a world of hard fact both outside and within, the world of the dynamics of potential action interpreted in the way of a behaviorist psychology, where man never acts, but only reacts, and we are little more than machines, either malfunctioning or in order! Compare this dismal image with that of the old myths and legends, where the hero of action is one who, through his own action, determines the shape of the world itself. What a contrast! And the occult, the hidden, the metaphysical, whether as God, the Devil, or man's own inward nature, is now something that has simply been refuted. There is no such thing. There are the laws only of hard outward fact and their methodically scientific translation inward.

Yet anyone falling in love will find that, while under the spell of this frenzy, the laws of hard fact are for him suspended. He becomes the creator of his own sweet world. They rightly say that Love is blind, Love does not see the crude, ugly fact that everyone else beholds and which it has turned into a radiant delight. Moreover, if Love presses on (or let it be anyone seized with a real passion), the laws that govern all prudent life will dissolve—as they did, let us remember, in that adventure of the rescued suicide at the Pali, in Hawaii, in an adventure that created, beyond reason, a new man.

Furthermore, as we are now finding at the ultimate outposts of our sciences, at the rim of modern physics research, what once had been thought to be the laws of a fact-hard nature have dissolved into mere statistical probabilities. Every fact, in itself, is an exception. Also, the authority of the Scriptures of those who preach the doctrine of a *supernatural* God has been pretty well unsettled. Their hard line, too, is dissolving, and we are now observing throughout our culture world a resurgence of the sense of the *immanence* of the occult, within ourselves and within nature. The Old Bronze Age realization of a micromacrocosmic unity is returning, and everywhere all the old arts that once were banned are coming back. I have myself been traveling about quite a bit, these years, from one college campus to another, and everywhere the first question asked me is, "Under what sign were you born?" The mysteries of the Tarot pack, the *I Ching,* and Transcendental Meditation. . . . Well, all this is just the beginning, the first signaling of a dawning realization of the immanence of the occult, and of this as something important for our living.

Furthermore, one can follow this trend in the novel as well, and in philosophy. With Schopenhauer, I introduced this question. Before him was Kant, who broke with a single hammer blow the claim of reason to absolute authority, and already in Schopenhauer's thought, the implications of Kant's *Critique of Pure Reason* were recognized as in easy accord with the non-dualistic thinking of the East.[5] He used properly and without strain the terminology of the *Upanishads* and Vedanta. Still further, there has been given to us, more recently, by the great physicist Erwin Schroedinger, an illuminating little book, *My View of the World,* in which the culminating word is the Indian *Tat tvam asi.* Historically we can say, therefore, that in our moment of time, there is a strong movement to be observed, on many levels, toward a rediscovery and re-recognition of the immanence of the occult.

In psychology, the great symbolic event in this context seems to me to have been that of the fantastic conversation between Freud and Jung, shortly after Dr. Freud had endowed the younger Dr. Jung with the crown of his psychoanalytic kingship. He wanted him to accept the presidency of his own international society for psychoanalysis, and Jung, in return, wished to know the other's attitude toward the study of occult phenomena; for the title of Jung's own first scientific paper had been "On the Psychology and Pathology of So-called Occult Phenomena"—possession, somnambulism, automatic writing, and the like.[6] As a young man he had once been seated in his room studying, his mother being in the next room, where there was a large, wooden dining table; and while he was sitting there at his books, he heard suddenly, in the other room, a startling pistol crack, and, dashing in to see what had happened, he found that the big table in that room had split in the middle. Two days later there was another great pistol crack in the house, and when they opened a bread cupboard in which there had been a breadknife lying upon a rectangular breadbasket, they found the breadknife shattered, in four parts, one part in each of the corners of the basket. And Jung kept those four broken parts to the time of his death.

Some little time after these two amazing occurrences, it was learned that there was a company of Jung's relatives who had been engaged for some months, nearby, in table-tapping. They also had a medium, a young girl of fifteen and a half. Jung was invited to join them and for some two and a half years took notes at their séances, of which he then made use in his doctoral dissertation. He was therefore, years later, greatly interested in learning what his new friend, Dr. Freud, would have to say about such things.

The Doctor had just been discoursing on the primacy of sexuality, when Jung seriously asked him for his opinions on precognition and on parapsychology in general. As Jung tells in his autobiography, *Memories, Dreams, Reflections,* Freud replied by rejecting the whole subject as nonsensical, and in terms of so shallow a positivism that it made Jung hot inside. He was, however, the younger man and respectful of his elder, and so suppressed the retort. But he then began to feel glowing in the region of his diaphragm a sort of red-hot plate of iron. He was literally burning inside with what the Indians call *tapas,* yogic heat, and to the two doctors' mutual astonishment there occurred an explosion in the bookshelves. Freud looked at Jung in alarm, and Jung said to him: "There, that is an example of a so-called catalytic exteriorization phenomenon." "Oh, come," exclaimed Freud, "that is bosh." "It is not," replied the younger, "and to prove my point, it is going to happen again." And it did. The new world had come.[7] And it is coming still, from the occult abyss. Or, as we read, again from an *Upanishad:*

> From that Abundance, this Abundance,
> And abundance remains.

So much, then, for the topic of my talk: The Occult in Myth and Literature. We commenced with a consideration of the idea of a hidden unity beyond or informing the apparent world of multiplicity and its phenomena. The first way of thinking of this unity was of an immanent power through all things; and the second view was of a conflict between the good occult and the evil: *our* God and all those others. A third point of view was that of the veneration of the hard world of fact against which Don Quixote rode and which exploded in Freud's bookcase. And we are coming now to a notion again of the immanence whereby the nineteenth-century novel can be seen to have already dissolved into the mythological novel.

Let me point, in this context, to two outstanding authors, whose works remarkably parallel each other both in time and in the stages of their passages from positivistic nineteenth- to metapsychological mid-twentieth-century styles. These two are Thomas Mann and James Joyce. They started out, Thomas Mann in *Buddenbrooks* and "Tonio Kröger," and James Joyce in *A Portrait of the Artist as a Young Man,* with what looked, to those who first read them, like nineteenth-century novels. But what concerned each author most deeply was the subjectivity of his main character: the world as that character experienced it—not the world as an unconditioned, character-conditioning "fact." They were interested in what might be termed the *psychological environments* of their characters. And their fluent styles were designed to reproduce the qualities of those ever-altering environments.

One readily recalls, for example, in the *Portrait,* how Joyce commenced in the style of someone talking to a very little boy. "Once upon a time and a very good time it was there was a moocow coming down along the road and this moocow that was coming down along the road met a nicens little boy named baby tuckoo." Now that certainly was not James Joyce's own style at the age of twenty-one. The style grows up with the boy, and two pages later has become that which Hemingway took over for his early stories of his boyhood; and so, on it grows, through prep-school and through college, where the style is in imitation of Cardinal Newman.

The next two productions of these two great authors appeared almost together, directly after the First World War: James Joyce's *Ulysses* in 1922 and Thomas Mann's *Magic Mountain* in 1924. And these again had the appearance of naturalistic novels. However, the structuring of both was of mythology, and mythological clues being given, first, in the titles, but then, in various ways, throughout.

For example, the number of the room in which Hans Castorp lives in the mountain sanatorium is thirty-four (he had come to spend three weeks, but remained for seven years: three plus four equals seven, the number of notes of the diatonic scale, through which one passes to rebirth in a higher octave). He takes the measure of his temperature by means of a glass "cigar" containing mercury: Mercury, the god Hermes, mystic guide to rebirth beyond death. He holds the guiding thermometer in his mouth for seven minutes. The first appearance in the sanatorium dining hall of the woman, Clavdia Chauchat, with whom he was to fall in love, was at the moment of the serving of the fish course: the fish-meal of Good Friday, day of the divine death before resurrection: fish, the symbolic animal of Venus-Aphrodite, goddess of love, and so forth. That is to say, every detail of the naturalistic world is seen to hide, and at the same time to reveal, occult, mythological messages. And the same device was employed by Joyce, independently, in *Ulysses*.

Then, finally, both authors—Thomas Mann in the Joseph novels and Joyce in *Finnegans Wake*—drop completely into the sea of myth, and regard the world in which we have our being from the point of view of its transpersonal, deeply unconscious, ground, both, meanwhile, having been profoundly influenced by Jung's publication of his theory of psychological archetypes in the work that finally brought about Freud's doctrinaire rejection of him in 1912: *Wandlungen und Symbole der Libido* (translated in its revision as *Symbols of Transformation*).

And so now, in conclusion, let me offer a little anecdote, an animal-fable from India, which epitomizes unforgettably the whole sense of this occult knowledge that is hidden within us, each and all. It tells of a tigress, both pregnant and hungry, who comes upon a little herd of grazing goats, and with great energy pounces upon them. They scatter and she misses. But her violent pounce has brought about the sudden birth of her cub, and her own death. She had overdone it.

The goats return to their grazing place, and what they there discover is this just-born little tiger with its dead mother. Having strong parental instincts, they adopt the little thing, which then grows up thinking it's a goat. He learns to eat grass, learns to bleat. But grass is not easily digested by a carnivore; his teeth cannot properly chew it, nor his digestive juices dissolve it. So he grows up into a pretty miserable specimen of his kind. And when he has come, in this way, to a scrawny estate of adolescence, a large male tiger pounces on the flock, and again it scatters. But this little fellow is a tiger; and he is standing there; and the big one looks at him in amazement.

"What! You are living here with these goats!" he exclaims. "Maaaa," replies the tiger. The big one is mortified—like a father returning home to find his son there with long hair. He cuffs him right and left a few times, and the little one responds only with those silly bleats, beginning, however, in his embarrassment, to nibble at blades of grass. The big fellow picks him up by the neck and carries him to a nearby pond, where the water is perfectly still. Still water is a favorite Indian image to symbolize the idea of yoga. The aim of yoga—so the lesson goes—is to make the mind stand still. When the surface of a pond is blown by a wind, the water is rippled and all that one can see in it are broken, moving reflections, appearing and disappearing. But make the wind die down. Clear the water, let the sediment settle, and let the pond stand still. Then all those broken reflections, coming and going, will disappear, and what will be seen will be a constant, steadily present form, a single reflection of the sky above, with its clouds, a view downward to the fish down there, and the sandy bottom beneath. So also in yoga, when the mind has been made to stand still. The ephemeral phenomena of this ego-world, which come and go in passing forms, disappear, and one beholds the constant form of forms that had been hidden, broken, in all. And the rapture of this revelation can so entrap the mind that one becomes lost in it—like Narcissus—and the wind never blows again. Or, on the other hand, having seen the one true image, one may allow the wind to blow again and take delight in the various inflections of its form, as they come and go.

And so it was in the case of this tiger cub, brought to gaze into the still pond. He looked in, and for the first time in his little long life beheld his own true face. It was not a goat face. And the big tiger, stretching his own neck out, was also reflected in the pond. "You see," he said, "you have the pot-face of a tiger. You're no goat. You're a tiger, like me. Now *be* like me." That's the way of the Oriental Guru, setting himself up, always, as the model.

Well, the little one is experiencing some new ideas running through his head. And when the big fellow is satisfied that the image has soaked in, he picks the cub up by the neck again and carries him to his den, where the bloody remains are lying of a recently slaughtered gazelle. The big fellow picks up a chunk of this stuff and says to the cub, "Open your face!" The little one backs away. "I'm a vegetarian," he argues. The big one roars: "None of this nonsense!" and shoves the gobbet down his student's throat. The little one gags, and the text declares: "As all do on true doctrine!" Gagging, frightened, he is nevertheless assimilating the juices of this food: his proper food: his true food. And it alerts within him his true nature, which is not a goat nature at all: his tiger nature. And he stretches a true tiger stretch, for the first time in his life. And from his throat there comes a kind of tiger roar: sort of an elementary tiger roar: Tiger Roar 101. And the big one says to him, showing satisfaction: "There we are! Good boy! Now let's go into the forest together and eat tiger food."

So now, the lesson that I would draw from this is that we are all tigers, living here apparitionally as goats. The sociologists deal with our goat nature, training it to the flock. The humanists try to refine it. But the function of yoga, and of the arts, and of mythic forms, is to reveal to us our tiger face. We are tigers in goats' clothing. And it is through the arts, therefore, through meditations, and through all those symbolic mysteries that have come down to us from primordial times, that we are introduced to that everlasting form of forms which underlies all these 432,000 reflections of our world of time and space. And so I am sure that in the course of this great conference on the occult, our tiger faces will emerge and all goat faces be abashed.

Erotic Irony and Mythic Forms
in the Art of Thomas Mann

In the year 1936 somebody in Vienna made a monumental mistake and invited Thomas Mann to deliver a festival address honoring the eightieth birthday of Sigmund Freud. How it could have been supposed that an artist would talk long about anyone or anything but himself and his work, I cannot imagine; and the interesting thing is that Mann expressed his own bewilderment in his first sentence. Why, he asked, should an artist, a maker, have been chosen to speak of a scientist, a knower? "An author," he declared, "is a man essentially not bent upon science, upon knowing, distinguishing and analyzing; he stands for simple creation, for doing and making, and thus may be the *object* of useful cognition without by his very nature having any competence in it as *subject.*" However, the great speaker then suggested, perhaps those who had made this selection had had in mind a festival—a Saturnalia, where the object becomes subject, and the subject the object; or to use again Mann's own turn of phrase: where "the knower and seer of dreams becomes himself, by our act of homage, the object of dreamlike penetration."

Now in the festival of the Roman Saturnalia social tables were reversed: masters served their slaves, and a mock king was appointed who could break rules as he pleased. A slave might insult his master, railing at him as he liked, and not even a word of reproof would be uttered for conduct that at any other season would be rewarded with a beating, imprisonment, or even death. Thus in Mann's mention of the Saturnalia there was a threat implicit of carnival-like lese majesty, which might not be altogether gentle. Indeed, in the term "useful cognition" itself there was already implied a certain depreciation (from the artist's point of view) of the psychoanalyst's approach to the reading of life's dream. And since Eros, "love," had long been a dominant theme in the writings no less of Thomas Mann than of Sigmund Freud, the celebrants at that birthday festival might have taken warning, that moment, that they were about to give audience to a not quite orthodox commentary on the science of their master.

Freud's own thoughts about art and artists were already well known to Mann, no less than to everyone else in that room, and they were certainly not Mann's own. They had been stated on many occasions and, most sharply, sixteen years before, in a lecture on "The Paths of Symptom-Formation" that had been published as Lecture Twenty-three of Freud's *General Introduction to Psychoanalysis.* There we find the artist diagnosed (from the point of view of "useful cognition") as one who desires intensely "honor, power, riches, fame, and the love of women," but lacks the means to attain them. Frustrated, he becomes introverted and turns with unsatisfied longing from reality to fantasizing—which, in the Freudian view, is always unconsciously predetermined by repressed infantile fears and desires. Since the artist, however, is gifted with what Freud in this passage terms the "mysterious ability" to reproduce his daydreams in such a way as to afford satisfaction to other frustrated souls, he earns their gratitude and admiration, and (to quote) "has won thus *through* his fantasy what before he could win only *in* fantasy, namely: honor, power, and the love of women."[1]

Thus the present artist, Thomas Mann, it would appear, had made such progress *through* his fantasy toward the winning at least of honor that he had been designated to pronounce the eulogy at Dr. Freud's eightieth birthday. However, as already remarked: of more interest than Freud to this particular artist were himself and his own great works.

In a fifteen-page edition of Mann's encomium hardly four pages go to Freud; the rest, to himself and those nineteenth-century authors by whom his own works had been chiefly inspired. Mann, at the time, was sixty-one; at the peak of his creative career. He had just published volume III of his magnificent *Joseph* tetralogy.[2] And the year was 1936: two years later came the *Anschluss,* Hitler annexing Austria. Freud took flight to London, to complete there his final works, and Mann, very shortly after, moved to Switzerland, then England, and finally, Hollywood. The terminal volume of his *Joseph* series had to wait to appear until 1943, and in the meantime there were published from his hand, not only a number of political tracts urging Americans into the war for what he termed "The Coming Victory of Democracy," but also two remarkable novels: one, a really beautiful thing treating of Goethe in his old age, *The Beloved Returns (Lotte in Weimar)*, and the other, an amusing fantasy, *The Transposed Heads,* on a grotesque Hindu theme with which Mann had become acquainted from the writings of the great Indologist (and close friend of C. G. Jung) Dr. Heinrich Zimmer.[3]

Now, on entering into his festival speech, directly following the announcement of his Saturnalia theme, Thomas Mann gave praise to Freud as a courageous, mighty spirit, who had trodden independently, and alone, as physician and natural scientist, the very steep and difficult path of his researches, in total ignorance of the fact that all of the essential ideas of the new branch of science he was founding had already been put forward by those great German Romantics with whose writings Mann himself had been familiar since early youth. Dr. Freud had not—said Mann—known Nietzsche, who had already recognized that the leading themes, ideas, and images of philosophy, mythology, and religion are psychologically grounded, the best method of exploring the psyche being through a study of disease. Freud had never read Novalis, "whose romantic-biologic fantasies," in Mann's words, "so often approach astonishingly close to analytic conceptions."[4] Nor had he read Kierkegaard. He knew nothing of Ibsen, who had shown that the lie—and little lies—of life are absolutely necessary in the interests of survival. And he had not read Schopenhauer, in whose *World as Will and Idea* the whole Freudian theme of the conflict of id and ego is already thoroughly worked out.[5]

Mann went on, then, to announce that *Freud* had come to *him*, not *he* to *Freud*—and rather late in his career, at that. Freud had been brought to his attention by a number of young scholars who were carrying his ideas into the fields of literature, history of art, religion, and pre-history; "and when," said Mann, "I began to occupy myself with the literature of psychoanalysis, I recognized, arrayed in the ideas and language of scientific exactitude, much that had long been familiar to me through my own youthful experiences."

"Perhaps," he then said, "you will kindly permit me to continue for a while in this autobiographical strain, and not take it amiss if instead of speaking of Freud, I speak now of myself." Which, indeed, he proceeded to do for the best part of the remainder of his hour.

Mann proceeded in his Saturnalian play to a discussion of Schopenhauer and the contribution of that philosopher's thinking to his own—as represented in his first long novel, *Buddenbrooks,* which he completed in 1900 (the year of Freud's first masterwork) and published in 1902.[6] Schopenhauer's characterization of the Will, Mann pointed out, as a blind, metaphysically grounded, general impulsion informing all of nature, shifted the accent of philosophy from rational idealism to a recognition of the primacy of instinct over reason in the psyche.[7] All thinking in this view (as later, in Freud's) responds to subliminal urgencies which are the actual determinants of our lives, the conscious ego being only provisionally competent to formulate and realize aims of its own. Mann compares this relationship to that of Europe to Asia: Europe, the province of the intellect and developed rational thinking; Asia of the unconscious. He again compares it—using a well-known mythic figure—to that of a rider and his mount: the mount, the power of the will in nature; the rider, guiding, reasoning mind. And in this connection he brings forward in his talk his first overt contradiction of Freud, reproaching him for his mistrust of the mount. For the steed may at times know better than its rider, and the best thing then is to let the mount (the wisdom of nature) bear one on.[8]

This had long been a leading theme, not only of Thomas Mann, but also of German literature generally. Already, for example, in the early thirteenth-century *Parzival* of Wolfram von Eschenbach, it was only when the young

Grail Knight let his reins lie slack on his powerful charger's neck that he was carried on his proper course. Such a basic trust—even to the length, sometimes, of letting nature tide one along in a perilous way dangerous to reason, morality, and possibly even to life—is opposed altogether to Freud's leading thesis, which he once epitomized in the sentence: "Where there is id there shall be ego." In Mann, on the contrary, there is very much of id, even though much, also, of ego. The two are not opposed, as in Freud, but complementary. And this conduces in the novelist's work to a quality of irony that is as different as can be from the deliberately "useful cognitions" of the medical man—who by profession, of course, is more strictly committed than the artist to what his intellect tells him is health. In fact, there is implied in the reckless turning over of the reins of prudence to nature a certain dubious strain of what Thomas Mann has called a "sympathy with death."

But, paradoxically, there is a death of opposite kind in store for those who would protect themselves from such a waking; and that is the leading lesson of *Buddenbrooks*—which Mann wrote, by the way, before he reached twenty-five. It is a tale of the psychological disorientation of a nineteenth-century North German business family, paralleling in its course the decline generally in Central Europe of the old conservative burgher class and the rise of a new-rich bourgeoisie. We are introduced to four generations, losing progressively their courage for adventure, each of the members of generation three—Thomas, Christian, and Tony (their sister)—sacrificing in the name of loyalty to the firm every youthful impulse to an individual life. And all lose thereby not only their feeling for life but also, disastrously, their heritage of feeling for success. They make one wrong decision after another, until Thomas, the eldest, increasingly conscious of the onerous weight of his duties and the unlikelihood of anything ever again coming off as it should, finally knows, one day, that all is lost. The firm is in desperate straits, misjudgments having all but wrecked it; and his only child, little Hanno, sickly, deeply afraid, sensitive, and with a gift for the arts but no will to pursue the disciplines, has no will to live and will shortly die. The moment has come (that is to say) that has come to many a good father in our time, of realizing that what he had lived and toiled for had been (to quote Mann's earlier novelette, *Little Herr Friedemann*) "all lies and imagination."

Thomas, however, does not drown himself. Instead, he one day chances on a copy of Schopenhauer's *World as Will and Idea,* and there learns that we are all embodiments of one universal Will and that our true being, moreover, is not in our temporal physical bodies, but in our metaphysical unity in that Will. He had been thinking of immortality only in temporal terms, as a continuation into future; and of his own immortality in social terms, as pertaining somehow to the family, to be passed on through a son. From Schopenhauer, however, he now learns of eternity as a presence, here and now, some kind of universal ground.

The chapter to which he had opened bore the title "On Death, and Its Relation to the Indestructibility of our True Being," and when he closed the book, he felt himself to have been both deepened and expanded.[9] Filled with the sense of a strange, sweet, vague allurement that reproduced somehow the feelings of early love, he that night slept more prodigiously than ever before in his life—to wake next morning sobbing, after what he immediately knew had been a wisdom-dream.

"I shall live!" he thought; "for *It* lives and I am *It*, living now and forever in all beings." And with that, from that time on, his brief remaining days were penetrated, consoled, and pacified by a deep "sympathy with death" and willingness to let go.

Mann associates such allure with the philosophies of Asia, the force of the Freudian id, and the rapture of music—especially Wagner's perfumed sea of sound. And he balances against all these the values of ego, the rational intellect, social duties, integrity of character, and what, in his celebration of Freud, he had referred to as "useful cognition."

Now one of the very great influences on Wagner's art was the philosophy of Schopenhauer, and during those years of Thomas Mann's growing up, Wagner's operas were the great new thing in the world.[10] The composer himself in his autobiography tells of the overwhelming effect upon him of his first reading of *The World as Will and Idea;* and Thomas Mann, in turn, describes in a number of passages the influence of Wagner's art on his own.[11] Schopenhauer had likened the appeal of music to the force of the Will in nature, and Wagner, seizing upon this thought, conceived the music of his operas to represent the motivation of his characters.[12] Mann, continuing in this vein, thought of the musicality of his prose (not always evident in translation) as suffusing with life the meticulously described details of his narrative.

There is a beautiful essay by Schopenhauer on *The Foundation of Morality* in which he asks the following question: How is it that one human being can experience the pain and danger of another as though it were his own, and to such a degree that he will forget himself and, putting his own life in jeopardy, go spontaneously to that other's rescue? Schopenhauer's answer is that such an act occurs because that other is in truth oneself, the notion of a separate ego served in the field of space-time by "useful cognition" being secondary only. You and I are in substance one, objectifications of the one Will and in the experience of compassion (*Mitleid*) this truth is immediately recognized. In Schopenhauer's own words:

As soon as this sentiment of compassion is aroused the weal and woe of another comes to lie directly on my heart in exactly the same way—though not always to the same degree—as otherwise only my own would lie, and therewith the difference between him and me is absolute no longer. And this surely is amazing—even mysterious. It is, in fact, the great mystery inherent in all morality, the prime integrand of ethics, and a gate beyond which the only type of speculation that can presume to venture a single step must be metaphysical.

Now right here, I would say, is the key, the nugget-thought and founding realization of the principle of irony in the novels of Thomas Mann. For although, as Schopenhauer maintains, this impulse of compassion is the basis of all morality, it is equally a basis of what must appear to the world to be immorality, since, like God, it makes no distinction between good and evil. According to the Gospel: the Father makes his sun to rise on the evil and on the good, sends rain on the just and on the unjust: judge not that ye may not be judged. Normally we think of ethics as a function of the principle of judgment, supporting right against wrong, good against evil, truth against falsehood, fair against foul, whereas here is a teaching that would know morality rather as a function of the principle of mercy. There is a word of Paul to the Romans in which this mystery is epitomized (and which supplied James Joyce, by the way, with the motto of his *Finnegans Wake*): "For God has consigned all men to disobedience, that he may have mercy upon all."[13] The very act of living is an affirmation of what is false—the illusion of separateness and distinction; and where this illusion is so recognized, there may follow a denial of the will to life: Hamlet's question, "To be or not to be . . . "; Mann's theme of the "sympathy with death"; the "love-death" theme, *mild und leise,* of Wagner's *Tristan and Isolde;* and more brutally, Calvin's doctrine of the "total depravity" of human nature.

The most forceful, thoroughgoing answer to such a baffled, guilt-ridden posture of negation, of course, is Nietzsche's ironic affirmation of life in all its ambiguity; and Mann immediately following his completion of *Buddenbrooks,* moved ahead to this in his next story, *Tonio Kröger,* which appeared in 1903; and as he has himself declared of this work, it was here that he truly found himself and the philosophy proper to his art.

The youthful hero, Tonio Kröger, whose name already tells of the mixture in him of two worlds—the North German of his father and the Latin of his mother—found himself set apart temperamentally as well as in appearance from his blue-eyed blond companions, and accordingly, on coming of age, left his northern home to fashion for himself in a city of the South a destiny of his own among others who, like himself, would have "dropped out" into a "Hippieville" of intellect and art—or, as it was termed in those days, Bohemia. The inhabitants were of two orders: first, those frightened by life, who, like Schopenhauer, had intuitively penetrated the veil of phenomenality and were wallowing now in Bunyan's "Slough of Despond," spiritual paralysis, existential "nausea," and sympathy with death; and then those, more like the majority of our current college "intellectuals," who had set up in their heads an ideal for human life and conduct to which no living thing had ever in the history of the human race conformed, and from the prospects of that unassailable tower of thought were demolishing with volleys of rhetoric every earthly institution and personage of public trust within reach of their winged words. Both were types of what Nietzsche had called "Decadents," people with little talent for life: girls who fell down when they danced and chaps who, like Tonio, had felt, one way or another, isolated, special, and apart—the very types, in short, that Freud was to characterize as "artists." Their motivation was self-defensive resentment, and the whole sense of their relentless talk, disparagement.

Tonio, however, soon found himself no more at ease among such critics of the commonality of the human race than he had formerly felt among the objects of their scorn; for although he had himself departed from the burgher world, he had not departed in resentment. He loved life, and he had even loved those handsome blue-eyed blonds among whom he had been a stranger—particularly a certain charming Hans and beautiful Ingeborg, to whom he had secretly pledged his heart. He presently realized, therefore, with a melancholy pang, that he was at home neither here nor there: a "lost burgher," as he termed himself, "between two worlds," that of people who could act without thinking, and this of critics who could think but not do very much.

Now he had become acquainted in his southern refuge with a young Russian woman, Lisaveta by name; and when he had quit her circle he sent back to her a letter setting forth his credo as an artist.

The right word, *le mot juste,* he had recognized, wounds and can even kill; yet the duty of the writer must be to name and to name exactly. But what chiefly have to be named in a person are his imperfections, since in human life perfection does not exist. Perfection is cold, impersonal, finally uninteresting. (All the Buddhas, they say, are alike. Having gained release from the imperfections of this world, they have left it, never to return.) Accordingly, what makes a person lovable are precisely his imperfections and what the "right word" names as an imperfection is exactly what is to be loved. The arrow of judgment, then, is to fly to its mark with a balm on its point of compassion; for the function of art is not annihilation, but celebration. Tonio Kröger wrote to his intellectual friend:

> I admire those proud and cold creatures who adventure on paths of great daemonic beauty and despise "mankind": but I do not envy them; for if there is anything capable of making a poet of a literary man, it is this burgher-like love that I feel for the human, the commonplace and what is alive. All warmth derives from this, all goodness and all humor; and to me it even seems that this must be that

very love of which it has been written that though I speak with the tongue of men and of the angels, if I have not this, I am as sounding brass or a clanging cymbal. . . .

"Erotic" or "plastic irony" is the name that Thomas Mann gave to this principle. It is basically a Nietzschean principle, recognizing first with Schopenhauer the inherent fault and injustice in every act of life, but then, with a courageous leap of faith, so to say, affirming all with a resounding "yea." And it was this profoundly compassionate, while equally ruthless, manner of seeing and naming that supported Mann, giving life to his art, throughout the better part of his career.

Now it appears to me that my principal aim should be to show how this guiding principle of "erotic" or "plastic irony" opened out in Mann's later writings to an extraordinarily rich appreciation and creative utilization of traditional mythic themes; and I might do this best by reviewing the main lines and themes of his great novel *The Magic Mountain.* This is a work that appeared in 1924, just two years following Joyce's *Ulysses.* The two men had developed independently, Joyce from an Irish Catholic background, Mann from a German Protestant. And it seems to me a matter of the greatest literary interest that these two paramount authors of the first decades of our century moved in their development, stage by stage in equal pace, along parallel courses—from the late-nineteenth-century manner of the naturalistic novel, through the mythologically suggestive, only apparently naturalistic stage of *Ulysses* and *The Magic Mountain,* on to the frankly mythological final masterworks of *Finnegans Wake* (1938) and the *Joseph* novels (1934–44).

Mann himself informs us that the inspiration that in time developed into the novel of *The Magic Mountain* first occurred to him in 1912, when with his wife he went for a visit of three weeks to a sanatorium in Davos, Switzerland. The idea that occurred to him there, as he tells, was to place a young man of somewhat delicate health and disposition between two questionable pedagogues in just such a morally dangerous environment. But he had hardly begun to develop this thought when along came the First World War, and for the next three or four years he remained emotionally caught in a great tangle of social-historical problems and analyses: of conservatism vs. progressivism, Germany vs. France and England, and again following the lead of Nietzsche, what sickness it was, of the European soul, that in this total war had broken to the surface. Now from this side, now from that, he reviewed and resolved these unresolvable questions, and in a great, tumultuous sea of a book, *Betrachtungen eines Unpolitischen,* brought his ruminations forward at the close of the war.[14] In *The*

Magic Mountain they are brought forward again, but in a balanced, harmonized, orderly way, attached ironically to that earlier thought of the two questionable pedagogues and morally dangerous environment—with a young German marine-engineer as hero, and the setting, of course, the same international sanatorium that he had visited, 1912, in the Alps.

The novel is in two volumes. The first tells of the arrival of its hero, Hans Castorp, in the Davos sanatorium Berghof, "Mountain Court," for a visit of three weeks with his cousin, a young army officer named Joachim, but where he was actually to spend seven years. Volume I, that is to say, is the tale of his relaxation to, and acquiescence in, a really dangerous adventure, and volume II then deals with his analysis, interpretation, and creative assimilation of the realizations gained, concerning disease and death, life and lust, love, society, nature, and the nature of man, as well as, of course, himself.

The visit had been suggested by his doctor, not because of any hint of illness, but simply for a change of air. He was not strong and his work was getting a little on his nerves. It was exacting. He respected it. But he enjoyed much more his holidays and the luxury of relaxing with a Maria Mancini cigar.

And so it was with considerable expectation that he boarded, one midsummer day, a train from the "flatland" of his daily tasks to the beautiful Swiss vacation-land, transferring there to one of those marvelous little toylike trains that go winding up incredible heights, up, and then up still more—leaving behind, at last, the deciduous trees that annually shed their leaves and so mark the years and the seasons, entering a region of eternal snows and unchanging evergreens. He had passed from time to a kind of eternity: a region, furthermore, of such rarefied air that his heart was beating like crazy when he arrived, and he was excited, like a lover about to be blessed.

Already his body has gotten ahead of him, so to say, and is leading his spirit—which is already the announcement of death and beginning of disintegration. When he steps from the little train he is greeted by his charming cousin: fresh, athletic, tanned, and looking so full of life! yet sick actually unto death. In other words, the arriving hero is being greeted here, in this land of the living dead, by King Death himself, wearing the mask of Life. And his educator here, for the next seven years, will be exactly this mythological figure, along with his consort, Lady Lust.

Death and disease, lust and lechery, as educators, disintegrators and transformers that tear apart programs and intentions, the mind as well as the body, and carry one away on a wild vertiginous adventure!

The room in the sanatorium to which Hans found himself assigned, and in which he thought he would spend three weeks, bore the number 34, which was already a prophecy of what awaited him. For three plus four is seven—seven years. Seven also is the number of those visible spheres (Moon, Mercury, and Venus, Sun, Mars, Jupiter, and Saturn) by which the soul ascends to heaven from earthly to eternal wisdom. It is the number, furthermore, of time (Past, Present, Future) plus space (North, South, East, and West), and so, of the Universe, totality. Thus we have started already with a magical note, not exactly proper to a good, old, down-to-earth, naturalistic novel.

The bed in that room, into which Hans, our hero, collapses at the end of his first exciting day, had been the deathbed, just before, of an American girl; so that, in falling asleep he is joined with her in mystic marriage, as it were, in the night of death, and in dreaming, picks up, so to say, where she left off. Suggested, also, in this image is the mythological androgyne motif. One thinks of Tiresias, for example, whom Odysseus found in the Underworld, who in life had been magically turned into a female and, after a spell of seven years, back into his male form again.

Now the guiding measure of Hans's stay in the mountain is to be his body-temperature as registered by the mercury of a thermometer. Mercury, the god, is the Roman counterpart of the Greek Hermes (Egyptian Thot), the guide of souls to the Underworld and, through death and corruption, to rebirth in eternal life. Mercurius in alchemy, furthermore, is the power that transmutes base matter into gold; and in order to be in this way transmuted, the raw material has to be *hermetically* sealed in a retort: sealed away by the god Hermes from all influences of the common world, so that the feverish process of interior transformation may proceed according to internal laws without outside interruption.[15] Thomas Mann has likened such an ideal of education, which he terms "hermetic pedagogy," to this figure of the alchemist's retort. Not the hue and cry of the moment, but the influences of perennial themes, the arts, philosophies, and sciences, are to be allowed to work for a time unhindered on the spirit, according to this reasoning. However, not all are in a condition of readiness for such influences. Not all on the Magic Mountain were, like Hans, in a condition, so to say, of spiritual pregnancy. Three, by the way, is an active, masculine number; four, a passive feminine; so that already in the number of his room, 34, success in the adventure is foretold.

Well, when our mystic bridegroom, aged twenty-three, woke the following morning and had shaved, he went out onto his balcony and, viewing the picturesque mountain-scene of eternal snows and peaks, heard strains of a music being somewhere played. He loved music and, when listening, would make his music-listening face: abstracted, stupid, sleepy, and pious. Below, in the garden, there was an old woman walking, deathly pale, in black: a Mexican, as Hans later learned, who had just lost, up here, her two sons. And as she walked, she was keeping time unconsciously to the music. Hans returned to his room, where, through the wall, he now heard from the room next door sounds of a wrestling, giggling, and panting, that brought to his countenance a flush which, very curiously, never left it again the whole period of his stay.

His cousin Joachim arrived to conduct him down to breakfast, and in the dining room, while meeting, greeting, and learning to know the other members of his table, he was rudely jarred and irritated when someone, entering, let the door slam, bang! right behind him. "Pfui!" he thought. "What kind of slob is that?" But he was held in conversation, unable to turn.

Then he was introduced to the two governing doctors: Behrens in a long white surgeon's coat, and Krakowski, the psychologist, in a smock of shiny black. White and black, these two, a brother-pair, like Minos and Rhadaman-thys, judges of the dead in the afterworld, were highly questionable fellows, unhealthy-looking shepherds, hosts and entertainers of a questionable flock.

Next, our adventuring innocent of delicate health and disposition, meets in this morally dangerous palace of Death the first of those two pedagogues whom Thomas Mann had had in mind when first conceiving this symbolic work. Appearing at the opening of a chapter entitled "Satana," he is Mann's counterpart of Goethe's Mephistopheles: an Italian, Settembrini, moderately tall, attractive with his black moustache, first seen by Hans standing in an easy posture, leaning on his can with his legs crossed. He is a writer of political tracts, a theoretical humanist and social disciplinarian, instinctively interested in capturing people's souls. He will be unstinting in instruction, companionship, and advice, his politics of the order that used to be known as "liberal." Not Marx and Engels, but Garibaldi, Carducci, and Mazzini, and before them, the eighteenth-century rhetoricians of the rights of man, were his models and antecedents.[16] His immediate advice to Hans, very shortly after meeting him, was to quit this mountain resort of corruption right away, before it trapped him, and to return to his social duties at home. Hans, however, saw him rather as one of those bowing, smiling, Italian hand-organ men who used to be seen on the streets grinding out familiar tunes, with an amusing little monkey on a string who would take your pennies in his little black hand and tip to you his little cap. Like his neatly kept ideas, his black-and-white checked trousers, a bit old and a bit threadworn, were always neatly pressed. And he was certainly civilized: there was no question about that.

But the startling carnival atmosphere of this Saturnalian health resort had already caught the young visitor's fancy. His cheeks were already flushed. And the way he would burst out laughing at every odd grimace of King Death gave notice that his character was unraveling. As Mann himself has pointed out, Death appears in this book as a comic figure. Hans had arrived with many romantic feelings of piety before death and about the special dignity of the sick, whereas here he soon learns of a club of jolly "half-lungers." Others, with punctured lungs, would lewdly whistle at him through the puncture. The dead were sent flying downhill on bobsleds. Death the Clown, as educator, was upsetting all his ideas. Moreover, Settembrini, with his Latin eye for the girls, had his own way of regarding the goings-on of this land of the walking dead. "Look," he would whisper as Krakowski passed by. "There he goes and knows all our women's secrets. He has only one idea in his head, and that's a dirty one."

Then it happened—in the dining hall: the door slammed again—at the fish course; and Hans turned in anger, to see.

Now the fish, you must know, is an animal sacred to Aphrodite. One eats fish on Friday, "Venus's Day." And we have also to remember that Christ, symbolized in early Christian art in the figure of the fish, was crucified on a Friday, immolated in love. The door slammed at the fish course. Hans turned—and there she was; and he was hooked.

A young woman of middle stature was gliding on her way to the Russian table with her red-blond hair wound simply about her head in braids. We think of Circe of the Braided Locks. And she moved without a sound, in wonderful contrast to the noise of her entrance, her head a little thrust forward, one hand in the pocket of a close-fitting white woolen sweater and the other, raised to the back of her head, supporting and ordering her hair. Her name was Clavdia, Clavdia Chauchat; and that evening there was a touch of blood on Hans's handkerchief.

He was not only psychologically hooked, but actually in physical danger, and the remaining chapters of this volume will treat of his separation from Settembrini's control and passage, fatefully, irresistibly, into Clavdia's keep and spell, Mann's model for the stages and symbolism of this transit being Part II, Act II, of Goethe's *Faust:* that marvelous passage known as the "Classical Walpurgisnight," where Faust, desiring Helen of Troy—who can be found only in Persephone's realm, the Classical land of the dead—flies on a magic carpet with the aid of Mephistopheles to a carnival scene of the ancient gods, there to unite with her in marriage. I am not going to review these scenes in detail, but shall point briefly to a few parallels, the first being that of the definite separation of Faust (Hans) from the guardianship and companionship of Mephistopheles (Settembrini).

This occurs in Goethe's work at the point where the two, Mephistopheles and his pupil, arrive before the figure of the Sphinx; not the great Egyptian

Sphinx, but the Greek: its forepart, the head and bust of a beautiful human female; its rear, a lithe animal form.[17] Mephistopheles, attracted to the animal aspect, turns in that direction and goes thereafter his own way among all the
leading half-animal freaks of the ancient pantheon: sirens, lamias, the vampire
Empusa, and the rest, ending finally with three old gray hags having but one
tooth and one eye between them; whereas Faust, turning to the human, personal aspect of the challenging symbol of the riddle of life, is lead by a succession
of guides to the chamber of that very one whose face (in the poet Marlowe's
words) "launched a thousand ships and burnt the topless towers of Ilium." In
The Magic Mountain the ways of the two go apart at the baseline of their experiences of the allure and mystery of love's body: Settembrini with his Latin eye for
the girls and Hans with his sense of a mystery through which he would learn of
the wonder of life.

The critical episode occurred when Dr. Behrens invited Hans with his
cousin to the X-ray laboratory of the sanatorium. Not the light-world of Settembrini's order of reason, but darkness here would be the medium of illumination. "We must first wash our eyes in darkness," Behrens said, "and get cat's
eyes" (Madame Chau*chat's* eyes!) He let Hans view his cousin's whole chest at
the fluoroscope and, after that, his own hand—where he looked as it were, into
his own grave. "Spooky, what?" remarked the doctor. "My God!" said Hans in
awe. "I see!" And he had indeed seen and realized something deeper about the
Sphinx-enigma of death in life and life in death than the clarity of Settembrini's thinking ever would have taught him.

His next adventure occurred when Behrens invited him to his rooms for a
talk where a portrait hung of Clavdia. It was not a very good portrait, painted by
the doctor himself, but good enough to excite Hans to a detailed examination
of its qualities. The two sat down to coffee, ground from a coffeemill apparently
of Indian manufacture, bearing an erotic ornamentation which, when Hans
took it in, made him blush. The doctor was descanting upon the advantage to
his art of his knowledge of anatomy. "If a man knows a bit," said he, "about what
goes on under the epidermis, it helps." And Hans, significantly stirred, with his
eyes attempting to penetrate the paint of Clavdia's lightly veiled bosom, resolved then and there to improve his time during the sanatorium rest-hours by
a regimen of readings in the science of anatomy, to learn, like Behrens, something of the mysteries to be known beneath Clavdia's interesting epidermis.

In Goethe's *Faust*, when the hero in quest of Helen of Troy has, at the
Sphinx, separated from Mephistopheles, he is met by the centaur Chiron
(teacher of many heroes of Antiquity), who conducts him to the goddess
Manto (daughter of the god of medicine, Aesculapius), who, as patroness of all

mystic wisdom, points him to Persephone's realm. In *The Magic Mountain* Behrens plays the role in this scene of Chiron, turning Hans from the insubstantial rhetoric of Settembrini's political lore to the life-wisdom and world-wisdom of the sciences. Beginning with anatomy, probing the epidermis for its treasures beneath—the oil glands, sweat glands, coursing of the lymph, etc.—the fascinated student is led on from the laws of Clavdia's interesting form to those of nature in general, organic and then physical, to astronomy, physics, and the universe: all in amplification of his initial interest in Clavdia's bosom, lightly veiled. Which leads him, finally, to a consideration of the mystery of death and dying. In his conversation with Behrens he had asked to know what caused decomposition. "Oxidation," he had been told. Then he asked to know what gave life, and again heard, "Oxidation." "So what is the difference?" he asked; and Dr. Behrens answered: "Form! Life is that which in the process of changing matter holds its form." Corruption follows from the loss of form. And Hans, with Clavdia's form on his mind, held his ruminating eye to her picture.

The title of the chapter of Hans's early conversations with Settembrini is "Encyclopaedics"; that of his talk with Behrens, "Humaniora"; the chapter of his avid readings, "Researches"; and that of his visits to the bedsides of the moribunds in the Mountain Court, "The Dance of the Death." Then comes the great chapter of his meeting with Lady Lust, Lady Beauty, the goddess of his stay up here, corresponding to Goethe's Act III of *Faust*, "The Marriage of Faust and Helen." Mann titled his own scene "Walpurgisnight." The occasion was a party at carnival time, when the basic health rules of the institution were for one evening disregarded. Everybody was in festival dress, and when Clavdia in a simple, modest, black frock appeared with her white arms bare to the shoulders, Hans had to catch his breath: *"Mein Gott! Mein Gott!"* he murmured.

A blindfold game was instituted, the aim, to try to draw a pig blindfolded. (We are exactly in Circe's isle.) And as Goethe's Faust was guided to Helen's palace by a magical key held in hand, so here, when it came time for Hans to attempt to draw, he turned directly to Clavdia for a pencil. *"Eh! Ingegnere! Aspetti! Che cosa fa!"* called Settembrini in dire warning. Hans addressed her even with "du": *Hast du nicht vielleicht einen Bleistift?"* She answered partly in French. And when the company later had dispersed, game and evening ended, he went down to her on his knees, a little drunk, altogether undone, and threw himself on her mercy. In a curious Germanic French, he told of his rapture in the wonder of her feverish mortal body, the symmetry of its white shoulders, hips, breasts, and ribs arranged in pairs, the delicacy of her backbone, and so on . . . *"Le corps, l'amour, la mort . . ."* he prayed. And she, wearing for the Saturnalian occasion a little three-cornered paper hat, like a child, set this on his head, and rising to go, called softly back, *"N'oubliez pas de me rendre mon crayon."*

That is the end of volume I, chronicling the variously dangerous, comical adventure of Hans from his flatland home to the mountain-palace of King Death, spurning the warnings of a concerned pedagogue, and coming to the very threshold and chamber of the Mountain Queen.

❦❦❦

"Well, Engineer," said Settembrini, some weeks later, "how did the pomegranate taste? Those who have eaten the fruit of the underworld don't often return."[18]

"Carducci, Latini, Humani, Spaghetti," thought Hans, "disappear!"

Volume II would be of his inward-turning and assimilation of what had been learned. Clavdia had departed for a visit to the flatland. He had returned the pencil and acquired thereby an X-ray portrait of her chest and infected lungs. He was now an old-timer, at home in the timelessness and irresponsibility of just-one-day-after-another. April had come, and it was about this time that Settembrini introduced him to the second of the two educators whom Thomas Mann had had in mind when first conceiving this work. We have already met and learned to enjoy the first: Satana, Settembrini, a scion of the light, the Renaissance, and the Enlightenment. The second, now, whose name is Naphta, is a Jew, a Jesuit and Communist: a compendium of the whole history of that other, righteously authoritarian, heretic-burning line of our mixed heritage, standing not for persuasive reason, but the authority of an incontestable sanctified Book of one kind or another. Mann's model for this figure was the Marxist theoretician Gyorgy Lukács, whose nimble changes of position to fit the line of whatever Communist clique chanced to be currently in the saddle enabled him to survive through the years one Party purge after another. (Mann himself had helped rescue Lukács from Budapest in 1929, when the times had changed quicker than he, and Lukács, in turn, in 1949, back safely in Budapest, brought forth an appreciative study of Thomas Mann.) In *The Magic Mountain,* Naphta is described as small and thin, of a piercing, corrosive ugliness, with a large hooked nose dominating his hard tight mouth, and pale eyes behind thick glasses. He was always excellently tailored in dark-blue flannel and dwelt in rented rooms in town above the shop of a ladies' tailor, by name, Lukacek.

Almost a quarter of the novel is given over to the philosophical and sociological arguments—for days and years—of these two irrepressible talkers: Joachim and Hans between them, listening now with this ear, now that. And there was much that Hans learned from each: from Settembrini, the rhetoric of reason, and from Naphta, the reign of death. "Not liberation and development of the individual are the secret and requirement of this present age,"

Naphta once declared to the assembled group. "What it needs, what it yearns for, and what it will create for itself is—the Terror."

But Settembrini's own revolution also had known something of the politics of terror. Hans, by accident one day, had mispronounced his name in such a way as to suggest the word "September": there is in French a word, *septembrisades*, referring to the "September" massacres of the French Revolution (1792), when the aristocrats in Paris jails were all mercilessly slaughtered. Ironically, too, Settembrini was a Freemason, so that, in spite of all his fine talk about spiritual freedom and the individual, there was in his own background a hidden tradition of oaths of secrecy and obedience, mystic orders, Oriental symbols, and ritual hocus-pocus. On learning of this from Naphta, Hans was amazed.

And so it came to pass, after he had been listening with both ears for a good quarter of the novel to these two contending men of words, that he went forth alone, one winter afternoon, on skis, impelled by he knew not what. And sliding along not skillfully, he began to be overtaken by fatigue. There was an abandoned hut ahead, he made for it and, standing, leaning hard against it, took a sip from a flask of port that he had brought along, which, however, instead of giving him strength, put him to sleep, still standing on his skis; and he dreamed there a marvelous dream.

It was of a Mediterranean landscape, where beautiful people moved harmoniously among trees and Classical buildings: children, people young and old, dancing, strolling, riding horses, and the like, with a noble dignity that drew from his heart the exclamation "Oh lovely, lovely!"

Then, however, he turned and behind him saw another scene—of horror: a dark temple wherein were two gray old hags, tearing in dreadful silence a child apart. He was appalled.

Now in Nietzsche's *Birth of Tragedy* there is an almost identical scene symbolizing, at the end of the work, the balance in Classical tragedy of Apollonian beauty and Dionysian horror; and I could only wonder, when this identity first struck me, how conscious Thomas Mann might have been of the similarity when he wrote this.[19] I had the good fortune to know at that time a lady very close to the Mann family, Mrs. Eugene Meyer, one of whose daughters had been a student of mine at Sarah Lawrence. Mann himself, at the time, was in Princeton. That was in 1941. And so on one occasion I asked Mrs. Meyer what she knew of this: whether Mann had possibly not realized how closely, in this scene in which the whole experience of the novel culminated, he was following Friedrich Nietzsche. She answered with a look of real interest: "When I see Tommy next, I'll ask him." And a week later there came in the mail the following note, which I have kept as my principal treasure of those years.

Showed him the passage toward the end of the *Geburt* [*The Birth of Tragedy*] upon which his vision is so obviously based. He was struck dumb with surprise: had forgotten it entirely and probably wrote the whole version without consciously recalling where he got it. Interesting.

There have been, of course, in the history of literature and art quite a number of instances of such unconscious acts of recall. Cryptomnesia, "hidden memory," the phenomenon is called, and Carl Jung, in his first important paper, "On the Psychology of So-called Occult Phenomena" (published in 1902, four years before he met Freud), produced an example from the writings of Nietzsche himself. In a second article on the same subject he wrote as follows:

> The brain never forgets any impression, no matter how slight. . . . Consciousness, on the other hand, operates with an unending loss of previous impressions. . . . Under special conditions the re-emergence of old memory traces with photographic fidelity is by no means impossible. . . . The work of genius fetches up these distant fragments in order to build them into a new and meaningful structure.[20]

Hans woke with a start from his sight of the horrible hags, but the spell of the earlier scene was still upon him and he thought—using a term, *Homo Dei,* that he had first heard from Naphta's lips: Man, *Homo Dei,* is the lord both of death and of life. He alone is noble, not they. More noble than life is the piety of his heart; more noble than death, the freedom of his thought. And love, not reason, is stronger than death. Love, not reason, gives gentle thoughts. And not reason but love and gentleness render form, form and civilization, in silent recognition of the feast of blood.

So now, having with that dream and thought transcended all the verbalizations of his two literary pedagogues, Hans, in the remainder of his days up there, was to be furnished two examples of his discovered hero, *Homo Dei.* The first would be his cousin Joachim, who, like Naphta, was vowed to an iron discipline, a life, as Hans playfully phrased it, of "poverty, chastity, and obedience." Unlike the other's dedication, however, the soldier's—though also under the sign of death—was to the ends of life in *this* world. His silent presence, always beside his cousin, inspired their nickname, Castor and Pollux: of which mythic pair, it will be recalled, Castor (Castorp) was the mortal brother, Pollux (Joachim), the immortal. And one of the most moving chapters of the novel is that in which this noble, soldierly young man does indeed pass to immortality. Like Hans, he had been smitten by the exotic glamour of a young Russian woman on the Mountain. However, unlike Hans, he did not let go, renouncing his duties to the flatland, but was so impatient for his career that he left before his cure was ended—only to have to return, to be put to bed, and to die. His body had won against his manly spirit; or, as Hans could not but wonder: "Had it not been perhaps the form of Marusya that had brought him back; so that it was, rather, his heart that had won?" There is a moral here—the main moral of the book; namely, that in yielding to the allure of his noble heart, the Man of God may fare better and more truly to Wisdom than through honoring hard and fixed rules.

The second example of the features of *Homo Dei* that Hans was to experience appeared with the return to the Mountain of his goddess. She was, one day, already in the dining room and the door had not slammed—because caught behind her and closed quietly by a robust but lean, white-haired gentleman who accompanied her to her table and there took his place by her side: Mynheer Peeperkorn, by name, a Dutch coffee-planter from the Indies, a truly marvelous character, of imposing presence and great mobility of gesture, but never a finished sentence: quite a change, in fact, from the arguing pair whom Hans, throughout all these months and years, had been studiously heeding. Peeperkorn, in short, was a personality, and his talk was fascinating rather as an expression of himself in play than as a reference to some valuable thought. And the amusing scene through which the wonder of this culminating symbolic figure of the novel is displayed is an incongruous picnic, to which he had invited an assortment of seven guests, including Settembrini and Naphta. He settled them all directly under a waterfall, the great noise of which made conversation impossible; and with that, of course, the two educators were wiped out. Nature took over and the exhilarated company, moving closer to the great cascade, communicated by looks and signs, mouthing unheard vocables of admiration. A few climbed up a rocky path alongside the waterfall, reached a bridge that went across, from which they could look up, then down, and wave to those below; after which they descended by the other side—having gotten nowhere, nowhere at all. Hans in his studies of astronomy had been impressed by the joyous though aimless circling of the planets, and this little round had been of the same kind. The elated company settled to their banquet and when all had been eaten, Peeperkorn, their host, imbibing from a silver cup, suddenly rose and began to speak: raising the cup, pointing to the waterfall, mouthing words nobody could hear. And his speech went on, directed now to one, now to another of the fascinated company, hanging on his unheard eloquence. And he seemed now to be some kind of heathen priest of wine and dance, now the image of the Man of Sorrows. He grandly flourished the cup, drank it down, and waved the party closed.

That is the climax of the book: a sort of Zen koan.

But to move along! The novel ends with a chapter of which the title, "The Thunderbolt," refers to the news of the guns of the First World War. Hans in

Switzerland was out of it, and he could have remained up there on his mountain, hermetically sealed away, or he could have entered the fray on the side of Settembrini's politics, of England, Russia, and France. But what, in fact, he decided to do was to enter and participate where his flesh and blood—his birth and his nature—called him. At the opening of the novel, he had been unable to endure even the harmless grind of an office job. Now, on the other hand, after a season of seven years of self-and-life discovery and testing, guided by the mercury of his own temperature through death and corruption to rebirth, he returns to the world as one capable of action out of his own directive center, not simply in reaction to the claims and calls of others. And he accepts life at its worst—at war—in its whole character, that is to say; for life is in fact a battlefield: life lives on life, life kills, life eats. Fire, burning, oxidation, is of its essence. Hans's return to the world is an act of love, a giving of himself, as to a marriage. And let me tell you, if you are going to marry someone to change and improve him, better not. Likewise, if you are saying yea to the world to improve it, please, just leave us alone. There is but one way to say yea in love, and that is to affirm what is there. That is true love; and, as Paul says, "Love bears all things."

And so now, in conclusion, let me return to that festival occasion of Thomas Mann's celebration of Freud. Exactly halfway through his Saturnalian talk, he let fall the unutterable name, he named Jung. He protected himself by referring to the man as an "ungrateful scion of the Freudian school," which he must have known was untrue. Jung never studied under Freud, but was himself an authority on the psychology of schizophrenia when he met Freud in 1907, at the age of thirty-two, and was immediately appointed Permanent President of the International Psychoanalytic Association. Moreover, it was not Jung who broke with Freud, but Freud who broke with Jung, when he realized that the younger man's psychology could never be identified with his own. Freud interpreted dreams as allegorical distortions of repressed infantile wishes, and when, in *Totem and Tabu*, he extended this view to the interpretation of myths and rites, he again looked back to infancy—now the infancy of the race—to explain the reference of their symbols. Jung, on the other hand, saw myth as symbolic, finally, not of occurrences in the past, but of structures and powers of the psyche and consequently antecedent to history; and Mann saw them this way too. Moreover, certain dreams (which Jung called "big dreams") might be interpreted, according to this view, as transcending personal experience and biography, pointing in the way of revelations of the great transpersonal mysteries of life and death, being, non-being, phenomenality and the like. The deep dream of Thomas Buddenbrook, after his dip into Schopenhauer, was a dream of this mythic sort, not to be read in Freudian terms—and not read by Mann in Freudian terms. Again, still more impressively, Hans Castorp's dream in the snow, which Mann (by cryptomnesia) had taken from Nietzsche, was interpreted by Mann himself, not in Freudian style, but Jungian. So it is no wonder that when he had progressed in his talk to a discussion of *Joseph and His Brothers* it was to Jung that he had finally to refer.

Mann spoke of Jung as providing a bridge between Occidental thought and Oriental esoteric, and launched then into an open attack on Freud for his ignorance of philosophy and overestimation of his own science. All that science can do, Mann declared, is to write the Q.E.D. to some philosophical proposition; and those that Freud had demonstrated, whether knowingly or unknowingly, were of the great German Romantics: Novalis, Schopenhauer, Nietzsche, and so on; whereas Jung had enlarged on the insights of such thinkers through his understanding not only of Oriental esoteric lore but also of the Greek and Egyptian hermetic mysteries. Schopenhauer's proposition, which Freud had scientifically demonstrated, that what happens to one is actually of one's own doing, Jung had recognized as already announced in *The Tibetan Book of the Dead*. . . . And from this point on, for the next two pages of his fifteen-page oration, Mann is quoting, nearly word for word, from Jung's important commentary on that text.[21]

Not only is what happens to one the effect (à la Freud) of one's own doing, but the world itself, as man knows it, is "given" by the nature of man's organs of knowledge. The psyche is the "giver" of the "given," i.e. the possibilities of experience; and among the "given"—as the East well knows—are the gods. Ergo: the soul, the human psyche, is the ultimate radiant godhead, transcendent of all such categories of temporal experience as I and Thou, This and That, Subject and Object. The soul itself is the giver of what is "known" as "God."

Such an idea, however, states Mann (quoting Jung), is intolerable to the Occidental religious sense, even though certain Christian mystics have recognized and proclaimed it; Angelus Silesius, for example, where he declares:

> I know that without me
>   God could not one moment be;
> Were I destroyed, then he
>   Would disappear instantly.

Such an alignment of God with the soul is *not* the same as Freud's idea of God as a projection into the universe of an infantile father-image. God is *not* an illusion here, to be explained away, but a symbol pointing beyond itself to the realization of a mystery of at-one-ment. What is here referred to is *not* to be discovered at the end of a "pudendascope" (as James Joyce names Freud's psychology) but is antecedent to all categories (even Sigmund Freud's) of thought and research.

Nor is it compatible with the biblical notion of God as a kind of fact, a personality (or, as Ernst Haeckel once quipped, a "gaseous vertebrate"), who in some distant past, the infancy of the race, appeared to certain Hebrews and arranged with them a Covenant. Mann alludes respectfully to this imagined prehistoric event and then proceeds to elucidate, in the final third of his lecture, the method by which in his *Joseph* novels he has dealt with it; namely, in such a way as to accord with both the Jungian approach and the Freudian, the Oriental-mystical and the Hebrew-pseudo-historical in such a way (as he declares) that "the concept of the soul as 'giver of the given' reaches an ironic pitch not authorized either in Oriental wisdom or in psychological perception." Mann, that is to say the artist-maker and dreamer of dreams, not given, like Freud, to "useful cognition," but to fantasizing only, had (in his own estimation) surpassed not only both Freud and Jung, but also the prophets and the mystics with his dreamlike ironic affirmation of both terms of the opposition simultaneously. He states in his talk,

> God's mighty qualities—and thus God Himself, are indeed something objective, exterior to Abram; but at the same time they are in him and of him. The power of his own soul is at times scarcely to be distinguished from them, it consciously interpenetrates and fuses with them—and such is the origin of the bond that the Lord then strikes with Abram, as the explicit confirmation of an inward fact.[22]

Having disclosed his Jungian affinities, Mann next gives witness to his Freudian, by citing a recent article in the Freudian journal *Imago*, where the very idea of mythic biography is described, which he, for some years already, had been developing in his *Joseph* novels: the idea, so to speak, of an individual life lived consciously on the model of a mythical archetype, and so, incorporating its values. This, in fact, has been an idea fundamental to all traditional cultures. The *Imitatio Christi* of Thomas à Kempis affords an example, and Christ himself, as the Matthew Gospel tells, went into and out of Egypt, spoke in parables, healed the sick, and so on, as prophesied of the Messiah, "so that the Scripture might be fulfilled." Cleopatra identified herself with Isis, Hathor, Ishtar, and Aphrodite. Or the model might be of some historical figure whose life has become legendary. Alexander the Great walked in the footsteps of Miltiades; Caesar imitated Alexander and Napoleon imitated Caesar. "Much that is extrapersonal, much unconscious identification, much that is conventional and schematic," declared Mann to the listening company, "is nonetheless decisive for the experience not only of the artist but of the human being in general." Indeed, every child imitates its parents. And at this point in his discourse Mann was pleased to remark that in the Freudian essay to which he was referring, his own *Joseph* novels had been favorably cited as examples: for, as he next went on to explain, "the 'myth' as lived is the epic idea embodied in my novel; and it is plain to me that when as a novelist I took the step in my subject-matter from the bourgeois and individual to the mythical and typical, my personal connection with the analytic field passed into its acute stage." —As indeed it did; for with that, he had passed from the sphere of the Freudian ego and "personal unconscious" to the Jungian (transpersonal) "archetypes of the collective."

Mann's hero, Joseph, played consciously the *imitatio* of that great Mediterranean god of many names, discussed by Frazer in *The Golden Bough,* who annually died and was resurrected (Tammuz, Adonis, Attis, Osiris); and since that is the very god whose image lives with us still in the mystery of the death and resurrection of Christ, and is set before us by the Christian Church as the model for us all, Mann was able to ring a great many bells simultaneously as he developed his Joseph theme, pointing both backward to our pre-Christian past, and forward to our present—it being evident, also, that this same fundamental myth had been the model of Hans Castorp's spiritual death and rebirth on the Magic Mountain.

Mann declared, in summation, now clearly much closer to Jung than to Freud:

> For the myth is the foundation of life; it is the timeless schema, the pious formula into which life flows when it reproduces its traits out of the unconscious. And when a writer has acquired the habit of regarding life as mythical and typical, there comes a curious heightening of his artist temper, a new refreshment of his perceiving and shaping powers, such as otherwise occurs only much later in life; for while in the life of the human race the mythical is an early and primitive stage, in the life of the individual it is a late and mature one. What is gained is an insight into the higher truth depicted in the actual; a smiling knowledge of the eternal, the ever-being and authentic; a knowledge of the *schema* in which and according to which the supposed individual lives, unaware, in his naive belief in himself as unique in space and time, of the extent to which his life is but formula and repetition, and his path marked out for him by those who trod it before him.[23]

Well, so much for Thomas Mann's birthday oration in celebration of Freud. Let me conclude by noting, now, what occurred shortly after 1936.

Asia moved into Europe, with the aid first of Hitler, then of England, France, and the United States; so that now a good half has been lost of that precious ego-world of the European progressive consciousness which, as Mann has said, has always maintained itself precariously against the overlapping sea of the id and of Asia. The world as it stood in 1936 has been wiped out, and indeed we now have Asia even more intimately among us in our current zeal for Zen, kibbutzim, Hinduism, Oriental mysticism, and meditation. This regressive Orientalization is something far more threatening to the civilization Mann stood for than anything he, or anyone else of his generation (except

Oswald Spengler), ever imagined. Mann himself soon left Germany and took refuge in the United States, where he set to work immediately writing political speeches to urge our country into the war. And I am sorry to say, but it seems to me all too evident, that his art from that moment declined.

And here I come to a great and final problem; that, namely, of the incompatibility of art and politics.

The first three of Mann's *Joseph* novels had been completed by 1936. The fourth appeared only seven years later, in 1943. And whereas in the earlier works—particularly volume II, *Young Joseph,* but also volume III, *Joseph in Egypt*—he had been developing with incredible skill a gorgeous art of mythic resonances, in volume IV, *Joseph the Provider,* the whole glorious balloon has collapsed to earth. All the wonderful mythic resonances are gone, and we have little more than a masterfully written family narrative telling of how a handsome son, thought dead, made a great success of it in Egypt as psychoanalyst to the Pharaoh, interpreting his dreams, and so found himself in a position to give substantial aid to his old father and numerous brothers when they flocked to the capital city to obtain what we call today "relief."

Mann himself, in his earlier days, had declared that the artist has to lead two lives, between two worlds: one participating in society, where blood and nature bind him, and the other, removed, as artist. "Politicians," Johan Strindberg once said in a statement that Mann himself quotes in his *Reflections of a Non-Political Man,* "are one-eyed cats." They see out of this eye, or that, either right or left, and in fact, one cannot live or act without standing for and representing one side or another. However, as artist one is to see with *both* eyes and (as Tonio Kröger told Lisaveta) to name ruthlessly, yet with affirming love. James Joyce, it is worth remarking, remained loyal throughout to the two-eyed view and his art held firm to the end. However (as we also know), Joyce had never to face quite such an experience as that which unsettled Mann, when his beloved Hans and Ingeborg were transformed under Hitler into what he could only regard as monsters. His love failed him at that point and his art declined.

Can one treat of such things with the balanced vision of an artist? Has a human heart such magnitude? "Love bears all things," Saint Paul has said. "Judge not that you may not be judged," said Christ. The limitation comes where your judgment comes. The revelation of art is not of ethics or a judgment—not even of humanity as one generally thinks of it—but a marveling recognition of the radiant Form of forms that shines through all things; and as our own great American master, Nathaniel Hawthorne, has said in a little story called *Fancy's Show Box* (telling of what dreams and fancies show of the innermost truth of each of us): "Man shall not disclaim his brotherhood even with the guiltiest."

Appendix 1: Select Bibliography of the Works of Joseph Campbell

Following is a select bibliography of Campbell's more important works, including the essays in this volume, arranged in chronological order.

"Heinrich Zimmer (1890–1943)." *Partisan Review*, 20 (July 1943): 415–416.

A Skeleton Key to Finnegans Wake. With Henry Morton Robinson. New York: Harcourt, Brace & Co., 1944. New York: Penguin Books, 1977.

The Hero with a Thousand Faces. Bollingen 27. New York: Pantheon Books, 1949. 2nd ed. rev. Princeton: Princeton University Press, 1968.

The Flight of the Wild Gander: Explorations in the Mythological Dimension. New York: Viking Press, 1951. 2nd rev. ed. New York: Harper & Row, 1990.

"Hinduism." In *Basic Beliefs: The Religious Philosophies of Mankind*. Ed. Johnson E. Fairchild. New York: Sheridan House, 1959. Subsequent ed. New York: Hart Publishing Co., n.d.

"The Historical Development of Mythology." *Daedalus: Journal of The American Academy of Arts and Sciences*, 88 (1959).

Renewal Myths and Rites of the Primitive Hunters and Planters. Eranos-Jahrbücher 28. Zürich: Rhein-Verlag, 1959. Reprint. Dallas: Spring Publications, 1989.

The Masks of God. 4 vols. New York: Viking Press, 1959–1968. Vol. 1, *Primitive Mythology*, 1959. Vol. 2, *Oriental Mythology*, 1962. Vol. 3, *Occidental Mythology*, 1964. Vol. 4, *Creative Mythology*, 1968. Pb. ed. Arkana, 1991.

Introduction to *Myth, Religion, and Mother Right* by J. J. Bachofen. Princeton: Princeton University Press, 1967. Pb. eds. 1973, 1992.

"Mythological Themes in Creative Literature and Art." In *Myth, Dreams, and Religion*. Ed. Joseph Campbell. New York, E.P. Dutton, 1970. Pb. reprint. Dallas: Spring Publications, 1988.

Myths to Live By. New York, Viking Press, 1972. New York: Bantam Books, 1973.

"Erotic Irony in the Art of Thomas Mann." In *Essays from the Sarah Lawrence Faculty*. Bronxville, NY: Sarah Lawrence College, 1973.

The Mythic Image. Bollingen 100. Princeton: Princeton University Press, 1974. Pb. ed. Princeton: Princeton Unversity Press, 1983.

"The Occult in Myth and Literature." In *Literature and the Occult: Essays in Comparative Literature*. Ed. Luanne Frank. Arlington, Texas: UTA Publications in Literature, 1977.

"The Interpretation of Symbolic Forms." In *The Binding of Proteus*. Ed. Marjorie W. McCune, Tucker Orbison and Philip M. Withim. Lewisburg, Pennsylvania: Bucknell University Press, 1980.

Inner Reaches of Outer Space: Metaphor as Myth and as Religion. New York: Alfred van der Marck Editions, 1986. New York: HarperCollins, HarperPerennial, 1988.

The Historical Atlas of World Mythology.

    Vol. 1, *The Way of the Animal Powers*. New York: Alfred van der Marck Editions, 1983. Reprint in 2 pts. Part 1, *Mythologies of the Primitive Hunters and Gatherers*. New York: Alfred van der Marck Editions, 1988. Reprint of Part 1. New York:

Harper and Row Perennial Library, 1988. Part 2, *Mythologies of the Great Hunt*. New York: Alfred van der Marck Editions, 1988. Reprint of Part 2. New York: Harper and Row Perennial Library, 1988.

Vol. 2, *The Way of the Seeded Earth*. 3 pts. Part 1, *The Sacrifice*. New York: Alfred van der Marck Editions, 1988. Reprint. Harper & Row Perennial Library, 1988. Part 2, *Mythologies of the Primitive Planters: The Northern Americas*. New York: Harper & Row Perennial Library, 1989. Part 3, *Mythologies of the Primitive Planters: The Middle and Southern Americas*. New York: Harper & Row Perennial Library, 1989.

"Creativity." In *C. G. Jung and the Humanities: Toward a Hermeneutics of Culture*. Eds. Karin Barnaby and Pellegrino D'Acierno. Princeton: Princeton University Press, 1990.

"The Mystery Number of the Goddess." In *In All Her Names*, Ed. Charles Muses and Joseph Campbell. San Francisco: HarperSanFrancisco, 1991.

The Power of Myth. With Bill Moyers. Ed. Betty Sue Flowers. New York: Doubleday, 1988. New York: Anchor Books, 1991.

Reflections on the Art of Living: A Joseph Campbell Companion. Ed. Diane K. Osbon. New York: HarperCollins, 1991.

Mythic Worlds, Modern Words: On the Art of James Joyce. Ed. Edmund L. Epstein. New York: HarperCollins, 1993.

Baksheesh and Brahman: Indian Journal 1954–1955. Eds. Robin and Stephen Larsen and Antony Van Couvering. New York: HarperCollins, 1995.

Appendix 2: Reading List for Joseph Campbell's Class on Mythology at Sarah Lawrence College

The following books were characteristically assigned by Joseph Campbell for his mythology course at Sarah Lawrence College. Eighty to eighty-five percent of these titles appeared each year as part of his course reading list. Where Campbell favored a particular edition, it is listed here, along with a modern edition if very old; otherwise, a good modern edition is shown.

Ovid. *Metamorphoses.* Trans. Allen Mandelbaum. New York: Harcourt Brace, 1993.

Frazer, Sir James George. *The Golden Bough.* One-volume ed. New York: The Macmillan Company, 1922. Also, abridged from the second and third editions, ed. Robert Frazer. Oxford and New York: Oxford University Press, 1994.

Durkheim, Emile. *The Elementary Forms of Religious Life.* Trans. Karen E. Fields. New York: The Free Press, 1994.

Levy-Bruhl, Lucien. *How Natives Think.* Trans. Lilian A. Clare. Princeton: Princeton University Press, 1985.

Freud, Sigmund. *The Interpretation of Dreams.* Trans. James Strachey. New York: Basic Books, 1995.

——. *Three Contributions to a Theory of Sex.* Trans. A. A. Brill. New York: E. P. Dutton, 1962.

——. *Totem and Taboo.* Trans. A. A. Brill. New York: Vintage Books, 1950.

——. *Moses and Monotheism.* Trans. Katherine A. Jones. New York: Vintage Books, 1967.

Jung, Carl Gustav. *Integration of the Personality.* Trans. Stanley M. Dell. New York and Toronto: Farrar & Rinehart, 1939.

The Secret of the Golden Flower: A Chinese Book of Life. Translated and explained by Richard Wilhelm, with a foreword and commentary by C. G. Jung. Revised and augmented edition. New York: Harcourt Brace Jovanovich, 1962.

The Tibetan Book of the Dead, or, The After-Death Experiences on the Bardo Plane: according to Lama Kazi Dawa-Samdup's English rendering. Compiled and edited by W. Y. Evans-Wentz. New York: Oxford University Press, 1960.

Coomaraswamy, Ananda. *The Dance of Śiva.* London: Simpkin, Marshall, Hamilton, Kent and Co., 1924. Reprint. New York: Dover Publications, 1985.

The Bhagavad Gita. Trans. W. J. Johnson. Oxford and New York: Oxford University Press, 1994.

Okakuru, Kazuko. *The Book of Tea.* Tokyo & New York: Kodansha International, 1989.

Watts, Alan. *The Way of Zen.* New York: Pantheon, 1957.

Herrigel, Eugen. *Zen in the Art of Archery.* Trans. R. F. C. Hull. New York: Vintage Books, 1989

Lao-Tze, *The Canon of Reason and Virtue* (Tao Te Ching). Chinese and English. Trans. D. T. Suzuki and Paul Carus. La Salle, Ill: Open Court, 1974.

Sun-Tzu, *The Art of War.* Trans. Thomas Cleary. Boston: Shambhala, 1988.

Confucius, *Analects.* Trans. and annotated by Arthur Waley. Reprint of 1938 Allen & Unwin edition. London and Boston: Unwin Hyman, 1988.

——. *The Great Digest and Unwobbling Pivot.* Trans. Ezra Pound. New York, 1951.

Chiera, Edward, *They Wrote in Clay; the Babylonian Tablets Speak Today.* Ed. George G. Cameron. Chicago: University of Chicago Press, 1938.

Nietzsche, Friedrich Wilhelm. *The Birth of Tragedy.* Trans. Walter Kaufmann. New York: Vintage Books, 1967.

Bible, New Testament, Book of Luke

Aeschylus. *Prometheus Bound.* Trans. James Scully and C. J. Herrington. New York: Oxford University Press, 1975.

Euripides. *Hippolytus.* Trans. Richard Lattimore, in *Four Tragedies.* Chicago: University of Chicago, 1955.

———. *Alcestis.* Trans. William Arrowsmith. New York: Oxford University Press, 1974.

Sophocles. *Oedipus Tyrannus.* Trans. and ed. by Luci Berkowitz & Theodore F. Brunner. A Norton Critical Edition. New York, Norton, 1970.

Plato. *Phaedrus.* Trans. R. Hackforth, in *The Collected Dialogues of Plato.* Ed. Edith Hamilton & Huntington Cairns. Bollingen Series LCXXI. Princeton: Princeton University Press, 1961.

———. *Symposium.* Trans. Michael Joyce, in *The Collected Dialogues of Plato.*

The Koran. Trans. N. J. Dawood. 3rd rev. ed. Baltimore: Penguin Books, 1968.

The Portable Arabian Nights. Ed. Joseph Campbell. New York: Viking Books, 1951.

Beowulf. Trans. Lucien Dean Pearson. Ed. Rowland L. Collins. Bloomington: Indiana University Press, 1965.

Prose Edda of Snorri Sturluson. Trans. Arthur Gilchrist Brodeur. New York: The American-Scandinavian Foundation, 1916. Also, trans. Jean I. Young. Berkeley: University of California Press, 1964.

Poetic Edda. Trans. Henry Adams Bellows. New York: The American-Scandinavian Foundation, 1926. Also, trans. Lee N. Hollander. 2nd ed., rev. Austin: University of Texas Press, 1962.

The Mabinogion. Trans. Jeffrey Gantz. New York: Dorset Press, 1985.

Grimm, Jacob and Wilhelm. *Grimm's Fairy Tales.* New York: Pantheon, 1944.

Adams, Henry. *Mont Saint Michel and Chartres.* Boston: Houghton Mifflin, 1932. Also New York: New American Library, 1961.

Boas, Franz. *Race, Language, and Culture.* New York: The Macmillan Co., 1940.

Mann, Thomas. "Tonio Kröger," trans. H. T. Lowe-Porter, in *Stories of Three Decades.* New York: Alfred A. Knopf, 1936.

Thompson, Stith. *Tales of the North American Indians.* Cambridge: Harvard University Press, 1929.

Opler, Morris Edward. *Myths and Tales of the Jicarilla Apache Indians.* New York: The American Folk-lore Society, 1938.

Benedict, Ruth. *Patterns of Culture.* Boston: Houghton Mifflin, 1934, 1989.

Stimson, John E. *Legends of Maui and Tahaki.* Honolulu: The Museum, 1934.

Melville, Herman. *Typee.* The Library of America. New York: Literary Classics of the United States, distrib. by the Viking Press, 1982.

Frobenius, Leo, and Douglas C. Fox. *African Genesis.* New York: B. Blom, 1966.

Radin, Paul. *African Folktales and Sculpture.* 2nd ed., rev., with additions. New York: Pantheon Books, 1964.

Deren, Maya. *Divine Horsemen: The Living Gods of Haiti.* New Paltz, NY: McPherson, 1983.

Endnotes

Editor's comments are placed within brackets. References to Campbell's works are given in short form for simplicity; full references may be found in Appendix 1 above.

COMPARATIVE MYTHOLOGY AS AN INTRODUCTION TO CROSS-CULTURAL STUDIES

[1] [For a complete listing of the books assigned by Campbell for his class at Sarah Lawrence, see Appendix 2.]

[2] [The interested reader is referred to Campbell's discussion of his intellectual background in "The Dialogue of Scholarship and Romance," *Primitive Myth*, pp. 8–18; for Tylor and Frazer see p. 14; for Müller, p. 17; for Radcliffe-Brown, pp. 33–34. See also *Flight of the Wild Gander*, pp. 30, 33, 43–51.]

[3] [See *Mythic Image*, pp. 450–81, esp. figs. 394, 397–99.]

[4] [For a discussion of this trans-Pacific influence, see *Mythic Image*, pp. 104–39, esp. map 2, pp. 134–35.]

[5] [For more on Job, see *The Joseph Campbell Companion*, pp. 164–67.]

[6] [See "The Signatures of the Four Great Domains" in *Oriental Mythology*, esp. pp. 30–34.]

[7] [Aeschylus, *Prometheus Bound*, 938–39.]

[8] [Some of these lectures were converted into the book *Myths to Live By*.]

[9] ["Mask, Myth, and Dream," WNET-TV, 1963.]

THE HISTORICAL DEVELOPMENT OF MYTHOLOGY

[1] [Campbell elaborated many of the ideas presented in this lecture in his series of books *The Masks of God*, especially in the early chapters of *Primitive Mythology*.]

[2] *Nonni Dionysiaca* 6.121; *Orphei Hymni* 39.7; 253. [See also *Primitive Mythology*, pp. 101–2.]

[3] O. Kern, *Orphicorum fragmenta* (Berlin, 1922), p. 34.

[4] Kern, *Orphicorum fragmenta*, pp. 34, 35.

[5] F. M. Cornford, *Greek Religious Thought from Homer to the Age of Alexander* (London: J. M. Dent & Sons, Ltd.; New York: E. P. Dutton & Co., Inc., 1923), pp. xv–xvi.

[6] Cornford, *Greek Religious Thought*, p. xiii.

[7] E. J. Rapson, ed., *The Cambridge History of India* (New York: The Macmillan Company, 1922), vol. I, pp. 434–61, 541–61.

[8] Leo Frobenius, *Paideuma, Umrisse einer Kulter- und Seelenlehre* (3 Aufl., Frankfurt, 1928), pp. 143–45.

[9] Cornford, *Greek Religious Thought*, pp. x–xii.

[10] *Brihadāranyaka Upanishad* 1.4.6–10.

[11] H. Diels, *Die Fragmente der Vorsokratiker*, vol. I, 4th ed. (Berlin, 1922).

[12] Cited by Clement of Alexandria, *Exhortation to the Greeks*, p. 61.

[13] *Kena Upanishad* 1.3.

[14] J. Huizinga, *Homo Ludens*, trans. R.F.C. Hull (London: Routledge & Kegan Paul Ltd., 1949), p. 5.

[15] Huizinga, *Homo Ludens*, p. 22.

[16] Huizinga, *Homo Ludens*, p. 23, citing R. R. Marett, *The Threshold of Religion* (New York, 1914), p. 45.

[17] Huizinga, *Homo Ludens*, p. 25.

[18] Heinrich Zimmer, *Philosophies of India*, ed. Joseph Campbell (New York: Pantheon Press, 1951), pp. 581 ff.

[19] Swami Nikhilananda, trans., *The Gospel of Sri Ramakrishna* (New York: Ramakrishna-Vivekananda Center, 1942), p. 396.

[20] Nikhilananda, *Gospel of Sri Ramakrishna*, p. 396.

[21] Nikhilananda, *Gospel of Sri Ramakrishna*, pp. 778–79.

[22] Huizinga, *Homo Ludens*, pp. 34–35.

[23]Kant, *Prolegomena zu einer jeden künftigen Metaphysik, die als Wissenschaft wird auftreten können* (Werke, Leipzig, 1838–1842, Theil 3), paragraph 58 (italics added). [See also *Inner Reaches*, pp. 55–58, for Kant's formula; also, "Identity and Relationship," in *Creative Mythology*, pp. 338–48.]

RENEWAL MYTHS AND RITES OF THE PRIMITIVE HUNTERS AND PLANTERS

[1]Emil Bächler, *Das alpine Paläolithikum der Schweiz* (Basel, 1940). [See also *Historical Atlas*, I.1, map 20, figs. 80–83, 85.]

[2]Konrad Hörmann, "Abhandlungen der Naturhistorischen Gesellschaft zu Nürnberg," *Die Petershöhle bei Velden in Mittelfranken* (1923).

[3]Henry Fairfield Osborn, *Men of the Old Stone Age*, 3rd ed. (New York: Charles Scribner's Sons, 1925), figs. 5–6, pp. 115–214.

[4]Osborn, *Men of the Old Stone Age*, pp. 115–214, citing H. Klaatsch and O. Hauser, "Homo aurignacensis Hauseri, ein paläolithischer Skelettfund aus dem untern Aurignacien der Station Combe-Capell bei Montferrand (Périgord)." *Prähistorische Zeitschrift* (1910), Bd. I, Heft 3–4, pp. 273–338. [See also *Historical Atlas*, I.1., figs. 71–76.]

[5]A. C. Blanc, "L'homme fossile du Mont Circé." *L'Anthropologie* 49:3 (Paris, 1939), pp. 253–64.

[6]Rudolf Otto, *The Idea of the Holy*, trans. J. W. Harvey (London: Oxford University Press, 3rd impression, revised, 1925), p. 7.

[7]Kyosuki Kindaiti, *Ainu Life and Legends*, Tourist Library 36 (Tokyo, 1941), p. 50. [See *Historical Atlas*, I.2, pp. 152–55, figs. 262–64 for the Ainu bear-cult.]

[8][See Spengler, "Herbivores and Beasts of Prey," ch. II, sec. 3 of *Man and Technics*, trans. Francis Atkinson (New York: Alfred A. Knopf, 1932), pp.19–27.]

[9]Leo Frobenius, "Atlantis," *Volksmärchen der Kabylen*, vol. I (Jena: Eugen Diederichs, 1921), p. 15.

[10][See Joseph Campbell, "Life's Delicate Child," *Saturday Review of Literature 28* (October 1945), pp. 56–58: a review of Géza Róheim's *The Origin and Function of Culture*.]

[11]Kindaiti, *Ainu Life*, pp. 51–52.

[12]I. Bachelor, "Ainus," *Encyclopedia of Religion and Ethics*, vol. I, ed. James Hastings (New York: Charles Scribner's Sons, 1928), pp. 249–50; and Kindaiti, *Ainu Life*, pp. 52–54.

[13]Luther Friedrich Zotz, *Die schlesischen Höhlen und ihre eiszeitlichen Bewohner* (Breslau, 1937); *Die Altsteinzeit in Niederschlesien* (Leipzig, 1939). Also, Wilhelm Koppers, "Künstlicher Zahnschliff am Bären im Altpaläolithikum und bei den Ainu auf Sachalin," *Quartar*, 1938, pp. 97 ff. [See *Historical Atlas*, I.2, map 34, p. 147 for distribution of the circumpolar bear cults; also, *Primitive Mythology*, p. 340.]

[14]Herbert Kühn, "Das Problem des Urmonotheismus," *Abhandlungen der Geistes-und Sozialwissenschaftlichen Klasse*, Akademie der Wissenschaften und der Literatur in Mainz, Nr. 22 (Wiesbaden: Franz-Steiner-Verlag, 1950).

[15]Kindaiti, *Ainu Life*, pp. 41–47.

[16]Otto, *Idea of the Holy*, pp. 16–17.

[17][In "The Awakening of Awe," *Historical Atlas*, I.1, p. 25, Campbell quotes Spengler briefly on the spiritual force of death. Spengler goes further:

> Man is the only being that knows death; all others become old, but with a consciousness wholly limited to the moment, which must seem to them eternal. They see death, not knowing anything about it. . . . Only fully awakened man, man proper, . . . comes to possess . . . the *notion* of transience . . . we so often find the awakening of the inner life in a child associated with the death of some relation. The child *suddenly* grasps the lifeless corpse for what it is, something that has become wholly matter, wholly space, and at the same moment it feels itself as an individual *being* in an alien extended world. . . . Here, in the decisive moments of existence, when man first becomes man and realizes his immense loneliness in the universal, the world-fear reveals itself for the first time as the essentially human fear in the presence of death . . . here too, the higher thought originates as meditation upon death. Every religion, every scientific investigation, every philosophy proceeds from it. Every great symbolism attaches its form language to the

cult of the dead, the forms of disposal of the dead, the adornment of the graves of the dead" (Oswald Spengler, *The Decline of The West*, trans. and ed. Charles Francis Atkinson, vol. I [New York: Alfred A. Knopf, 1926], pp. 166–67).]

[18]Jean Piaget, *The Child's Conception of the World* (New York: Harcourt, Brace & Company, 1929), p. 362.

[19]["The lord of the animals breaks a horn off one of the antelopes and hands it to the hunter. In the future, he must allow some drops of blood to run into this horn from every animal he kills ... this horn of blood is a survival of the days when human beings pictured themselves praying before the image of the great buffalo. It is a symbol of a predominantly *magical culture.*" (*Leo Frobenius 1873–1973: An Anthology,* ed. Eike Huberland, trans. Patricia Crampton (Wiesbaden: F. Steiner, 1973), p. 65). For the horn, or "calabash," see *Historical Atlas,* I.1, fig.109.]

[20]George Bird Grinnel, *Blackfoot Lodge Tales* (New York: Charles Scribner's Sons, 1916), pp. 104–7, 220–24. [Also, see *Historical Atlas,* I.2, p. 234.]

[21]["It is 'Lord Buffalo' who ... bestowed on the favored hunter the right to kill animals from specific herds. We often hear about a 'lord of the animals' who rules the congregation of all animals as their highest embodiment" (Leo Frobenius, *An Anthology,* p. 65).]

[22][For an illustration of this scene, see *Historical Atlas,* II.1, fig. 3, p. 8.]

[23]["The Pygmy of the Central African forests who shot his arrow into the picture and then into the body of the antelope—the first at the very moment when the eye of day cast its first glance upon the picture—who then mixed the blood from the horn with his picture—was releasing himself from the curse of blood. An attitude to life which has become quite alien to us is being expressed here ... to this attitude everything becomes spiritualized matter; the name, the glance, the blood. The seat of life is not in the blood but the blood is life. The name is not a sound, it is matter, and as such a part of its bearer. The glance is matter, its effect is material. Hence the constant fear of the evil eye. And accordingly, the image of an object, a man, an animal is also part of the thing portrayed and the influence it exerts on the image extends to the living exemplar, the object portrayed itself ... the part stands for the whole. This is the philosophy of the ancient hunter civilization." (Frobenius, *An Anthology,* pp. 66–67.)]

[24][*Historical Atlas,* I.1, fig. 136.]

[25]Knud Rasmussen, *Across Arctic America* (New York & London: G. P. Putnam's Sons, 1927), p. 80.

[26]*Bhagavad Gītā* 2:17–18.

[27]Ovid, *Metamorphoses,* XV, 165–68.

[28]["It is the intimate attachment to plant life, whether through root, grain, or juice, which works on the culture and gives it its shape. The outlook which arises from the hunting life, the battle for blood and death, culminates in intoxication and in a sensually-based magic. But the creative spirit arising from plant life sheds its dream over the mystery of life." (Frobenius, *An Anthology,* p. 71.)]

[29][See *Primitive Mythology,* p. 167, for Frobenius's map of equatorial distribution of ritual regicide; also, *Historical Atlas,* I.2, map 33 (for diffusion of bisexual mythic beings) and II.1, map 7 (for the range of ritual cannibalism).]

[30][See "The Descent and Return of the Maiden," *Primitive Mythology,* pp. 173–76.]

[31]Adolf E. Jensen, "Die mythische Weltbetrachtung der alten Pflanzer-Völker," *Eranos-Jahrbuch* XVII/1949 (Zürich: Rhein-Verlag, 1950); also, Jensen, *Das religiöse Weltbild einer frühen Kultur* (Stuttgart: August-Schröder-Verlag, 1949).

[32][For an elaboration of this people and their myths, see "The Festival" and "The Offering," *Historical Atlas,* II.1, pp. 53–73, and accompanying illustrations.]

[33]Paul Wirz, *Die Marind-anim von Holländisch-Süd-Neuguinea,* vol. II (Hamburg: L. Friedrichsen & Co., 1925), pp. 40–44.

[34]Cf. Henri Frankfort, *Kingship and the Gods: A Study of Ancient Near Eastern Religion as the Integration of Society and Nature* (Chicago: University of Chicago Press, 1948), pp. 400–401, n. 12.

[35]Sir Leonard Woolley, *Ur of the Chaldees* (London: Ernest Benn, Ltd., 1929), pp. 46–56. [For illustrations of these materials, see *Historical Atlas,* II.1, figs. 166–81.]

[36][See *Historical Atlas,* I.1, figs. 77–79; II. 1, fig. 100.]

[37]Genesis 3:1–24.

[38][See *Historical Atlas,* II.1, fig. 97.]

[39]Duarte Barbosa, *A Description of the Coasts of East Africa and Malabar in the Sixteenth Century* (London: Hakluyt Society, 1866), p. 172, cited by Sir James G. Frazer, *The Golden Bough,* one-volume edition (New York: The Macmillan Company, 1922), pp. 274–75.

[40]Woolley, *Ur of the Chaldees.*

[41]["The northern philosophy expressed in animal pictures was matched by the southern sensitivity to the plant world. The northern experience of frenzy and the oscillation between high tension and deep relaxation is matched here by a twilight existence, a dream state; here a surrender to life, there a life subservient to the will" (Frobenius, *An Anthology,* p. 70). See also "The Sacrifice," *Historical Atlas,* II.1, pp. 32–33.]

[42]Leo Frobenius, *Der Kopf als Schicksal* (München, 1924), p. 88, as cited by Carl Kerényi in *Essays on a Science of Mythology* by C. G. Jung and C. Kerényi (New York: Pantheon Books, 1949), pp. 141–42.

[43][See "Men and Tools of the Old Stone Age," in *Historical Atlas,* I.1, pp. 22–23.]

[44]Raymond Dart, "Some Aspects of the Significance of the Australopithecine Osteodontokeratic Culture," in *Fifth International Congress of Anthropological and Ethnological Sciences* (Philadelphia: September 1956).

[45]Raymond Dart, "The Makapansgat Australopithecine Osteodontokeratic Culture," in *Third Panafrican Congress of Prehistory,* ed. J. Desmond Clark (London: Chatto & Windus, 1957), pp. 161–71.

[46]Joseph Epes Brown, *The Sacred Pipe: Black Elk's Account of the Seven Rites of the Oglala Sioux* (Norman: University of Oklahoma Press, 1953), p. 80.

[47]Brown, *Sacred Pipe,* p. 4, n. 2.

[48]Brown, *Sacred Pipe,* p. 5, n. 4.

[49]Brown, *Sacred Pipe,* p. 108.

[50]Frazer, *Golden Bough,* p. 386.

[51]Exodus 32:1–20.

[52]Exodus 34:29–35.

[53]Brown, *Sacred Pipe,* pp. 3–7.

[54]Brown, *Sacred Pipe,* p. 23.

[55]Brown, *Sacred Pipe,* p. 25.

[56]Brown, *Sacred Pipe,* p. 21, citing Francis La Flesche, *War Ceremony and Peace Ceremony of the Osage Indians,* Bureau of American Ethnology Bulletin No. 101 (Washington, D.C., 1939), pp. 62–63.

[57]Carl G. Jung, *The Integration of the Personality* (New York & Toronto: Farrar & Rinehart, Inc., 1939), p. 189.

[58]Brown, *Sacred Pipe,* pp. 5–6, nn. 6, 7.

[59]Brown, *Sacred Pipe,* p. 7, n. 10. [In alchemy, red and black also signify two different stages of the process of transfiguration. Black is the color of the first stage, the *nigredo,* in which the substance to be transformed must first be broken down into a *prima materia,* or primordial mass. In the individuation process, this corresponds to the disintegration of the ego under the impact of the repressed energies of the unconscious. It is appropriate that the Indian who took the black road of the senses and their earthly attachments was turned into a pile of bones. Red, on the other hand, signifies the third stage, the *rubedo,* or reddening, which is the spiritual goal of the entire alchemical opus: gold is produced as the direct product of the fusion of the opposites sulfur and mercury, or Sol and Luna. In the individuation process, this corresponds to the formation of a stable and unified personality, configured in the unconscious by the production of a uniting symbol, such as a mandala, signifying the attainment of a new attitude born of the fusion of conscious and unconscious elements. The red road of the Sioux myth, correspondingly, leads to the way of spiritual illumination, the black road only to earthly entanglement and, ultimately, death.]

[60]Brown, *Sacred Pipe,* pp. 7–9.

[61]George E. Hyde, *Red Cloud's Folk, A History of the Oglala Sioux* (Norman: University of Oklahoma Press, 1936).

[62]Hyde, *Red Cloud's Folk.*

[63]Gordon R. Willey and Philip Phillips, *Method and Theory in American Archeology* (Chicago: University of Chicago Press, 1958), pp. 158–66.

[64]Carl O. Sauer, "Cultivated Plants of South and Central America," *Handbook of South American Indians,* ed. Julian H. Steward, Smithsonian Institution, Bureau of American Ethnology, vol. VI, Bulletin 143 (Washington, D.C., 1950), pp. 487–543. [See also, "Agricultural Origins and Dispersals," *Historical Atlas,* II.1, pp. 12–17, esp. map 3 ("The Americas") and figs. 5, 6.]

[65]Cf. George F. Carter, "Plants across the Pacific," *American Antiquity,* vol. XVIII, no. 3, pt. 2 (January 1953), pp. 62–63, 71; and Frederick Johnson, "Radiocarbon Dating," *Memoirs of the American Society for American Archaeology,* no. 8 (Salt Lake City, 1951), p. 10, Sample no. 321; also, Sauer, "Cultivated Plants of South and Central America," pp. 506, 537–38.

[66]["Leo Frobenius announced a new approach to the study of primitive cultures (the *Kulturkreislehre,* 'culture area theory'), wherein he identified a primitive cultural continuum, extending from equatorial West Africa, eastward through India and Polynesia, across the Pacific to equatorial America and the northwest coast. This was a radical challenge to the older "parallel development" or "psychological" schools of interpretation, such as Brinton, Bastian, Tylor, and Frazer had represented, inasmuch as it brought the broad and bold theory of a primitive transoceanic "diffusion" to bear upon the question of the distribution of so-called "universal" themes" (*Primitive Mythology,* p. 15).]

[67][See *Historical Atlas,* I.2, fig. 379 for illustration.]

[68]Willey and Phillips, *Method and Theory,* pp. 163–70.

[69]Gordon F. Eckholm, "A Possible Focus of Asiatic Influence in the Late Classic Cultures of Mesoamerica," *Memoirs of the Society of American Archaeology,* vol. XVIII, no.3, pt. 2 (Washington, D.C.: 1953), pp. 72–89; also, Gordon F. Eckholm, "The New Orientation Toward Problems of Asiatic-American Relationships," in *New Interpretations of Aboriginal American Culture History: 75th Anniversary Volume of the Anthropological Society of Washington* (Washington, D.C.: 1955), pp. 95–109.

[70][See, for example, *Historical Atlas,* I.2., p. 156, figs. 269–272.]

[71][See *Historical Atlas,* I.1, pp. 64–65, figs. 103–4.]

[72][See *Historical Atlas,* I.1, p. 76, fig. 132.]

[73][See *Historical Atlas,* I.1, p. 65, fig. 105.]

[74][See *Historical Atlas,* I.1, p. 77, fig. 134.]

[75][See *Primitive Mythology,* p. 387.]

[76]Brown, *Sacred Pipe,* p. 6, n. 8; p. 9, n. 15. Also, George A. Dorsey, *The Pawnee: Mythology,* Pt. 1, The Carnegie Institute of Washington (Washington, D.C.: 1906), p. 134.

[77][See "The Parade of Ants," *Myths and Symbols,* pp. 3–11; for Hairy and the circle of hair, see p. 9.]

[78][See "The Enigma of the Inherited Image," *Primitive Mythology,* pp. 30–49.]

[79]A. R. Radcliffe-Brown, *The Andaman Islanders* (Cambridge: Cambridge University Press, 1933), pp. 233–34.

[80]Adolf Portmann, "Die Bedeutung der Bilder in der lebendigen Energiewandlung," *Eranos-Jahrbuch* XXI/1952 (Zürich: Rhein-Verlag, 1953), pp. 333–34.

[81]H. Ostermann, "The Alaskan Eskimos, as Described in the Posthumous Notes of Dr. Knud Rasmussen," in vol. X, no. 3 of *Report of the Fifth Thule Expedition 1921–24* (Copenhagen: Nordisk Forlag, 1952), pp. 97–99.

[82]Ostermann, "The Alaskan Eskimos," p. 99.

[83]Ostermann, "The Alaskan Eskimos," p. 128.

JOHANN JACOB BACHOFEN

[1][Stefan George (1868–1933) believed that the poet's role was to preserve traditional spiritual values in a crumbling society. Associated with the George circle were the poets Rainer Maria Rilke and Hugo von Hofmannsthal.]

[2][Spengler articulated the concept of the "informing idea" or "prime symbol" as follows: "Thus, the Destiny-idea manifests itself in every line of a life. With it alone do we become members of a particular culture, whose members are connected by a common world-feeling and a common world-form derived from it . . . and thenceforth this symbol is and remains the *prime symbol* of that life, imparting to it its specific style and the historical form in which it progressively actualizes its inward possibilities. From the specific directedness is derived the specific prime symbol of extension, namely, for the Classical world view, the near, strictly limited, self-contained Body, for the Western infinitely wide and infinitely profound three-dimensional Space, for the Arabian the world as Cavern" (*The Decline of the West*, vol. 1, p. 174).]

[3]Bronislaw Malinowski, *The Sexual Life of Savages* (New York: Halcyon House, 1929), pp. 3–7.

[4]Quoted from Loren Eiseley, *The Firmament of Time* (New York: Atheneum, 1962), p. 93.

[5]Vol. 8, pp. 859 and 858, respectively.

[6]Vol. 1, p. 71.

[7]From a letter to Heinrich Meyer-Ochsner, May 25, 1869, quoted by Rudolf Marx in his introduction (p. xxvi) to the volume of selections of which the present is a translation. [J. J. Bachofen, *Mutterrecht und Urreligion*, ed. Rudolf Marx (Stuttgart: Alfred Kröner Verlag, 1926. Enlarged ed., 1954.) The present essay is the introduction to the English translation *Myth, Religion, and Mother Right*, trans. Ralph Mannheim (Princeton: Princeton University Press, 1967).]

[8]*Literarisches Zentralblatt*, Nr. 27, 1860; cited by Carl Albrecht Bernoulli, ed., J. J. Bachofen, *Versuch über die Gräbersymbolik der Alten*, 2nd ed. (Basel: Helbing & Lichtenhahn, 1925), p. vi.

[9]Robert H. Lowie, *History of Ethnological Theory* (New York: Farrar & Reinhart, 1937), p. 41.

[10]Robert R. Marett, *Tylor* (London: Chapman & Hall, 1936), pp. 180–1.

[11][See "The Wonder Child," *Mythic Image*, pp. 32–49, esp. figs. 28, 29.]

[12][For Dionysus, see *Mythic Image*, pp. 248–253.]

[13]From a letter quoted by Rudolf Marx, p. xxvii. (Cf. above, n. 7).

[14]Ernst Curtius, *The History of Greece*, trans. A. W. Ward, 3 vols. (New York: Charles Scribner & Company, 1871).

[15]Quoted from Morgan MSS by Leslie A. White, ed., Lewis H. Morgan, *Ancient Society* (Cambridge, Mass.: Belknap Press of Harvard University Press, 1964), p. 297, n. 5.

[16]Morgan, *Ancient Society*, pp. 297–8.

[17]Schurtz, *Altersklassen und Männerbünde* (Berlin: G. Reimer, 1902), pp. iv–v.

[18]Sir James G. Frazer, "The Succession to the Kingdom in Ancient Latium," chap. xiv, *The Golden Bough*, one-volume ed. (New York: The Macmillan Company, 1922), pp. 152–58.

[19]Leonard R. Palmer, "The Mycenaean Religion" in *Mycenaeans and Minoans* (New York: Alfred A. Knopf, 1962), pp. 119–31.

[21]Sigmund Freud, *Totem and Taboo*, trans. James Strachey (London: The Hogarth Press & The Institute of Psychoanalysis, 1955), p. 149.

[22]Ludwig Klages, Introduction to J. J. Bachofen, *Versuch über die Gräbersymbolik der Alten* (Basel: Helbing & Lichtenhahn, 1925), pp. x–xi.

THE MYSTERY NUMBER OF THE GODDESS

[1]Grimnismäl 23, translated by Henry Adams Bellows, *The Poetic Edda* (American-Scandinavian Foundation, Oxford University Press, 1923), p. 93.

[2]Völuspá 59–62 in Bellows, *Poetic Edda*, pp. 24–25, abridged.

[3]The recognition of this number in the Book of Revelation I owe to the Icelandic scholar Einar Pálsson, whose *Roetur íslenskrar menningar* (*The Roots of Icelandic Culture*, 7 vols. [Reykjavík: Mímir, 1969–1985]) argues that the culture of Pagan/Celtic-Christian Iceland during the period c. A.D. 870–1000 was of a piece with that of contemporary medieval Europe and not, as has been commonly supposed, of a separate and distinct, specifically Nordic source and

context. His argument has been summarized in English in three brief monographs: *The Dome of Heaven: The Marking of Sacred Sites in Pagan Iceland and Medieval Florence* (Reykjavík: Mímir, 1981), *Hypothesis as a Tool in Mythology* (Mímir, 1984), and *Celtic Christianity in Pagan Iceland* (Mímir, 1985).

[4]For this dating of the tablet, see Samuel Noah Kramer, *Sumerian Mythology* (Philadelphia: American Philosophical Society, 1944), p. 9.

[5]I have followed primarily Arno Poebel, *Historical Texts* (Philadelphia: University Museum, Publications of the Babylonian Section, vol. 4, no. 1, 1914), pp. 17–20, but with considerable help from the later renditions by Stephen Herbert Langdon, *Semitic Mythology*, vol. 5 of The Mythology of All Races, 13 vols. (Boston: Marshall Jones, 1931), pp. 17–20, and Samuel Noah Kramer, *From the Tablets of Sumer* (Indian Hills, Colorado: Falcon's Wing Press, 1956), pp. 179–81.

[6]Julius (Jules) Oppert, "Die Daten der Genesis," Königliche Gesellschaft der Wissenschaften zu Göttingen, Nachrichten 10 (1877), pp. 201–27.

[7][See *Oriental Mythology*, p. 129.]

[8]Samuel Noah Kramer, *The Sumerians* (Chicago: University of Chicago Press, 1963), pp. 42, 59.

[9]Kramer, *Sumerians*, pp. 59–68.

[10]Kramer, *Sumerians*, pp. 144–45.

[11]Kramer, *Sumerians*, p. 42.

[12]Kramer, *Sumerians*, pp. 40–41; Alain Daniélou, *Shiva et Dionysos* (Paris: Librairie Artheme Fayard, 1982); English translation by K. F. Hurry, *Shiva and Dionysus* (New York: Inner Traditions International, 1984), pp. 20–23.

[13]Gimbutas, *The Goddesses and Gods of Old Europe, 7000–3500 B.C.* (Berkeley & Los Angeles: University of Calfornia Press, 1974), p. 195.

[14]Gimbutas, *Goddesses and Gods*, p. 196.

[15]Daniélou, *Shiva and Dionysus*, p. 32.

[16][See *Occidental Mythology*, pp. 42–43.]

[17]Apuleius, *The Golden Ass*, bk. 11, trans. W. Adlington.

[18]Kramer, *Sumerians*, p. 122. [For the design on the signet ring, see *Occidental Mythology*, pp. 45–54.]

[19][See *Primitive Mythology*, pp. 413–18.]

[20][For Iris and Osiris, see *Mythic Image*, pp. 21–31; for Demeter and Persephone, see *Primitive Mythology*, pp. 183–90.]

[21][See "Four Episodes from the Romance of the Goddess," in pt. 2 of *The King and the Corpse: Tales of the Soul's Conquest of Evil*, by Heinrich Zimmer, 2nd ed. (Princeton: Princeton University Press, 1956, pb. ed., 1971), pp. 239 ff.]

[22]*The Gospel of Sri Ramakrishna*, trans. Swami Nikhilananda (New York: Ramakrishna-Vivekananda Center, 1942), p. 336.

[23]Gimbutas, *Goddesses and Gods*, p. 196.

[24]*Muṇḍaka Upanishad* 1.1.7.

[25]*Vedāntasāra* 56.

[26]Gimbutas, *Goddesses and Gods*, p. 38.

[27]Gimbutas, *Goddesses and Gods*, p. 89. [For an example, see fig. 11 in "The Symbol Without Meaning," *Flight of the Wild Gander*.]

[28]Gimbutas, *Goddesses and Gods*, p. 236.

[29][For *anodos/kathodos*, see *Primitive Mythology*, p. 185.]

[30]Gimbutas, *Goddesses and Gods*, pp. 19–34.

[31]Gimbutas, *Goddesses and Gods*, pp. 85–87.

[32]Kramer, *Sumerians*, p. 93.

[33]Kramer, *Sumerians*, p. 94.

[34]Kenneth H. Cooper, M.D., M.P.H., *Aerobics* (New York: Bantam Books, 1968), p. 101.

[35]Arthur Avalon (Sir John Woodroffe), *The Serpent Power*, 3rd rev. ed. (Madras: Ganesh, 1931), p. 215.

[36]H. V. Hilprecht, *The Babylonian Expedition of the University of Pennsylvania, Series A:*

Cuneiform Texts, vol. 20, pt. 1 (University of Pennsylvania: University Museum, 1906), p. 215.

37Alfred Jeremias, *Das Alter der babylonischen Astronomie* (Leipzig: J.C. Hinrechs'sche Buch-handlung, 2 Aufl., 1909), p. 68, n. 1.

38Jeremias, *Das Alter der babylonischen Astronomie*, pp. 71–72.

39[For the diffusion of astronomy, see fig. 126 of *Mythic Image,* p. 147.]

40D. R. Dicks, *Early Greek Astronomy to Aristotle* (Ithaca: Cornell University Press, 1970), pp. 62–63.

41Alain Daniélou, *Introduction to the Study of Musical Scales* (London: India Society, 1943), p. 7. (Text italics, mine.)

42*Li Chi* 28.97–99, trans. Derk Bodde, in Fung Yu-lan, *A History of Chinese Philosophy,* 2 vols. (Princeton: Princeton University Press, 1952), vol. 1, p. 343.

43Tung Chung-shu, trans. by Daniélou in *Introduction to the Study of Musical Scales,* pp. 6–7; André Preau, "Lie Tseu," in *La Voile d'Isis* (Paris: Chacornac), no. 152–53 (1932), pp. 554–55.

44[For more on Pythagorean-hermetic symbolism, see *Inner Reaches*, pp. 126–29.]

45Daniélou, *Introduction to the Study of Musical Scales,* p. 12.

46Tao Te Ching 42, trans. James Legge, *Sacred Books of the East,* ed. F. Max Müller, vol. 39, *The Texts of Taoism,* part 1, p. 85.

47[For the *Sānkhya* philosophy, see Heinrich Zimmer, *Philosophies of India,* ed. Joseph Camp-bell (New York: Pantheon Press, 1951), pp. 314–22, esp. the diagram on p. 327.]

48*La Vita Nuova* II, III, and XXX, abridged, translated by Charles Eliot Norton as *The New Life of Dante Alighieri* (Boston & New York: Houghton Mifflin, 1967), pp. 1–4, 65–66.

49Gimbutas, *Goddesses and Gods,* p. 205.

50[That is, the *Shri Yantra.* See "The Shri Yantra" in Heinrich Zimmer, *Artistic Form and Yoga in the Sacred Images of India,* ed. and trans. Gerald Chapple, James B. Lawson, and J. Michael McKnight (Princeton, N.J.: Princeton University Press, 1984), pp. 158–80 and accompany-ing figures.]

51[See *Joseph Campbell Companion,* pp. 155–58.]

52Hesiod, *Theogony* 116–34, abridged, trans. Richard Lattimore (Ann Arbor: University of Michigan Press, 1959), pp. 130–31. [Also see *Occidental Mythology,* pp. 234–35.]

53See *The Jerusalem Bible* (Garden City, NY: Doubleday, Imprimatur, 1966), 943, note h.

54Dom Gaspar LeFebure O.S.B., *Daily Missal with Vespers for Sundays and Feasts* (Lophem-near-Bruges, Belgium: Abbey of St. Andre; Saint Paul, Minnesota: The R.M. Lohmann Co., 1934), p. 187.

55These are recorded in Asoka's Rock Edict XIII. Cf. Vincent A. Smith, *The Edicts of Asoka* (Lon-don, 1909), p. 20. This is an exceedingly rare book, only one hundred copies having been printed. It revises the translations given by the author in his earlier volume, *Asoka: The Buddhist Emperor of India* (Oxford, 1901).

56[See *Creative Mythology,* pp. 99–105, and fig. 13, p. 100.]

57*Conclusiones . . . de modo intelligendi hymnos Orphei,* no. 8., as cited by Edgar Wind, *Pagan Mysteries in the Renaissance,* rev. and enlarged ed. (New York & London: W. W. Norton, 1968), p. 36.

58Wind, *Pagan Mysteries,* p. 36.

59Wind, *Pagan Mysteries,* pp. 37–38 and n. 9.

60Wind, *Pagan Mysteries,* p. 259.

61Wind, *Pagan Mysteries,* p. 266.

62[For the Three Graces and Wind's accompanying quote see *Historical Atlas,* II.1, fig. 2.]

63[See *Inner Reaches,* fig. 9; also, *Historical Atlas,* II.1, p. 104, fig. 216.]

64*Shatcakranirūpanam* 49; Avalon, *The Serpent Power,* p. 448.

65 Wind, *Pagan Mysteries,* p. 38, n. 9, citing Proclus, *Elements of Theology,* prop. 35 (ed. Dodds [1933], p. 18f.).

66Wind, *Pagan Mysteries,* p. 38, n. 9.

67Wind, *Pagan Mysteries,* p. 43.

68Translation by J. L. Stocks, in *The Complete Works of Aristotle,* ed. Jonathan Barnes, Bollingen

Series LXXI. 2 (Princeton: Princeton University Press, 1984), 1:447.

[69]B. Jowett translation, 4th. ed., revised, 1953.

[70]Gimbutas, *Goddesses and Gods,* p. 93. [See, also, *Historical Atlas,* I.1, figs. 66, 109.]

[71]"The Woman with the Horn" in *Historical Atlas,* I.1, figs. 66, 109.

[72]Alexander Marshack, *The Roots of Civilization* (New York: McGraw-Hill, 1972), p. 335 and n. 17.

[73]*Historical Atlas,* I.1, fig. 111.

[74]*Historical Atlas,* I.1, fig. 112.

[75]Gimbutas, *Goddesses and Gods.*

[76]James Mellaart, *Çatal Hüyük: A Neolithic Town in Anatolia* (New York: McGraw-Hill, 1967). [See, also, "The Symbol without Meaning," figs. 7–9, in *Flight of the Wild Gander.*]

[77][See *Occidental Mythology,* p. 161, fig. 22.]

[78]Gimbutas, *Goddesses and Gods,* p. 224.

[79]Gimbutas, *Goddesses and Gods,* p. 227.

[80][See *Historical Atlas,* I.1, figs. 114–124.]

[81][For shamanic figures, see *Historical Atlas,* I.2, figs. 269–272.]

[82][See *Historical Atlas,* I.1, fig. 110.]

[83]*Kena Upanishad,* 3–4. [For this episode see *Oriental Mythology,* pp. 204–5.]

[84]See Gimbutas's fundamental articles on this subject in *The Journal of Indo-European Studies,* 1:1 (Spring 1973), "Old Europe c. 7000–3500 B.C.: The Earliest European Civilization before the Infiltration of the Indo-European Peoples"; and 1:2 (Summer 1973), "The Beginning of the Bronze Age in Europe and the Indo-Europeans 3500–2500 B.C."; also, 8:3 and 8:4 (Fall/Winter 1980), "The Kurgan Wave #2 (c. 3400–3200 B.C.) into Europe and the Following Transformation of Culture."

[85]For an introduction to the works and career of Georges Dumézil, see Edgar C. Polomé, ed., "Homage to Georges Dumézil," *Journal of Indo-European Studies,* monograph no. 3 (1982).

[86]The earliest archaeological strata of this important site date back to c. 8000 B.C. See Kathleen M. Kenyon, *Archaeology in the Holy Land* (New York: Frederick A. Praeger, 1960), p. 42.

[87]Völuspá 42–49 in Bellows, *Poetic Edda,* pp. 18–21.

[88]Snorri Sturluson, "The Beguiling of Gylfi" 51; adapted from Arthur Gilchrist Brodeur, *The Prose Edda of Snorri Sturluson* (New York: American-Scandinavian Foundation, Oxford University Press, 1929), 77–81.

[89]Einar Pálsson, *Hypothesis as a Tool in Mythology* (Reykjavík: Mímir,1984), p.11, referring to his *Roetur íslenzkrar menningar,* 7 vols. (Reykjavík: Mímir, 1969–85).

[90]As reported in *News from Iceland,* Reykjavík (August 1985) pp. 1, 22; also, *Morgunblathith* (July 16, 1985), p. 52.

[91][For Erigena, see *Occidental Mythology,* pp. 466–67.]

[92][Emanation, as articulated by Plotinus in *The Enneads,* is an unfolding of spiritual substance from the One, or unitary ground of being, to the World Intellect, or realm of Platonic Forms, and ultimately down into the dualistic world of Soul entrapped in materiality.]

[93]Pálsson, *Celtic Christianity in Pagan Iceland* (Reykjavík: Mímir, March 1985), pp. 22–23.

[94]Pálsson, *Hypothesis as a Tool in Mythology,* p. 24.

[95]Pálsson, *Celtic Christianity in Pagan Iceland,* pp. 8–9.

[96][See "The World Mountain" in *Mythic Image,* pp. 76–103.]

[97]Pálsson, *The Dome of Heaven: The Marking of Sacred Sites in Pagan Iceland and Medieval Florence, A Report on Studies in Florence in May 1980* (Reykjavík: Mímir, 1981), p. 47.

[98]Pálsson, *Celtic Christianity in Pagan Iceland,* p. 7.

[99]Franz Rolf Schröder, *Altgermanische Kulturprobleme,* Trübners Philologische Bibliothek Band 11 (Berlin und Leipzig: Walter de Gruyter, 1929), pp. 64, 69–70.

[100]Hávamál 139, 140, 142, trans. Bellows, *Poetic Edda,* pp. 60–61.

[101][For discussion of the *Tunc* page of the *Book of Kells,* see *Occidental Mythology,* pp. 467–73.]

[102]A critical review of the scholarship of this subject appears in Schröder, *Altgermanische Kulturprobleme,* pp. 21–39. [For further diffusion into Mexico, see *Mythic Image,* pp. 120–35; also see

fig. 110 for Chinese (Shang) animal mask.]
[103] *Mythic Image,* fig. 308. [Also, *Inner Reaches,* fig. 13.]
[104]Elaine Pagels, *The Gnostic Gospels* (New York: Random House, 1979), pp. xx and *passim.* [Also see "The Interpretation of Symbolic Forms," below, pp. 169–70.]
[105] [See *Inner Reaches,* fig. 1.]
[106] *Mythic Image,* figs. 53, 54.
[107] [See Zimmer, *The King and the Corpse,* fig. 4, pp. 174–75; also, "Foreword" and "Symbolism of the Marseilles Deck" in Joseph Campbell and Richard Roberts, *Tarot Revelations* (San Francisco: Alchemy Books, 1974).]
[108] [*Mythic Image,* fig. 164.]
[109] *The Gospel According to Thomas,* Coptic text established and translated by A. Guillaumont, H.-Ch. Puech, G. Quispel, W. Till, and Yasah abd al Masih (Leiden: E. J. Brill; New York: Harper & Brothers, 1959), pp. 3, 55, 57.
[110]Völuspá 27 and 28/29 combined and abridged, Bellows, *Poetic Edda,* pp. 12–13.
[111]Snorri Sturluson, Gylfaginning 27. Brodeur, *The Prose Edda of Snorri Sturluson,* p. 40.
[112]Schröder, *Altgermanische Kulturprobleme,* ch. 17. [See *Occidental Mythology,* pp. 260–63.]
[113]Pálsson, *Hypothesis as a Tool in Mythology,* p. 31, citing Ernest G. McClain, *The Myth of Invariance* (New York: Nicolas Hays, 1976), pp. 104–5.
[114]Pálsson, *Hypothesis as a Tool in Mythology,* pp. 32–35.
[115]Daniélou, *Introduction to the Musical Scales,* pp. 6–7.
[116]Sermon on "Riddance" in Franz Pfeiffer, *Meister Eckhart,* trans. C. de B. Evans, 2 vols. (London: John M. Watkins, 1947), sermon 96, vol. 1, p. 239.

CREATIVITY
[1] [Friedrich von Schiller (1759–1805), the German poet and dramatist whose early writings were associated with the *Sturm und Drang* movement. Along with Goethe, he helped to shape the movement known as Weimar classicism. He is the author of many important essays on aesthetics, the most famous of which is "On Naïve and Sentimental Poetry" (1795). His poetical theories were highly influenced by his studies of Kantian metaphysics. He is the author of such plays as *Wallenstein, Mary Stuart, The Maid of Orleans, Don Carlos,* and *Wilhelm Tell.*]
[2] [For more on Dionysus see above, "Historical Development of Mythology," pp. 15–17.]
[3] [The story of Pentheus is the subject of one of the last plays of Euripides, *The Bacchae* (c. 405 B.C.). Pentheus is the grandson of Cadmus and the son of Semele, who was also the mother of Dionysus. As King of Thebes, Pentheus refuses to allow the cult of Dionysus to enter his city, dreading its orgiastic madness and worship of the vital forces of nature. When the god Dionysus appears in Thebes, Pentheus has him imprisoned. Dionysus, however, arranges for him to view a group of Bacchant women performing their ecstatic rites one night in the forest. Dionysus reveals that Pentheus is present, and the women tear him to pieces.]

THE INTERPRETATION OF SYMBOLIC FORMS
[1] [See *Creative Mythology,* pp. 17–21, esp. fig. 8, for alternate interpretations of the crucifixion.]
[2] [For a picture of this cross, see *Mythic Image,* figs. 151–52.]
[3] [For the skull of Adam at the foot of the cross, see *Mythic Image,* fig. 150, and *Inner Reaches,* p. 71, fig. 4; for a bird at its top, see *Mythic Image,* fig. 231, and the cover of *Historical Atlas,* II.1.]
[4]Bellows, *The Poetic Edda* (New York: The American-Scandinavian Foundation, 1923), pp. 60–61. [See also "Europe Resurgent," in *Occidental Mythology,* esp. pp. 482–83.]
[5] [See "Concerning Mandala Symbolism" and "Appendix: Mandalas" in *The Collected Works of C. G. Jung* (Princeton, N.J.: Princeton University Press), vol. 9; for Campbell's critique, see "The Symbol Without Meaning" in *Flight of the Wild Gander.*]
[6]T. S. Eliot, *Collected Poems, 1909–1962* (New York: Harcourt, Brace & World, 1963), p. 177.
[7] [An understanding of the term *homologous,* which Campbell drew from biology, is essential for illuminating Campbell's comparative method. The distinction betweeen *homology* and *analogy* was formulated by Sir Richard Owen in the mid-nineteenth century as follows:

... the former [homology] as the same organ in different animals under every variety of form and function (e.g., forelimbs of *Draco volans* and wings of a bird); the second [analogy] as a part or organ in one animal which has the same function as another part or organ in a different animal (e.g., parachute of *Draco* and wings of a bird).]

[8]Questions and answers for Lessons Fifth and Sixth of *A Catechism of Christian Doctrine,* Kindead's Baltimore Series of Catechisms, no. 3 (New York, Cincinnati, Chicago, San Francisco: Benzinger Brothers, 1885), pp. 54, 57–60. [See also *Joseph Campbell Companion,* pp. 159–62.

[9][See *Inner Reaches,* pp. 99–100 for an amplification.]

[10][See *Historical Atlas,* II.1, p. 104, fig. 216.]

[11][Blake, *The Marriage of Heaven and Hell.* See also *Inner Reaches,* p. 115.]

[12][For a picture of these door guardians, see *Inner Reaches,* p. 81, fig. 9.]

[13] *The Gospel According to Thomas,* Coptic text established and translated by A. Guillaumont, H.-Ch. Puech, G. Quispel, W. Till, and Yasah abd al Masih (Leiden: E. J. Brill; New York: Harper & Brothers, 1959).

[14][For further discussion of the *Kuṇḍalinī,* see "Metaphor as Myth and as Religion," *Inner Reaches,* pp. 63–92. Also see "Transformations of the Inner Light" (pt. 5) and "The Lotus Ladder," in *Mythic Image* (pp. 330–82); Joseph Campbell, "Seven Levels of Consciousness," *Psychology Today 9* (December 1975), pp. 77–78; and "The Lamb, the Hero, and the Man-God," in Heinrich Zimmer, *The Philosophies of India,* ed. Joseph Campbell (Princeton: Princeton University Press, 1951), pp. 582–95]

[15]Franz Pfeiffer, *Meister Eckhart,* trans. C. de B. Evans, 2 vols. (London: John M. Watkins, 1947), 1:221. [See also "Europe Resurgent," *Occidental Mythology,* pp. 510–14; figs. 31, 32.]

[16][For Hallaj, see *Occidental Mythology,* pp. 447–53.]

[17]R. A. Nicholson, "Mysticism," citing Sir Thos. Arnold, Alfred Guilaume, eds., *The Legacy of Islam* (Oxford: Oxford University Press, 1931), p. 217.

[18]Pfeiffer, *Meister Eckhart,* 1:239.

[19]Pfeiffer, *Meister Eckhart,* 1:422.

MYTHOLOGICAL THEMES IN CREATIVE LITERATURE AND ART

[1][See *Oriental Mythology,* p. 36: "... the crucial moment that I shall term the great reversal—when, for many in the Orient as well as in the West, the sense of holiness departed from their experience both of the Universe and of their own nature, and a yearning for release from what was felt to be an insufferable state of sin, exile, or delusion supervened ..."]

[2]Géza Róheim, *The Eternal Ones of the Dream* (New York: International Universities Press, 1945), p. 232, citing K. Langloh Parker, *The Euahlayi Tribe* (London: A. Constable & Co., 1905), pp. 72–73.

[3]A. R. Radcliffe-Brown, *The Andaman Islanders* (Cambridge: Cambridge University Press, 1933), pp. 233–34.

[4]William Wordsworth, "Intimations of Immortality from Recollections of Early Childhood," ll. 64–65.

[5]Wordsworth, "Intimations of Immortality," ll. 158–71.

[6]Sir Arthur Keith, in *Living Philosophies,* a symposium (New York: Simon & Schuster, Inc., 1931), p. 142.

[7]Albert Pauphilet, ed., *La Queste del Saint Graal* (Paris: Champion, 1949), p. 26.

[8][In *Creative Mythology,* p. 35, Campbell makes the distinction between "intelligible character" and "earned character":

The inborn, or, as Schopenhauer terms it, *intelligible* character is unfolded only gradually and imperfectly through circumstance; and what comes to view in this way he calls the *empirical* (experienced or observed) character. Our neighbors, through observation of this empirical character, often become more aware than ourselves of the intelligible, innate personality that is secretly shaping our life. We have to learn through experience what we are, want, and can do, and "until then," declares Schopenhauer, "we are characterless, ignorant of ourselves, and have often to be thrown back onto our proper way by hard blows from without. When finally we shall have learned, however, we shall have gained what the world calls 'character'—which is to say earned character. And this, in short, is neither more nor less than the fullest possible knowledge of our own individuality."]

[9] *Bṛihadāraṇyaka Upanishad* 1.4.1–5.

[10] Genesis 2 and James Joyce, *Finnegans Wake* (New York: The Viking Press, 1939), p. 255.

[11] Plato, *Symposium* 189d–193d, trans. Michael Joyce, in *The Collected Dialogues of Plato*, ed. Edith Hamilton and Huntington Cairns, Bollingen Series LXXI (New York: Pantheon Books, 1961), pp. 542–46.

[12] *Bṛihadāraṇyaka Upanishad* 1.4.10.

[13] Genesis 3.

[14] [See *Mythic Image*, pp. 370–71, fig. 340, and *Historical Atlas* II.1, p. 104, fig. 216.]

[15] Aquinas, *Summa Theologica*, Part I, Question 102, Article 1, Reply 3.

[16] [See also "Art as Revelation" in *Historical Atlas*, I.2, esp. pp. xiii–xvii.]

[17] [Campbell elucidated these terms slightly differently in *Inner Reaches*, pp. 131–32:

Integritas. . . . To appreciate the effect of this principle, the function of which is to create an enclosed hermetic field of self-defined and self-defining, impractical relationships, one may regard any collection of objects whatsoever, say, a clutter of things on a table, and in imagination put a frame around them . . . "You see it," says Stephen, "as a whole." You apprehend its wholeness. That is *integritas*.

Consonantia. . . . This is the esthetic instrument: rhythm.... The parts may be objects, colors, words, and their sounds, musical intervals, architectural features and proportions. "You pass," says Stephen, "from part against part within its limits; you feel the rhythm of its structure."

Claritas. . . . The radiance of which [Aquinas] speaks is the scholastic *quidditas*, the whatness of a thing. This supreme quality is felt by the artist when the esthetic image is first conceived in his imagination. The mind in that mysterious instant Shelley likened beautifully to a fading coal. . . ."]

[18] [In an interview on September 24, 1985, Campbell explained:

The *katharsis* is cleansing you of man's fear and desire in terms of merely temporal purposes and opening then the great experiences of pity, compassion for the other. And I think when [Aristotle] speaks of *katharsis* as following from pity and terror, he's speaking of going past fear and desire into a deeper realm. James Joyce has discussed this magnificently in *A Portrait of the Artist as a Young Man*. What Joyce calls the kinetic emotions, the emotions that move you to desire something or to loathe and fear it, are erased in the tragedy, where the emotions which he calls static emotions, of pity: participation and identification with the suffering of another; and terror: the experience and identification with the secret cause behind all things, the Being of beings. These are static emotions that arrest the mind and cleanse it of the mere temporal interests of fear and desire.

For the concept of "human suffering," see *Inner Reaches*, p.132: "Not the poor, the black, the jobless sufferer, be it noted, but the human sufferer. We are penetrating the local, ethnic, or social mask to the human being."]

[19] James Joyce, *Finnegans Wake*, p. 92.

[20] Wolfram von Eschenbach, *Parzival*, ed. Karl Lachmann, 6th ed. (Berlin & Leipzig: Walter de Gruyter & Co., 1926), Book XV, p. 740, ll. 26–30, and p. 741, ll. 21–22.

[21] Matthew 7:1.

[22] Heraclitus in Diels, *Fragmente der Vorsokratiker* (1922), Fragments 80, 102, and 58; *Greek Religious Thought from Homer to the Age of Alexander*, trans. F. M. Cornford (London & Toronto:

J. M. Dent & Sons; New York: E. P. Dutton & Co., 1923), p. 84.

[23]Diels, *Fragmente der Vorsokratiker*, Fragment 51.

[24]Wolfram, *Parzival*, XV:740, ll. 2–5.

[25]See Matthew 6:19–21, of which the parenthesis is a paraphrase.

[26]Ovid, *The Metamorphoses*, trans. Horace Gregory (New York: The Viking Press, 1958), pp. 211–12.

[27]C. G. Jung, *Analytical Psychology, Its Theory and Practice* (New York: Pantheon Books, 1968), pp. 11–14.

[28]Jung, *Analytical Psychology*, pp. 21–25.

[29]Jung, *Analytical Psychology*, p. 8.

[30]Jung, *Analytical Psychology*, pp. 40–41.

[31]James Joyce, *Ulysses* (Paris: Shakespeare & Company, 1924), p. 552; (New York: Random House, 1934), p. 574.

[32]Innocentii III, *Epistolae*, bk. VII, no. 75, in Migne, *Patrologia Latina*, vol. CCXV, pp. 355–57.

[33]T. S. Eliot, *Collected Poems 1909–1962* (New York: Harcourt, Brace & World, 1963), p. 55.

[34]*Brihadāranyaka Upanishad* 5.2.

[35]Robinson Jeffers, *Roan Stallion, Tamar, & Other Poems* (New York: Horace Liveright, 1925), p. 232.

THE OCCULT IN MYTH AND LITERATURE

[1][See "The Sacrifice" in *Mythic Image*, pp. 450–81.]

[2][See *Creative Mythology*, pp. 17, 204.]

[3][For the Gothic Black Mass, see *Creative Mythology*, pp. 165–66, 595.]

[4][See *Creative Mythology*, pp. 213–14, 604–6.]

[5][See *Creative Mythology*, p. 340.]

[6][See *The Collected Works of C. G. Jung* (Princeton, N.J.: Princeton University Press), vol. 1, "Psychatric Studies."]

[7][See also Campbell's account of Freud and Jung in the "Editor's Introduction" to *The Portable Jung*, ed, Joseph Campbell, trans. R.F.C. Hull (New York: Viking, 1971), pp. vii–xxxii.]

EROTIC IRONY AND MYTHIC FORMS IN THE ART OF THOMAS MANN

[1][For more of Freud's paper on artists, see *Inner Reaches*, pp. 143–44.]

[2][*Joseph in Egypt*.]

[3][See Campbell's "Heinrich Zimmer," *Partisan Review* 20 (July 1953), pp. 444–51:

> . . . with *The Transposed Heads* (1940) [Mann] discovered Zimmer, Nietzsche's vision announced in the *Birth of Tragedy* and echoed by Castorp's snow-dream in integration of a time-and-space-shattering insight into the ground of being, Zimmer had perfectly matched with an elucidation of a collection of Indian stories, *Vetahapanchavinshati*, "Twenty-five Tales of the Ghost in a Corpse." And Mann, ever enchanted by life's promise of a transcendent knowledge in which subject and object will have become identical, was seduced. The tale sounded motifs akin to those that he was developing symphonically in *Joseph and His Brothers*. In a playful, very sophisticated excursion, therefore, he composed, with plastic irony, an erotic idyll much reminiscent of his own earlier *Tristan*, yet catching wonderfully many of Zimmer's themes and through these a glimpse of the timeless East.

See also Heinrich Zimmer, *The King and the Corpse: Tales of the Soul's Conquest of Evil*, ed. Joseph Campbell, 2nd ed. (Princeton: Princeton University Press, 1956), pp. 202–35, esp. p. 210, for the source of Mann's inspiration.]

[4][Novalis (1772–1801), poet of early German Romanticism. Novalis believed that mankind's mystical harmony with nature had been lost, and that its primary ideal ought to be to regain it. He wrote the novel *Heinrich von Ofterdingen* (1801), a *Bildungsroman* which treats of the growth of a poet in medieval Europe. The Blue Flower, the famous symbol of Romanticism, first

appeared here, in the form of a dream to young Heinrich, symbolizing an unobtainable ideal, the romantic goal of yearning for infinity. See Heinrich Heine, *The Romantic School and Other Essays,* ed. Jost Hermand and Robert C. Holub (New York: Continuum, 1985), esp. pp. 77–80 for Novalis.]

[5][See Thomas Mann, *Essays* (New York: Alfred A. Knopf, 1957), pp. 304–5.]

[6][*The Interpretation of Dreams* (1900).]

[7][See Mann's essay "Schopenhauer" in *Essays.* See also Spengler, *Decline of the West,* vol. I, pp. 373–74 for Schopenhauer as inaugurating a new epoch of philosophy.]

[8][See Mann, *Essays,* p. 311: ". . . I take leave to add what Freud's rational morality prevents him from saying, that under some circumstances, it {the ego} makes more progress by this illegitimate means" {i.e. by allowing the id to lead it, rather than vice versa}.]

[9][Arthur Schopenhauer, *The World as Will and Representation,* trans. E.F. J. Payne, 2 vols. (New York: Dover Publications, 1966), vol. 2, p.463.]

[10][For the significance of Wagner's work in Europe during the nineteenth century, see the 1861 essay by Baudelaire, "Richard Wagner and Tannhauser in Paris," in *Baudelaire: Selected Writings on Art and Artists* (New York: Penguin, 1972).]

[11][See *Creative Mythology,* pp. 73–83, for Wagner and Schopenhauer, and "The Sufferings and Greatness of Richard Wagner" in Mann, *Essays,* esp. pp. 226–33, for the effect of Schopenhauer on Wagner.]

[12][See Schopenhauer, "On the Metaphysics of Music" in *World as Will and Representation,* vol. 2, p. 447 ff. In *Creative Mythology,* Campbell notes (p. 83): "in the art of Wagner's opera, therefore, the music is meant to render the inward time-sense of the scenes presented on the outward space-field of the stage. It is related to those scenes as the will is to the body. . . ."]

[13][Romans 11:32.]

[14][*Reflections of a Non-Political Man,* trans. Walter D. Morris (New York: F. Ungar, 1983).]

[15][See "Phoenix Fire" in *Creative Mythology,* pp. 257–97. Also see "The Golden Seed" in *Mythic Image,* pp. 254–63, esp. pl. 226, "The Transformations of Mercurius."]

[16][E.g. Thomas Paine (1737–1809), Thomas Jefferson (1743–1826), and Jean-Jacques Rousseau (1712–1778).]

[17][Goethe, *Faust,* II, Act II, ll. 7080–245.]

[18][When Zeus demanded Persephone's release to the upper world, Hades assented. However, right before Persephone's departure, one of Hades' gardeners gave her seven pomegranate seeds to eat. These seeds were called, according to the myth, "the food of the dead." See Robert Graves, *The Greek Myths,* 2 vols. (New York: George Braziller, Inc., 1957), p. 91, item 24j.]

[19][The passage is as follows:

> That this effect should be necessary, everybody should be able to feel most assuredly by means of intuition, provided he has ever felt, if only in a dream, that he was carried back into an ancient Greek existence. Walking under lofty Ionic colonnades, looking up toward a horizon that was cut off by pure and noble lines, finding reflections of his transfigured shape in the shining marble at his side, and all around him solemnly striding or delicately moving human beings, speaking with harmonious voices and in a rhythmic language of gestures—in view of this continual influx of beauty, would he not have to exclaim, raising his hand to Apollo: "Blessed people of Hellas! How great must Dionysus be among you if the god of Delos considers such magic necessary to heal your dithyrambic madness."
>
> To a man in such a mood, however, an old Athenian, looking up at him with the sublime eyes of Aeschylus, might reply: "But say this, too, curious stranger: how much did this people have to suffer to be able to become so beautiful! But now follow me to witness a tragedy, and sacrifice with me in the temple of both deities!" (Nietzsche, *The Birth of Tragedy,* p. 144).]

[20]C. G. Jung, "Cryptomnesia," *Collected Works,* vol. I, pp. 103–5.

[21]C. G. Jung, "Psychological Commentary on *The Tibetan Book of the Dead,*" *Collected Works,*

vol. II, pp. 509–26; the precise passages from which Mann is quoting will be found on pp. 513–14.

[22][Mann, *Essays*, pp. 314–15.]

[23][Mann, *Essays*, p. 317.]